D0580645

The WILLOW CREEK GUIDES Series includes

North America's Greatest Fishing Lodges

North America's Greatest Bird Hunting Lodges and Preserves

North America's Greatest Big Game Lodges and Outfitters

North America's Greatest Waterfowling Lodges

North America's
GREATEST
Bird Hunting
Lodges
and Preserves

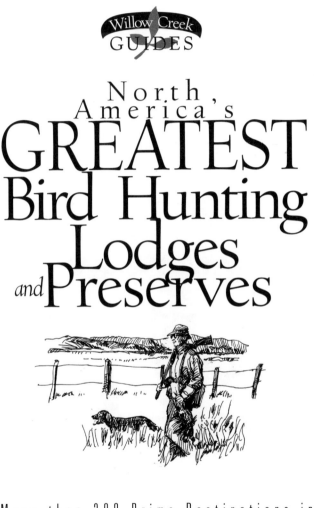

Willow Creek GUIDES

North America's
GREATEST
Bird Hunting
Lodges
and Preserves

More than 200 Prime Destinations in
the United States, Canada & Mexico

BY JOHN ROSS

Copyright 2000

John E. Ross

ALL RIGHTS RESERVED

No part of this book may be reproduced or transmitted in any form by any
means, electronic or mechanical, including photocopying, recording, or by
any information storage and retrieval system without permission in writing
from the Publisher, except in the case of brief excerpts in critical reviews
and articles. All inquiries should be addressed to:

Willow Creek Press

P.O. Box 147

Minocqua, Wisconsin 54548

www.wcguides.com

Printed in the United States of America

EDITED BY CHUCK PETRIE

DESIGNED BY GRETTER DESIGNS

Maps and Illustrations by R. L. Gretter

Cover Photograph by Andy Anderson

Library of Congress Cataloging-in-Publication Data

ROSS, JOHN, 1946-
    North America's greatest bird hunting lodges : more than 250 prime des-
tinations in the United States, Canada & Central America / by John Ross.
        p. cm.   (Willow Creek Guides)
    ISBN 1-57223-279-X
    1. Fowling--United States. 2. Fowling--Canada. 3. Hunting lodges--
United States. 4. Hunting lodges--Canada. 5. Shooting preserves--United
States. 6. Shooting preserves--Canada. I. Title. II. Series.

SK313 .R78 2000
799.2'4'0257--dc21   00-021961

Published by
WILLOW CREEK PRESS
PO Box 147
Minocqua, WI 54548

Acknowledgements

A S A KID, I had jumped a few quail along the honeysuckle entwined fences separating fallow fields in east Tennessee, but I didn't know what bird hunting was really like until I moved to Plymouth, New Hampshire, and met up with Tom Fowler. Tom's a preacher with a fondness for side-by-sides and Brittany spaniels, one of which attached himself firmly to my right calf when we first met. You don't quickly forget a thing like that, nor Tom's gentle education in the ways of Parkers and woodcock in those tiny coverts along the Baker. Later, in Carlisle, Pennsylvania, Jim Peterson and his setter Jake broke me in on pheasants, and then Tom Cornicelli introduced me to Long Island ducks and New Jersey geese. These gentlemen have given me a gift that I can never reciprocate. And a special thanks goes to my editor, Chuck Petrie. Chuck, who knows more about bird hunting than I ever will, hauled me out of the swamps when I stumbled in over my head. His edits are as true as a clean double on teal.

John Ross
Upperville, VA 2000

C o n t

e n t s

Early season on the Delaware River,
where local ducks aren't as wary as their
migratory cousins who will show up later on.

Among the hallmarks of a great lodge are
fine guides, great dogs, and wild birds, such as this trio
from the Miramichi Inn in New Brunswick.

Introduction

IT WAS THANKSGIVING. My brother Sam had driven up to our mom and dad's house near Sivierville, Tennessee, and I'd come down from New Hampshire. While our kids, whose ages had yet to reach double digits, tumbled over each other like puppies, and our wives commiserated over our transgressions, Sam and I slipped out of the house to kick up a rabbit or two and maybe some quail.

We hunted without a dog, as we always did. We poked into thickets of brush because they simply looked like they had to hold game. About mid-morning, I dropped down into a shallow weed-choked draw, and stepped smack dab into a covey of quail. Around my feet scuttled brown bodies the size of my fist. "Hey Sam," I hollered, "something's gonna happen here!" And boy did it ever! Like the grand finale on the Fourth of July, quail erupted everywhere.

Some years later I was living in Carlisle, Pennsylvania. In the cornfields there, friend Jim Peterson and I hunted pheasants over his old wonderful English setter, Jake. On this day, a few weeks after the blush of the season opener, we were working an alfalfa field behind a dairy barn. Jake, almost too feeble to be hunting, tottered to a standstill. His right leg was raised, head and neck turned slightly to the left, and his tail was straight as a gun barrel. His long white hairs fluttered in the whispering breeze. When the cock flushed, it left an iridescent trail across the sky. Bird hunting at its best.

It was good then and it is good now, but different. Today, here in the mid-Atlantic where I live, native quail and pheasants are all but a memory. Farming techniques, a proliferation of feral dogs and cats, and yes, the post-DDT-era return of high populations of raptors have all but erased huntable stocks of ring-necks and bobwhite. However, our grouse are much more numerous — probably because our shooting is so bad — and we see more ducks than anytime in the decade past. Why some years produce great flights of doves, and other years nothing, continues to be a mystery. Canada geese are reaching nuisance proportions. And wild turkey abound. In all, bird hunting is good, though changed from what it once was.

This book is not so much about bird hunting as it is about places to shoot birds. It's a book about lodges and preserves that offer bird hunting for a fee. That, then, presupposes that birds are available in huntable populations throughout a season that's long enough to make a lodge or guiding operation commercially viable.

In North America, there are few locations indeed where you'll find such native stocks: grouse and woodcock in the Canadian and U.S. maritimes and in the cut-over woods of the Great Lakes states; pheasants, prairie chickens, Hungarian partridge and sharp-tailed grouse in the broad prairies; quail and dove in Texas; ducks and geese in all of the great flyways; and wild turkey wherever there are warm summers and dense woods or swamp. In this book, you'll find lodges that offer hunts for native birds.

But in the main, the enterprises profiled here offer hunting for birds that are hatched in incubators, raised in pens, and turned loose sometime before you set foot in the field. At some preserves — or regulated shooting areas as they're called by some states that license them — the birds do not fly well. We've all hunted at such places. After your dog finds them, you have to nudge them with your foot to make 'em fly. Not very exciting. On other preserves, though, you'll be hard pressed to tell the difference between birds reared in the wild from those raised in a flight pen. The manner of releasing the birds and available cover make all the difference.

I don't think of preserves as hunting preserves but as **shooting** preserves. Some days when I hunt native birds, I get no shooting. But when I go gunning on a preserve, I always get shooting. More often than not, I get hunting as well. Preserves are locales where I can take my dog and run her on live birds. There are enough birds to reinforce lessons. Preserves give me the chance to work the kinks (and lord, there's enough of 'em) out of my swing and my legs. Preserves extend my gunning season. And they offer opportunities for fine group outings where everyone is pretty well assured of shooting, and thus a good time. Shooting preserves are fun, as are the game bird dinners that often result.

In this book, you'll find a wide range of lodges and preserves, from the pricey to those that even I can afford. You'll find operations that cater to corporations, as well as small and charming inns where you and your spouse can enjoy an intimate hunt and more. Read the profiles, contact the owners, question them thoroughly and check their references. And then pack up your shotgun and dog and go get some birds. Such hunting is good for the soul.

John Ross
Upperville, Virginia
2000

How to Pick a Lodge

I CY SLEET SCRATCHES A FINE TATTOO on the window. Blue flames from an apple-wood fire dance in the fireplace, and the noble head of your big old Lab lies in your lap. You absent-mindedly work your finger beneath his ear just the way he likes it, and your thoughts wander off to hunts for the coming year.

Where? Pheasants in the Dakotas? Quail down south? Great waterfowl in the Sacramento Valley? Or grouse and woodcock among the flaming maples of New Brunswick? Do you like to hunt over flashy pointers and slip down from the mule cart each time they freeze in the broom grass? Do you prefer poking behind a Brit, fending your way through the poplar as her bell tinkles merrily in the frosty New England air? How 'bout the way a German shorthair busts through cornstalks raising bloody hell to nail those ringnecks before they leak out the end of the field?

There's gunning from a butt as high-flying pheasant after pheasant soars overhead, released mallards sailing into the pond as your offspring gets the hang of duck shooting for the first time — the preserve where a three-hour hunt loosens your stride and frees your soul and puts birds in the freezer for sure. Well, almost for sure.

Some lodges and preserves cater to corporate groups, others to families. Many offer purely pen-raised birds, others only native and some a combination of both. At some, accommodations and cuisine satisfy the most sophisticated of tastes, and you'll find locations that feel just like home. Most provide guides, dogs and instruction, to greater or lesser degree. At others, you're pretty much on your own.

Gunning preserves can be found near almost every major American city. Bird hunters who travel on business might toss boots and brushpants into their carry-on; a number of preserves rent guns as well as guides with dogs. More than one deal has been cemented in a patch of milo or sorghum, or on a course for sporting clays.

Picking a lodge or preserve depends on decisions. Choices of birds, cover,

3

terrain, dogs, room and meals are legion. It all depends on what you like to do, where you want to go, and how much you want to spend.

❖ *"Wild" birds*

I met him on the high plains, a salesman from the East come to Montana to hunt pheasants, chukar, Hungarian partridge and sharp-tailed grouse. We hunted behind springers who first worked talus below the stubby cliff for chukar. The birds flushed, and the salesman hit some and missed others. And every half an hour or so, he asked the guide if these were "wild" birds. Well, yes and no. Were they born in the wild? Probably not. Did they flush and fly with such demonic spirit that our shots often went awry? Yep.

The business about wild versus pen-raised birds is overblown. Very few commercial hunting operations—save those with vast tracts of acreage situated in the heartland, and those that offer gunning for migratory birds—can rely on sustainable populations of game birds that are bred, hatched and reared outside of captivity. If hunting wild rather than pen-reared birds makes a difference to you, here are a few hints:

• Check the state's hunting regulations. If seasons and bag limits are established for the bird you want to hunt, you'll know that huntable populations of the species exist in the area you're interested in hunting. For instance, you won't find pheasant listed in the upland game section of Florida's hunting regs. Ringnecks in the Sunshine State are only available on a few preserves.

• If the hunting season at the lodge you're considering begins no earlier and extends no later than that for the surrounding area of the state or province, you'll probably be hunting natural birds.

• If the bag limits are no greater than those imposed by the state for the species you want to hunt, that's another good indication that the birds there weren't raised in a pen.

• Migratory birds such as woodcock, dove and waterfowl (with the exception of flighted mallards), as well as ruffed grouse, are almost always "natural."

Some preserves will tell you they "flight condition" their birds before releasing them in the field. That may or may not be true, and it may not mean much if it is. Most preserves release the number of birds you pay for within an hour or so of when you're scheduled to start your hunt. Some will dizzy a bird or lull it to sleep before setting it down in that patch of sorghum. Others just open the crate and let 'em fly. There's no guarantee, of course, that the bird you flush was one of those just released.

A third method of stocking is to release scores of birds periodically throughout the season. Those that survive hawks, feral dogs and cats, and other predators, become acclimated to their new surroundings within a few days. As the season progresses, it's incredibly hard to tell these from "natural" birds. On the other hand, preserves that follow this course lose more birds to depredation, thus you'll pay a higher price to gun these grounds than you will at those places that release six cocks just for you and your buddy.

A number of preserves offer "scratch" hunts. This means that no birds are released for you, but that you're hunting for birds that were released for other gunners who failed to find them or kill them if they did. Often, scratch hunts are only offered to shooters well known to a preserve's managers. Such hunts can be a nice fringe benefit that accrues only after a long-term friendship has been established.

❖ A word about cover

Second to the quality of birds, ask about cover at the preserve. That which is plush and thick when the season opens in September, may be sparse and threadbare come the tail end of March. Often, but not always, preserves mow walking paths through their cover crops. That makes it easy for the gunners. Dog and guide generally work the plantings while gunners walk the edges. The only way to check out a preserve's cover is to hunt it yourself. If you aren't enamoured by what you see, you don't have to come back.

Lodges that offer gunning for natural birds normally do so on so much acreage (either owned or leased) that they don't have to worry about whether hunters will trod the cover into the ground. But remember, those wonderful fields of prairie grasses that hunt so well in October and November become very different after two or three weeks of winter snow and ice. You'll find birds, then, where cover is sheltered from wind. In a sense, the birds become concentrated, but finding those concentrations becomes a bit of a challenge.

❖ And filthy lucre

You can pay a little or a lot to hunt birds. Generally you get what you pay for. Virtually all of the preserves and lodges in this book rely on repeat business. The difference between the most expensive and the least has a great deal to do with services that are really peripheral to hunting—but certainly a part of it. It takes bucks, and a lot of them, to maintain a kennel of 40 or more well-bred and trained pointers. Guides don't work for nothing (though sometimes it seems as if they do). Then there's the horse-drawn cart, the four-by-four bird buggies, leases, insurance (no mean expense), etc., etc. The greater the number and quality of services, the more you can expect to pay. Also, the more exclusive a lodge, the more it's apt to charge. The thing to remember about a shooting lodge or preserve is that you're not just paying for the birds, but the ambience. It's a total hunting experience.

❖ What you can expect

The most professional of the lodges and preserves understand one simple truth: commercial hunting is part of the hospitality business. Their job is to satisfy the needs of their guests in any manner that's safe, legal, and yes, moral. Once you tell them what you want in a bird hunt, they have an obligation to provide what they promise. Not all do. It's not unheard of for a group to pay for a 20 bird hunt and for the preserve to release only 15 ringnecks. How will you know? Don't worry, the word will get around. Check references religiously, and also talk to sporting goods stores, and game and fish departments. Learn to listen between the lines. Any but the most enthusiastic endorsement, ought to be a bit of a warning flag.

Lodges and preserves are licensed by the state. They also carry extensive liability insurance. You should be able to see evidence of both. If either is unavailable, flee for the hills.

Most lodges and preserves will not mix parties, meaning that if you and your buddy make reservations for a hunt, you won't be teamed with another pair of guys without your approval. If, on the other hand, you show up without reservations—a breach of etiquette as well as common sense—you may be squadded with other hunters on whom the owner or manager feels he can prevail. Reservations are important.

In the main, you should have exclusive rights to hunt a parcel of land described to you by the hunt manager. If you find others on your ground, leave the area and go talk it over with the manager.

If you hire a dog and guide as part of the package, you can expect the guide to be knowledgeable and the dog to be suitably trained. If either fall short of your expectations, withholding the tip is certainly appropriate. Be wary of the guide who carries a shotgun "just to back you up."

You can also expect to have your birds cleaned and bagged, ready for freezing. If you've traveled a long distance to a lodge, the odds are that your birds will not only be skinned or plucked (the former much more likely than the latter), but frozen and packed in a styrofoam or other insulated cooler.

❖ What your host expects of you

Imagine that you're a manager of a shooting preserve and the season's about to begin. Along with some old friends who come back year after year, there'll be a new crop of folks you've never seen before. They'll be toting loaded shotguns. Some will be very competent. Others will have never handled a gun before in their lives. Mixed in, there will be guys who admit they know nothing about the sport, and guys who think they know it all. It's the latter group that scares you to death.

The preserve manager has every right to expect you to follow his directions. He'll assign you to a field or two, and expect you to confine your hunting therein. At the very least, to do otherwise risks ruining another party's hunt; at the worst, it increases the risk of tragic accident. If you hunt with a guide and dog, let the guide control the dog. Tell the guide how you like to hunt, but follow the guide's recommendations. Tip the guide in cash if the hunt was good, even though you may not have harvested all the birds for which you paid. By all means, keep the muzzle of your shotgun pointed in a safe direction, especially when birds are flushing and the pointer may be leaping to catch a jumping cock. Firearms safety is paramount.

Be punctual. Most preserves operate two, half-day sessions per day. Lateness screws up the schedule and knocks all other logistics into a cocked-hat. If you're running behind, call the preserve and give an accurate estimate of your new arrival time, and permit the manager to make appropriate adjustments.

About Agents

SHOULD YOU BOOK a wingshooting trip through an agent? Yes and no. If you haven't done much traveling wingshooting, an agent can be very helpful. And if you're hunting an area about which you have no first-hand knowledge, using an agent might really be the right thing. The best agents work for you, not a lodge or outfitter. They want your repeat business. Good ones treat you like a client. They'll learn where and how you like to hunt. They'll know whether you prefer pointers or setters or all-purpose Labs. They'll understand your physical condition and recommend hunts accordingly. And they can help steer you through the wilds of traveling across international boundaries with firearms.

Good agents know lots of lodges and they'll match you to the kind of trip you want and can afford.

Following is a list of agents who give good information and service:

AGENTS

CABELA'S OUTDOOR ADVENTURES
1 Cabela Dr. Sidney NE 69160 800/346-8747
Web: www.cabelas.com

FRONTIERS
305 Logan Road PO Box 959 Wexford PA 15090-0959
800/245-1950
Web: www.frontierstrvl.com

GAGE OUTDOOR ADVENTURES
10000 Hwy 55 Plymouth MN 55441 800/888-1601
Web: www.gageoutdoor.com

OFF THE BEATEN PATH
27 E. Main St. Bozeman MT 59715 800/445-2995
Web: www.offbeatenpath.com

ORVIS ENDORSED WINGSHOOTING LODGES
(

ORVIS TRAVEL
Historic Rt. 7A Manchester VT 05224-0798 800/547-4322
Fax: 802/362-8795
Web: www.orvis.com

ROD & GUN RESOURCES, INC.
206 Ranch House Road Kerrville, TX 78028
800/211-4753 Fx: 830/792-6807
E-mail: venture@rodgunresources.com
Web: www.rodgunresources.com

TREK SAFARIS
PO Box 1305 Pointe Verde Beach FL, 32004
800/654-9915 Fax 904/273-0096
E-mail: trek@treksafaris.com
Web: www.treksafaris.com

ORGANIZATIONS

DUCKS UNLIMITED
One Waterfowl Way
Memphis TN 38120
901/758-3825
Web: www.du.org

PHEASANTS FOREVER
PO Box 75473
St. Paul, MN 55175
612/773-2000
Fax:612/773-5000

**NATIONAL WILD
TURKEY FEDERATION**
PO Box 530
Edgefield, SC 29824
803/637-3106 or 800/843-6983
Fax: 803/637-0034
E-mail: nwtf@nwtf.net
Web: www.nwtf.org

QUAIL UNLIMITED
31 Quail Run
PO Box 610
Edgefield SC 29824-0610
803/637-5731
Fax: 803/637-0037
Web: www.qu.org

**THE RUFFED
GROUSE SOCIETY**
451 McCormick Rd.
Corapolis PA 15108
888/564-6747
Web:
www.ruffedgrousesociety.org

And if the trip turns sour, they'll help you get any recompense that's coming to you. Best of all, it costs you nothing to use an agent. You'll generally pay the same for a hunt whether you book it directly yourself, or through an agent.

On the other side of the coin, if you're an old hand at traveling with bird dogs and shotguns and you know want you want, then it just might be easier to book your trips yourself. The advantage is that you make the contacts on your own schedule, and you don't have to wait for a middleman to return phone calls, and the time lag such always entails. Planning trips well in advance, of course, mitigates this problem. But who has time to plan ahead?

Other references:

❖ *Organizations:*

Organizations like Ducks Unlimited and Pheasants Forever provide a rich trove of information for traveling wingshooters. Most of those listed to the left have some regional or local chapters that might be sources for unbiased intelligence about places you're thinking about hunting. Memberships, by the way, are very inexpensive. They're worthwhile investments in the future of the sport we all love.

❖ *Books:*

Only now are regional wingshooting guides beginning to appear on book store shelves. And books that describe practical aspects of bird hunting are not as prevalent as one might expect.
To the right is a short list of some I've found to be particularly helpful.

USEFUL REFERENCES

**AMERICAN
WINGSHOOTING:**
A 20th Century Pictorial Saga, by Ben Williams,
Willow Creek Press, 1998.

BLACK'S WING & CLAY,
Black's Sporting Directories (annual)

GROUSE AND WOODCOCK,
by Don L. Johnson, Krause Publications, 1995.

**QUAIL HUNTING
IN AMERICA,**
by Tom Huggler, Stackpole, 1987.

**THE GAME BIRD
HUNTER'S BIBLE,**
by Robert Elman, Doubleday, 1993.

WILDFOWLER'S SEASON,
by Chris Dorsey, The Lyons Press, 1995.

A Shooting School or Not

MOST OF US learned to shoot shotguns by imitating our fathers or uncles or friends. With hand-traps in the back field, or rounds of trap, skeet or sporting clays, we tried to figure out how to drive that string of shot through a target whirring through the air at 60 miles per hour plus.

Some of us are naturals, blessed with that hand-eye coordination and an internal mental calculator that intuitively swings the shotgun, and fires the shot so pellets arrive where they're supposed to be to do the job. These gunners are a joy to watch and a source of deep frustration to those of us who cannot consistently hit a going-away pheasant, let alone a pair of highballing geese.

What's the answer? Perhaps a shooting school or series of lessons (unless you're very gifted, a single lesson won't do it). Throughout the country are a number of shooting schools, and at virtually every sporting clays course, you'll find instructors.

Just like with other kinds of schools, curriculum will vary from one place to the next. Also, the style of teaching changes with the personalities and experiences of each instructor. Finding the right shooting school and the right teacher requires very careful shopping. The wrong teacher can only make a lifetime of bad habits worse.

Here are some tips to separate the wheat from the chaff:

What are your objectives in attending a shooting school? Do you want to consistently shoot in the 70s and 80s on good sporting clay's courses? Do you want to become a better shot in the field. If so, what kind of birds do you hunt primarily—pheasants, ducks, grouse? Your primary objective makes a difference in the kind of instruction from which you'll benefit most.

Not too long ago I attended the Orvis shooting school at Sandanona, one of the nation's oldest shooting preserves. I was teamed with Scot Jones, whom I'd never met before. My goal was to learn how to shoot a fine old 20-gauge Parker on grouse hunts in the thick fox-grape and bittersweet tangles that crown the tops of the Shenandoahs near my house. Scot is a trap shooter. He came to Sandanona to learn to shoot sporting clays.

While there are many similarities between sporting clays and hunting, you'll discover an equal number of differences as well. The primary difference is the position of the gun preliminary to the flush or release of the bird. I generally carry my shotgun at something approximating high port arms—shotgun diagonally left to right across my chest with my right hand clutching the pistol grip close to my breast bone.

On the other hand, a sporting clay's shooter must be ready to mount his gun in an instant. He may be schooled to call for the bird with his shotgun at a high-ready position, with the heel of the butt just below the junction of arm and shoulder, and the muzzle pointing at the place where he will first see the bird. The safety will be off … that is, the gun is ready to fire.

Hard by the sea on Maine's rocky coast, the Eggemoggin offers splendid duckin' with warm, down-east hospitality.

If you are a wing shooter, the school and instructor you choose must understand the distinctions between sporting clays and hunting. And the converse is equally true.

Ask the school's director about the goals of other shooters who have attended there. Did they come primarily for sporting clays or wing-shooting? Ask for the names of instructors who teach the kind of shooting you seek to strengthen. Call them up and talk to them about your goals. Ask for names of previous students whom you can call as references. And, by all means, call them as well.

Shooting schools are generally one-day or two-days in duration. Opt for the two-day school if finances and time permit. During the first day, you'll become almost overwhelmed by new concepts and techniques. But during the intervening evening and night, you'll think consciously and subconsciously about what you experienced. On the second day, you'll put into practice what you learned the day before, and the instructor will be there to reinforce your successes and offer pointers where needed. And between the two days, the instructor will have had a chance to think about how you learn and your physical and mental capabilities. I brought to Sandanona 30 years of bad shooting habits and a lack of discipline. On the first day, I just could not do exactly what Geoff Kerr, my oh-so-patient instructor, wanted me to do. Geoff figured me out and improved my shooting immeasurably. It takes a couple of days to achieve a real gain in performance. You owe it to yourself not to settle for half a loaf.

Travel Tips

GETTING THERE can be half the fun, but tough travel can cast a pall over even the finest trip. You can mitigate potential travel disasters through good planning and by allowing yourself enough time (which I seldom do, of course). Planning begins in your mind when you begin thinking about a trip to Texas for quail or to New Brunswick for grouse. It only gets serious after you've made a commitment to a lodge. Then comes the big question: how are you going to get there?

Flying vs. Driving

OCTOBER 15 IS BUT A MONTH AWAY and you're eager to head for South Dakota, where the birds are. You and your bud have been planning this hunt for a year. After you picked a lodge, you told the guys at the gun club. Not only had they heard of it (maybe they lied), but they told you good things about it. The question foremost in your minds right now was, do we fly or drive? With two of you sharing driving chores, it'll take no more than a day or two to drive half way across the country for a bird shoot. On the other hand, it'll take as long to drive home.

So the debate plays itself out in your mind: driving adds four days to your trip, but that's only two weekends, leaving the week in between for hunting. If you drive, you'll be able to bring Ginger, your Brittany, and not have to worry about whether she'll be ok in an airliner's baggage hold. And you can haul as much gear as you need — a couple of extra shotguns, those bulky waders, coolers for birds on the return trip, and your camcorder and tripod.

The key to the answer to the debate may lie in your decision about bringing your dog on the hunt. If you do, you'll more than likely want to drive, if possible. While airlines make provisions for traveling with pets, it's not easy, nor is there any iron-clad guarantee that Ginger won't end up in Tulsa while you land in Pierre, where you're supposed to be. In fairness to the airlines, thousands of pets make cross-country trips every year and arrive none the worse for wear.

You can increase the odds of a successful flight for your pooch by booking a direct flight. But what if there isn't a flight from New York's LaGuardia to Lubbock, Texas? One solution is to fly directly to Dallas/Ft. Worth and rent a car from there. As it is with baggage, the greater the number of connections, the greater the chance that the dog and crate can go astray.

11

Airlines are pretty particular, with good cause, about the temperatures along the route the aircraft will take. If a dog is likely to spend more than 45 minutes outside at an airport in temperatures exceeding 85°F or below 45°F, the airline will not accept it. It is possible to obtain a waiver for the lower temperature limit from your veterinarian.

Size and weight restrictions also come into play. Cody, that big old loveable lummox of a Lab of yours, may be too large and too heavy to fit in a kennel of the size that an airline will transport. Normally 36" L x 24" W x 26" H is the maximum size kennel that can be transported on most commonly used commercial aircraft. If your flight to Pheasant Land Ranch requires a transfer to a feeder airline, it may not be possible to take your pet as baggage, because baggage used for such flights is limited.

And airline requirements for kennels vary. While all require that kennels be constructed so waste does not leak out, some mandate that kennels be equipped with false floors, and that bowls for water and food be permanently affixed to the kennel and accessible without opening the kennel's doors. While airlines do not feed or water dogs in transit (and they insist that you sign a statement saying that they haven't eaten within four hours of the flight time), they'll provide food and water if the flight encounters a long delay. If your dog is sensitive to diet (my American water spaniel is allergic to chicken), provide appropriate emergency feed to the airline.

When you and your pooch arrive at the airport (two hours before flight-time, because of the dog), you'll be required to show documentation from your vet that all of the dog's immunizations are current. The statement needs to have been obtained within 10 days of your flight. There is some difference between airlines on this. Check with your carrier.

Flying can be a traumatic experience for dogs, yet the debate over whether to sedate hunting dogs for travel rages. Jerome Robinson of *Field & Stream* makes a good point: Who wants to go to all the trouble of flying a dog into the best bird hunting its ever seen, only to have it reacting dopey on drugs? Talk to your vet about this. The cost of sending your dog as baggage on your flight is usually reasonable, around $50 on most airlines. However, if for some reason you opt not to travel at the same time as your dog, Bowser will be shipped as priority freight, which can cost several hundred dollars.

Along with making a decision about whether you want to fly your dog, you may want to think about what you'll do with your dog when you arrive at your wingshooting lodge. Many advertise the availability of kennel facilities for guests' dogs. But are those kennels maintained to the same standards of cleanliness as a vet's? Maybe, but maybe not. If your dog can stay in his traveling kennel in your room, he and you will probably be much happier.

Traveling with firearms

YOU'LL WANT TO TAKE TWO SHOTGUNS on a wingshooting trip. You may want a pair of gauges, say a 12 for ducks and geese and a 20 for quail. Or you may want a back-up gun in case something goes awry with your favorite. Unless you're driving, you may want to consider buying ammo at your destination — unless you're shooting a 28-gauge or a 16-gauge. You'll have no trouble finding more popular loadings for those bores in major cities, but in the hinterlands, forget it. Check airline regulations on the number of rounds you're allowed to carry in baggage. You may want to send ammo via UPS (and your guns as well) to your destination two or three weeks in advance of your trip.

Airlines are fairly consistent in their policies for checking firearms as baggage: unloaded in a locked, hard case with the firearms waiver and a card with your name and address on it. Ammunition generally cannot be contained in the same case as the firearm, even though it is unloaded.

If you travel to Canada, you'll want to be aware of changes in law governing importing of firearms by hunters. Essentially, you'll be required to file a written Firearms Declaration with Canadian Customs upon entering the country. As of this writing (Summer, 1999), plans call for the forms to be available by mail and from outfitters and lodges. You will complete the form and have it verified *in person* when you enter the country. A fee of $50 (Canadian) will be charged, and the form is good for a year. More information can be obtained by calling 800/731-4000.

Traveling with firearms to Mexico poses its own problems. Permits to bring sporting arms into the country are very high, even if (as is best) they are handled by your outfitter or booking agent. Plan to spend about $200 per gun, maybe more. As an alternative, many outfitters rent loaner guns to their clients for $15 or so per day. Bring your own shotgun to Mexico only if you can't bear to shoot any other.

And, when you're traveling out of the U.S. with a firearm, don't forget to register it with U.S. Customs. The procedure is simple, it's good for as long as you own the gun, and it costs you nothing (what a deal!). However, don't count on getting the form completed on the day of your flight. Best strategy is to make a separate trip to the airport some weekday, take your guns to customs, and register them all then.

I've heard enough stories about firearms that have been lost or damaged as baggage to be reluctant to use long hard cases — easily identified as carrying guns — when I travel. Instead, I make sure that all my traveling shotguns break down into pieces that fit inside a locking aluminum hard case that slides inside my duffel. That way only a few of us — me, the ticket agent and the lady who runs the airport baggage scanner — know what's inside.

❖ Bringing home the game

There's nothing better than pheasant breast with a raspberry salsa and a glass of chilled Riesling, or a quail potpie with an Octoberfest brew. Most outfitters clean and package birds for the trip home. Wise hunters bring along a cooler, a roll of freezer paper, a box of one-gallon plastic bags, and a roll of duct tape. They get and read a copy of the game rules for the state in which they're hunting and they abide scrupulously by the regulations there-in. You may think it a pain to leave wing or foot attached, but that may be the law. Freeze the game if you like; you can always thaw it at home. But a better course is to wrap each bird in freezer paper, seal them in Ziplock bags, and layer them in your cooler with ice as you would build a lasagna with a level of noodles, a level of cheese, and another of noodles, etc. Place your name inside of the cooler and seal it with duct tape. Thus packed, gamebirds will stay fresh for more than 24 hours, unless left in blazing sun.

Other Basic Tips

❖ The essentials

When packing for a hunt, ask yourself: What are the most important items I must, and I mean MUST, not be without?

❖ Medications and prescription glasses.

Lay in an emergency supply of medications. Carry one supply with you, pack the other in your luggage. Be sure to have current copies of prescriptions. In addition to prescription sunglasses, you should take a spare pair of glasses and extra sets of contact lenses if you use them.

❖ Money.

Traveler's checks, ATM cards and credit cards have pretty well reduced the need for cash on the road. But not with outfitters. For any outstanding balance due for the hunt, carry a money order or a certified check. While guides prefer cash for tips, give them a check. That way you have a record of your expenditure. If you're hunting in Canada or Mexico, carry the equivalent of $100 (U.S.) in local currency, and another $300 in traveler's checks. Take only two or three credit cards (American Express, MasterCard or Visa). In addition, stash $200 in emergency cash and traveler's checks and a list of all your credit cards (card numbers and phone numbers if you have to cancel them) in a place separate from where you carry your main funds. That way you won't be out of luck if your wallet is lost or stolen.

❖ Identification.

Even though it's not required, if you're traveling to Canada or Mexico, get a passport. If you don't have one, apply when you pay the deposit for the hunt. If you neglect to get a passport, a photo ID, such as a driver's license and your birth certificate, will suffice. Also, make a list of any medical conditions and allergies you haveand keep it with your identification. A copy of your identification should be cached with your emergency money.

❖ Airline tickets

Outfitters with sophisticated operations will offer to assist in booking your flight, but you may do better to have the outfitter tell you where and when to arrive, and then book the flights yourself. Sometimes a travel agent can get you a good deal, but again, you can sometimes do better yourself. It depends, mainly, on whether you're willing to spend the time to do it. Advance-purchase tickets can save you a bundle, but not if the no-refund, no-alteration policy is so strict as to limit flexibility in the case of missed connections due to weather, primarily on the return leg of your trip. Beware of connections that are too tight —l ess than an hour — particularly at international airports. Though baggage may be checked through, you'll have to take it through customs yourself. When entering or leaving Canada or Mexico, two hours between planes isn't too much. Booking agents have shepherded thousands of clients through the intricacies of international travel. If you're new to the traveling hunter game, they can be a big help.

Tickets do get lost or stolen. Make two copies of your ticket before leaving home. Keep one with your packet of emergency cash, the other folded in your wallet. If your ticket vanishes mysteriously, the copy will help you cancel the ticket and may help secure a replacement. And don't carry your ticket sticking out of a travel bag. Sure, it's convenient, but it's also easily swiped.

❖ Insurance

Outfitters book far in advance and require payment of up to 50 percent to hold a reservation. In some cases the balance is due in advance; others want it on arrival. In any event, you will have contracted for services; should you not be able to make the trip, you'll be liable for the full cost. If you cancel more than 90 days in advance, there's a fairly good chance that the lodge or outfitter will be able to fill the space. (Each has its own refund policy. Check them out thoroughly.) Travel insurance is available, too. Should illness, accident or a death in the family prohibit you from making the trip, travel insurance will pay up to the full amount of your obligations. Available coverage varies extensively among insurance companies, as do premiums. However, you can expect to pay about five percent of the total coverage, or roughly $350 for a policy worth $6,500.

While we're on the subject of insurance, if you're traveling to another country, you'll want to check with your medical insurance carrier to determine coverages. If you're stricken with an acute medical problem while in the bush, will your insurance pay for air evacuation to the closest hospital? It's also a good idea to determine the applicability of automobile insurance and loss/theft provisions of homeowner's or business insurance in Canada or Mexico.

Other Fundamentals

IF YOU'VE TAKEN CARE OF THE ESSENTIALS, you'll survive your trip and most likely won't go broke. But what about luggage, clothing and traveling hunting gear?

❖ *Baggage*

Add it up: hunting boots, heavy and light hunting clothes, raingear, sweaters, hats, gloves, socks, long underwear, binoculars, camera, shotgun etc., etc. None of it's light and most is bulky. Take only what you need. Most lodges provide lists. Follow them religiously. Unfortunately, hunters are obvious prey for baggage thieves. For bags that you check, use tough, nondescript, soft-sided luggage. Put your name, address and phone number on a luggage tag outside and inside each bag.

Fine old homes like the Burge Plantation steep gunners in the genteel traditions of bird hunting down South.

Checked baggage does get lost. In your carry-on, pack things you absolutely cannot do without: medications, extra glasses, Gore-Tex hat (wear the parka and one of your two pairs of boots), mini-shaving kit, camera, gloves, flashlight, a Ziploc bag with two pairs of heavy socks and lightweight polypropylene long underwear, a woolen or fleece shirt and sweater, and wool hunting pants, plus your brand-new Swarovski 10x50 binoculars. Jam in a couple of paperback books. All this, stuffed into a large waterproof kit bag, such as the one from Orvis, weighs about 20 pounds and slings comfortably over your shoulder. It fits in most overhead bins and can be shoved under most seats. Leave cotton clothing at home.

Also consider wearing a fannypack for extra supplies. It's unobtrusive and secure, and you'll soon forget you're wearing it, but you'll be glad you've got it.

A Word about Vital Statistics

A LONG WITH EACH PROFILE is a list of pertinent information about each lodge or preserve. It's a kind of shorthand. Gives you the skinny quickly. One glance and you should gain a sense of whether this is a place you want to consider visiting. If so, forge ahead and read the profile. If not, turn the page.

Since the Vital Statistics information is abbreviated, a little explanation may be helpful.

❖ Source of birds:

Like the old controversy about native versus hatchery trout, upland hunters debate the merits of pen-raised versus birds born in the wild. To me, a "wild" bird is one that was born and raised out of captivity. Though it seems strange to define a natural critter in terms of its lack of confinement, pen-raised birds are the norm on preserves, and truly wild birds are not. Still, some birds released from flight pens go wild in a hurry, and I'll defy anyone to tell with 100 percent reliability which is always which.

❖ Land:

Generally, the more land that's available to a lodge or preserve, the higher the quality of the hunting experience and the greater the odds that you'll hunt for wild birds.

❖ Accommodations:

While the focus of this book is lodges, a number of good preserves offer lodging in town. Given the choice of bunking with four other guys and sharing a bath, I'm old enough and so set in my ways that I'll opt for a motel room with a private bath almost anytime. Motels aren't all bad.

❖ Conference groups:

Meat and potatoes for most bird hunting lodges are corporate and business groups. Second come armies of vendors entertaining customers. Bird hunting is a small-group sport and thus conducive to building relationships between vendors and clients.

❖ *Guides:*

Most preserves offer guide services. Their fees are usually in addition to the price of a hunt. Many are skilled dog handlers, and most are employed in other ways (they'd go broke if they only depended on guiding). Tips are always appreciated.

❖ *Dogs and facilities:*

Bird hunting is as much about dogs as it is about birds. Many preserves offer good, dry, warm kennels for visiting dogs. Others have a barrel and chain staked out back. Ask about a lodge's kennel facilities. If you have any doubt, leave your dog at home or go elsewhere. If not, be sure your dog's Parvo and other immunizations are up to date, and bring old Beau along.

❖ *Other activities:*

In this list you'll notice golf and tennis. Few lodges (I can think of only one, but I'm going bald and my memory leaks out) actually offer golf on site. But often it's close enough so a hunter can shoot birds in the morning and then get in 18 holes in the afternoon. Listed here are sports that are available close to the lodge or preserve.

❖ *Rates:*

While not quite as complicated as fees charged for hunting big game, rate structures at preserves can be kind of complex. Most are based on the number of birds released before you hunt. Sometimes room and board are included; other times they're not. Rates included here are for the 1999 year. Best rule of thumb: Check rates before you go.

❖ *Contacts:*

Names, addresses, phone, fax, e-mail, web sites . . . once this book goes to press, some start becoming out of date. If you can't contact a lodge or preserve through the data provided here, try information. If that still doesn't work, send me an e-mail message (jross@crosslink.net) and I'll help you hunt 'em down.

Tom Cornicelli calls the shot over a little freshwater marsh on the eastern tip of Long Island, a land short of hunting lodges but replete with bed-and-breakfasts and motels where hunters stay.

EAST

CONNECTICUT, MAINE, MASSACHUSETTS, NEW HAMPSHIRE, NEW JERSEY, NEW YORK, PENNSYLVANIA, RHODE ISLAND, VERMONT

FROM NEW ENGLAND, where clumps of golden-leaved birch split century-old stone fences that once framed meadows, west to the second growth woodlands of oak, maple and fir, and south to the broad rolling fields of corn and beans, the East retains much of its traditional wingshooting promise. Ruffed grouse and woodcock are abundant in New England's forests and those 30-minute coverts (so called because that's as long as it takes two to hunt them), the locations of which are tightly held among one's dearest friends.

Rugged highlands of New York, New Jersey and Pennsylvania also offer marvelous grouse hunting, though it's apt to be more arduous than in New England. This is the land of the light 20 gauge, and a cocker or Brittany. Valley farmlands may offer some gunning for ring-necks, but that game is largely played out on preserves.

Lodges:

Maine

1	ALLAGASH GUIDE SERVICE
2	CEDAR RIDGE OUTFITTERS
3	COASTAL MAINE OUTFITTERS
4	CONKLIN'S LODGE & CAMPS
5	EGGEMOGGIN LODGE
6	FOGGY MOUNTAIN GUIDE SERVICE
7	GENTLE BEN'S LODGE
8	KING & BARTLETT FISH & GAME CLUB
9	POINTERS RUN HUNTING PRESERVE
10	THE BRADFORD CAMPS

New Hampshire

11	TALL TIMBER LODGE

New Jersey

12	SHORE WINDS HUNTING FARM & KENNEL

New York

13	FORRESTEL FARM HUNTING PRESERVE
14	LUCKY STAR RANCH
15	ORVIS SANDANONA
16	R. L. SHELTRA'S SALMON RIVER OUTFITTERS
17	SNO-FUN HUNTING PRESERVE

Pennsylvania

18	HILL'S TWIN SPRUCE LODGE
19	HILLENDALE HUNT CLUB
20	JUNIATA RIVER GAME FARM
21	WING POINTE

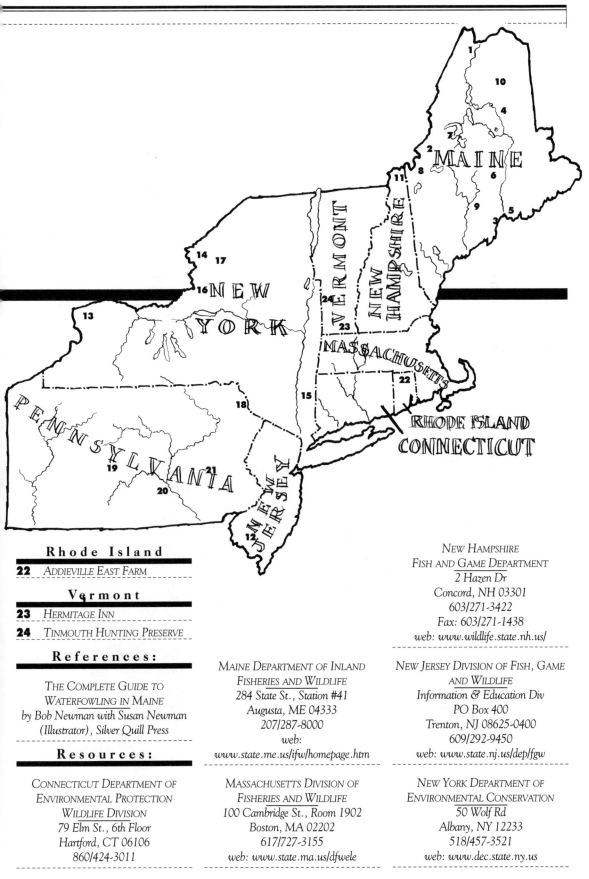

References:

THE COMPLETE GUIDE TO
WATERFOWLING IN MAINE
by Bob Newman with Susan Newman
(Illustrator), Silver Quill Press

Resources:

CONNECTICUT DEPARTMENT OF
ENVIRONMENTAL PROTECTION
WILDLIFE DIVISION
79 Elm St., 6th Floor
Hartford, CT 06106
860/424-3011

MAINE DEPARTMENT OF INLAND
FISHERIES AND WILDLIFE
284 State St., Station #41
Augusta, ME 04333
207/287-8000
web:
www.state.me.us/ifw/homepage.htm

MASSACHUSETTS DIVISION OF
FISHERIES AND WILDLIFE
100 Cambridge St., Room 1902
Boston, MA 02202
617/727-3155
web: www.state.ma.us/dfwele

NEW HAMPSHIRE
FISH AND GAME DEPARTMENT
2 Hazen Dr
Concord, NH 03301
603/271-3422
Fax: 603/271-1438
web: www.wildlife.state.nh.us/

NEW JERSEY DIVISION OF FISH, GAME
AND WILDLIFE
Information & Education Div
PO Box 400
Trenton, NJ 08625-0400
609/292-9450
web: www.state.nj.us/dep/fgw

NEW YORK DEPARTMENT OF
ENVIRONMENTAL CONSERVATION
50 Wolf Rd
Albany, NY 12233
518/457-3521
web: www.dec.state.ny.us

Wood ducks and teal open the waterfowl season, but mallards are the most popular ducks. Black ducks, pintails, and canvasbacks are also fairly common. Gunners hunting inland bays do well on scaup (bluebills) and scoters. The resident population of Canada goose is thriving with very liberal limits set early and late in the season. Snow goose populations are burgeoning and there is excellent brant hunting along the New Jersey coast.

Pennsylvania Game Commission
2001 Elmerton Ave
Harrisburg, PA 171100-9797
717/787-4250
Fax: 717/772-2411
web: www.pgc.state.pa.us/

Rhode Island Division of Fish and Wildlife
4800 Tower Hill Rd
Wakefield, RI 02879-2207
401/789-8281
web: www.state.ri.us/dem

Vermont Fish and Wildlife Department
103 South Main St
Waterbury, VT 05676
802/241-3700
Web: www.state.vt.us/anr

Sandanona, that great Orvis shooting preserve in Millbrook, New York, has instructors, like Geof Kerr, who teach willing pupils the secrets to high crossingshots.

Allagash Guide Service

A l l a g a s h ,   M a i n e

Ruffed grouse are knights of this realm, and woodcock, jesters of the court.

VITAL STATISTICS:

GAME BIRDS:
GROUSE, WOODCOCK
Source of Birds: Wild
Seasons:
GROUSE: October and November
WOODCOCK: October
Land: Unlimited private acres
Accommodations:
WOODEN CABINS
NUMBER OF ROOMS: 17
MAXIMUM NUMBER OF HUNTERS: 35
Meals: Solid chops, stews, pasta, and turkey
Conference Groups: No
Guides: Trained dogs and guides
Dogs and Facilities:
Bring kennels for your dogs
Other Services:
Birds cleaned and packed for travel
Other Activities:
Big game, bird-watching, canoeing, fishing, wildlife photography
Rates:
$500 / week per hunter; guide service additional
Gratuity:
Hunter's discretion
Preferred Payment:
Cash or check
Getting There:
Fly to Presque Isle and rent a car.

Contact:
Sean Lizotte
Allagash Guide Service
RR 1, Box 131D
Allagash ME 04774
207-398-3418
EMAIL: allaguide@ainop.com
WEB: www.maineguides.com/allagash-guide-service

GROUSE. RUFFED GROUSE. *Bonasa umbellus.* Pa'tridge or Pa'ts for short. Call 'em any name you please, but of all the upland birds, ruffs are king. They're the salmon of the forests: wily, resilient, and oh so challenging. Grouse hunters go though season after season without harvesting a bird. They talk of points and jumps. Of timberdoodle, which frequently shares cover with grouse, they say: "Oh, it was only a woodcock." Grouse hunters wear their badges proudly. One "shoots" quail and ducks, but one "hunts" grouse. Their guns are apt to be lively 20s or 28s; but savvy, old-school, woodswise grouse hunters often carry 16s. If a guy's toting a 16-bore, watch out. There's a likelihood, come nightfall, you'll find partridge in his pot.

Of all the territory in the northeastern quadrant of the U.S., Maine may well have the best populations of ruffed grouse. Why? Most of the state is heavily forested and managed for timber. While environmental folk get damn mad at the cutting of even a single tree, were it not for clearcutting and the thick tangles of underbrush that mark the first stages of a forest's rebirth, there would be no grouse (to say nothing of fewer deer and moose). And were it not for the timber companies, there would be no abandoned logging roads tawny now with the dried grasses of summer. Logging roads are avenues for grouse.

Sean Lizotte, owner and operator of Allagash Guide Service, sits in the catbird seat with his lodge near the northern end of the Allagash Wilderness Waterway. This is Maine at its most rural. Roads are of sand and cobble. Stands of birch, larch and firs roll over the glacial landscape. In October and November, there's no better country for ruffed grouse. The population is so thick that meat hunters drive logging roads and bag birds without leaving their cars (illegal, by the way). It would seem that an average wingshooter with a pointing or flushing dog would stand a pretty good chance of bagging a limit of four birds. True enough. Trick is finding concentrations of birds, and that's where Sean's guides come in. They know the real estate. Hunt over their dogs or yours. Oh yeah, if you happen to flush a woodcock, it's ok.

Cedar Ridge Outfitters

J a c k m a n ,   M a i n e

In the back of Maine's beyond lies a friendly camp with new cabins and great grouse.

VITAL STATISTICS:

GAME BIRDS:
GROUSE, WOODCOCK
Source of Birds: Wild
Seasons:
GROUSE: October through mid-December
WOODCOCK: October
Land: Unlimited private and public acres
Accommodations:
PRIVATE LODGE AND FRAME CABINS
NUMBER OF CABINS: 8
MAXIMUM NUMBER OF HUNTERS: 60
Meals: Family-style
Conference Groups: Yes
Guides: Trained dogs and guides
Dogs and Facilities:
Bring you own kennel if you bring a dog
Other Services:
Birds cleaned and packed for travel
Other Activities:
Big game, biking, bird-watching, boating, canoeing, fishing, golf, hiking, horseback riding, skiing, wildlife photography
Rates:
From $160 / person / week, minimum group of 3; guiding $135 / day / person
Gratuity:
$10 - $20 / day
Preferred Payment:
Cash, MasterCard, Visa or check
Getting There:
Fly to Bangor and rent a car.

Contact:
Deborah Blood
Cedar Ridge Outfitters
PO Box 744
36 Attean Rd
Jackman ME 04945
207/668-4169
Fax: 207/668-7636
EMAIL:
info@cedarridgeoutfitters.com
WEB: www.cedarridgeoutfitters.com

JACKMAN IS ONE OF THOSE TOWNS that you'd be most unlikely to visit unless you really wanted to go there. Twenty miles south of the Quebec border on US 201, Jackman lies in a valley beneath Burnt Jacket Mountain and between Wood and Long ponds. A low basin, the area round the town is boggy and then rises to ridges of beech and birch. Woodcock thrive here and a sizable population summers in this neck of the woods. But when the weather turns tough in Canada, flight birds begin to filter across the border. On mornings after the passage of a cold front, you'll find new chalking in the woods.

That's the time to uncase your 20-bore, bell your Brittany, and probe the coverts along beaver flowages and abandoned logging roads. Grouse, of course, are resident here year-round. Other locales may hold more birds at any given time, but few are more pleasurable to hunt. Flushes should be plentiful, and your dog will get lots of work. So will you.

Grouse and woodcock hunting overlap with seasons for bear and deer. And some hunters who fill their tags early with bows take advantage of woodcock in October. Woodcock closes in November, but rifle hunters might consider bringing a shotgun for grouse.

Recently, Cedar Ridge opened six beautiful housekeeping cabins that boast all the modern conveniences. Located five minutes from town down a secluded road, each cabin offers privacy and convenience. Most have complete kitchen facilities. If you stay in a cabin, you may not want to overlook the cooking of Debbie Blood, co-owner with husband Hal of the operation. Her turkey, pork roast, stews, veggies and baked goods would founder you were it not for the walking. Bird hunting guides are available if you wish, but you're not required to use one. However, if you haven't hunted here before, a guide is a great idea.

Coastal Maine Outfitters

Belfast, Maine

Hunt classic abandoned farms through orchards long overgrown where grouse still come to feed.

VITAL STATISTICS:

GAME BIRDS:
DUCKS, GROUSE, WOODCOCK
Source of Birds: Wild
Seasons:
GROUSE: October through early December
WOODCOCK: early October through early November
DUCKS: October through late January
Land: Unlimited private and public acres
Accommodations:
CLAPBOARD FARM HOUSE
NUMBER OF ROOMS: 4
MAXIMUM NUMBER OF HUNTERS: 8
Meals: Regional cuisine with lobster and beef
Conference Groups: Yes
Guides: Trained dogs and guides
Dogs and Facilities:
Kennel for hunters' dogs, dog training
Other Services:
Birds cleaned and packed for travel
Rates:
$300 / day
Gratuity:
$50 - $100
Preferred Payment:
Cash or check
Getting There:
Fly to Bangor, Maine, and the lodge van will pick you up.

Contact:
Joe Lucey
Coastal Maine Outfitters
RR#4, Box 4140
Belfast ME 04915
207/722-3218
WEB: www.maineguides.com/members/coastal

ONCE UPON A TIME, those glacially rounded hills of coastal Maine were covered with prosperous farms. A family could live then on a few milk cows, apples, potatoes and squash. But before long, the thin soils got tired, the War Between the States siphoned men to military and to mills in the cities, and others went off to the big woods to log. By the 1900s, only a few families struggled with subsistence farms, and by the 40s, even they'd gone south. Hampered by a short growing season, it took decades for stands of poplar, maple and beech to eat away at the pastures. But eat away they did, and the resulting riot of limber thickets, punctuated here and there with an abandoned orchard, provide ruffed grouse with marvelous habitat.

Pa'tridge is to Maine (and Michigan) what bobwhite is to the South. The latter is a gentlemen's sport of mule-drawn wagons and mounted gunners, of white-flanked pointers slashing through broomsedge, of lively side-by-sides. Grouse hunting is different. Coverts are so thick that you can rarely see the dog, especially early in the season. Tangled brush clutches your ankles at each step. Birds won't hold for longer than a minute to two. And when they flush, they seem to have a knack for finding that one escape route where you can't get a shot no matter what. Grouse hunters learn perseverance and patience, and take it with a great dose of humility. And that's why the only trophy in some hunters' dens is the black-banded fan of a ruffed grouse tail.

For the better part of 20 years, Joe Lucey has been guiding hunters for grouse and woodcock in the hills northwest of Belfast on Penobscot Bay. He hunts overgrown farms, working hunters along stone walls and through thickets bordering creeks or beaver ponds. You'll get gunning here, no doubt of that. And if a flight of woodcock's in, you may fill your tag with them. Getting a limit of grouse is akin to winning the Irish Sweepstakes. One bird is a fair day, two is great. Grouse season overlaps with hunting eider, oldsquaw, scoter, bufflehead, goldeneye, and big black ducks off the rocky coastal points. Combo hunts are popular. Bring your own dogs or hunt with setters or spaniels from Joe's kennel.

Joe and partner Brenda Haley put up hunters in their remodeled 1840s farmhouse with an ell attached to a huge, shingled barn. Meals feature lobster and beef, and those hors d' ouervres you're eating are eider with a piquant sauce.

[E A S T]

Conklin's Lodge & Camps

P a t t e n ,   M a i n e

Hunting these foothills for partridge is best just after Columbus Day, when leaves have left the trees.

VITAL STATISTICS:

GAME BIRDS:
GROUSE, PHEASANT, WOODCOCK
Source of Birds: Wild, pen-reared
Seasons:
GROUSE and WOODCOCK: October through November
PHEASANTS: September through December
Land: Unlimited private and public acres
Accommodations:
LOG CABINS
NUMBER OF ROOMS: 6
MAXIMUM NUMBER OF HUNTERS: 35
Meals: Family-style roasts
Conference Groups: Yes
Guides: Guides and dogs available
Dogs and Facilities:
Kennel for hunters' dogs
Shotgun Sports:
Driven birds, shooting schools, tower or release shoots
Other Services:
Birds cleaned and packed for travel
Other Activities:
Big game, bird-watching, boating, canoeing, fishing, golf, hiking, skiing, wildlife photography
Rates:
From $425 / week
Gratuity:
Hunter's discretion
Preferred Payment:
Cash or check
Getting There:
Fly to Bangor and rent a car.

Contact:
Lester Conklin
Conklin's Lodge & Camps
PO Box 21
Patten ME 04765
207/528-2901
EMAIL: guideonc@hotmail.com

LOCATED ON THE ROAD to the north entrance of Baxter State Park, Conklin's Lodge & Camps sits on the fringe of Maine's great wilderness. The land does more than roll; it climbs rocky hills and falls off the other side into twisting drainages that are one part water and three parts swamp. Here and there are clearings where farmers in the early 1900s tried vainly to grow a living from harsh yet lovely land. They're gone now. So too is the primal spruce fir forest. In its place is second-growth scrub, cover much favored by grouse and woodcock.

From his camp, Les runs hunts for those birds in October and November. Bring your own dog and hunt without a guide (he'll give you good directions and a bag lunch and your off on your own). Best bet, though, is to spring for a guide at $150 per day. Your chances of bagging a grouse or two will be infinitely improved. The best time for grouse in this section of Maine is late October. By then, leaves have fallen from the trees, and it's actually possible to follow the flight of a flushed grouse. Any earlier, and you play now-you-see-'em-and-now-you-don't. Snow-shoe, or varying, hares are also legal game and can be hunted with or without a dog.

If you want some fowl to take home to the family, Les will release pheasants for you on his preserve. Tower shoots and driven bird shoots can also be arranged upon request. And bird hunting overlaps with baited bear and deer. If either of those whet your appetite, book a big game hunt and add a day or two of bird hunting.

Conklin's camps are clean, but not fancy. Five log cabins and one house-keeping chalet are scattered beneath the trees surrounding the main lodge. Two of the cabins sleep four, and the others six. A shared shower and bath facility is near-by. Meals are hardy affairs as befits the Maine woods. Bookings are by the week, generally speaking, but depending on occupancy, special arrangements may be possible.

Eggemoggin Lodge

When winter's winds turn the bay the color of pewter, then Down East duckin' shines.

VITAL STATISTICS:

GAME BIRDS:
DUCKS
Source of Birds: Wild
Seasons:
October through mid-January
Land: Unlimited public acres
Accommodations:
PRIVATE LODGE
NUMBER OF ROOMS: 11
MAXIMUM NUMBER OF HUNTERS: 15
Meals: Elegant regional cuisine
Conference Groups: Yes
Guides: Included
Dogs and Facilities:
Kennel for hunters' dogs
Shotgun Sports:
Sporting clays, informal shooting
instruction
Other Services:
Birds cleaned and packed for travel
Other Activities:
Bird-watching, boating, fishing,
hiking, swimming, wildlife
photography
Rates:
From $250 / day
Gratuity:
$50 per day/per guide
Preferred Payment:
Cash, MasterCard, Visa or check
Getting There:
Fly to Bangor and rent a car, or
arrange for the lodge van.

Contact:
Susan Lemoine
Eggemoggin Lodge
HC 64 Box 380
Brooklin ME 04616
888/559-5057
Fax: 207-359-5057
EMAIL: mainecoast@hypernet.com
WEB: maincoastexperience.com/duck-hunting/index.htm

EGGEMOGGIN REACH is a northwest to southeast channel that connects Penobscot and Blue Hill bays. Penobscot is the heart of Maine's sea duck hunting. American eider, oldsquaw, and American, surf, and white-winged scoters are the primary quarry. While the season stretches from October to late January, the best hunting occurs in December and January. *Brrr.*

But that's the way it is. Bundled in layers of polypropylene, wool, fleece, and Gore-Tex, you'll hunker among the ledges and boulders of the bay's outer islands. You may or may not hunt over decoys, depending on wind and tide conditions. Sea duck hunting is a fast and furious business. Birds can jet in like teal on after- burners, screaming past before you know they've been there. A 12-gauge auto is the best medicine with #4 steel shot. Ounce and a quarter loads are all you need, and three-inch shells offer very little advantage. Keep in mind, however, that salt water is extremely hard on shotguns and, no matter how careful you are, during your hunt your gun's stock is bound to come into contact with granite boulders. If you're heading off on a sea duck hunt, consider investing in a synthetic stocked Remington or Bennelli with matte-finished metalwork. With barrels of 26 inches (nothing longer is of any advantage), these semiautos are equally at home in a goose pit.

The lodge ferries gunners and guides out to the islands in a 36-foot cruiser, which tows tenders behind it. The same cruiser collects you at the end of the hunt and warms you on the return run to the lodge. You'll love the lodge. It sits by itself on a bit of Maine Coast with stunning views of the reach and Little Deer Isle beyond. After the hunt, you'll toast yourself two ways…one ,before the fire, and two, with a welcome libation. Meals feature local seafood, beef, pasta and organic vegetables. Rooms feature a pair of queen-sized beds, or a king if you prefer, and private baths. Combination packages including deer hunting are available.

As you've guessed by now, there's more to Eggemoggin than sea ducks and deer. In more temperate seasons you'll paddle the bays in sea kayaks, watch whales, fish for lobster, and hike islands where nobody lives. Bird-watching can be fantastic, and sitting on the deck watching sailboats ply the reach is just about as therapeutic as relaxation can get.

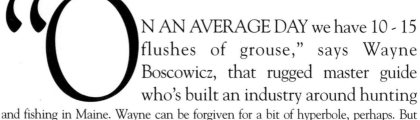

Foggy Mountain Guide Service

D o v e r - F o x c r o f t ,   M a i n e

So where do you find grouse when you're hunting 6 million acres? Right where they're s'posed to be.

VITAL STATISTICS:

GAME BIRDS:
GROUSE, WOODCOCK
Source of Birds: Wild
Seasons:
GROUSE: October through November
WOODCOCK: October
Land: Unlimited private and public acres
Accommodations:
LOG HOUSEKEEPING COTTAGES
NUMBER OF ROOMS: 10
MAXIMUM NUMBER OF HUNTERS: 25
Meals: Self-catered
Conference Groups: Yes
Guides: Trained dogs and guides
Dogs and Facilities:
Kennel for hunters' dogs
Other Services:
Birds cleaned and packed for travel
Other Activities:
Big game, fishing, wildlife photography
Rates:
$990 / 3 days for two
Gratuity:
Hunter's discretion
Preferred Payment:
Cash or check
Getting There:
Fly to Bangor and rent a car.

Contact:
Wayne A. Boscowicz
Foggy Mountain Guide Service
RR2 Box 1140
Dover-Foxcroft ME 04426
207/564-3404
Fax: 207/564-8209
WEB: www.foggymountain.com

"**O**N AN AVERAGE DAY we have 10 - 15 flushes of grouse," says Wayne Boscowicz, that rugged master guide who's built an industry around hunting and fishing in Maine. Wayne can be forgiven for a bit of hyperbole, perhaps. But with some six million acres at his disposal, there's no doubt that the birds are there. And Wayne and his guides are quite adept at finding them. They've been doing it for more than a generation.

You'll meet your guide after breakfast, discuss the day's plans and load up in the four-by-four pickup with the dog boxes in back. Following old logging roads deep into land Wayne leases from paper companies, you'll aim for the plot selected for this morning's hunt. It may be an old abandoned farm with overgrown orchards and pasture land. You might be striking out for a patch that's been clear-cut and now filled with saplings and young firs. You may hunt edges of swamps. You'll work one covert in the morning, break for lunch, and then work another in the afternoon. Each day you'll see different country, and it will stay in your mind forever. It's all prime habitat for grouse and woodcock. Grouse season opens in October and runs through November, but Wayne only hunts woodcock in October.

Some big game hunters in the know sign up for archery hunts for deer or bear. Deer are not nearly as plentiful as they are in the South, but those that you see will be pretty good size. Spend three of four days deer hunting and add a couple of days for grouse and woodcock. Why not? A 20-gauge and a couple boxes of shells doesn't add much to your baggage.

At Foggy Mountain, you'll stay in cabins where bedding and all kitchen utensils are provided. All you need to do is bring your own grub. If no one in your party cares to cook, there are plenty of good restaurants within an easy drive.

Under leaves so gold they make your heart swell, a trapper looses a bird for a gunner who will hunt the rolling fields of Tinmouth, one of Vermont's finest preserves.

Coastal Main Outfitters' Lodge in Maine harkens back to the days when dairying was the cash crop. Now pa'tridge hide in abandoned orchards, and woodcock lurk by the brook.

Gentle Ben's Lodge

R o c k w o o d ,   M a i n e

Lodgin', guide and dog won't break your bank at this family camp. A' yup.

VITAL STATISTICS:

GAME BIRDS:
GROUSE, WOODCOCK
Source of Birds: Wild
Seasons:
GROUSE: October through November
WOODCOCK: October
Land: Unlimited private and public acres
Accommodations:
PRIVATE LODGE
NUMBER OF ROOMS: 3
MAXIMUM NUMBER OF HUNTERS: 12
Meals: Family-style
Conference Groups: Yes
Guides: Optional at $150 / day
Dogs and Facilities:
Bring your own dog box
Other Services:
Birds cleaned and packed for travel
Other Activities:
Big game, bird-watching, boating, canoeing, fishing, hiking, wildlife photography
Rates:
$300 / week
Gratuity:
$25 / day
Preferred Payment:
Cash, credit cards or check
Getting There:
Fly to Bangor and rent a car.

Contact:
Bruce Pelletier
Gentle Ben's Lodge
PO Box 212
Rockwood ME 04478
800/242-3769
Fax: 207/534-2236
EMAIL: info@gentleben.com
WEB: www.gentleben.com

IN SOME PARTS OF MAINE, grouse hunting is laborious. In others, it's a little easier. One of the best places is the western shore of Moosehead Lake. Here, according to Maine guide Bruce Pelletier, who with wife Cheryl owns and operates Gentle Ben's, you'll encounter an unusual number of birds. Getting your limit of four each day is fairly well certain—assuming you shoot reasonably well. Most hunters bring their own dogs; Bruce runs hounds for bear, but you won't find a pointing, flushing or retrieving dog in his kennel. Even though hunters without dogs seem to do just fine. "You can kick up four birds in a mile's walk," says Bruce.

Woodcock, of course, go hand in hand with grouse. Heavy flights of migratory birds move down through the Moosehead region in the first three weeks of October. That's the best time to hunt this reclusive, long-beaked, big-eyed bird. You'll know when you're in woodcock cover, for you can see white splashes— "chalking" it's euphemistically called—on leaves and, occasionally, beak holes in soft ground. Streamside coverts are heavily used by woodcock, but you'll also find them on higher ground mixed in with grouse. In any event, terrain is not steep here. It's more a land of rolling hills.

Gentle Ben's only hosts about a dozen grouse hunters each year. Some hunt with a guide throughout their five-day stay, but some hire a guide for the first day or two and then hunt on their own. Both are equally successful. A number of hunters sign up to hunt bear with dogs or deer with bows, and they add a few days of grouse and woodcock on the side. When not in the field, hunters hang out in the lodge, getting fat on Cheryl's family-style cooking. Accommodations are comfortable, but by no means plush. However, if it's a bargain you're seeking, look no further: Where else can you get a warm and dry bed, three meals a day, and a week of excellent grouse hunting for a mere $300 plus license? A guide will cost you $150 per day additional.

King & Bartlett Fish & Game Club

E u s t i s ,   M a i n e

If you wander far enough into Maine's north woods, you'll reach this rustic lap of luxury.

VITAL STATISTICS:

GAME BIRDS:
GROUSE, WOODCOCK
Source of Birds: Wild
Seasons:
October
Land: 100,000 public and private acres
Accommodations:
TRADITIONAL LOG CABINS WITH MODERN AMENITIES
NUMBER OF ROOMS: 11
MAXIMUM NUMBER OF HUNTERS: 12
Meals: Fine mid-Maine fare of seafood and beef
Conference Groups: Yes
Guides: Optional at $140 / day
Dogs and Facilities:
Kennel for hunters' dogs
Shotgun Sports:
Sporting clays
Other Services:
Birds cleaned and packed for travel
Other Activities:
Big game, bird-watching, boating, canoeing, fishing, golf, hiking, tennis, wildlife photography
Rates:
From $165 / day
Gratuity:
$25 / day / person
Preferred Payment:
Cash, MasterCard, Visa or check
Getting There:
Fly to Portland and rent a car.

Contact:
Buzz Cox
King & Bartlett Fish & Game Club
PO Box 4
Eustis ME 04936
207/243-2956
Fax: 207/246-7029
EMAIL: buzz@somtel.com
WEB: www.kingandbartlett.com

BENEDICT ARNOLD PASSED THROUGH this country on his way to fight the French at Quebec in the Indian wars of the 1760s, and you'll follow a portion of his rag-tag army's route along the Diamond River before turning right into the wild western mountains of Maine. The private and gated road runs for 15 miles through a troubled landscape of granite knobs, swamp, and fast-flowing black-water brooks and lakes where landlocked salmon and brookies play. Endorsed by Orvis, King and Bartlett is known for its fishing, and it has been since it was established in the late 1800s.

After fishing season closes in September, the camp settles into its fall ritual. Deer and bear hunting tops the docket, and a few knowledgeable grouse hunters manage to find their way as well. Cover, as you'd expect, is superb. In this region, you'll find few abandoned farms, but thickets here are aplenty along lake shore and streams and in areas that were cut-over a generation ago. It's not uncommon to flush a dozen or more grouse in a day (hitting them is another matter), and woodcock are definitely a bonus. At King and Bartlett, birds are only hunted in October. The lodge does not provide setters or pointers. You'll be better served if you bring your own. But guides and kennel facilities are available, and there's a sporting clays course which may help you figure out why you missed.

Cabins at this venerable camp date back more than a century. They've all been remodeled to include wall-to-wall carpeting, electricity and private baths. For dinner, you'll have your choice of a pair of entrees, while special dietary needs are easily accommodated with advance notice. Though far, far of the East's beaten path, a number of corporate groups of 20 to 25 find King and Bartlett an ideal retreat. The rest of us who leave business at home spend our spare time lounging in front of the fire with a book.

Pointers Run Hunting Preserve

O a k l a n d ,   M a i n e

'Tis fine fields that lie below the mountains, where pheasant and chukar please gunners of all ages.

VITAL STATISTICS:

GAME BIRDS:
CHUKAR, GROUSE,
PHEASANT, QUAIL
Source of Birds: Wild and
pen-reared
Seasons:
GROUSE: October through early
December
WOODCOCK: October
PRESERVE BIRDS: Year-round
Land: 245 private acres
Accommodations:
IN NEARBY TOWN
Guides: Trained dogs and guides
Other Activities:
Big game, fishing
Rates:
From $120 / gun
Gratuity:
$20
Preferred Payment:
Cash or check
Getting There:
Fly to Augusta and rent a car.

Contact:
Malcolm Charles
Pointers Run Hunting
Preserve
RR3, Box 32090
Oakland ME 04963
207/397-4868
EMAIL: pointers@mint.net
WEB: www.mint.net/pointersrun

AT ITS WIDEST EXPANSION, the range of ringneck pheasant included Vermont and New Hampshire, and it kissed the southeastern corner of Maine. But no more. State efforts to stock pheasants were never more than put-and-take operations, similar to some trout release programs. Yet the lure of ringneck hunting whets the imagination of hunters in the increasingly suburbanized counties northeast of Boston. The best preserves are those that give you the feeling of hunting wild birds on your grandmother's farm.

So it is with Pointers Run, a 245-acre preserve just east of Waterville. The land here rolls gently. In places you'll find stands of ancient apple trees, a one-time orchard abandoned to grouse and deer. A small trout brook issues forth from a beaver pond and flows through pasture tufted with thick clumps of grass. Raspberry, blackberry and grape vines abound. Fence rows are heavily brushed. Stands of maple and beech edge open fields. In the distance rise the rounded tops of French and Vienna mountains and Hampshire Hill.

The normal bill of fare is a half-day hunt which includes four pheasant and a pair of chukar for $120. Full day hunts provide twice as many birds for twice the price. Guides and dogs are available for $50 for half-day hunts and $75 for full-day hunts. Owner Malcolm Charles is a stickler for gun safety, a fact especially appreciated by parents who bring their daughters and sons to the preserve for their first hunting experiences.

The season at Pointers Run spans the entire year. Thus it's not unreasonable to combine a morning of upland hunting with fishing for trout, landlocked salmon or smallmouth in the Kennebec River, one of TU's 100 best trout streams in America. As yet, Pointers Run offers no accommodations or restaurant for clients, yet Waterville and the lovely Belgrade Lakes region around Oakland are replete with a wide range of hostelries. Take your pick from classic Victorian bed-and-breakfasts to modern motels near the interstate.

The Bradford Camps

Ashland, Maine

This camp carries you back to the way it was a century ago (with a little luxury on the side).

VITAL STATISTICS:

GAME BIRDS:
GROUSE, WOODCOCK
Source of Birds: Wild
Seasons:
October through November
Land: Unlimited private and public acres
Accommodations:
PRIVATE LODGE AND CABINS
NUMBER OF ROOMS: 8
MAXIMUM NUMBER OF HUNTERS: 24
Meals: Prime rib and lobster
Conference Groups: Yes
Guides: Available on request at $135 per day for two hunters
Dogs and Facilities:
Bring your own portable kennel
Shotgun Sports:
Sporting clays
Other Services:
Birds cleaned and packed for travel
Other Activities:
Big game, bird-watching, boating, canoeing, fishing, hiking, wildlife photography
Rates:
$105 / night
Gratuity:
$10 - $30 per day
Preferred Payment:
Cash, MasterCard, Visa or check
Getting There:
Fly to Presque Isle and rent a car or arrange for an air charter at extra cost.

Contact:
IGOR SIKORSKY
THE BRADFORD CAMPS
PO BOX 729
ASHLAND ME 04732
207/746-7777
OFF SEASON:
PO BOX 778
KITTERY ME 03904
EMAIL: maine@bradfordcamps.com
WEB: www.bradfordcamps.com

IN THE BEGINNING, when the cabins were first opened in the 1890s, sportsmen and women spent five days just getting to the camp. Two days on the train were followed by a day's wagon trip to the waters of the Aroostook. Guides then paddled canvas canoes upstream to a set of rude lean-to camps for a night's rest before pushing on to the final destination on Munsungan, a lake due north of Baxter State Park. Too long a trip? Outdoorsmen and women of that era didn't think so. Of course, once they arrived, they settled in for at least two weeks and sometimes for a whole season.

Today, a flight of less than an hour in a Beaver, that great radial-engined bush plane, will lift you from Presque Isle to the dock in front of the main lodge at Bradford camp. Or you can drive. Staff will help you with your luggage into comfortable gas-lit cabins, each with its own bath. Ice cut from the lake will cool your drinks, maple crackling in the massive fieldstone hearth will restore your spirit, and hearty meals of prime rib, lobster, and turkey will make you think you should never eat again.

On the morrow you'll hunt for grouse with your dog, working along skid rows with grass still green under birches yellowed by nightly frosts. If you follow your dog's nose, you'll poke though stands of spruce and pine, and climb ridges of beech and maple. You'll wade through thickets and skip across tussocks of grass where you cross boggy streams. All the while your ears will live for the instant that your setter's Swiss bell ceases to ring. With luck, you'll hustle up, flush the bird and add another grouse or woodcock to your bag. Bird hunting stretches from October though November, but the best time is the middle weeks of October. For it's then that flights of woodcock should be at their peak and enough leaves will have fallen from the trees so you can see that at which you're shooting. The camp's sporting clays course is always available for tune-ups, and guides are available should you so desire.

*Cheerful accommodations at Cedar Ridge,
near Jackman, Maine, host gunners with
a taste for grouse and woodcock.*

*Check out the cabins and birds at Bradford Camps;
there's nothing that says you gotta rough it when
hunting Maine's northwoods.*

Tall Timber Lodge

Pittsburg, New Hampshire

This historic lodge caters to grouse and woodcock hunters and fishers of fine brown trout.

VITAL STATISTICS:

GAME BIRDS:
DUCKS, GEESE, GROUSE, PHEASANT
Source of Birds: Wild
Seasons:
GROUSE: October through December
WOODCOCK: early October through early November
PHEASANT: October through December
Land: Unlimited public acres
Accommodations:
PRIVATE WOOD SPORTING LODGE
NUMBER OF ROOMS: 25
MAXIMUM NUMBER OF HUNTERS: 120
Meals: Extensive menu
Conference Groups: Yes
Guides: Possibly available by prior arrangement
Dogs and Facilities:
Bring your own kennel
Other Activities:
Fishing, hiking
Rates:
From $38 / per person;
meals additional
Gratuity:
7% billed with room
Preferred Payment:
Cash, MasterCard, Visa or check
Getting There:
Fly to Manchester and rent a car.

Contact:
Tom Caron
Tall Timber Lodge
231 Beach Rd.
Pittsburg NH 03592
800/835-6343
Fax: 603/538-6582
EMAIL: tom@talltimber.com
WEB: www.talltimber.com

PACK YOUR COPY of *The Best of Corey Ford*, slip your Brittany in the kennel in the back of your truck, and beat a path as far up into New Hampshire as you can go. Do it in the first two weeks of October. That's when the first flights of migratory woodcock arrive. For a brief period, migrating birds merge with local populations. Add to that substantial numbers of grouse, the comeback kid over the past decade or so. Here, in the upper valley of the Connecticut River, you'll find upland bird hunting almost as good as the storytellers of old remember it.

Two massive tracts of land, one privately held by Champion Paper and the other by Perry Stream Land and Timber, are open to public hunting. Birch, poplar, spruce and fir are the mainstays of this forest, but harvesting practices create scores of plots in varying stages of succession. You'll hunt on your own and with your own dogs, but most folks from New England seem to like it that way. If you're desperate for help, the Caron's, who own Tall Timber, will see what they can do to get you a guide. Limits are generous: four grouse and three woodcock per day. There is some duck and goose hunting, but it's more of a bonus than anything else. And the state of New Hampshire runs a pheasant-stocking program at two sites near Pittsburg.

Since you're up in this neck of the woods, don't forget to bring a fly rod. Waters have cooled and brookies and browns are active in their prespawn patterns. Landlocked salmon are again in the river. Life among the flaming maples, russet-hued oaks, and fluttering golden-leaved birch cannot become better.

Neither could the accommodations at Tall Timber Lodge on Back Lake. For more than half a century, Tall Timber has been hosting hunters, anglers and others who enjoy wild woods and waters. Accommodations range from ridiculously inexpensive rooms upstairs in the main lodge to rustic cabins with fireplaces and Jacuzzi's. Cabins' capacities range from two to nine. Dogs are allowed in most of the cabins for an additional charge of $10 per day, with hunters assuming responsibilities for any damages. Meals are hearty and plentiful.

[E A S T]

Shore Winds Hunting Farm & Kennel

M i l l v i l l e , N e w J e r s e y

Hunt the western Pine Barrens and then sample the pleasures of Atlantic City or Cape May.

VITAL STATISTICS:

GAME BIRDS:
CHUKAR, PHEASANT, QUAIL
Source of Birds: Pen-reared
Seasons:
September through April
Land: 170 private acres
Accommodations:
IN NEARBY TOWN
Meals: Restaurant
Conference Groups: Yes
Guides: Trained dogs and guides
Dogs and Facilities:
Kennel for hunters' dogs, dog training
Other Services:
Birds cleaned and packed for travel
Rates:
From $80
Gratuity:
Hunter's discretion
Preferred Payment:
Cash or check
Getting There:
Drive from Philadelphia or
Atlantic City.

Contact:
Jerry Lynch
Shore Winds Hunting Farm
& Kennel
5392 Rt. 49
Millville NJ 08332
609/327-4949

SOUTH JERSEY is one big glacial plain. At places the sandy soil is hundreds of feet deep. Stunted oaks and pines (hence the Pine Barrens moniker) constitute forest with an understory of laurel and some holly. Some of the swamps have been converted into cranberry bogs, others ooze tannin streams that coalesce into black-water rivers that meander wildly as they turn tidal.

At one time, South Jersey supported a thriving population of wild pheasants and quail, but with the exception of a few isolated and carefully guarded locales, such is no longer the case. That's where preserves like Shore Winds come in. For $80, you can spend a morning hunting pheasants, chukar or quail. An additional $45 adds a guide and dog. Half of the preserve's 170 acres is in open fields striped with swaths of sorghum. A third is open pine and laurel cover, perhaps a little lusher than the heart of the Pine Barrens to the north and east. And the balance is deep woods that hide small fields that offer some of the most exciting hunting on the preserve. Reservations are needed for weekend hunts.

Bird hunters and watchers alike benefit from an accident of geography and climate that pours millions of migrating species into South Jersey each fall. Increasingly cold westerlies—the harbingers of winter—drive game and song birds across the country to the Atlantic Coast. Once they reach the ocean, the birds turn south. Bounded on the east by the Atlantic and the west by Delaware Bay, south Jersey acts as a funnel that concentrates birds at Cape May. Woodcock hunting in the wildlife management areas to the west of the town is some of the best in the country. Later, waterfowling can be quite good, too.

Shore Winds is less than an hour from Atlantic City, Cape May and Philadelphia. It's ideally located for hunters who want to chase birds while spouses gamble in Atlantic City or go antiquing in Cape May—a lovely resort of stunning Victorian bed-and-breakfasts. And if your interests don't range so widely, the little village of Millville offers reasonable accommodations.

Forrestel Farm Hunting Preserve

M e d i n a ,   N e w   Y o r k

Step back in time to a place like the one where your dad first took you hunting.

VITAL STATISTICS:

GAME BIRDS:
CHUKAR, DUCKS, PHEASANT, QUAIL

Source of Birds: Pen-reared

Seasons:
September through March

Land: 600 private acres

Accommodations:
MOTELS ALONG RT. 31 AND BED AND BREAKFASTS IN NEARBY TOWNS

MAXIMUM NUMBER OF HUNTERS: 25

Meals: Restaurants

Conference Groups: Yes

Guides: Trained dogs and guides

Dogs and Facilities:
Dog training

Shotgun Sports:
Tower or release shoots

Other Services:
Birds cleaned and packed for travel

Rates:
Packaged hunts from $210

Gratuity:
Hunter's discretion

Preferred Payment:
Cash or check

Getting There:
Take exit 48A north from Interstate 90.

Contact:
Bill Keppler
Forrestel Farm Hunting Preserve
4660 Water Works Rd
Medina NY 14103
716/798-0222

YOU WORRY ABOUT IT, SOMETIMES. Your kids are reaching the age where they're mature enough to hunt. And you'd like to share with them the joy you feel every time your Brittany points a pheasant. Just being in the field with the Brit makes you alive in ways that you can't really describe. And when you swing on a risking cock, and crumple it with a dose of #6s from that old 16-gauge that belonged to your dad, it's as if you're hunting with him.

For him, hunting was very different. The farms along Lake Ontario were larger. Fields were separated by fences, overgrown with weeds two feet on either side. Your dad and his friend, whom you called Uncle Al, would go out when the season opened in October and walk the fence lines and return with a pheasant or two and sometimes a rabbit. They didn't have a dog. It was just the two of them. Then one Saturday Uncle Al couldn't go, and your dad said, "Well, takes two to hunt the Johnson place. Think you can keep from shooting me?" Could you ever!

That was your first hunt, 30 years ago. Now it's your turn. Sandy, your eldest child, loves walking in the woods with you when you go birding or to see the wildflowers of spring. She enjoys helping you cook pheasants when you bring them home, and the recipe she made up for the cranberry glaze is really good, delicious. And she is always up and kind of hanging around, and not acting goofy, when you're getting ready for an early morning hunt. But where to take her on her first hunt?

A preserve like the Forrestel Farm, half way between Rochester and Buffalo just off Rt. 31A, is just such a place. With nearly 600 acres, this farm, run by Bill Keppler, offers traditional hunts for pheasant, chukar and quail. Some preserves are of the "put, punt and pull" variety. The manager dizzies the birds and puts them in the field. When you find them, you have to punt them up with a kick of your boot. Only then can you pull on them to bring them down. Bill turns the birds loose in the general area of the overgrown fields where you'll hunt. Then it's up to you. Hunter with dogs do better here, and if you don't have your own, you can arrange for a dog and handler. In addition to its field hunts, Forrestel also offers shoots for flighted pheasants and mallards.

Lucky Star Ranch

C h a u m o n t ,   N e w   Y o r k

Driven bird shoots, done in continental fashion, are the highlight of the Baron's gunning estate.

VITAL STATISTICS:

GAME BIRDS:
DUCKS, PHEASANT
Source of Birds: Wild and pen-reared
Seasons:
UPLAND BIRDS: September through March
Land: 1,200 private acres
Accommodations:
A PAIR OF CHARMING COUNTRY HOUSES
NUMBER OF ROOMS: 8
MAXIMUM NUMBER OF HUNTERS: 10
Meals: Elegant game in European-style
Conference Groups: Yes
Guides: Trained dogs and guides
Dogs and Facilities:
Bring your own kennel for your dog
Shotgun Sports:
Driven birds, sporting clays, tower or release shoots
Other Services:
Birds cleaned and packed for travel
Other Activities:
Big game, bird-watching, fishing, skiing, wildlife photography
Rates:
From $225 / gun
Gratuity:
Hunter's discretion
Preferred Payment:
Cash, credit cards or check
Getting There:
Fly to Syracuse and rent a car.

Contact:
Penny Fitzgerald
Lucky Star Ranch Crop.
13240 Luck Star Rd.
Chaumont NY 13622
315/649-5519
Fax: 315/649-3097
EMAIL: lucky@luckystarranch.com
WEB: www.luckystarrranch.com

W**ANT TO HUNT A EUROPEAN ESTATE,** but have no time for the trip? There's an operation near Watertown, New York, that just might fit the bill. It's called the Lucky Star Ranch, and the name conjures up images of Texas. Nothing could be further from the truth. The ranch is named for a lake of more than a mile in length that borders the property. Here are 4,500 acres of mixed hardwoods, spruce and pine, and fields awash in lush grasses managed for big game and shotgun sports. The owner is Baron Josef Kercherinck zur Borg, and that gives you a clue about the culture of this fine country estate.

As you'd expect, American-style pheasant hunting is quite popular. Packaged hunts begin at $100 for five birds. You and two other hunters will work one or two fields where the birds have been released. Because of its more than ample size, fields are rotated to preserve cover through the long winters. Lake-effect snows plague this country, and from late December into February, heavy snows are the rule rather than the exception. The best upland bird hunting occurs from September through December. While kennel facilities for guests' dogs are lacking, Lucky Star will arrange for you to hunt with a trained dog and a handler if you wish. Hunting for wild ducks in accordance with state regulations is also available.

And it could come as no surprise that shoots for flighted mallards and pheasants also rank highly among guests. Gunners stand in blinds or butts waiting for birds to appear over the brush and trees in front. Those high overhead shots look easier than they are, and you'll get lots of practice. Depending on the nature of the shoot, you may be aided with a dog and handler to retrieve birds. Generally 15 birds are flown per gun, for $300 for each shooter. Four gunners is the minimum for most shoots, but special arrangements may be made. The estate also boasts a 10-station sporting clays course.

Roughly a quarter of the estate, some 1,200 acres, is fenced for trophy and big game. Fallow, red, Sitka and whitetail deer roam the game park along with mouflan ram and, from January through March, European wild boar. Two lovely, impeccable houses provide accommodations, and dinners of game have a distinctly European flavor. Lucky Star is well known as a corporate retreat, and a membership program for individuals ensures access and provides a significant break on prices.

Orvis Sandanona

Millbrook, New York

Work the kinks out of your swing at this fine old shooting ground.

VITAL STATISTICS:

GAME BIRDS:
CHUKAR, HUNGARIAN PARTRIDGE, PHEASANTS
Source of Birds: Pen-reared
Seasons:
Year round
Land: 400 private acres
Accommodations:
IN VILLAGE OF MILLBROOK
Meals: Gourmet lunches
Conference Groups: Yes
Guides: Trained dogs and guides
Shotgun Sports:
Shooting schools, sporting clays
Other Services:
Birds cleaned and packed for travel, proshop
Other Activities:
Fishing
Rates:
Schools from $450;
Field memberships: $1,000 after initiation
Gratuity:
Hunter's discretion
Preferred Payment:
Cash, credit card or check
Getting There:
Fly to Stewart and rent a car.

Contact:
Orvis Sandanona
PO Box 450
Millbrook NY 12545-0450
914/677-9701

FOR CLOSE TO A CENTURY, the house of umber-hued shingles at Sandanona has catered to wingshooters. In those early days you found London guns and those of Ithaca, Parker, and LeFever lineage. Tatterstall shirts and ties, and tweed shooting jackets were *de rigueur*. And before the hearth when the shooting was done came the drams of whiskies, rich with the aura of peat dried grain. Gentlemen, and some ladies, too, shot trap and that new game called skeet, and hunted for pheasants released on acreage farmed for more than 200 years.

Sandanona is still this. Though guns, dress and games have changed, Sandanona is the quintessential wingshooting grounds. Weaving along a low ridge of mixed hardwood and pine, a sporting clays course of 30 stations offers shots that challenge the pros and yet are easy enough for mortals like you and me to make. The course is annually listed among the best in the nation by *Gray's Sporting Journal* and *Esquire*. Below the ridge stretch fields planted and managed for pheasants, chukar and Hungarian partridge. A membership is required to hunt them.

While the sporting clays course and preserve hunts draw fugitives from New York, Albany and their environs, it's the shooting school added by Orvis that makes Sandanona doubly special. This shooting school focuses on sporting clays, but if you're an upland bird hunter, chief instructor Geoff Kerr adapts easily. Orvis offers one and two day programs. After a short indoor session where Geoff checks the fit of your gun and how you mount it, you'll view an instructional video and then it's off to the course. You'll begin with the easy going-away shots as you're reminded to touch your cheek to stock, swing through the target ("touch bird"), and touch trigger. "Touch stock, touch bird, touch trigger." It's a mantra that plays in your sleep. After breaking for an exquisite lunch in the club house, it's back to the course for more gunning.

Is a shooting school worth the investment? Look at it this way. If you're traveling to an upscale bird hunting lodge, you're going to fork over three or four grand. Investing in a two-day shooting school gives you the tools to make great shots, not excuses. There are no accommodations at Sandanona, but the nearby town of Millbrook is a resort community of long standing and filled with eclectic lodgings and restaurants to match.

R. L. Sheltra's Salmon River Outfitters

P u l a s k i ,   N e w   Y o r k

Hunt grouse over Brittanies and chase steelhead or salmon with the fly. Does life get better than this?

VITAL STATISTICS:

GAME BIRDS:
GROUSE, WOODCOCK
Source of Birds: Wild
Seasons:
GROUSE: September through February
PHEASANT: October through December
WOODCOCK: October through November
Land: 10,000 private and public acres
Accommodations:
IN NEARBY TOWN
Meals: Local restaurants
Conference Groups: Yes
Guides: Yes
Dogs and Facilities:
Bring your own portakennel
Other Services:
Birds cleaned and packed for travel
Other Activities:
Big game, biking, bird-watching, boating, fishing, hiking, skiing, wildlife photography
Rates:
$225 / gun
Gratuity:
Hunter's discretion
Preferred Payment:
Cash or check
Getting There:
Fly to Syracuse and rent a car.

Contact:
R.L. Sheltra
R.L. Sheltra's Salmon River Outfitters
40 North St.
Pulaski NY 13142
315/298-3803

THEY CALLED IT the "vest pocket gun dog," that auburn-and-white spaniel, so svelte that it could slip through tangled coverts as easy as you please. Brits were bred for grouse and woodcock of New England and New York's northern tier. Oh sure, they were fine on pheasants, eagerly retrieved ducks, and would even wrestle geese back to the blind. Hunting over a Brittany is poetry, especially if your shotgun's a side-by-side 20-gauge or a 16-gauge with Parker, L.C. Smith or LeFever on the lock plate.

Such dogs and guns call up memories of abandoned farms, alder swamps, and orchards gone unpruned for a generation or more. Such is the 10,000 acres that Robin Sheltra hunts in the neighborhood of Pulaski, a town better known for salmon fishing below the ancient dunes of Lake Ontario. You'll find this sporting town half way between Syracuse and Watertown on Interstate 81, and as you hustle along the four-lane, your eye will be drawn to miles and miles of open woodland. A transplant from northern Vermont, Robin and his Brits took to this country like migrating woodcocks take to a dense stand of poplar.

Flight birds filter down from Quebec in late September and the season opens in October. By then, grouse have been in for a month, making October the best month to carry a smoothbore in the woods. Grouse populations are on the rise—four-bird limits are quite possible—and it's nothing to flush a dozen woodcock along the way. Pheasants are also on the menu.

The prudent gunner packs a fly rod in his dunnage. Chinook, steelhead and lake-run browns are moving up the rivers and streams that drain into Ontario. Combination trips are increasingly popular. Hunt one day, fish the next, and add a few more grouse for the freezer on the third. At Robin's rates of $225 for two per day, plus less than $100 for room and board at a local hotel, this cast-and-blast is one of the best bargains going.

Sno-Fun Hunting Preserve

Evans Mills, New York

While the name suggests otherwise, hunting on this little preserve is a lot of fun.

VITAL STATISTICS:

GAME BIRDS:
CHUKAR, PHEASANT, QUAIL
Source of Birds: Wild and pen-reared
Seasons:
September through March
Land: 500 private acres
Accommodations:
WOOD-SIDED LODGE
NUMBER OF ROOMS: 1
MAXIMUM NUMBER OF HUNTERS: 4
Meals: Game dinners by special arrangement
Conference Groups: No
Guides: Trained dogs and guides
Dogs and Facilities:
Kennel for hunters' dogs
Other Services:
Birds cleaned and packed for travel
Other Activities:
Big game, fishing
Rates:
From $100 with guide and accommodations
Gratuity:
Hunter's discretion
Preferred Payment:
Cash or check
Getting There:
Fly or drive to Watertown, and the Farr's will have you picked up.

Contact:
Richard Farr
Sno-Fun Hunting Preserve
26809 Keyser Rd
Evans Mills NY 13637
315/629-4801
EMAIL: rfarr@gisco.net
WEB: www.1000islands.com/snofun

FLAT. LIKE THE BLANKET on a bunk in the old-time army. That's the way the land lies here north and a little east of Watertown. Reservists and national guardsmen throughout the Northeast have an intimate acquaintance with this countryside. Each summer, thousands of soldiers journey to Fort Drum for training. Less than a mile northwest of the town of Evans Mills, you'll find Sno-Fun Hunting Preserve.

Contrary to the name, hunting here is fun. Opened by a physician in the mid-1960s, Dick and Valerie Farr bought the preserve ten years later and have been running it ever since. During the summer, Dick raises corn, oats and barley. Come fall, when he harvests the crops, he leaves a bit for the birds and plenty of bent-over stalks. This, along with feed plots of sorghum and buckwheat, goes a long way in keeping birds on the property year-round. Patches of brush grow at field-edges, but stands of timber are few. Gunners like the openness of the preserve; they can see birds that flush and don't have to master the art of shooting around trees. Because of the flat land, it's possible for wheelchair-bound hunters to chase pheasant. Dick will be glad to accommodate by rocking the birds to sleep before setting them out.

But generally he does not set birds by dizzying them. For $60, you get three pheasants, four chukar, or 10 quail. The odds are you'll jump more than that, and if you're a good shot, taking your quota is a reasonable expectation. If you want to harvest birds beyond those for which you paid initially, you'll pay a slightly discounted per-bird rate. Many hunters bring their own dogs, but Dick keeps a kennel stocked with setters, pointers, shorthairs, springers and labs. Just let him know which you prefer.

A wood-sided lodge with four bunk beds provides accommodations, and the rate is down right reasonable: $20 per night per person. You have your choice of dining out in Watertown or asking Valerie to work her magic on quail or pheasant for dinner. That's fun too!

*A bird in the bag, a pause for a moment's conversation,
then back to work in the corn. What more could you ask from
an afternoon's hunt on the flanks of a hill in Vermont?*

Hill's Twin Spruce Lodge

Equinunk, Pennsylvania

The big "D" is known for excellent fishing, so much so that birds on the farms along its banks are often overlooked.

VITAL STATISTICS:

GAME BIRDS:
CHUKAR, DUCKS, GEESE, GROUSE, PHEASANT, TURKEY
Source of Birds: Wild and pen-reared
Seasons:
PHEASANT and CHUKAR: September through April
GROUSE: October through January
TURKEY: May and November
Land: 1040 private acres
Accommodations:
VICTORIAN BED & BREAKFAST
NUMBER OF ROOMS: 15
MAXIMUM NUMBER OF HUNTERS: 35
Meals: Breakfast
Conference Groups: Yes
Guides: Trained dogs and guides
Dogs and Facilities:
Kennel for hunters' dogs, dog training
Shotgun Sports:
Skeet, sporting clays, tower or release shoots
Other Services:
Birds cleaned and packed for travel
Other Activities:
Big game, biking, bird-watching, boating, canoeing, fishing, golf, hiking, skiing
Rates:
Packages from $125; lodging $55 night, double occupancy
Gratuity:
Hunter's discretion
Preferred Payment:
Cash, MasterCard, Visa or check
Getting There:
Fly to Avoca-Scranton; transfer to the lodge is $25.

Contact:
Adam Hill
Hill's Twin Spruce Lodge
Box 212
Equinunk PA 18417
570/224-4191
WEB: www.twinsprucelodge.com

SWINGING DOWN from a pair of water supply reservoirs for New York City, the Delaware River runs clean and cold along the border separating the Keystone and Empire states. Equinunk is one of those forgotten railroad towns that sprang up where a road crossed the tracks at the river. Here, too, was the last Lenapi Indian reservation in the region, vacated in the 1880s. As you hunt, you'll still find arrowheads, broken points and occasionally parts of rock bowls.

As the last century waned, dairy farming reached its zenith along the river. Fields were cleared and fenced. Meadows were small as was the custom of that day. Economy of scale killed small farms, and many next to the river were left to grow wild in the 1950s and 1960s. Such is the case of the first of three separate preserves operated by Adam Hill. On his 230 acres of river-bottom land, you'll hunt hedgerows for pheasants, chukar and the occasional grouse who wanders in by mistake. The second of the trio is one and a half miles away: 360 acres planted in switch grass with strips of millet and sorghum. Fields are bigger, and it pays to be long-legged to cover the ground behind your pointer. The third preserve is larger still, about 450 acres. Grouse love thick cover, and chukar and pheasants are released in open pastures left to go fallow.

Early in the duck season, which opens in October, gunning for woodies can be exceptional. Adam hosts no more than 12 to 18 duck hunters per season. Before sun-up, they're gunning from blinds in swamps along Little Equinunk Creek and other watersheds. Mid-day finds them going from pond to pond on a mission of "poke and hope." At night, it's back to the blinds. Waterfowlers also enjoy goose hunting on the river during the September and January seasons for resident birds.

As one of the nation's premier trout rivers, the upper mileage of the Delaware overshadows fishing in ponds and lakes near Twin Spruce. Adam regularly lands record class striped bass from Lake Wallenpaupack. Heavy browns of eight pounds or more are also found. Fishing here is uncommonly good during September and October, and in May during spring gobbler season. Guests are accommodated in the lodge, a turn-of-the-century Victorian farmhouse with a modern addition. Breakfast is provided and dinners can be arranged by special request. A number of good restaurants are also found in the small towns along the river.

[E A S T]

Hillendale Hunt Club

T y r o n e ,   P e n n s y l v a n i a

A complete wingshooter's retreat lies near some of the finest trout fishing in the country.

VITAL STATISTICS:

GAME BIRDS:
CHUKAR, DUCKS, PHEASANT, QUAIL

Source of Birds: Pen-reared

Seasons:
UPLAND BIRDS: September through mid-April
DUCKS: November through mid-April

Land: 475 private acres

Accommodations:
1900s FARM HOUSE
NUMBER OF ROOMS: 5
MAXIMUM NUMBER OF HUNTERS: 12

Meals: Available on request

Conference Groups: Yes

Guides: Trained dogs and guides

Dogs and Facilities:
Kennel for hunters' dogs, dog training

Shotgun Sports:
Driven birds, shooting schools, sporting clays

Other Services:
Birds cleaned and packed for travel

Other Activities:
Fishing, golf

Rates:
From $140 / day / gun (includes lodging)

Gratuity:
Hunter's discretion

Preferred Payment:
Cash, MasterCard, Visa or check

Getting There:
Fly to Altoona or State College and rent a car.

Contact:
Tom Crawford
Hillendale Hunt Club
RD 1, Box 390
Tyrone PA 16686
814/684-5015

I F YOU LOOK AT A MAP of Pennsylvania, you'll see a huge arc of folded mountains that run hard up against the flat rocks of the Allegheny Plateau. What you are seeing is the effect of the collision of continental plates. Pressure from the mid-Atlantic rift, roughly 2,000 miles to the southeast, has pushed up these folded ridges and valleys. Between the ridges are broad, almost level valleys, often underlain here by limestones and watered by spring creeks.

Hillendale Hunt Club is located about half way between Altoona and State College just to the southeast of Interstate 99. On 475 acres, Tom Crawford and his wife Pam operate a traditional shooting preserve. In fields planted with corn and wheat, and some running riot with weeds, gunners chase pheasants, chukar and quail from September through mid-April. You and your party will have a section of the acreage to yourself; it's like visiting the family farm of an uncle. There's no pretension here. Everything's sort of laid back. This preserve is less than a day's drive for more than a quarter of the country's population. It's easy to bring your own dog. If not, hunt over one of the Crawford's English springers. Sporting clays and shooting schools are also on the docket here. So too are release shoots for pheasants from behind a grassy hilltop, and for ducks from deep in the woods.

At the center of the preserve is a farmhouse so typical of those built in the late 1890s and early 1900s. In it are five bedrooms with shared baths. You're welcome to cook your own meals or hie yourself into Tyrone, a few miles northwest. The best time to hunt this preserve may be in early fall. The cover is best then, and the fishing is great. Fishing? Well, within an hour's drive are a number of Pennsylvania's great spring creeks. For more information about fishing in this neck of the woods, contact Dan Shields at Flyfisher's Paradise, 2603 E. College Ave., State College, Pennsylvania 16801. His phone is 814/234-4189. Hunt in the morning and catch an afternoon hatch. Pennsylvania's trout seasons continue into the fall, but they vary by stream. Dan can give you the info you need.

Juniata River Game Farm

McClure, Pennsylvania

*Hidden beneath high ridges is a quaint game farm
with fine pheasant and wild duck hunting.*

VITAL STATISTICS:

GAME BIRDS:
CHUKAR, DUCKS, GEESE, PHEASANT, QUAIL
Source of Birds: Wild and pen-reared
Seasons:
PRESERVE BIRDS: September through March
GEESE: September and November through mid-February
Land: 542 private acres
Accommodations:
In Lewiston
Meals: Restaurants
Conference Groups: Yes
Guides: Trained dogs and guides
Dogs and Facilities:
Kennel for hunters' dogs
Shotgun Sports:
Driven birds, sporting clays, tower or release shoots
Other Services:
Birds cleaned and packed for travel
Rates:
$65 / 4 pheasants;
$25 / gun / ducks and geese
Gratuity:
Hunter's discretion
Preferred Payment:
Cash or check
Getting There:
Drive from Harrisburg.

Contact:
Doug Boreman
Juniata River Game Farm
52 Goose Lane
McClure PA 17841
717/543-6281

LIKE A THROW RUG rumpled against the wall by a running kid, vast beds of limestone and shale are folded and faulted and pushed up against the Allegheny Plateau. Ridges are made up of more resistant rocks and the valleys are often underlain by limestone, making them rich and fertile. Their grasses nourished dairy cows for generations of farmers, but the small farms are all but gone now.

On a pair of these historic old farms hidden between a pair of ridges just over the hill from the town of McClure, Doug Boreman runs the Juniata River Game Farm. He plants corn, sorghum, Sudan grass and some cold weather species such as timothy and orchard grass. Greenbrier and multiflora rose entwine old fence rows. To hunt these farms is like pulling on an old comfortable pair of jeans.

Doug didn't intend to get into the preserve business. It's just that one thing kind of led to another. He needed to train his Chesapeake retriever for an AKC hunting test. So he needed pheasants. Unable to buy any locally, he bought three dozen day-old chicks and raised them. That, of course, set him to thinking . . . always dangerous for a man who lives in a narrow valley. Next thing you know, he's bought the farm next door and launched into the preserve business. His Chessies consistently finish well in AKC and National Hunting Retriever Association trials. Clients like the way the dogs work pheasants and geese, hunted on a pair of fields a mile from the junction of the Juniata and Susquehanna rivers.

His plans call for a small lodge on the farm, but that's in the future. Right now, guests stay in motels and eat in restaurants in Lewistown, 12 miles to the southeast. Penn State fans know Lewistown well. It's the place where US 322 becomes four-lane again, ending those mammoth traffic jams on Nittany Lion football weekends.

Wing Pointe

H a m b u r g ,   P e n n s y l v a n i a

*Antiquing and bird hunting go hand in hand
in the Pennsylvania Dutch country.*

**VITAL
STATISTICS:**

GAME BIRDS:
CHUKAR, PHEASANT, QUAIL
Source of Birds: Pen-reared
Seasons:
September through March
Land: 200 private acres
Accommodations:
GLASS AND TIMBER LODGE
NUMBER OF ROOMS: 5
MAXIMUM NUMBER OF HUNTERS: 9
Meals: Restaurant at the preserve
Conference Groups: Yes
Guides: Trained dogs and guides
Dogs and Facilities:
Kennel for hunters' dogs
Shotgun Sports:
Five-stand, shooting schools, sporting
clays, tower or release shoots
Other Services:
Birds cleaned and packed for travel
Other Activities:
Antiquing, swimming
Rates:
Hunts from $96 / gun;
accommodations from $370 /
minimum group of four
Gratuity:
Hunter's discretion
Preferred Payment:
Cash, MasterCard, Visa or check
Getting there:
Fly to Reading/Allentown and rent
a car.

Contact:
Allen Sanders
Wing Pointe
1414 Moselem Springs Rd.
Hamburg PA 19526
610/562-6926
Fax: 610/562-6999

NORTHWESTERN BERKS COUNTY has always been someplace special when it comes to hunting. The good Pennsylvania Dutch in their adherence to the old ways would cut corn by hand and leave the shocks standing in the field. Even those who were more liberal tended to strip ears from the stalks, which were left broken at knee height to rot as organic fertilizer for the following year. Swales too damp to plant grew heavy with dense grasses. It was farm country made for pheasants, and somehow pheasants seemed made for it.

Isolated pockets of such cover do exist here and there in the Berks County corridor bounded by Interstate 78 and U.S. Route 222. And it was just this sort of cropland that Joe Solana sought to preserve when he built and opened Wing Pointe on 200 acres at the head of Lake Ontelaunee. The lodge is 30 minutes from Redding and about an hour and a half from both Philadelphia and New York. Planted in sorghum and other thickly growing grains, fields undulate like the swells in a quiet ocean. Woodlots and waterways are grown up with brush. And that's where flushed quail and chukar will head. Pheasants will sail to another field or fool you and head for the woods, too. A 20-station sporting clays course filters in and out of the forest. Continental shoots are available by prior arrangement. Remember, though, there's no hunting in Pennsylvania on Sunday.

Wing Pointe boasts a better than good restaurant—try the Chicken la Port, a breast cooked with sweet red peppers and portobello mushrooms—and a modern lodge of wood and glass that sleeps nine comfortably. A complete pro shop is also available on site.

Nonshooting spouses will find much to do in the area. Antique shops abound, particularly near Kutztown. Redding is famed (or infamous, depending on your take of things) for its profusion of outlet malls. And numerous bed-and-breakfasts are found in small towns and on farms in the tranquil countryside.

Addieville East Farm

Smithfield, Rhode Island

Not more than an hour south of Boston is a wonderful old-time lodge and preserve.

VITAL STATISTICS:

GAME BIRDS:
CHUKAR, HUNGARIAN PARTRIDGE, PHEASANT
Source of Birds: Pen-reared
Seasons:
September through April
Land: 900 private acres
Accommodations:
PRIVATE LOG LODGE
NUMBER OF ROOMS: 3
MAXIMUM NUMBER OF HUNTERS: 12
Meals: Self-catered or hire chefs from Johnson & Wales
Conference Groups: Yes
Guides: Trained dogs and guides
Dogs and Facilities:
Kennel for hunters' dogs, dog training
Shotgun sports:
Shooting schools, sporting clays, tower or release shoots
Other services:
Birds cleaned and packed for travel, proshop
Other Activities:
Fishing
Rates:
From $260 for 12-bird hunt
Gratuity:
$20 - $40
Preferred Payment:
Cash or check
Getting There:
Fly to Providence and rent a car.

Contact:
Geoff Gaebe
Addieville East Farm
200 Pheasant Dr
Smithfield RI 02839
401/568-3185
Fax: 401/568-3009
EMAIL: addievil@ir.netcom.com

S O THE WAG TOOK ONE LOOK at the preserve. He saw meadows lush with switchgrass and bounded by tangled hedgerows. He saw feed strips of wild grains and bits of all-but-impenetrable brush. Woods of spruce, pine, oak and maple frame dark-water ponds stocked with drag-smoking trout. "Beautiful," he mused. "Just what Mother Nature would have done if she'd been a bird hunter!"

That's Addieville East Farm, an hour south of Boston and half that north of Providence. With more than 900 acres, this vintage farm is slowly being wrested from Mother Nature's untutored hands and fashioned into one of the premiere membership shooting retreats in the country. When Goeff Gaebe purchased the farm nearly 20 years ago, it was all but abandoned. Today, four fields of 100 acres or so each are regularly used by hunters, and more are on the way. English pointers do dog duty. Or bring your own.

Goeff takes considerable and justifiable pride in the 65,000 or so pheasants raised on the preserve each year. He aims for high-flying, richly colored birds of four to four-and-a-half pounds. "Bigger birds," he says, "frankly, don't fly as well." As soon as they are mature enough, young birds are turned loose into 14 acres of flight pens with netting 15 feet high. About half of the birds are harvested on the preserve (with 20,000 chukars and Huns), and the remainder are sold to other preserves and to chefs throughout New England. All stocked birds on the preserve are yearlings, which are as tough to hit as they are tender to the palate.

Sporting clays is a very important part of the Addieville East picture. Two courses provide amply challenging (read that frustrating) shots. Jack Mitchell, a legendary instructor from England, and his American protégé Russ Jette, do their best to unravel years of bad shooting habits among experienced gunners and to start young shooters off with the right mount and swing. In addition, there's a lovely old log lodge on the property. Three rooms with shared baths sleep up to a dozen or so. Guests can either pull k.p. themselves, or arrange for gourmet chefs from nearby Johnson & Wales culinary school to handle kitchen chores. Annual membership runs $400. During week days, the club is open to the public, but on weekends it's normally fully booked with members.

Hermitage Inn

W i l m i n g t o n ,   V e r m o n t

An intimate New England inn with exquisite service and bird hunting to match.

VITAL STATISTICS:

GAME BIRDS:
GROUSE, PHEASANT, and WOODCOCK

Source of Birds: Wild and pen-reared

Seasons:
GROUSE: Late September through December
WOODCOCK: Early October through early November
PHEASANT: September through November

Land: 500 private acres

Accommodations:
SECLUDED NEW ENGLAND LODGE
NUMBER OF ROOMS: 29
MAXIMUM NUMBER OF HUNTERS: 60

Meals: Gourmet game

Conference Groups: Yes

Guides: Trained dogs and guides

Dogs and Facilities:
Kennel for hunters' dogs

Shotgun Sports:
Shooting schools, sporting clays

Other Services:
Birds cleaned and packed for travel, proshop

Other Activities:
Biking, boating, fishing, golfing, hiking, horseback riding, tennis, skiing

Rates:
Hunts from $295 / for up to 4 guns; accommodations from $225 for two

Gratuity:
Hunter's discretion

Preferred Payment:
Cash, credit card or check

Getting There:
Fly to Hartford, CT, or Albany, NY and rent a car.

Contact:
Jim McGovern
Hermitage Inn
PO Box 457
Wilmington VT 05363
802/464-3511
FAX: 802/464-2688
EMAIL: hermitage@sover.net

THROUGH THE ORCHARD beyond a wall of grey stone rise the immaculate buildings of the inn, white clapboard against the russets and flame of autumn. Your visit to this bit of tranquility was timed with equal perfection. You left the city a little later than you wanted. Dinner, you knew, would be over by the time you arrived, but that didn't matter. You'd ordered deli before you left and picnicked, as it's sometimes fun to do, in the car on the drive. Arriving at the inn, you'd been helped to your room. It is as you remembered. Wing chairs flank the brick hearth where apple logs blaze merrily. On a pewter tray sits a bottle of port, two Granny Smiths, a modest hunk of Stilton, a spread of water crackers, a knife and a pair of crystal goblets. You and your wife unpack and then settle in before the fire with the snack. You don't remember going to bed in the four-poster, lulled by the sound of the wind in the trees.

Breakfast finds you both in the dining room, looking out through small-paned windows at the farm glowing a bit in the apricot light of early morning. It is hard to rush breakfast—grapefruit and eggs Benedict and rich, black coffee—but you do. On the morning's agenda are woodcock and grouse. Jim McGovern, owner of the Hermitage, told you that the birds might be in when you made reservations, and last night he'd left you a confirming note. You would hunt over a pair of his English setters this morning. And after lunch, the work would turn to a few fields for released pheasants.

Located halfway between Bennington and Brattleboro about five miles northwest of Wilmington in the southern Green Mountains, the Hermitage Inn is about three hours from Manhattan and Boston. Albany and Hartford are the closest airports with commercial service. Along with hunting for wild and released birds, you'll find an excellent sporting clays course and a wobble trap. Nonshooting guests will enjoy horseback riding, hiking, museums, antique and craft shops, and life performances ranging from chamber music to contemporary guitar or piano. Reservations for hunts in mid-October are best booked well in advance.

Tinmouth Hunting Preserve

T i n m o u t h ,   V e r m o n t

Just half an hour north of Manchester is wingshooting the way it used to be in old New England.

VITAL STATISTICS:

GAME BIRDS:
CHUKAR, PHEASANT, QUAIL
Source of Birds: Wild and pen-reared
Seasons:
Year round
Land: 800 private acres
Accommodations:
HISTORIC EQUINOX HOTEL
Guides: Trained dogs and guides
Dogs and Facilities:
Kennel for hunter's dogs, dog training
Shotgun Sports:
Driven birds, sporting clays, tower or release shoots
Other Services:
Birds cleaned and packed for travel
Other Activities:
Fishing, golf, tennis
Rates:
$300/ 1/2 day hunt
Gratuity:
Hunter's discretion
Preferred Payment:
Cash or check
Getting There:
Fly to Albany and rent a car.

Contact:
Rick Faller or Joe Palombo
Tinmouth Hunting Preserve
403 North End Road
Tinmouth VT 05773
802/446-2337
Fax: 802/446-2337

BIRD HUNTING was born in New England. Only they don't call them birds, but "buuds," a word where the "r" hides in the back of your throat like the hint of peat in good whisky. And when you call for a clay at Tinmouth Preserve, you don't say "pull" as you might at those hard driven commercial courses, but "buud," spoken as if you were calling to your partner to tell him the dog had gone on point.

Tinmouth Preserve is the quintessential north country farm. Lying on the west flank of a low ridge, its 800 acres run for about a mile on either side of a gravel road. West of the road are corn and hay fields, sloping down to second growth oaks, maples and overgrown meadows thick with brambles, goldenrod and grasses. Here, manager Rick Faller releases pheasants, chukar and bobwhite quail. For the for-fee hunts, Rick divides up the farm into 200 to 300 acre sections. Each party is given a section for half a day. To hunt it is like visiting your uncle's place. You don't own it, but it's all yours when you're there.

East of the road, where the hillside steepens through birches and beech trees, is Tinmouth's 14-station sporting clay's course. The course winds up an old woods road, cuts across a bench under the brow of the hill, and wraps its way back to the beginning under a trio of glorious maples.

Nearby accommodations can be as splendid and the dining as sumptuous as the recently refurbished Equinox (802/362-4700) in Manchester, 45 minutes south of Tinmouth. This grand hotel incorporates the original structure of the Marsh Tavern, established in 1769. Lee Bowden, manager of The Equinox and an ardent sporting clays competitor, has put together what he calls the "Vermont Sportsman's Package," which, for $500 per person, double occupancy, provides two days' meals and lodging, two rounds of sporting clays at Tinmouth, fishing in the resort's private waters and falconry lessons. There are worse ways to spend a fall weekend.

SOUTH

ALABAMA, DELAWARE, FLORIDA, GEORGIA, KENTUCKY, LOUISIANA, MARYLAND, MISSISSIPPI, NORTH CAROLINA, SOUTH CAROLINA, TENNESSEE, TEXAS, VIRGINIA, WEST VIRGINIA

A REGION OF extreme diversity, the Appalachian highlands offer some of the toughest and most rewarding grouse and woodcock hunting in the United States, while the vast swamps of Florida can be stunning for ducks. But when you say "bird" here, you're talking bobwhite quail, and sadly, native coveys are an increasing rarity. The odds just don't favor this gentleman of the broom sedges. On one hand, cover-limiting farming techniques, exploding populations of feral dogs and cats, and resurging numbers of hawks and owls (thanks to the ban on DDT) are thinning native stocks at an alarming rate. On the other, the new gentry is buying vast tracts of fallow farmland, managing it for quail which can be hunted only by the owner or guests. Leased lands are the way of the new South. Still, lowland national and state forests, along with state wildlife management areas offer some "free" hunting for quail.

Alabama

1 DIXIELAND PLANTATION
2 DOUBLEHEAD RESORT & LODGE
3 PARCHES COVE HUNTING PRESERVE
4 ROCKFENCE STATION
5 WHITE OAK PLANTATION

Delaware

6 OWENS STATION

Florida

7 BIENVILLE PLANTATION
8 IRON-WOOD PRESERVE
9 PLANTATION OUTFITTERS

Georgia

10 BOGGY POND PLANTATION
11 BOLL WEEVIL PLANTATION
12 BROUGHTON PLANTATION
13 BURGE PLANTATION CLUB INC
14 CHARLANE PLANTATION
15 GILLIONVILLE PLANTATION
16 QUAIL COUNTRY LODGE & CONFERENCE CENTER
17 RIVERVIEW PLANTATION
18 ROCKY CREEK PLANTATION
19 SHIRAHLAND PLANTATION
20 THE LODGE AT CABIN BLUFF
21 WHITEWAY PLANTATION

Kentucky

22 DEER CREEK OUTFITTERS

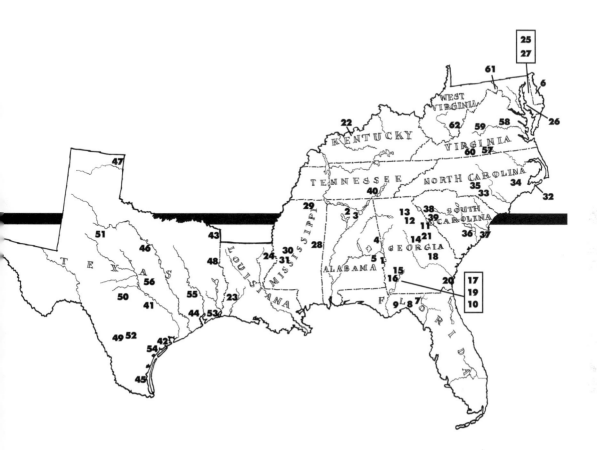

Louisiana
23 DRY CREEK RANCH
24 PIN OAK MALLARDS

Maryland
25 FAIR WINDS GUN CLUB
26 PINTAIL POINT
27 SCHRADER'S HUNTING

Mississippi
28 CIRCLE M PLANTATION
29 DUNN'S SHOOTING GROUNDS
30 ROSE HILL PLANTATION
31 TARA WILDLIFE MANAGEMENT

North Carolina
32 ADAMS CREEK GUNNING LODGE
33 GEORGE HI PLANTATION
34 QUAIL RIDGE SHOOTING PRESERVE
35 TOBACCO STICK HUNTING PRESERVE & KENNEL

South Carolina
36 BROXTON BRIDGE PLANTATION
37 DEERFIELD PLANTATION
38 HARRIS SPRINGS
39 LITTLE RIVER PLANTATION

Tennessee
40 QUAIL VALLEY HUNT CLUB

Texas
41 74 RANCH HUNTING RESORT
42 B-BAR-B RANCH
43 CIRCLE ROCKING N RANCH
44 EAGLE LAKE & KATY PRARIE OUTFITTERS
45 EL CANELO RANCH
46 GREYSTONE CASTLE SPORTING CLUB
47 HARPER'S HUNTING PRESERVE
48 HAWKEYE HUNTING CLUB
49 HERRADURA RANCH INC

50 JOSHUA CREEK RANCH
51 KROOKED RIVER RANCH OUTFITTERS
52 LOS CUERNOS RANCH
53 LOS PATOS LODGE & GUIDE SERVICE
54 MARIPOS RANCH-SK CORPORATION
55 POSSUM WALK SHOOTING PRESERVE
56 TEXAS WINGS SPORTING CHARTERS

Virginia
57 FALKLAND FARMS
58 FFF KENNELS HUNTING PRESERVE
59 OAK RIDGE ESTATE
60 PRIMLAND RESORT

West Virginia
61 PROSPECT HALL
62 THE GREENBRIER WINGSHOOTING PRESERVE

51

Dove, the secondmost popular southern bird, is more egalitarian in its habitats. Find a good field of cut corn near water and a patch of gravel early in September, and you and your pals may have some great gunning. It's still there and yours for the finding. Offering a farmer a couple of days' labor in exchange for hunting rights pays dividends beyond belief.

Grouse hunting is good, and on the upswing, from the mountains of western Maryland all the way to Alabama. Waterfowling for ducks in coastal areas is also on the wax, as is gunning for resident Canadas. Arkansas and Louisiana can't be beat for ducks, and Texas, at the tail end of the Central Flyway, is the one state that has it all, sans ruffed grouse.

Resources:

ALABAMA DEPARTMENT OF CONSERVATION AND NATURAL RESOURCES
Div. of Game and Fish, Wildlife Section
PO Box 301456
Montgomery, AL 36130
334/242-3469
web: www.dcnr.state.al.us/agfd

DELAWARE DIVISION OF FISH AND WILDLIFE
Wildlife Section
Dover, DE 19901
302/739-3441
web: www.dnrec.state.de.us

FLORIDA GAME AND FRESH WATER FISH COMMISSION
620 S. Meridian
Tallahassee, FL 32399-1600
904/488-1960
web: www.state.fl.us/gfc/

GEORGIA WILDLIFE RESOURCES DIVISION
2070 U.S. Hwy. 278 SE
Social Circle, GA 30025
770/918-6400
web: www.dnr.state.ga.us/

You hunt birds in Texas as much to see a flashy pointer strut her stuff amid the dried grasses, cacti and mesquite, as to shoot a bird.

KENTUCKY DEPARTMENT OF FISH
AND WILDLIFE RESOURCES
#1 Game Farm Rd
Frankfort, KY 40601
502/564-3400
web:
www.state.ky.us/agencies/fw/kdfwr.htm

LOUISIANA DEPARTMENT OF
WILDLIFE AND FISHERIES
Box 98000
Baton Rouge, LA 70898-9000
504-765-2800
web: www.wlf.state.la.us

MARYLAND DEPARTMENT OF
NATURAL RESOURCES
Wildlife & HeritageDivision
E-1 580 Taylor Ave.
Annapolis, MD 21401
410/260-8540
web: www.dnr.state.md.us

MISSISSIPPI DEPARTMENT OF WILDLIFE,
FISHERIES AND PARKS
Box 451
Jackson, MS 39205
601/362-9212
web: www.mdwfp.com

NORTH CAROLINA WILDLIFE
RESOURCES COMMISSION
Division of Wildlife Management
512 N. Salisbury St
Raleigh, NC 27604-1188
919/733-7291
web:
www.state.nc.us/wildlife/management

SOUTH CAROLINA DEPARTMENT
OF NATURAL RESOURCES
Division of Wildlife and Freshwater
Fisheries
Box 167
Columbia, SC 29202
803/734-3889
web: www.dnr.state.sc.us

TENNESSEE WILDLIFE
RESOURCES AGENCY
Box 40747
Nashville, TN 37204
615/781-6500
web: www.state.tn.us/twra

TEXAS PARKS AND WILDLIFE
DEPARTMENT
4200 Smith School Rd
Austin, TX 78744
512/389-4505
web: www.tpwd.state.tx.us/

VIRGINIA DEPARTMENT OF GAME
AND INLAND FISHERIES
4010 W. Broad St
Box 11104
Richmond, VA 23230-1104
804/367-1000
web: www.dgif.state.va.us

WEST VIRGINIA DIVISION OF
NATURAL RESOURCES
Building 3, Room 819
1900 Kanawah Blvd. E
Charleston, WV 25305
304/558-2771
web: www.dnr.state.wv.us

[S O U T H]

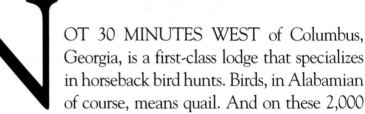

Dixieland Plantation

H a t c h e c h u b b e e ,   A l a b a m a

VITAL STATISTICS:

GAME BIRDS:
QUAIL
Source of Birds: Wild and pen-reared
Seasons:
Late November through February
Land: 2,000 private acres
Accommodations:
MODERN YET RUSTIC LODGE
NUMBER OF ROOMS: 4
MAXIMUM NUMBER OF HUNTERS: 8
Meals: Southern-style
Conference Groups: Yes
Guides: Trained dogs and guides
Dogs and facilities:
Kennel for hunters' dogs, dog training
Shotgun Sports:
Skeet
Other Services:
Birds cleaned and packed for travel
Other Activities:
Bird-watching, hiking, horseback riding, wildlife photography
Rates:
$688 / hunter / day; minimum group of four
Gratuity:
$30
Preferred Payment:
Cash or check
Getting There:
Fly to Columbus, Georgia, and rent a car.

Contact:
Don Dixon
Dixieland Plantation
PO Box 168
Hatchechubbee AL 36858
334/667-7876
EMAIL: dondixon@mindspring.com
WEB: www.outdoorsusa.com/dixieland

If you can pronounce the name of this town, you'll get extra birds in your bag.

N OT 30 MINUTES WEST of Columbus, Georgia, is a first-class lodge that specializes in horseback bird hunts. Birds, in Alabamian of course, means quail. And on these 2,000 acres, coveys are abundant. Fields are farmland left to grow fallow and now protected under the Conservation Reserve Program. Broomsedge carpets the ground beneath widely spaced pines. Fighting encroaching brush is a perennial battle. Laugh's Bo Dixon, "We burn every year." Bo's mom and dad own the plantation.

On a typical morning, hunters work through a southern breakfast of legendary proportions before preparing for the day's hunt. After breakfast, you'll meet your horse (well, you can walk if you want, but few do). Bred from Tennessee walker strains, these mounts are gentle and easy to ride. Some hunters always worry if there's time to dismount and get up to dogs on point. The answer is, yes. Normally, birds will hold for the Dixon's well-trained pointers.

In small groups of three or four, you'll ride out with your guide and dog handler to the section of the plantation chosen for the day's merriment. The land rolls gently; it's neither hilly nor flat, but sort of in the middle. A brace of the plantation's two dozen pointers will cut figure-eights through the grass in front of you. When on point, you'll slip off your mount and go in behind the dogs. The rest is up to you.

Then comes lunch and a nap if you're pleased with your shooting, or a trip to the skeet range if you're not. An afternoon hunt is always on the agenda unless you choose otherwise or managed to get your state limit of 12 birds per day. Though pen-raised birds are released, the Dixons opted out of the accounting nightmare implicit in preserves that bill by the bird. Dinner is another fine southern meal, and afterwards there may be cigars and brandy on the front porch if its warm enough, and in the lodge if it isn't. Nothing's rushed here, and everyone seems to have a good time, and that's just what's in your mind as you climb upstairs to your bedroom with private bath.

Doublehead Resort & Lodge

Town Creek, Alabama

Bring the family to this lakeside lodge; there's lots to keep them entertained.

VITAL STATISTICS:

GAME BIRDS:
CHUKAR, PHEASANT, QUAIL
Source of Birds: Wild and pen-reared
Seasons:
October through March
Land: 2,500 private acres
Accommodations:
MODERN LAKESIDE CEDAR RESORT
NUMBER OF ROOMS: 35 CABINS
MAXIMUM NUMBER OF HUNTERS: 50
Meals: Fine hotel dining
Conference Groups: Yes
Guides: Trained dogs and guides
Dogs and Facilities:
Kennel for hunters' dogs
Shotgun Sports:
Five-stand, sporting clays
Other Services:
Birds cleaned and packed for travel
Other Activities:
Biking, boating, canoeing, fishing, hiking, horseback riding, tennis
Rates:
From $250 / 1/2 day
Gratuity:
Hunter's discretion
Preferred Payment:
Cash, credit cards or check
Getting There:
Fly to Huntsville or Muscle Shoals and rent a car.

Contact:
Jimmy Waddell
Doublehead Resort & Lodge
145 County Rd 314
Town Creek AL 35672
800/685-9267
Fax: 256/685-0224
EMAIL: info@doublehead.com
WEB: www.doublehead.com

WILSON LAKE, which winds through northern Alabama, is one of the oldest of TVA's impoundments on the Tennessee River. On its shores near Huntsville and the famed Redstone Arsenal is a full-service resort which features five-stand sporting clays and quail hunting, along with fishing, horseback riding and tennis. Thirty-five three-bedroom, two-bath cedar cottages are scattered along the lake's edge. Each features a full kitchen, wood-burning fireplace, washer and dryer. On the point jutting into the lake is Doublehead's main lodge, also of cedar. The dining room is of pine log, reminiscent of historic western hotels. The restaurant is known for its first-class cuisine (breakfast: poached eggs and smoked salmon with hollandaise on English muffin; dinner: lobster paella or stuffed mutton chop). This is a resort where people come just to eat.

With 1,100 acres managed expressly for bobwhite quail hunting, Doublehead combines the best of southern resort hospitality with quality bird shooting. Most hunters begin with a round of clays from the seven-trap, five-stand trap. Instruction is available if you want it. Four-by-fours, specially modified to carry four hunters and a couple braces of pointers, are driven to the field du jour. Or, if you prefer, you can ride horseback. There, a pair of dogs are loosed and the Jeep idles down the road as you watch the action. When the dogs get birdy, your guide will stop the truck, and you'll alight and follow the dogs on foot. Comes the point, you'll bust it with your guide and with luck (the most important element of shotgunning), you'll bag a double. For half-day hunts, Doublehead's crew will place 20 birds per gunner, each of whom is limited to 12 quail. On full-day hunts, 40 birds are released. Pheasants and chukar are available on request, and special hunts can be arranged for corporate or group clients.

Doublehead is half way between Huntsville and Nashville via Interstate 65. With outstanding conference facilities equipped with up-do-date technology, this is one of those convenient locations where you can combine business with lots of pleasure. And, if bass fishing is your bag, boats and guides are available from the marina. Families will enjoy riding and tennis as well as the food.

Parches Cove Hunting Preserve

U n i o n   G r o v e ,   A l a b a m a

Ancient Cherokee hunting grounds now teem with pheasants and quail.

VITAL STATISTICS:

GAME BIRDS:
DUCKS, PHEASANT, QUAIL
Source of Birds: Wild (ducks) and pen-reared
Seasons:
PHEASANTS and QUAIL: October - March
DUCKS: December and January
Land: 3000 private acres
Accommodations:
RUSTIC LODGE AND CABIN
NUMBER OF ROOMS: 9
MAXIMUM NUMBER OF HUNTERS: 12
Meals: Hearty steaks and chicken
Conference Groups: Yes
Guides: Trained dogs and guides
Dogs and Facilities:
Bring your own kennel with your dog
Shotgun Sports:
Skeet
Other Services:
Birds cleaned and packed for travel
Other Activities:
Big game
Rates:
$350 / day
Gratuity:
Hunter's discretion
Preferred Payment:
Cash or check
Getting There:
Fly to Huntsville and rent a car or arrange for the lodge van at $75 round trip.

Contact:
Houston Lindsay
Parches Cove Hunting Preserve
4415 Parches Cove Rd
Union Grove AL 35175
256/498-2447
Fax: 256/498-1039

WITH SWIFT AND DELICATE feather-tufted darts, fired with amazing accuracy from blowguns made from hollowed out reeds, the Cherokee hunted quail and ducks near their village at the confluence of Pigeon Roost Creek and the Tennessee River. They lived in houses of log and wattle, and around their villages, they cultivated corn which was their staff of life. Much of this preserve 35 miles southeast of Huntsville was once the village of Chief Corn Parch. During spring plowing, arrowheads, an occasional axe, and bits of flint and pottery are turned up with the rich red soil.

This 3,000-acre preserve sprawls along four miles of river bottom just downstream from the Tennessee Valley Authority's Guntersville Dam. Rock bluffs climb more than 600 feet behind the floodplain. Fields are cropped with corn, soybeans, hay and alfalfa. Damp swales grow brush, and it's thickest along meandering wet-weather streams. Pointers or setters (yours or theirs) work through the cover, probing for quail or pheasants. A dog handler offers suggestions, but the gunning is up to you. Most hunters find it easy to walk this land.

While the preserve program operates from October through March, and hunting for wild ducks (blinds and decoys in the bottomlands) runs from December into January, there's more to Parches Cove than birds. You'll find big Alabama bucks in this country. During the day, they hide out in the thick timber filling draws between the bluffs. Morning and evening will find them in the fields, maybe beneath your stand. Bass fishing in Guntersville Lake can be excellent in the fall, and a number of nearby marinas offer guides and boats. Parches Cove offers accommodations in a rustic house and cabin on the preserve. Huntsville, site of Redstone Arsenal, offers excellent restaurants for those who desire fancier fare than steaks and grilled chicken at the lodge. You can mix and match hunting packages at Parches Cove, but the most popular finds guests arriving about noon. They'll hunt the afternoon, enjoy a lazy dinner, and then walk the dogs again in the morning.

Rockfence Station

Lafayette, Alabama

Plant cover and grow birds — that's the motto of Rockfence.

VITAL STATISTICS:

GAME BIRDS:
CHUKAR, DOVE, QUAIL, TURKEY
Source of Birds: Pen-reared
Seasons:
QUAIL and CHUKAR: October through March
DOVE: September
TURKEY: mid-March through mid-April
Land: 3,500 private acres
Accommodations:
MODERN LODGE WITH RAILROAD MOTIF
NUMBER OF ROOMS: 8
MAXIMUM NUMBER OF HUNTERS: 16
Meals: Beef, venison, fish, quail
Conference Groups: Yes
Guides: Trained dogs and guides
Dogs and Facilities:
Kennel for hunters' dogs, dog training
Shotgun Sports:
Five-stand, sporting clays, trap and skeet
Other Services:
Birds cleaned and packed for travel, proshop
Other Activities:
Big game, golf, wildlife photography
Rates:
$450 / gun
Gratuity:
$40 / 1/2 day
Preferred Payment:
Cash, credit card or check
Getting There:
Fly to Atlanta and rent a car or arrange for the lodge to pick you up at $50 per person.

Contact:
Kane Hadmon
Rockfence Station
4388 County Rd 160
Lafayette AL 36862
334/864-0217
Fax: 334/864-0235
EMAIL: rmclendon@rockfence.com
WEB: www.rockfence.com

ONE OF THE SECRETS of a great quail hunting preserve is cover. Not only must it provide food and shelter, for that encourages the propagation of native birds, but it must stand up to the ravages of six months of hunting. On its 3,500 acres just across the Georgia border north of Interstate 85, Rockfence goes to great lengths to create and maintain outstanding habitat. Selective burns are employed to condition fields. They're planted with a variety of grains and grasses: bahia, bicolor, fescue, millets, corn, cowpeas, lespedeza, partridge pea, sunflower and rye. Cover crops and native plants are fertilized to provide optimum growth. The result is cover that's hard to beat.

In operation, most quail preserves are fairly similar. At Rockfence, your morning will open with a breakfast of fried quail and biscuits, juice and coffee, and eggs should your cholesterol be feeling low. At eight, you'll meet your guide who, before he picks you up, will have selected two to four dogs from the lodge's kennel of Brittany's, pointers and setters. You and your partner will climb aboard the shootin' Jeep and head out to the first field of the day. You can pick the kind of terrain that suits you best: open timber or food plots. Then comes lunch and an obligatory snooze. (Well, you don't have to; in fact, given the way you shot this morning, a session at the sporting clays or five-stand course may be in order.) Next, you'll saddle up for the afternoon's festivities.

Drinks and dinner are served in a main lodge that's quite modern, yet rustic at the same time. A huge open fireplace juts into the great room and on those grey, chill days of January, there's no better place to warm your backside, sip a favored libation, and swap yarns about other shoots. After a fine dinner of venison cooked the southern way, you'll head for the sack—in a converted railroad box car. No hobo haven this, your car contains two beds and a shared private bath.

In addition to its mainstay, quail, Rockfence offers dove shoots in September and turkey hunting in March and April. In December and January, combo hunts for quail and deer can be arranged. You'll also find regulation trap and skeet ranges, and among guests, friendly competitions are wont to develop.

*At Bienville Plantation in north Florida, there are ducks on
the lake, quail in the piney sedge, trap, deer, hogs and, heaven help
us, bass for those who get bored.*

*The wraparound porch at Broughton Plantation near
Atlanta is tailor-made for watchin' the fog lift from the pond,
and contemplating just how you missed that easy double on quail
before dinner yesterday.*

White Oak Plantation

T u s k e g e e ,   A l a b a m a

Oh, no. Ain't it awful. Guess we'll have to hunt quail, or ducks, or deer.

VITAL STATISTICS:

GAME BIRDS:
QUAIL, TURKEY
Source of Birds: Wild and pen-reared
Seasons:
QUAIL: October through March
TURKEY: Mid-March through April
Land: 16,000 private acres
Accommodations:
PRIVATE RAMBLING WOODEN LODGE
NUMBER OF ROOMS: 10
MAXIMUM NUMBER OF HUNTERS: 20
Meals: Southern cooking
Conference Groups: Yes
Guides: Trained dogs and guides
Dogs and Facilities:
Kennel for hunters' dogs
Shotgun Sports:
Five-stand, shooting schools, sporting clays
Other Services:
Birds cleaned and packed for travel
Other Activities:
Big game, bird-watching, fishing, golf, tennis, wildlife photography
Rates:
$300 / day
Gratuity:
Hunter's discretion
Preferred Payment:
Cash, MasterCard or Visa
Getting There:
Fly to Montgomery, AL, or Atlanta, GA, and rent a car.

Contact:
Robert Pitman
White Oak Plantation
5215 B County Rd 10
Tuskegee AL 36083
334/727-9258
Fax: 334/727-3411
EMAIL: whiteoakhunts@mind spring.com
WEB:
www.americaoutdoor.com/woak/

YOU KNOW ALABAMA'S black belt, that midstate swath of deep, rich earth, for its legendary whitetail. And you know Robert Pitman's plantations—White Oak and its sibling Red Oak—for their legendary deer hunting. Trophy-quality bucks of eight points plus are harvested with clockwork regularity. But what you may not know is that among those stands of hardwoods and pine and miles of boggy lowlands are hundreds of acres of feed plots. These are mainly for deer, but quail dine here too.

A regulated shooting preserve, White Oak offers gunning for wild and pen-raised bobwhite from October through March. Fields offer mixed cover: some corn, milo, sedge and enough briars to make a pair of brush pants essential. Groups of up to six gunners, a passel of pointers, and a guide or two comprise each hunt. Walking or riding the wagon as your pleasure or the situation dictates, you and your partner will work in behind the dogs when they go on point. Hunts include 15 birds per hunter; additional birds may be added in advance.

Quail, of course, is not the only bird found on Pitman's 16,000 acres. In the fall, wood ducks filter through the trees into a charming 200-acre swamp ringed with water oak and thick clumps of willow. Mallards like these waters as well, and you can fill your limit with greenwing teal as long as you don't think about each shot. And come March, when the grays and browns of Alabama's mild winters give way to the frothy green of spring, big ol' toms begin to sound off in the woods. If you time it right, combo hunts for deer, ducks, turkey and quail can be arranged.

White Oak is a consummate sporting resort. Shotgunners enjoy the 16-station sporting clays course that winds around Pitman's 13-acre bass lake. Then there's NSCA five-stand for prehunt warm-ups. Accommodations are rustic yet modern and very comfortable, and the meals, well, you know about southern cookin'. White Oak is a family-run operation and it caters not only to serious trophy hunters, but also to parents with youngsters new to the shooting sports. Conference groups will also find facilities ideal for strategic planning retreats.

Owens Station

G r e e n w o o d ,   D e l a w a r e

Bird hunting and great sporting clays far from the maddening crowd.

VITAL STATISTICS:

GAME BIRDS:
CHUKAR, HUNGARIAN PARTRIDGE, PHEASANT, QUAIL

Source of Birds: Pen-reared

Seasons:
UPLAND BIRDS: mid-October through March

Land: 300 private acres

Accommodations:
REMODELED MOBILE HOME
NUMBER OF ROOMS: 4
MAXIMUM NUMBER OF HUNTERS: 4

Meals: Self-catered or eat in restaurants

Conference Groups: Yes

Guides: Trained dogs and guides

Dogs and Facilities:
Kennel for hunters' dogs, dog training

Shotgun Sports:
Five stand, sporting clays, tower or release shoots

Other Services:
Birds cleaned and packed for travel

Rates:
$50 night / person (lodging); hunts by the bird

Gratuity:
$25 - $50 per hunt

Preferred Payment:
Cash, MasterCard, Visa or check

Getting There:
Fly to Georgetown and rent a car or drive down US 13 from Wilmington.

Contact:
William Wolter
Owens Station
RD1, Box 203
Greenwood DE 19950
302/349-4478

IT ISN'T ONLY THOSE LARGE corporations that seek tax advantages that love Delaware, but it's guys like you and me who've had it with droves of people. Delaware is one of those charming out of the way places with lots of huge coastal plain farms. Stately mansions of the Federal period rise at the end of tree-lined lanes. Fields of beans and corn stretch from tree line to tree line. Black-water creeks hide ducks and in the fall, snow geese and Canadas trade raucously overhead.

But it's not waterfowl that draw gunners to this bit of bucolic tranquility. It's sporting clays, one of the most impressive layouts in the East. "We can provide any kind of shot you want," says Bill Wolter, owner of the spread. With 43 stations, the number of courses is infinite. Make it as hard or easy as you like. National Sporting Clays Association shoots are held regularly here.

While gunners come for the sporting clays, they soon learn that Owens Station boasts some of the best upland bird hunting along the Mid-Atlantic Coast. Pheasants, chukar, Hungarian partridge, red-legged partridge and bobwhite quail (once native but no more) fill the menu here. Prices are by the bird.

The first thing most gunners notice is that the cover seems to hold up better at Owens Station that on other preserves. There's good reason for that. When Bill was working for USDA, he helped develop and market a hybrid strain of switchgrass, native to eastern prairies. Called "panic" grass by USDA, the hybrid's leaves and stems are slightly thicker than parent varieties. Some towns like Ocean City bought tons of seed to establish cover on sand dunes. For preserves, the panic grass stands up better to snow and the foot falls of man and dog. You'll find cover here in February and March that other preserves would brag about in December and January.

And the second thing hunters learn about Owens Station is that Bill knows dogs. He's bred, trained and shown trial dogs all his life. His kennels carry championship pointers, setters and German shorthairs. You'll also find German wirehairs among his stock. All are well trained and some are available for purchase.

Lodging here is pretty straight forward: a remodeled mobile home with a comfortable porch and kitchen. Fancier digs and restaurants are available in small towns nearby. However, when it comes to vittles, you won't do better than Yoder's Dutch Oven in Greenwood. It's a family restaurant with good food reasonably priced.

Bienville Plantation

W h i t e S p r i n g s , F l o r i d a

When it comes to full-service hunting and fishing retreats, you can't beat Bienville.

VITAL STATISTICS:

GAME BIRDS:
CHUKAR, DUCKS, PHEASANT, QUAIL
Source of Birds: Wild and pen-reared
Seasons:
CHUKAR, PHEASANT, QUAIL: October through April
DUCKS: November through April
Land: 15,000 private acres
Accommodations:
FIVE LAKESIDE LODGES
NUMBER OF ROOMS: 25
MAXIMUM NUMBER OF HUNTERS: 50
Meals: Country elegant
Conference Groups: Yes
Guides: Trained dogs and guides
Dogs and Facilities:
Kennel for hunters' dogs
Shotgun Sports:
Shooting schools, skeet, tower or release shoots, trap
Other Services:
Birds cleaned and packed for travel, proshop
Other Activities:
Big game, fishing, wildlife photography
Rates:
From $596 inclusive / gun /day, double occupancy
Gratuity:
$20 - $50
Preferred Payment:
Cash, credit cards or check
Getting There:
Fly to Jacksonville and rent a car.

Contact:
Scott Thomas
Bienville Plantation
PO Box 241
White Springs FL 32096
912/755-0205 or
904/397-1989
Fax: 904/397-1988
Off Season:
111 Orange St., Suite 101
Macon GA 31201
EMAIL: bienville@aol.com
WEB: www.bienville.com

ON THE ONE HAND, you have sportsman's resorts and, on the other, retreats. What's the difference? A resort is one of those fast-paced places where, in addition to bird hunting and maybe fishing, you may find a golf course, tennis courts, boat dock and marina, restaurant and a whole lot of folks with other things on their minds besides swinging a shotgun. A retreat, on the other hand, is a kind of get-away-from-it-all place, a refuge from the hustle and hype of business. Sure, you may do some business at a retreat, but if you do it at all, it'll be in an atmosphere so relaxed you'll hardly notice it.

Bienville is a first-class sporting retreat. Once a huge phosphate mine, today the ponds and fields have been reclaimed into some of the finest habitat for bass, quail and ducks you can imagine. Fields are burned and replanted every spring to ensure feed for wild and supplemental birds. Some fields are thick with broomsedge. Others feature open pines with thick grasses and patches of brush. Briars and brambles are few, but where you find them, you'll also find quail. Mule-drawn wagons carry some hunters afield. Modified jeeps transport others. Always, you're accompanied by a knowledgeable guide who handles Bienville's dogs as well as if they were his own. A 12-bird limit prevails. Quail is the main event here, but pheasants and chukar are available on request, and tower/release shoots can be scheduled for groups.

The best time to visit Bienville is between November and January: duck season. Ringnecks, mallards, woodies and an occasional canvasback drop into black water ponds with first light. Hunting is from long skiffs pushed by Go-devils, those wacky air-cooled outboards that drive a boat in water no deeper than a tea cup. Retrievers are seldom used. No sense feeding the 'gators. Deer hunting hits the calendar at the same time as ducks, and if you've a hankering for some wild bacon, sign up for a hog hunt. Traditional trap and skeet ranges are also available.

Not only does Bienville's acreage and abundance of game make it attractive, but accommodations are unparalleled. Beneath the pines, five cottages, each with kitchen, five bedrooms (with private baths), and screened porches flank the lakefront lodge and pro shop. Dining is country elegant with an understated penchant for game and seafood.

[**S O U T H**]

Iron-Wood Preserve

L a k e   C i t y ,   F l o r i d a

If you're one of the few that hunts Iron-Wood, consider yourself among the most blessed.

VITAL STATISTICS:

GAME BIRDS:
QUAIL, TURKEY
Source of Birds: Wild and pen-reared
Seasons:
QUAIL: November through February
Land: 2,500 private acres
Accommodations:
RUSTIC WOODEN LODGE
NUMBER OF ROOMS: 4
MAXIMUM NUMBER OF HUNTERS: 10
Meals: Quail, venison and trimmings
Conference Groups: Yes
Guides: Trained dogs and guides
Shotgun Sports:
Six-stand wobble clays
Other Services:
Birds cleaned and packed for travel
Other Activities:
None
Rates:
From $575 / person / day; 4-person minimum
Gratuity:
Hunter's discretion
Preferred Payment:
Cash, MasterCard or Visa
Getting There:
Fly to Jacksonville or Gainesville and rent a car.

Contact:
Penny Livingston
Iron-Wood Preserve
PO Box 1949
Lake City FL 32056
904/555-0220 x834
Fax: 904/752-7897
WEB: www.iron-wood.com

ET YOURSELF A GROUP of four or six pals (two or three couples is fun, too) and hie yourself down to Iron-Wood, a secluded lodge on 2,500 acres of pine, hardwood and tended game fields. Your day begins with breakfast, as late and leisurely as you like it, and then a "tune-up" on the six-stand wobble clays course. If you're not totally humiliated by your score (Hey, among friends, who keeps count, right? Wrong!), you'll mount up and head out for quail.

A pair of matched graying mules pulls the rubber-tired wagon along a soft track through the grasslands while a brace of pointers casts first to the right and then left. When one goes on point, you slip down from your seat on the wagon and walk up behind the dog. Your guide will motion you in and when the bird flushes . . . that's your chance. There's much to soothe the soul as you ride through the open pines, sunlight dappling on the needle-carpeted wagon trail. The dogs are working well and all's right with the world. Equestrians may forego the wagon in favor of a gentle Tennessee walker. Quail, both wild and pen-raised, are the main event here, but in the spring you may find some outstanding gobblers.

Iron-Wood is a very private preserve, created by owner Floyd Messer for the exclusive use of his friends and business guests. To preserve the quality of the birds and habitat, Floyd limits the number of groups that hunt Iron-Wood each year. Only one party of at least four and no more than 10 hunters books the two-story rustic lodge at any given time. For safety, and to maintain the intimacy of a truly southern-style quail hunt, no more than four gunners can hunt at one time.

Each tastefully decorated guest room boasts its own private bath. Meals are served family style on the long wooden table downstairs. Afterwards, have a cigar and watch the moon rise from the front porch that runs the length of the lodge. Iron-Wood provides everything that its guests need except shells and guns. And nonhunting members of any group are included at no extra charge.

Plantation Outfitters

Quincy, Florida

This old farm has been a quail hunter's dream for more than a century and a half.

VITAL STATISTICS:

GAME BIRDS:
DUCKS, GEESE, PHEASANT, QUAIL
Source of Birds: Wild and pen-reared
Seasons:
QUAIL and PHEASANTS: October through March
DUCKS and GEESE: late November through late January
Land: 1,000 private and public acres
Accommodations:
PRIVATE LODGES
NUMBER OF ROOMS: 2 IN THE PRESERVE / 3 AT THE LAKE
MAXIMUM NUMBER OF HUNTERS: 10
Meals: Country cooking
Conference Groups: Yes
Guides: Trained dogs and guides
Dogs and Facilities:
Kennel for hunters' dogs, dog training
Shotgun Sports:
Driven birds, shooting schools
Other Services:
Birds cleaned and packed for travel
Other Activities:
Big game, bird-watching, boating, canoeing, fishing, golf, hiking, wildlife photography
Rates:
QUAIL: $275 / day with meals and lodging; $175 without
PHEASANT: $125 / gun
DUCKS: $195 / day with meals and lodging; $125 without
Gratuity:
Hunter's discretion
Preferred Payment:
Cash or check
Getting There:
Fly to Tallahassee and rent a car.

Contact:
David Avant III
Plantation Outfitters
14 N Cone St.
Quincy FL 32351
904/575-1260
Fax: 850/576-1327
EMAIL: davidavant@aol.com

THE COUNTRYSIDE NORTH AND WEST of Tallahassee, Florida's capitol, is flat and piney. Sluggish black-water streams meander through narrow bottoms, and cleared land is usually in grasses of one variety or another. Grasses and seed-bearing weeds are favorites with quail native to this area, and they provide cover for pen-reared pheasants as well. This is fine country for a laid-back bird hunt with faintly Anglophile flavors. Double guns, and that means side-bys, are especially welcome here, as are kilts and knickers. Gentry wear ties.

Plantation Outfitters comes by this legacy naturally. The property has been in the Avant family for more than 175 years. The plantation dates from 1823, and the house—known locally as the Joshua Davis House—is of clapboard over log construction. It was built in 1827 and is the oldest documented building in Gadsden county. The British, who settled this area and the state of Georgia to the north, were quite delighted to find bobwhite when they arrived. They missed, of course, their driven grouse, but kept their fowling pieces warm on quail.

You will too during half-day hunts where the number of birds you take is determined only by the skill with which you wield your scattergun. (Since there's no limit, there's no extra charge for additional birds. Now, how's that for English logic?) And, while you're out for quail, you can harvest the odd dove, woodcock or rabbit for free (assuming you're properly licensed). Hunt over your own dogs or with those belonging to the preserve. Along with flight-conditioned quail, the preserve also features driven pheasant shoots. You'll arrive about 8 a.m., enjoy a light breakfast, and work the kinks out of your mind and muscles with a round or two of clay pigeons. Gunning begins at 9:00 sharp, with released birds soaring high over the heads of gunners. The morning concludes with a barbecue.

If ducks are on your agenda, Plantation will take you to its recently remodeled lodge on Lake Seminole. The 37,000-acre lake marks the corner where Alabama, Florida and Georgia meet. Gunning is from blinds and camouflaged boats. During the season, hunters limit on wood ducks, ringnecks, teal and mallards. More than occasionally, Canada geese find their way into the game bag. Guests stay in one of two lodges: at the preserve if quail or pheasant hunting, or on Lake Seminole for ducks.

Boggy Pond Plantation

M o u l t r i e , G e o r g i a

*Quail buggies take you to a field,
then you gotta go to work.*

VITAL STATISTICS:

GAME BIRDS:
CHUKAR, PHEASANT, QUAIL
Source of Birds: Wild and pen-reared
Seasons:
October through March
Land: 3,000 private acres
Accommodations:
FOUR TURN OF THE CENTURY COTTAGES
NUMBER OF ROOMS: 15
MAXIMUM NUMBER OF HUNTERS: 19
Meals: Friend chicken, ham, pork, and vegetables
Conference groups: Yes
Guides: Trained dogs and guides
Dogs and Facilities:
Kennel for hunters' dogs
Shotgun Sports:
Five-stand, sporting clays
Other Services:
Birds cleaned and packed for travel
Other Activities:
Fishing, golf
Rates:
From $350 / day
Gratuity:
Hunter's discretion
Preferred Payment:
Cash or check
Getting There:
Fly to Tallahassee and rent a car.

Contact:
Mack W. Dekle, Jr.
Boggy Pond Plantation
1084 Lanier Rd
Moultrie GA 31768
912/985-5395

AMONG THOSE THINGS that go hand in hand on the southern piedmont is growing timber and gunning for birds. And that's what this easy-going, no-nonsense quail plantation is all about. Located half-way between Albany, Georgia, and Tallahassee, Florida, Boggy Pond encompasses about 3,000 acres of longleaf yellow pine. The terrain rolls ever so gently with thick stands of new-growth woods giving way to feed plots and the brushy floor of mature pine forest.

Hunting here is a leisurely affair. Gunners ride in the high seats over twin dog boxes mounted on the backs of Jeeps. You can see the dogs working, and when they lock on point, all you do is slide down from your perch, slip a shell in the chamber and walk up behind the dog. With luck, the covey will flush, and at least one bird will give you that piece-of-cake going-away shot that everyone loves and misses. Once you've busted up the covey, you can hunt singles afoot or go back to the Jeep, as terrain and your disposition so dictate. You'll also hunt pheasant and chukar.

A dozen birds is considered a day's bag at Boggy pond, but you're not forced to shoot all of 'em before dinner. Most hunters peck away at their limit in the morning, come in for a lunch of fried chicken or quail with green beans and iced tea, and then, after a short siesta (you can go shoot a round of clays or seduce largemouth from the stocked pond if you're of mind and energy to), don their hunter's orange and return to the field for the afternoon hunt.

The main lodge at Boggy Pond was once a country school. But the only ciphers any one does there now is the cook figuring out how to double that recipe for spoon bread. Overnight guests sleep in one of four cottages, the sizes of which vary from five to two bedrooms. Corporate groups are welcome and so are children when accompanied by parents. Pricing is flexible, based on day, overnight or week. Weather in south Georgia can be as fickle as it can be fair. Often, days during the season—October through March—see the thermometer rise into the 70s. But occasionally it doesn't even clear the 30s. Layered, lightweight clothing is the rule here.

Boll Weevil Plantation

Waynesboro, Georgia

When it comes to birds and dogs, this resort is an all-time champ.

VITAL STATISTICS:

GAME BIRDS:
QUAIL, TURKEY
Source of Birds: Wild and pen-reared
Seasons:
QUAIL: October through March
TURKEY: mid-March through mid-May
Land: 6,200 private acres
Accommodations:
MODERN LODGE
NUMBER OF ROOMS: 15
MAXIMUM NUMBER OF HUNTERS: 30
Meals: Country-style game
Conference Groups: No
Guides: Trained dogs and guides
Dogs and facilities:
Kennel for hunters' dogs, dog training
Shotgun Sports:
Five-stand, sporting clays, trap
Other Services:
Birds cleaned and packed for travel
Other Activities:
Big game, fishing
Rates:
$495 / day
Gratuity:
Hunter's discretion
Preferred Payment:
Cash, MasterCard, Visa
Getting There:
Fly to Augusta, Georgia, and rent a car.

Contact:
Ben Seay IV
Boll Weevil Plantation
4264 Thompson Bridge Rd
Waynesboro GA 30930
706/554-6227
Fax: 706/554-0892
WEB: http://bollweevil.home.ml.org

WITH NEARLY 6,200 ACRES and more than 1,000 food plots of corn, sorghum, millet, lespedeza, peas, rye and clover, it's small wonder that both game animals and hunters beat a path to its door. This is one well-run operation. A fleet of 11 Jeeps, each modified to carry a tandem dog box under a pair of high-seated gunners, does most of the leg work for you. Dogs—pointers and setters—are raised and trained on the property. If you find one you like especially, you may be able to buy a pup or a started dog if you want. Bird cleaning is fast, professional and very inexpensive in comparison to other quail-hunting plantations.

But what of the hunting itself? You'll enjoy it. Though Boll Weevil serves a large number of hunters each season, fields are rotated so that the cover holds up throughout the season from October through March. A typical day's hunt begins after a full southern-style breakfast of the kind that makes you want to walk all day rather than ride in the Jeep. You and three pals will climb aboard the four-wheeler, and the guide will drive you to the field for the morning's merriment. There you'll watch pointers switching back and forth until one slams into a point. Two of you will dismount. Both should get shooting if the birds flare left and right. After a covey is flushed, you'll all take turns on the singles. A full day afield is seven hours with a limit of 12 birds. There's a break in the middle for dinner (only a city boy would call it lunch). Half-day hunts include the noon meal as well. On half-day hunts, gunners are allowed eight birds.

From mid-March through mid-May, turkey hunting tops the agenda here. While quail hunting is a high-and-dry affair, calling in gobblers may not be. Bring waders. Swamps along Brier Creek offer some of the best hunting. You'll also find that quail hunting overlaps with whitetails in the later weeks of October. Most hunting is from covered stands overlooking feed plots and escape routes. Midday quail hunts can be arranged.

Long, low and shielded by shrubs, the lodge contains 30 rooms for two with private baths. Meals, country-style and distinctly southern, are served in the dining room, off which is a richly furnished lounge with pool and poker tables. On the wall are mounts of some of the deer harvested at Boll Weevil. But they aren't the biggest. Those went home with their owners.

65

[S O U T H]

Broughton Plantation

N e w b o r n ,   G e o r g i a

Family-style hunting and family-style dining at an easy-goin' preserve not far from Atlanta.

VITAL STATISTICS:

GAME BIRDS:
CHUKAR, PHEASANT, QUAIL
Source of Birds: Pen-reared
Seasons:
UPLAND BIRDS: October through March
TURKEY: mid-March through mid-May
Land: 2,000 private acres
Accommodations:
PRIVATE LOG LODGE
NUMBER OF ROOMS: 4
MAXIMUM NUMBER OF HUNTERS: 10
Meals: Bona fide country cooking
Conference Groups: Yes
Guides: Trained dogs and guides
Dogs and Facilities:
Kennel for hunters' dogs, dog training
Shotgun Sports:
Five-stand, shooting schools, sporting clays, tower or release shoots
Other Services:
Birds cleaned and packed for travel
Other Activities:
Big game, fishing, wildlife photography
Rates:
From $225 / half-day for 2 guns minimum
Gratuity:
Hunter's discretion
Preferred Payment:
Cash, check or credit card
Getting There:
Fly to Atlanta and rent a car.

Contact:
Jim Babcock
Broughton Plantation
PO Box 172
Newborn GA 30056
706/342-2281
Fax: 706/342-9810

ROUGHTON'S A FAMILY OPERATION—a one-time dairy operation that was too big to sell and too small to operate economically. So, with the blessing of their mom and dad (whom you may have the good fortune to meet in the kitchen), sons Warren and Ken Howard turned the farm into a hunting preserve. Native birds are augmented with flight-conditioned pen-raised stock, and pheasants are released either in continental or field-style, as gunners prefer.

The keys to good quail hunting over pen-raised birds are two: good cover and good cover. Broughton, two hours east of Atlanta via Interstate 20, seems to have found the mix of sorghum, milo and other feed crops that stand up throughout the long preserve season. And with more than 2,000 acres, fields are rotated regularly. This said, it's important to remember that even on the best managed preserves, the later in the season one hunts, the more worn the cover. The best fields are to the east of the main lodge. From the top of a round-shouldered hill, they roll down to a brushy slough and then rise again up the other side. Here and there stand clumps of shrubbery and an isolated oak or two. Though walkways have been strategically mown, you'll have to get out of the Jeep to hunt this patch. You'll love it. This preserve is serious about safety on its hunts, and it really does cater to families with children who are old enough to hunt.

As is the norm, you'll find a kennel of pointers and a few Labs at Broughton, but you can hunt with your own dog if you wish. Manager Jim Babcock has put together a number of packages to meet the needs of corporate as well as individual clients. Overnighting guests sleep in a new log lodge, in rooms for two with private baths. Downstairs, in the morning, you'll find a cracking fire on the hearth, and the breakfast table, covered with a red-checked table cloth, will be laden with all those vittles that are so bad for us to love. What the hell, have one more biscuit and another ladle of sausage gravy. You're gonna walk it off, right?

Burge Plantation Club, Inc.

Mansfield, Georgia

Lookee here what grew up in the wake of ol' Billy Sherman's boys.

VITAL STATISTICS:

GAME BIRDS:
CHUKAR, PHEASANT, QUAIL, TURKEY
Source of Birds: Pen-reared
Seasons:
UPLAND BIRDS: October through March
TURKEY: mid-March to May
Land: 1,100 private acres
Accommodations:
PLANTATION HOUSE AND LOG CABINS
NUMBER OF ROOMS: 24
MAXIMUM NUMBER OF HUNTERS: VARIES
Meals: Exquisite regional cuisine
Conference Groups: Yes
Guides: Trained dogs and guides
Dogs and facilities:
Kennel for hunters' dogs
Shotgun Sports:
Driven birds, five-stand, shooting schools, skeet, sporting clays, tower or release shoots
Other Services:
Birds cleaned and packed for travel
Other Activities:
Bird-watching, fishing, golf, horseback riding
Rates:
$135 / person American Plan; $150 / gun
Gratuity:
Hunter's discretion
Preferred Payment:
Cash or check
Getting There:
Fly to Atlanta and rent a car.

Contact:
A.G. Morehouse
Burge Plantation Club Inc
200 Morehouse Rd.
Mansfield GA 30255
770/787-5152
Fax: 770/786-9963
EMAIL: burgeplan@aol.com

AFTER SHERMAN RAZED ATLANTA, he divided his troops, sending the right wing south toward Macon and the left wing, which he accompanied, southeast in the direction of Augusta. The left wing moved along a railroad line, laying waste to the country in mid-November, 1864. Among the plantations in the path of Sherman's soldiers was Burge, about midway between Covington and Madison. Houses and barns were burned, livestock slaughtered, and foodstuffs devoured by the Union's troops. Dolly Lunt Burge was an avid diarist, and her account of the conflict is the highly acclaimed *Women's Wartime Journal*, excerpts from which were included in Ken Burn's PBS series on the Civil War. The University of Georgia Press has recently published a complete version of Mrs. Burge's diary.

It took almost 60 years for the farm to recover from the war and for the family to construct the charming white clapboard plantation house in the 1920s. The farm prospered into the 1970s, but then as inflation soared and markets for agricultural products declined, the family sought other means to preserve and maintain the farm and its buildings. The happy solution was a members-only shooting club dedicated to the hunting of quail (with pheasants and chukar on the side). Fields are small. Some is CRP land and others are enhanced with feed strips. A 17-station sporting clays course was added later, as was a skeet range with a high tower behind station four. The trap on the high tower can be synchronized with high and low houses for fast and frustrating shoots which delight everyone.

Accommodations are absolutely first rate. Polished hardwood floors gleam on the perimeters of Persian rugs. Antiques and period reproductions grace the main lodge and guest cabins. Linen-draped tables are set with china and crystal for dinner, and the favorite entrée is a full tenderloin soaked in jalapeño sauce. Called Nicky's Road Kill, there's some debate whether the appellation refers to the beef or the fate of those who partake. Only members and their guests can avail themselves of Burge Plantation, and the number of local members is fairly controlled at 200. However, openings for nonresident members are available. The initiation fee is $2,500, and annual membership $600. That entitles you to stay at the club for $75 a night, enjoy quail hunts for $150 per day, and eat Nicky's Road Kill. Burge Plantation enjoys reciprocal arrangements with several other shooting clubs.

[S O U T H]

Charlane Plantation

D r y   B r a n c h ,   G e o r g i a

Ride horse, Jeep, or shank's mare to your destiny with feisty bobwhite quail.

VITAL STATISTICS:

GAME BIRDS:
DUCKS, QUAIL, TURKEY
Source of Birds: Wild and pen-reared
Seasons:
DUCKS: late November through mid-January
QUAIL: October through March
TURKEY: mid-March through mid-May
Land: 1,700 private acres
Accommodations:
HISTORIC CLAPBOARD LODGE AND COTTAGE
NUMBER OF ROOMS: 5
MAXIMUM NUMBER OF HUNTERS: 12
Meals: Gourmet country cuisine
Conference Groups: Yes
Guides: Trained dogs and guides
Dogs and Facilities:
Kennel for hunters' dogs
Other Services:
Birds cleaned and packed for travel
Other Activities:
Bird-watching, fishing, hiking, horseback riding, wildlife photography
Rates:
$475 / day
Gratuity:
$50 - $100
Preferred Payment:
Cash or check
Getting There:
Fly to Macon or Atlanta; round trip to the lodge is $100.

Contact:
Rose Lane Leavell
Charlane Plantation
Rt 1, Box 377
Dry Branch GA 31020
912/945-3939
Fax: 912/945-6566
EMAIL: charlane@mindspring
WEB: Charlane.com

WHERE DOES THE ROLLING STONES' keyboardist hang out when he's not doing gigs with Mick and company? At a 1,700-acre spread a little ways south of Macon deep in the piney woods. When he was 15, Chuck Leavell dried his ears as a session pianist at a small recording studio in Alabama. He went on to record with some of the best jazz and soul musicians—B.B. King, Aretha Franklin and Ray Charles. But when he's not on the road, you can find him flipping omelets at Charlane, where rock, birds, dogs, horses and a strong conservation ethic come together in a most inviting milieu.

You'll hunt bobwhite afoot, via Jeep or on Tennessee walkers, as tastes and weather suggest, working through thick grasses under mature pines and in open fields tufted with clumps of bush. Dogs will be Chuck's own strain of pointers developed from Elhew and Gunsmoke blood lines. If you prefer Brittany's or setters, Chuck keeps a few of those on hand. Or you may bring and hunt your own. That's cool, too. Along with quail, there's a little spring gobbler hunting, and a few ducks as well.

Chuck and his wife, Rose Lane, are dedicated to the plantation; it's been in her family since the 1920s, and today it is a model of the multiple-use stewardship. Charlane is a tree farm, but that doesn't tell the story at all. With projects such as the soul-soothing trail through native flora, which Rose Lane works to propagate, the plantation has earned the Nature Conservancy Conservation Award and the National Arbor Day Foundation's Stewardship Award, among others.

And the lodge where you may stay, the Bullard House, raised in the 1840s and a classic example of an early clapboard farmstead, is on the National Register of Historic Places. Hunting prints share the walls with gold albums and CDs from the Allman Brothers and the Stones. Bullard house contains three bedrooms, another cottage holds an additional three, and there's a loft over the stable. Hunters are treated like family here. Meals are lush affairs of game, vegetables and vintage wines. You'll long to come back to this place.

Draped with Spanish moss, these old live oaks shade modern cabins for clients who've come to Cabin Bluff to hunt Georgia quail and chase sea-trout in the bay.

*Taking birds down South means talkin' turkey
like this fine gobbler collected from Falkland Farms near
Danville, Virginia. Come fall, you'll find ducks, quail and
deer on Falkland's 7,600 acres.*

Gillionville Plantation

Albany, Georgia

Beneath the spreading oaks sprawls one of the finest quail lodges in the world.

VITAL STATISTICS:

GAME BIRDS:
QUAIL
Source of Birds: Wild and pen-reared
Seasons:
Late October through early March
Land: 9,000 private acres
Accommodations:
HISTORIC PLANTATION HOUSE
NUMBER OF ROOMS: 7
MAXIMUM NUMBER OF HUNTERS: 10
Meals: Exquisite regional cuisine
Conference Groups: Yes
Guides: Trained dogs, handlers and scouts
Shotgun Sports:
Sporting clays, trap
Other Services:
Birds cleaned and packed for travel, proshop
Rates:
On request
Gratuity:
Not appropriate
Preferred payment:
Check
Getting There:
Fly to Albany and you will be met.

Contact:
Chip Hall
Gillionville Plantation
PO Box 3250
Albany GA 31706
912/888-2500
Fax: 912/888-3453

SOME PLACES YOU KNOW ABOUT before you ever go there. Gillionville is one of those. For more than a century, folks have been unlimbering 20s and 16s, walking up behind a brace of liver-and-white pointers, one back standing, and sending a dose of 7 1/2s after one, maybe two, bobwhite quail. It is a game played with grace and style. There is no rush. Nobody's in a hurry. Hunters come to Gillionville to steep themselves in the essence of gentility, a lovely tonic that replenishes the soul and the spirit.

Once known as the first largemouth lodge ever to be endorsed by Orvis, this place is as far away from a fishing camp as The Waldorf is from a Motel Six. Liveried staff greets you at the door when you arrive, taking your luggage and replacing it with a cold potable if that's your desire. You may be led through the gun room, with its shelves of books and the Purdys and Parkers racked on the wall, to your bedroom. Yours may be the one of sunny, yet muted, lemon. Rooms are appointed with fine antiques and shooting prints from the days when hunters wore ties, and doubles had just lost their ears. The air of subtle stateliness is no accident; Gillionville was designed by Edward Vason Jones—a specialist in 18th and 19th century southern architecture—who went on to remodel the White House.

You'll find comfort before the fire in the long room with exposed beams, or if you'd rather and the weather permits it (as is often the case in November and December here in south Georgia), sit outside on the patio and wait for dusk to bring deer in to crop the manicured grounds. And with dusk comes dinner, fine regional cuisine with continental flare, and wine from a reasonably good cellar.

On the morrow you'll take the horse-drawn wagon with three others or ride horseback, if that's what you'd like. You may want to warm up with a round of sporting clays and, if there's time afterwards, somebody might escort you through the rolling piney woods to a bass pond. Most parties who book the lodge are members or guests of Gillionville's hunting club. They enjoy exclusive use of the lodge for a week. Typically, groups of eight or so reserve Gillionville well in advance and return year after year. While there is little turnover among parties who hunt here, there is some. Chip Hall, who manages the operation, will give you a tour if you ask, and advance your name to the club's executive committee for consideration. Egalitarian, the process is not. But would this be the finest quail lodge in the South if it were?

Quail Country Lodge & Conference Center

A r l i n g t o n ,   G e o r g i a

An ideal retreat for business meetings, with more than a few quail on the side.

VITAL STATISTICS:

GAME BIRDS:
DOVE, PHEASANT, QUAIL, TURKEY
Source of Birds: Wild and pen-reared
Seasons:
DOVE: September to January
NATIVE QUAIL: late November through February
PRESERVE BIRDS: October through March
Land: 2,500 private acres
Accommodations:
MODERN LODGE
NUMBER OF ROOMS: 15
MAXIMUM NUMBER OF HUNTERS: 30
Meals: Quail, chops, steak and all the trimmings
Conference Groups: Yes
Guides: Trained dogs and guides
Dogs and Facilities:
Kennel for hunters' dogs
Shotgun Sports:
Skeet, sporting clays, tower or release shoots
Other Services:
Birds cleaned and packed for travel, proshop
Other Activities:
Big game, biking, bird-watching, boating, canoeing, fishing, golf, hiking, wildlife photography
Rates:
From $250 / 1/2 day hunt; lodging and meals from $100 / person / day
Gratuity:
$50 / day
Preferred Payment:
Cash, credit cards or check
Getting There:
Fly to Albany and rent a car.

Contact:
Paschal Brooks
Quail Country Lodge &
Conference Center
Rt. 1, Box 745
Arlington GA 31762
912/725-4645
Fax: 912/725-5443
WEB: www.quailcountry.com

SOUTHWEST GEORGIA has been mecca for bobwhite hunters for decades. But loss of habitat and increasing numbers of hunters have pretty well limited acreage where wild, native quail can be found. Kay and Paschal Brooks, owners of Quail Country Lodge, decided to do something about it. On their 9,500-acre plantation, they've set aside 1,500 acres strictly for natural populations. Over the last six years, selective plantings, predator control, and virtually no hunting have resulted in numerous self-sustaining coveys. Here, albeit on a limited basis, you can actually hunt quail that have never seen a pen.

Most hunters have no complaints with pen-raised birds (pheasants, too) released on Quail Country's 1,000-acre regulated shooting area. You'll hunt from Jeeps or "hunting buggies," over fine pointers, and with guides who've been at it for years. Extensive feed plots and cover crops create habitats that hold birds. You can be assured of busting a handful of coveys during a typical half-day hunt. A limit of 12 birds is included with the price of the hunt, and additional birds may be harvested at $7 each. Quail Country runs tower shoots for pheasants as well. Dove hunts over fields of milo, millet, corn and pea fields are also on the agenda here, and the gunning can be frantic. Check out also the lodge's skeet and sporting clays facilities. The lodge also conducts deer hunts in the fall, and turkey hunts come spring.

Along with individuals and small groups, corporate guests find the facilities at Quail Country top notch. A new, 11,000-square-foot lodge (built in 1996) contains 15 guest rooms, each with private bath. Two lounges, appointed with antiques, fireplaces and country furnishings, offer relaxation after the day's hunt. A section of the lodge is devoted to meeting rooms, with data and voice communication. Meals at Quail Country are often built around smoked steaks, pork loin, and, of course, quail. Outdoor dining and related events are often held at the "Cookhouse," a pavilion on spring-fed Mill Creek. Albany, 30 miles to the northeast, is the closest airport with commercial service.

Riverview Plantation

Camilla, Georgia

Here, you'll never hunt the same field twice, no matter how long you stay.

VITAL STATISTICS:

GAME BIRDS:
QUAIL
Source of Birds: Pen-reared
Seasons:
October through March
Land: 12,000 private acres
Accommodations:
PRIVATE ROOMS IN COTTAGES
NUMBER OF ROOMS: 42
MAXIMUM NUMBER OF HUNTERS: 30
Meals: Elegant country-style
Conference Groups: No
Guides: Trained dogs and guides
Other Services:
Birds cleaned and packed for travel
Rates:
$715 / day
Gratuity:
Hunter's discretion
Preferred Payment:
Cash or check
Getting There:
Fly to Albany or Tallahassee, Florida, and engage a limousine through the lodge.

Contact:
Cader Cox
Riverview Plantation
Rt 2, Box 515
11991 Riverview Rd
Camilla GA 31720
912/294-4904
Fax: 912/294-9851
EMAIL: cbcox@surfsouth.com
WEB: www.riverviewplantation.com

IT'S BEEN A GOOD DAY, you reflect, sitting on the patio, watching the Flint River slide by stands of cypress and mossy oaks that are just now taking on the umber hues of fall. That double was really something. The setter held like a statue. You stepped down from your seat in the Jeep, dropped a pair of shells in your 20-gauge and walked in. Without a sound, there they were—a pair. They banked hard to your left and you nailed the first bird, and continuing your swing, you picked up the second pretty as you please. With due grace, you accepted praise from your guide and from Mac, your long-time hunting pal who really knows how modestly you shoot. And then, of course, on the next flush, you proved Mac right by missing that single straight-away.

In the morning, you hunted the fields' weeds and broomsedge and their thick borders where singles sought cover. After lunch, the Jeep took you and Mac into the open woods where pines grow tall and their sparse canopy allows mixed grasses to thrive in summer. You've been here for two days and you'll stay one more and never will you hunt the same fields. Better than this, bird hunting does not get.

And the accommodations are of equal caliber. Yours is one of 42 single rooms contained in the eight frame cottages that surround the main lodge. Each pair of rooms shares a bath. Dining is country elegant—Riverview Quail (the secret is a dash of Worcestershire and a peel of lemon), catfish, and pecan pie—all accompanied by wines from the well-stocked cellar. Jackets are required for dinner; hunting attire is appropriate for breakfast and lunch.

With 12,000 acres of forest and farmland planted in grains, vegetables and peanuts, Riverview is located in the southwestern corner of Georgia. Riverview is 35 miles south of Albany and 60 miles north of Tallahassee. The Delta Connection, a regional carrier, services Albany and Delta, while American and U.S. Air provide service to Tallahassee. Limousine service from airports to the lodge is available. Riverview caters to corporate clients as well as individuals, and reservations are frequently made a year or more in advance.

[S O U T H]

Rocky Creek Plantation

L y o n s ,   G e o r g i a

This vest pocket plantation in the heart of onion country delivers fine birds.

VITAL STATISTICS:

GAME BIRDS:
DUCKS, PHEASANT
Source of Birds: Pen-reared
Seasons:
October through March
Land: 260 private acres
Accommodations:
MOTELS IN VIDALIA
Guides: Dogs and guides
Shotgun Sports:
Shooting schools, tower or release shoots
Other Services:
Birds cleaned and packed for travel
Rates:
From $100 / gun
Gratuity:
Hunter's discretion
Preferred Payment:
Cash, MasterCard, Visa or check
Getting There:
Fly to Savannah, Georgia, and rent a car.

Contact:
Chuck Thompson
Rocky Creek Plantation
237 Joe Harden Rd
Lyons GA 30436
912/526-4868

O N THE OUTSKIRTS OF VIDALIA—the town for which the world's sweetest onions are named—lies the little village of Lyons, a wide spot in the eastern-central Georgia countryside where farming is a way of life. Here you won't find the pine woods of the southern part of the state. No, hardwoods mixed with some conifers make up the forests, while rolling fields are in pasture and, sometimes, beans.

As plantations go, Rock Creek is not large (only 260 acres or so). And lodging is offered in Vidalia, not on the plantation. But what sets Rock Creek apart from other hunting preserves is its released bird shoots for pheasants and ducks. Parties of up to 20 hunters rotate through 10 blinds, each 70 yards apart. Pheasants are released from a blind 110 yards from the gunners. Flights of four to eight cocks and hens climb over the trees and sail across the shooting butts. The action is fast. Once you shoot this way, you'll understand why the Brits have gun loaders in their blinds. During a two-hour shoot, 160 birds are typically taken.

Duck shoots are the same, yet different. Before sun-up, you're escorted to a blind on a pond where decoys bob in the freshening breeze. As dawn breaks, pairs of mallards wheel and turn and try to settle into your spread. While this shoot lacks the uncertainty of wild duck hunts, it's an excellent opportunity to introduce new hunters to the joys and challenge of hunting ducks over decoys. Steel or other approved nontoxic shot is required, and camouflage face masks are also needed, else mallards will veer away from your upturned face.

Rocky Creek also offers typical preserve-style pheasant hunts in strips of standing cover. Bring your own pointer, setter or flushing dog or hunt with one of Rocky Creek's guides and his dog. Here you'll also find an informal clays course and occasional shooting clinics staffed by a NSCA Level III instructor.

Shirahland Plantation

Camilla, Georgia

*They may come for the bird hunting,
but, oh, that chicken pot pie.*

VITAL STATISTICS:

GAME BIRDS:
QUAIL
Source of Birds: Wild and pen-reared
Seasons:
QUAIL: November through February
Land: 5,000 private acres
Accommodations:
PRIVATE LODGE
NUMBER OF ROOMS: 9
MAXIMUM NUMBER OF HUNTERS: 11
Meals: Excellent family cooking
Conference Groups: Yes
Guides: Trained dogs and guides
Dogs and Facilities:
Kennel for hunters' dogs
Shotgun Sports:
Five-stand, sporting clays
Other Services:
Birds cleaned and packed for travel, pro shop
Other Activities:
Big game, fishing, golf
Rates:
$595 / day
Gratuity:
Hunter's discretion
Preferred Payment:
Cash, credit card or check
Getting There:
Fly to Albany and rent a car or hire the lodge van for $50 / trip.

Contact:
Tim Shira
Shirahland Plantation
3093 Shirahland Rd
Camilla GA 31730
912/294-4805
Fax: 912/294-7651
EMAIL: shiraland@surfsouth.com
WEB: shiraland.com

AN ARMY, THEY SAY, travels on its belly. Not so with wingshooters. They don't care what they eat, as long as the birds hold and flush well and not too many shots go astray. Right? Well, maybe not. Lots of places provide good to great bird hunting, and Shirahland, with its 6,000 acres of broomsedge and feed plots, is in the top tier. But here you've got Willene Shirah's old family recipes, handed down from generation to generation of plantation farmers. Food here is simple and good.

Take the flaky, crusted chicken pot pie, or quail 'n gravy, or her pork loin roast that's so tender you can almost eat it with a spoon. Think of vegetables, grown fresh on nearby farms and put up in Shirahland's own kitchen; there's no Green Giant on those labels. And then there's piquant mayhow jelly, running red in butter, melting between the halves of a biscuit not two minutes from the oven. If you talk nice, you may be able to liberate a jar of the jelly to take home. And afterwards, you'll amble out to the front porch and sit, and let your gaze wander over miles and miles of mossy oak and piney woods. The talk will be of quail and guns and how 'n hell Bob managed to miss both those birds in that straight-away sure-shot double. Must 'a had cornmeal in his shells.

Shirahland is one of those places that gets in your mind. With more than 5,000 acres broken into plots of about 150 acres each—some planted with corn, milo, millet or sorghum, and all with grass waving tawny under the pines—the cover here is better than good. You'll ride a Jeep with one other hunter, and the guide will bring along four to six dogs of your preference: pointers, setters or springers. The game here is birds, and by that, the Shirah's mean bobwhite quail. There's no really bad time to hunt here, but December and January seem to be the best months. Check out, too, the opportunity to hunt bucks of eight points or better from stands.

Here, the emphasis is on friendly, personal service. Shirahland is not a large lodge; it caters to groups that often book the entire facility. Sometimes, however, manager Tim Shirah will meld two groups, but only if both agree and the chemistry is right. Every guest has a private room, though two rooms have twin instead of queen beds. All rooms have private baths.

[S O U T H]

The Lodge at Cabin Bluff

H a r i e t t s   B l u f f ,   G e o r g i a

Private, secluded, charming—everything that a sporting lodge should be can be found at Cabin Bluff.

VITAL STATISTICS:

GAME BIRDS:
QUAIL, TURKEY
Source of Birds: Pen-reared
Seasons:
QUAIL: October through March
TURKEY: late March through mid-May
Land: 48,000 private acres
Accommodations:
RUSTIC LODGE AND CABINS
NUMBER OF ROOMS: 16
MAXIMUM NUMBER OF HUNTERS: 16
Meals: Classic southern coastal cuisine
Conference Groups: Yes
Guides: Trained dogs and guides
Shotgun Sports:
Driven birds, shooting schools, sporting clays
Other Services:
Birds cleaned and packed for travel
Other Activities:
Big game, bird-watching, boating, fishing, golf, hiking, horseback riding, tennis, wildlife photography
Rates:
$1,495 / 3 days, 2 nights / person
Gratuity:
Hunter's discretion
Preferred Payment:
Cash, credit cards or check
Getting There:
Fly to Jacksonville and rent a car.

Contact:
Karen Cate
The Lodge at Cabin Bluff
PO Box 30203
Sea Island GA 31561
800/SEA-ISLA
Fax: 912/638-5897
Off Season:
PO Box 999
Woodbine GA 31569
WEB: cabinbluff.com

MERE 40 MINUTES NORTH OF Jacksonville on a spit of land facing Cumberland Island is one of the South's finest and most secluded hunting and fishing lodges. Here, two miles by gated drive from the nearest paved road on beautifully manicured grounds beneath oaks heavy with Spanish moss, is the descendant of the Camden Hunt Club, founded in 1827. Yet, while history is palpable here, it does not overwhelm you. Nothing does. You slip into the ambience of the Lodge at Cabin Bluff with the same comfort that you mount your custom Arietta. It fits.

Six cabins of rustic wood, each with stone fireplace for chilly nights, are scattered in an arc on either side of the main lodge. All front the narrow reach of the Intercoastal Waterway, which separates this forested neck from the national seashore preserve across the way. Cabin Bluff features dockage for guests who arrive by boat. To the north of the main lodge is a completely equipped conference center, and beyond that a championship golf course. Nature trails ideal for birding or evening strolls wind through the course.

With 48,000 acres jointly owned by Mead Paper and the Sea Island Company, the property is managed for forest products. Yet, among the stands of pine are fields of palmetto and grasses, ideal terrain for traditional bobwhite quail shoots. Hunters ride in high seated Jeeps as agile pointers sweep the fields. When birds are pointed, you'll dismount and walk toward the covey. What happens next is up to you. While operated as a preserve, daily limits on harvested birds match those of the state of Georgia. Turkeys are hunted in the spring.

An absolutely exquisite sporting clays course is situated on a finger of land well separated from the lodge proper. Traps are powered by solar charged battery, and reports from the firing are scarcely heard at the lodge. As seasons progress, a variety of saltwater and freshwater game fish become available for guests who use fly or conventional tackle. At times, the lodge will hold saltwater fly-fishing schools, and advice from skilled anglers is readily available.

Whiteway Plantation

Dry Branch, Georgia

No better place in Georgia to hunt deer early and late, and quail at midday.

VITAL STATISTICS:

GAME BIRDS:
QUAIL, TURKEY
Source of Birds: Wild and pen-reared
Seasons:
QUAIL: October through March
TURKEY: March through May
Land: 3,500 private acres
Accommodations:
RUSTIC LOG LODGE
NUMBER OF ROOMS: 4
MAXIMUM NUMBER OF HUNTERS: 10
Meals: Southern country cooking
Conference Groups: Yes
Guides: Trained dogs and guides
Other Services:
Birds cleaned and packed for travel
Other Activities:
Big game, biking, bird-watching, fishing, hiking, wildlife photography
Rates:
From $200 / 1/2 day;
room and board $75 / gun
Gratuity:
$20 - $50 / day
Preferred Payment:
Cash or check
Getting There:
Fly to Macon and rent a car or arrange to be picked up at additional cost.

Contact:
Alton White
Whiteway Plantation
Rt. 1, Box 349
Dry Branch GA 31020
912/945-3069

IF YOU'RE LOOKING FOR A PLACE where quail, convenience and laid-back country hospitality converge, check out Whiteway Plantation, just 20 miles southeast of Macon at exit 7 on Interstate 16. Since the depths of the Great Depression, Alton White's family has owned the plantation's 3,500 acres. In the last few years he's turned from cultivating row and forage crops to planting for wildlife, and guiding hunters for bobwhite, turkey and deer. And he's having fun doing it.

Feed plots of rye and wheat are planted in winter, and come spring, sorghum, corn and chufa go into the ground. Add scores of acres of pine forest with an understory of sedge and native brush along with open stands of white and red oak, and you've got a blend of outstanding habitat. Most hunting here is on foot. Normally, you'll walk with a guide who's running a brace of pointers, but hunting from four-wheel-drive vehicles can be arranged. In any event, when the dogs do their thing, it's up to you to do yours. Harvested birds are cleaned, packed and iced for travel. Full-day hunts include a 16-bird limit; half-day hunts include eight. Additional birds are, as you'd suspect, available for an extra fee.

In the fall, deer and quail seasons overlap. It's possible to spend the early morning and late afternoon in tree stands and work the birds during midday. And during March, a similar duo with turkey and quail can be put together, but only by special advance arrangement.

Accommodations at Whiteway are comfortably rustic. Alton has remodeled an old log barn into a rustic lodge with four bedrooms and two baths that sleeps up to 10 hunters. Dinners here feature the staples of country cooking: ham and greens, fried chicken, ribs and cornbread. After dinner, when the weather's warm, those old chairs on the long front porch look mighty inviting. Otherwise, there's a comfy living room that's heard its share of tall tales.

Deer Creek Outfitters

S e b r e e ,   K e n t u c k y

Ducks, geese and a one-price no-limit quail hunt make Deer Creek worth a look.

VITAL STATISTICS:

GAME BIRDS:
DOVE, DUCKS, PHEASANT, QUAIL, TURKEY
Source of Birds: Wild and pen-reared
Seasons:
QUAIL: October through April
PHEASANT and PARTRIDGE: November through April
DUCKS and GEESE: December through mid-January
DOVE, WOOD DUCKS and TEAL: September
TURKEY: mid-April into early May
Land: 5,000 private acres
Accommodations:
PRIVATE LODGE
NUMBER OF ROOMS: 5
MAXIMUM NUMBER OF HUNTERS: 9 W/LODGING
Meals: Steaks, pork chops, salads
Conference Groups: Yes
Guides: Trained dogs and guides
Dogs and Facilities:
Kennel for hunters' dogs, dog training
Shotgun Sports:
Sporting clays
Other Services:
Birds cleaned and packed for travel, proshop
Other Activities:
Big game, fishing, golf, wildlife photography
Rates:
From $675 / gun / double occupancy, all inclusive
Gratuity:
10% of package
Preferred Payment:
Cash, MasterCard, Visa or check
Getting There:
Fly to Evansville, Indiana, and rent a car.

Contact:
Tim Stull
Deer Creek Outfitters
8160 St. Rt. 132 E.
PO Box 39
Sebree KY 42455
502/835-2424

JUST SOUTH OF THE OHIO RIVER AT Evansville, Indiana, the terrain rises a bit and takes on a gentle undulation like long ocean swells on a very calm day. About 20 miles south of Evansville on the Pennyrile Parkway is the crossroads town of Sebree, and a mile or two further, Deer Creek flows into the Green River.

While you'll find some waterfowling at Deer Creek—woodies and teal in the early season and mallards later on—this preserve earned its stripes as one of the nation's premiere whitetail destinations and is gaining recognition for outstanding upland bird hunting. The preserve encompasses 5,000 acres of open and grassy fields planted with cover crops, corn and grains, and mixed hardwoods. Tributaries of its namesake creek make swampy, boggy patches that pheasants love, on some days.

The distinctive feature at Deer Creek is that there's no limit on quail. Depending when you hunt, you'll flush a dozen coveys a day. Sure, the coveys are supplemented with stocked birds. But they're introduced to coveys a week or so before the property is hunted—ample time for a pen-raised bobwhite to go wild. And, along with quail, you can also take pheasants and red-legged partridge. You'll find other birds here as well. In September, dove shooting gets hot and heavy. December brings geese and ducks, hunted from heated pit blinds overlooking flooded fields in the bottoms along the Ohio River. Among the best hunts at Deer Creek is the three-day waterfowl and no-limit quail hunt for $1,250, which includes everything except your bottle of Henry McKenna. If you can't get away for the combo hunt, check out the brief three- to four-week window in late April and early May that means turkey.

Tim Stull and his crew are bird hunters above all else. Their kennels contain champion Elhew pointers and English setters. Labs too, of course. You can hunt over adult dogs and, if they turn your fancy, you may be able to buy a pup or a started dog. Sporting clays is on tap at Deer Creek. The 10-station course is challenging enough to give you a real workout, but not so difficult that only champions can enjoy it. Accommodations are on the modest side, but they're clean, comfortable, and each room has a private bath—a real plus in my book. As for meals, let it be said that nobody's ever lost weight eating at Tim Stull's table.

Dry Creek Ranch

Ragley, Louisiana

Hunt quail and pheasant in this land that's better known for ducks.

VITAL STATISTICS:

GAME BIRDS:
CHUKAR, DUCKS, QUAIL
Source of Birds: Pen-reared
Seasons: October through April
Land: 1,500 private acres
Accommodations:
PRIVATE LODGE AND THREE CABINS
NUMBER OF ROOMS: 5
MAXIMUM NUMBER OF HUNTERS: 16
Meals: Cajun
Conference Groups: Yes
Guides: Trained dogs and guides
Dogs and Facilities:
Kennel for hunters' dogs,
Shotgun Sports:
Sporting clays, tower or release shoots
Other Services:
Birds cleaned and packed for travel
Other Activities:
Big game, boating, canoeing, fishing, golf
Rates:
From $395 / gun
Gratuity:
$20 - $25 / half-day
Preferred Payment:
Cash, MasterCard, Visa or check
Getting There:
Fly to Lake Charles and the lodge will collect you.

Contact:
Josh Sills
Dry Creek Ranch
1925 Kingrey Rd
Ragley LA 70657
318/666-2657

DRAINED BY THE WINDING marshy course of the Calcasieu River and bounded on the west by the Sabine River, southwestern Louisiana sees more than its share of ducks and geese during fall migrations. They flock into half a dozen large lakes and a trio of National Wildlife Refuges—Rockefeller, Lacassine and Sabine—to winter. North of the city of Lake Charles the land rises and becomes the province of farmers who grow row crops. The land, then, becomes ideal for birds whose feet are not webbed.

A preserve of about 1,500 acres, Dry Creek Ranch is located about 20 miles north of Lake Charles and east of U.S. Rt. 171. This is open, piney woods with sedge and other grasses and food plots planted to support quail. As the name implies, you won't need other than leather boots here; there's no swamp. You'll hunt over pointers or setters as your mood and availability dictate. Parties of two to three guns are the norm, but special needs can be accommodated. Released mallard hunts are available at Dry Creek, and you can also jump-shoot birds that made it to the ponds. Wild duck hunts in nearby bayous can be arranged by special request, and the price of $225 per hunter is quite reasonable. For that, you receive the services of a guide and dog as well as meals and lodging.

Dry Creek provides overnight accommodations for guests in its rustic lodge and three new cabins. Two rooms are located in the lodges, and each cabin sleeps three or four. A modern conference room in the main lodge provides space for business meetings, and afterwards guests lounge near the big stone fireplace sipping libations of their choice. Here, it's strictly BYOB, because the ward in which the ranch is located is dry. Meals are long, leisurely and, as you'd suspect, feature a distinctive Cajun flare. And if you want to excite more than your palate, head up the road to Grand Casino Coushatto, where you hope the cards are hot.

[S O U T H]

Pin Oak Mallards

R a y v i l l e ,   L o u i s i a n a

Heated blinds and hundreds of teal, woodies and mallards. How could life get better?

VITAL STATISTICS:

GAME BIRDS:
DUCKS
Source of Birds: Wild
Seasons:
Mid-November through mid-January
Land: 2,700 private acres
Accommodations:
PRIVATE WATERFRONT LODGE
NUMBER OF ROOMS: 10
MAXIMUM NUMBER OF HUNTERS: 18
Meals: Cajun with wild game
Conference Groups: Yes
Guides: Included in price
Dogs and Facilities:
Kennel for hunters' dogs
Shotgun Sports:
Sporting clays
Other Services:
Pro shop
Other Activities:
Fishing
Rates:
$250 / gun
Gratuity:
Hunter's discretion
Preferred Payment:
Cash or check
Getting There:
Fly to Monroe, Louisiana, and rent a car.

Contact:
Ace Cullum
Pin Oak Mallards
711 Hwy 15
Rayville LA 71269
318/248-3549
Fax: 318/248-3549

I F THERE'S A MOMENT IN HUNTING more magic than the dark hour before dawn, I'd love to know what it is. Maybe a boat carried you to the blind. Maybe you rode on the back of a jouncing ATV with your arms filled with bags of decoys, shotguns and lunch. Maybe as we all have, yours was a slog through a muddy swamp where the mud sucked at your ankles and you wondered, really wondered, why you left that nice warm bed. But then, sitting in the blind, gun loaded, safety on, guide leaning on the rail and dog on the pad in the corner, head cocked and looking with his ears, you know that there's no other place to be. Not now, not in December, not with the aftermath of the front lingering in the neighborhood, not with all those new birds that arrived with the freshening northwest wind.

In the predawn, silhouettes of trees stand cobalt against the sky. It's too early for mallards to laugh at the beginning of day. You hear teal slice the air (what else could they be?) and splash into the slough. A susie gabbles her way in, and you can tell there are pintails in the neighborhood by their whistle. So intent are you on looking for what your ears are showing you that you fail to see the sky turn pewter, and almost miss the guide's soft call to get ready. That pulls you back to reality, and your hand automatically reaches for the semiauto.

These are the best mornings at Pin Oak, one of the world's finest duck clubs in northeastern Louisiana. On nearly 2,700 acres, you'll hunt in flooded fields and timber from heated blinds, shallow johnboats, or your waders. Woodies will slip through the trees and surprise you; gadwall and wigeon will tease you before they settle into the decoys. But come they will, and you'll gun yourself happy.

For more than a generation, Ace Cullum has been hunting these waters, and a decade ago, he decided to build a lodge and sporting clays facility. Six bedrooms with private baths host up to 18 hunters. Meals are country, faintly Cajun, and focused on game and regional cuisine. Gear and licenses are available at the lodge if you've forgotten something. Guides will have their own retrievers, but if you want to bring your own, that's cool too.

Pintail Point

Queenstown, Maryland

Pheasants, quail, ducks, striped bass: you can do it all less than an hour from Washington D.C.

VITAL STATISTICS:

GAME BIRDS:
CHUKAR, DOVE, DUCKS, GEESE, PHEASANT

Source of Birds: Wild and pen-reared

Seasons:
DOVE: First week of September
WILD DUCKS and GEESE: October through late January
UPLAND BIRDS: October through March

Land: 500 private acres

Accommodations:
ON-SITE BED AND BREAKFASTS
NUMBER OF ROOMS: 8
MAXIMUM NUMBER OF HUNTERS: 20

Meals: Breakfast with lodging, restaurant on site

Conference Groups: Yes

Guides: Trained dogs and guides

Dogs and Facilities:
Kennel for hunters' dogs, dog training

Shotgun Sports:
Five-stand, sporting clays, tower or release shoots

Other Services:
Birds cleaned and packed for travel, proshop

Other Activities:
Big game, biking, bird-watching, boating, fishing, golf, hiking

Rates:
From $125 / gun / minimum 2; accommodations from $200 / night

Gratuity:
Hunter's discretion

Preferred Payment:
Cash, American Express, MasterCard, Visa or check

Getting There:
Fly to Baltimore/Washington International and rent a car.

Contact:
Reservations
Pintail Point
511 Pintail Point Lane
Queenstown MD 21658
410/827-7029
Fax: 410/827-7052
WEB: www.pintailpoint.com

JUST 45 MILES FROM both Washington and Baltimore is what may be the quintessential sporting resort. Endorsed by Orvis and handicapped accessible, this is one place where you can do it all. And if your timing's right, you can sample most of Pintail Point's charms in just one day. Here's how.

Book your group into one of Pintail's two on-site bed-and-breakfasts. Arise just before dawn for a duck shoot. You'll sit in a blind as drakes and hens are released deep in the woods. They'll climb and circle and make a beeline for a pond that's also fringed with trees. While the gunning isn't as simple as it looks, even newcomers to the sport will have good success. It's an ideal location for introducing a youngster or spouse to duck shooting.

Return to your room, doff your waterfowling duds and don brush pants and a field coat with blaze orange. Head for the main lodge and a late breakfast, after which you'll meet your guide with his pointers. Together you'll work food plots of milo, millet and sorghum for pheasants, quail, Hungarian partridge, or chukar. The morning hunt finishes about noon—just in time for lunch.

If you're a real glutton for punishment, you'll forego the arms of morpheus at midday, and instead head for the championship sporting clays course with its 22 stations along the banks of the Wye River. A five-stand course is also available, as are lessons. Special programs can be arranged to meet the needs of corporate groups; sporting clays can be a fabulous team-builder.

During the day, you will have noticed half a dozen ponds on Pintail Point. They contain bass of either fresh or saltwater variety. You don't have to change your shooting clothes to get in a little fly or spin fishing when you're through with sporting clays.

If you follow this regimen, you'll miss hunts for wild ducks, geese and dove. In addition, you'll be really pressed to squeeze in a round of golf on Pintail Point's new Scottish-style links. Guess you'll have to stay another day.

Schrader's Hunting

M i l l i n g t o n ,   M a r y l a n d

Up on the northern Eastern Shore lies this full-service hunting emporium of 20,000 acres.

VITAL STATISTICS:

GAME BIRDS:
CHUKAR, DUCKS, GEESE, PHEASANT, QUAIL
Source of Birds: Wild and pen-reared
Seasons:
DOVE: September to December
WILD QUAIL: November through February
WILD DUCKS: October through January
SNOW GEESE and RELEASED BIRDS: October through March
Land: 20,000 private acres
Accommodations:
VICTORIAN BED AND BREAKFAST
NUMBER OF ROOMS: 15
MAXIMUM NUMBER OF HUNTERS: 32
Meals: Regional cuisine
Conference Groups: Yes
Guides: Trained dogs and guides
Dogs and Facilities:
Kennel for hunters' dogs
Shotgun Sports:
Five-stand, sporting clays, tower or release shoots
Other Services:
Birds cleaned and packed for travel
Other Activities:
Big game, bird-watching, boating, canoeing, fishing, golf, hiking, wildlife photography
Rates:
From $80 / gun; full meals and lodging from $80 / day
Gratuity:
15%
Preferred Payment:
Cash or check
Getting There:
Fly to Baltimore\Washington International and rent a car.

Contact:
Kenneth Schrader
Schrader's Hunting
900 Red Lion Branch Rd.
Millington MD 21651
410/778-1895
WEB: www.schradershunting.com

KENNETH SCHRADER is something of a visionary. Unlike some of his peers among Eastern Shore waterfowl guides, he saw the declining numbers of Canadas overhead and read the handwriting in the sky. So he switched emphasis from birds of which there were too few to birds that are fairly ample (and not as well known as they might have been). Quail. Mr. Bob. What's this symbol of Southern gunning doing hanging out on that neck of Maryland between Chesapeake Bay and the Atlantic? He's always been there—part of his native range. Only because everybody was hot for corn-fat Canadas, nobody paid much attention to a little ol' bobwhite.

It's different now, and Ken hunts for wild quail on some of the 20,000 acres he leases. While the season runs from November through February, the best gunning occurs in December and January. The season on native birds overlaps with the preserve ("Regulated Shooting Areas," in fish and wildlife speak) season. So if wild birds are hard to come by, then you can fill your game bag on pen-raised birds. Don't turn up your nose at these babies, not until you hit every one you flush. On the preserve grounds, you'll also have opportunities to shoot pheasant, chukar, Huns and mallards.

Among the other wild species on Ken's agenda are dove, wild ducks and snow geese. The latter can be particularly exciting, especially if you've never lain among a couple hundred decoys and watched as 1,000 snows wheel and circle and wheel again, all the time descending over your decoys. Deafened by their cacophonous calls, you'll be mesmerized by the beauty of their alabaster bodies and black-tipped wings. Sometimes, it's tough to remember to shoot. Ken hunts snows from pit blinds as well. A full range of clays game is also available, as is instruction.

Hunters have the option of staying in a grand old Victorian home, operated as a bed-and-breakfast on the Chester River near Chestertown. Maryland's Eastern Shore is known for its abundance of wonderful old inns, some of them authentically historic. Good restaurants suiting any pocketbook are in equally good supply.

Perhaps the epitome of fine quail plantations
is Gillionville, in the piney woods
not far from Albany, Georgia.

At Schrader's on Maryland's eastern shore, gunners hunt
snows, Canadas, ducks and pheasants. When
they're done, they find their rooms in this
turn-of-the-last-century mansion.

Circle M Plantation

M a c o n ,   M i s s i s s i p p i

A most genteel retreat for gentlemen and ladies who appreciate the best gunning, southern style.

VITAL STATISTICS:

GAME BIRDS:
QUAIL, TURKEY
Source of Birds: Pen-reared
Seasons:
QUAIL: mid-October through March
TURKEY: Late March through April
Land: 6,000 private acres
Accommodations:
THREE TASTEFULLY DECORATED PRIVATE HOMES
NUMBER OF ROOMS: 14
MAXIMUM NUMBER OF HUNTERS: 22
Meals: Fine southern game
Conference Groups: Yes
Guides: Trained dogs and guides
Dogs and Facilities:
Kennel for hunters' dogs, dog training
Shotgun Sports: Five-stand
Other Services:
Birds cleaned and packed for travel
Other Activities:
Fishing, horseback riding
Rates:
$500 / day inclusive / double occupancy
Gratuity:
Hunter's discretion
Preferred Payment:
Cash or check
Getting There:
Fly to Columbus and the van from the lodge will pick you up.

Contact:
Lanier Long
Circle M Plantation
Route 3, Box 710
Macon MS 39341
601/726-5791
Fax: 601/726-9300

THE PRESIDENTS of General Mills, Archer-Daniels, and Weyerhauser knew a good thing when they saw it: 6,000 acres of forest and field in east-central Mississippi not far from the Alabama border. Not only was this convenient to reach by train (in the early days) and plane, but populations of native bobwhite, turkey and deer were astounding. So they threw in together and bought it.

The oldest house on the property was built in the 1920s for the governor of Oklahoma as his private hunting lodge. Recently, two other houses were added. These are spacious homes used by visitors. Each can accommodate up to five guests and contain private kitchens and fireplaces. Here, when it's bird hunting time, the living is indeed easy. If you do not feel like serving as your own chef, walk over to the main lodge for a dinner of quail or venison prepared as only a southern cook knows how.

Hunting here is likewise in the finest southern tradition. You'll choose among hunting on horseback via specially adapted four-by-fours, or from the mule-drawn wagon. Two or three pairs of bird dogs—graceful setters of aristocratic breeding and poise or svelte pointers whose muscles ripple as they course back and forth before you—will accompany you in the field under the watchful gaze of a completely professional guide. They'll hand you the birds you shoot. To tune up before your bird hunt, you'll be offered a round of five-stand sporting clays or skeet (or both, why not?).

As you work back through the fields, you're eye will scan the woods and you'll wonder about deer and turkey hunting. Both are superlative here. Big game hunts are fully guided, and hunter success is correspondingly high.

Owing to the quality of its service, attention to detail, outstanding facilities and good hunting, Circle M is earning an enviable reputation as a corporate retreat and a locale for private business meetings. Families will also find this a soothing getaway, a place to come, relax and unwind.

Dunn's Shooting Grounds

Holly Springs, Mississippi

Mule-drawn wagons carry hunters to quail fields,
all less than an hour from Memphis.

VITAL STATISTICS:

GAME BIRDS:
PHEASANT, QUAIL
Source of Birds: Wild and pen-reared
Seasons:
October through March
Land: 900 private acres
Accommodations:
MODERN, SOUTHERN-STYLE LODGE
NUMBER OF ROOMS: 8
MAXIMUM NUMBER OF HUNTERS: 16
Meals: Fine regional cuisine
Conference Groups: Yes
Guides: Trained dogs and guides
Dogs and Facilities:
If you bring your own dog, bring a kennel
Shotgun Sports:
Driven birds, shooting schools, sporting clays
Other Services:
Birds cleaned and packed for travel, proshop
Other Activities:
Golf
Rates:
Hunts from $225;
room and board $135 / person
Gratuity:
Hunter's discretion
Preferred Payment:
Cash, credit card or check
Getting There:
Fly to Memphis, Tennessee, and rent a car.

Contact:
Tom McDonald
Dunn's Shooting Grounds
532 Quailwood Ave.
Holly Springs MS 38635
601/564-1111
Fax: 601/564-2770
EMAIL: DSG@century.net
WEB: www.shootinggrounds.com

THE CREAK AND JANGLE of old leather harness danced a melody while the clop of mule shoes on the pine needle road carried the rhythm. It would have been tempting to loll on the padded bench in the wagon, but excitement, to say nothing of the morning's dose of caffeine and sugar from flapjack syrup, kept you on the edge of your seat. Ahead, a pair of pointers named Forrest and Davis slashed through broomsedge and brush. Forrest skidded into a point before a vine-tangled clump of thin trees, leafless in the late autumn morning. Davis whoaed as he should (this was probably the only time that the President of the Confederacy deferred to one of his proud generals). Forrest must think of the birds as blue-bellied Yankees, and when they flushed from cover, he relied on his artillery (that's you with your shotgun) to bring them to bag. Once done, these canine comrades sped off looking for more quail, and you returned to the wagon and your not-so-leisurely ride in their pursuit.

This describes a typical morning at Dunn's Shooting Grounds in Holly Springs, about 45 miles southeast of Memphis, Tennesee, via U.S. Route 78. The land here has a little heft to it; sluggish creeks drain cutover woods. Fields, once farmed or pastured, are allowed to lie fallow, sprouting native grasses augmented here and there by feed plots. Brush is selectively bush-hogged to make it easy for gunners to get around.

In this neck of the woods, Dunn's sets the standard for shooting resorts. Its modern lodge is styled in the classic Ante Bellum tradition. Two-story verandas shade eight guest rooms, each with private bath. Meals are hearty and cooked with all the care you'd expect from southern cuisine. Through the woods behind the shooting pavilion winds a quarter-mile sporting clays course. Shooting schools are regularly held, and Dunn's guarantees that novices will shoot 75 percent on the course by the end of the school.

Rose Hill Plantation

B e n t o n i a ,   M i s s i s s i p p i

What's surf and turf Mississippi style? Doves, bass and deer!

VITAL STATISTICS:

GAME BIRDS:
DOVE, TURKEY
Source of Birds: Wild
Seasons:
DOVE: September through November
TURKEY: Mid-March through early May
Land: 2,000 private acres
Accommodations:
CEDAR LODGE
NUMBER OF ROOMS: 3
MAXIMUM NUMBER OF HUNTERS: 6
Meals: Fine dining with a country flare
Conference Groups: Yes
Guides: Available on special request
Other Activities:
Big game, biking, bird-watching, fishing, hiking, horseback riding, wildlife photography
Rates:
From $60 / gun
Gratuity:
10% - 15%
Preferred Payment:
Cash, credit card or check
Getting There:
Fly to Jackson and the lodge van will pick you up.

Contact:
Tom Shipp
Rose Hill Plantation
1079 Passons Road
Bentonia MS 39040
601/755-8383
Fax: 601/755-2020
WEB: www.rosehillplantation.com

O K. THIS IS A HUNTING LODGE that caters to archers so focused on trophy bucks with spreads in the 16-inch to 18-inch range that they forget the names of their spouses and first-born offspring during the height of the season. It's a place where deer bed down in high cotton and come out during the evening to dine on soybeans, peas and corn. So what's it doing in a book about bird hunting lodges?

Doves. Owner Tom Shipp, whose family has been farming these 2,000 acres more or less since the ugly days of Reconstruction, plants a couple 50-acre fields in sunflowers each year. For weekends in September, he leases out his entire three-bedroom lodge and the fields to groups of up to 20 dove hunters for $800 a day. Contrary to other locales farther north in the South (which sounds like a contradiction in terms, but it isn't), the best dove hunting here in central Mississippi opens with sunrise and continues 'til midday. Sure, doves are flying in the afternoons too, but often it's just too blamed hot to go sit around a field.

The first dove season generally runs the month of September. Then, later in the year when the feds so deem it right, the season opens again. This time, the shooting—when doves are in—is reasonably good all day. Even archers come out of the woods for a midday break. Those who want to take a break from the rigors of using their minds to turn every woods sound into the footfall of a trophy buck may recover a little sanity with a couple hours of dove shooting. Generally, the season is open for two or three weeks in November and for a couple of weeks in December. It is possible to combine bass and bream fishing with deer and dove hunting. Adds a whole new dimension to surf and turf. And if you come in the spring for gobblers, there may be fish in your future as well.

Tom's lodge at Rose Hill is a comfortable modern red-cedar-and-glass home with a wide porch that overlooks fields and lakes. Meals revolve around fine cuts of beef, shrimp scampi and sauces that complement angle hair pasta. Ain't nobody loses weight in Tom's kitchen.

Tara Wildlife Management

Vicksburg, Mississippi

An environmental preserve where quail and duck hunting is without peer.

VITAL STATISTICS:

GAME BIRDS:
DUCKS, QUAIL

Source of Birds: Wild and pen-reared

Seasons:
DUCKS: December and January
QUAIL: October through May

Land: 20,000 private acres

Accommodations:
Four lodGES
NUMBER OF ROOMS: 28
MAXIMUM NUMBER OF HUNTERS: 55

Meals: Hearty and healthy

Conference Groups: Yes

Guides: Trained dogs and guides

Dogs and Facilities:
Kennel for hunters' dogs

Shotgun Sports:
Shooting schools, sporting clays

Other Services:
Birds cleaned and packed for travel

Other Activities:
Big game, bird-watching, boating, canoeing, fishing, golf, hiking, wildlife photography

Rates:
DUCK: $250 / gun inclusive
QUAIL: $300 / minimum, lodging and meals additional

Gratuity:
Hunter's discretion

Preferred Payment:
Cash, MasterCard, Visa or check

Getting There:
Fly to Jackson and rent a car or have Tara's Suburban provide transportation at $150 round trip.

Contact:
Sidney Montgomery
Tara Wildlife Management
6791 Eagle Lake Shore Rd
Vicksburg MS 39180
601/279-4261
Fax: 601/279-4227

TARA IS A 20,000-ACRE WILDLIFE management area down in the wide meander channel carved by the Mississippi River and its tributary, the Yazoo. A few miles to the east the channel's boundary is marked by bluffs that rise 250 feet above the river bottom. The bottom itself is a maze of oxbow cutoffs, swamp, hardwood forest and cultivated fields. It is a haven for waterfowl, whitetails, quail and turkey.

Make no mistake: Tara is very unusual in the realm of hunting preserves. It's one of less than a handful of operations (Teller in Montana is another) that is managed primarily for ecosystem conservation and the reintroduction of native species where hunting is permitted, let alone encouraged. Tara's founder, Maggie Bryant, is chairperson of the National Fish and Wildlife Foundation and has received numerous national and state awards for her conservation efforts.

Best known for its trophy whitetails—more than 130 Pope & Young bucks have been harvested here in the past decade—Tara is almost without peer as a serious destination for dedicated archery hunters. Duck hunting is equally good in December and January, and turkey can be outstanding in the spring. Quail are pen-reared and released in fallow fields, cropland and other suitable covers from October through May, with February and March being the best months for hunting. Dogs and guides are required. A minimum of 50 bobwhite at $6 each must be purchased for a quail hunt. When you figure that the fee includes a dog and guide, the price becomes very reasonable indeed.

Four modern lodges can accommodate a total of 55 guests. Rates are very inexpensive: $50 for a single and $55 for two. Meals are similarly priced: $5 for breakfast and $10 each for lunch and dinner. Meeting facilities are available for business or conference groups, and an airstrip can handle smaller corporate aircraft. Otherwise, the airport at Jackson provides the closest commercial service.

Adams Creek Gunning Lodge

H a v e l o c k ,   N o r t h   C a r o l i n a

An old-time gunning lodge offers fine hunts for ducks, quail and pheasants.

VITAL STATISTICS:

GAME BIRDS:
DUCKS, PHEASANT, QUAIL
Source of Birds: Wild and pen-reared
Seasons:
PHEASANT and QUAIL: November through March
DUCKS: November through January
Land: 800 private acres; unlimited public acres
Accommodations:
HISTORIC LODGE
NUMBER OF ROOMS: 8
MAXIMUM NUMBER OF HUNTERS: 10
Meals: Fine regional cuisine
Conference Groups: Yes
Guides: Trained dogs and guides
Dogs and Facilities:
Kennel for hunters' dogs
Shotgun Sports:
Skeet, sporting clays, tower or release shoots
Other Activities:
Bird-watching, boating, fishing
Rates:
From $225 / gun
Gratuity:
Hunter's discretion
Preferred Payment:
Cash, MasterCard, Visa or check
Getting There:
Fly to New Bern or Raleigh-Durham and rent a car.

Contact:
Rusty Bryan
Adams Creek Gunning Lodge
6240 Adams Creek Rd
Havelock NC 28532
252/447-7688
Fax: 252/447-6902

REAT NECK POKES OUT into the Neuse River north of Morehead City, and on the neck facing Adams Creek is an old-style hunting lodge known for ducks, pheasants and quail since the 1930s, and more recently for its sporting clays course. Marine vets once stationed at Cherry Point will recognize this neck of the woods in an instant. Havelock is the town by the air station's main gate. To the east is the Cape Lookout National Seashore. In the fall, Great Neck and its miles and miles of tidal creeks collect ducks like a vacuum sweeper. Duck hunting is the main business at this fine old lodge.

Divers, puddlers and sea ducks are hunted from a wide range of blinds, depending on the season, weather and where the birds are working. You may hunt blinds over tidal fingers that probe salt marshes. Or if sea ducks and divers are your meat, floating blinds or blinds atop stakes driven deep in the black muck may fill the need. Back from the tidal areas is prime habitat for sweet-tasting puddle ducks. Here, too, blinds are maintained. You may also hunt some flooded timber.

Adams Creek maintains an 800-acre regulated shooting area where it runs quail and pheasant hunts. Terrain includes open pines, where prescribed burns are used to condition undergrowth for each coming fall. You'll also hunt open fields and their edges. Continental pheasant and duck hunts are also scheduled throughout the year. Guides and dogs are provided for all hunts, but you may use your own dog if you like. Hunts are scheduled Monday through Saturday; there's no hunting here on Sundays.

In addition to feathered fowl, the lodge runs a fine sporting clays course that winds through woods and fields. Additionally, there is an abbreviated version of sporting clays—super sporting—which is tailor-made for individuals who have difficulty walking. A regulation skeet range is also found on the property.

Accommodations take you back to the turn of the last century. You'll stay in an 1870s plantation home and dine on fine, home-cooked regional cuisine.

George Hi Plantation

Roseboro, North Carolina

You and your friends will be the only hunters on this classic piedmont plantation.

VITAL STATISTICS:

GAME BIRDS:
CHUKAR, DUCKS, PHEASANT, QUAIL

Source of Birds: Pen-reared

Seasons:
October through March

Land: 2,000 private acres

Accommodations:
PLANTATION HOUSE CIRCA 1855
NUMBER OF ROOMS: 4
MAXIMUM NUMBER OF HUNTERS: 8

Meals: Southern cuisine

Conference Groups: No

Guides: Trained dogs and guides

Dogs and Facilities:
Kennel for hunters' dogs

Other Services:
Birds cleaned and packed for travel

Other Activities:
Canoeing, fishing, horseback riding

Rates:
$450 / gun / day

Gratuity:
$50

Preferred Payment:
Cash or check

Getting There:
Fly to Fayetteville, and rent a car or arrange for the lodge van at additional cost.

Contact:
Chas. DuBose
George Hi Plantation
PO Box 1068
Roseboro NC 28382
910/525-4524
Fax: 910/525-5684
WEB: www.georgehi.com

TUCKED IN A LITTLE TOWN 30 miles west of Fort Bragg and Fayetteville is an intimate plantation that caters to small groups. At the core of the plantation is the lodge, an antebellum farmhouse with a white columned front porch. The lodge has been remodeled to accommodate eight hunters, and groups of at least four can have it to themselves. Dinners are fine southern cooking—hey, what else?—and one of the better reasons to go hunting is to work off the biscuits and gravy from breakfast. As you're beginning to gather, the living here is genteel.

So is the gunning. Behind staunch setters or flashy pointers—yours or theirs, it makes no difference—you'll walk with a guide through open pine woods carpeted with sedge and other wild grasses. If you'd prefer, you can hunt from horseback, mule-drawn wagon, or four-by-four. They'll do it anyway you want it. Quail is the signature bird here, of course. But pheasants and chukar are also released. The plantation uses 200 acres regularly, but has access to another 1,800, which it keeps in reserve.

In addition to upland birds, the preserve runs mallard shoots. Hunting is from a floating blind. Birds are released from the woods nearby. They'll sift through the trees with none of the hesitation of wild birds, but on the other hand, they're faster—more like carrier pilots anxious to catch the first wire. Gunning can be hyper.

At George Hi, you won't find much that is high pressure. The plantation does not cater to conference groups. There's no trap, skeet or sporting clays. No shooting schools with instructors with accents from the north of Britain. All this is, is a quiet little gunning club off the main road, where nobody but you cares how many birds you harvest.

[S O U T H]

Quail Ridge Shooting Preserve

H o o k e r t o n ,   N o r t h   C a r o l i n a

A plethora of small farms offers plenty of old-style bird hunting.

VITAL STATISTICS:

GAME BIRDS:
QUAIL
Source of Birds: Pen-reared
Seasons:
October through March
Land: 500 private acres
Accommodations:
IN NEARBY TOWN
Meals: Catering available on request
Conference Groups: No
Guides: Trained dogs and guides
Dogs and Facilities:
Kennel for hunters' dogs
Shotgun Sports:
Devil's Triangle
Other Services:
Birds cleaned and packed for travel
Rates:
From $150 / 2 guns
Gratuity:
$15
Preferred Payment:
Cash or check
Getting There:
Drive to Greenville, then south to Hookerton.

Contact:
Robert Carraway
Quail Ridge Shooting Preserve
Rt. 1, Box 165
Hookerton NC 28538
252/747-5210

BEFORE HE RETIRED from Dupont, Robert Carraway yearned for the weekends when he could hunt. As a farm boy, he grew up with that springtime sweet whistle of bobwhite and saw those little chicks following the hens along fencerows. In the fall, he worked the fencerows and fields of harvested corn where the stocks were bent over and broken after the ears had been picked. Nothing afield pleasured him more than a flushing covey and taking a bird or two.

So when he cashed in his chips at the plant, he decided he'd run a preserve on a handful of farms 20 miles south of Greenville. Land holdings are not large here, nor is the soil as rich as it is elsewhere. Years of inheritances broke up the holdings, and a general depression in the markets for produce made farming less than lucrative for all but the largest, mechanized spreads. The result is a patchwork of small farms of 50 to 100 acres in size where quail hunters are a major cash crop.

If you come to Quail Ridge, Robert will start you and your buddy in a field of maybe 20 acres. It'll be lush with sorghum and millet, and maybe corn. You'll work the main part of the field and then hunt your way along brush lining a narrow creek. Crossing at the end of the field, you'll come up the other side into a plot of 30 acres or so. With more certainty than luck, you'll flush birds. Hunting here is mainly on foot, except, as Robert says, "We have a golf cart for older gentlemen. They can ride it to the point." There are places where the cart can't go, heavy swaths of waist-high reeds, for instance. You may find some birds there, but only if they've been pushed. All told, Quail Ridge encompasses more than 500 acres, including four farms.

Quail Ridge boasts a stock of good pointers and offers an 18-station clays course known as the "Devil's Triangle." While accommodations are found in Greenville and Farmville, local restaurants can cater lunches or special dinners upon request. Fees for hunting here are quite reasonable: two hunters will pay $75 each for a 20-bird hunt with a dog and guide.

Tobacco Stick Hunting Preserve & Kennel

Candor, North Carolina

Birds—chukar, pheasant and quail—have replaced burley and bright on this old southern farm.

VITAL STATISTICS:

GAME BIRDS:
CHUKAR, DUCKS, PHEASANT, QUAIL

Source of Birds: Pen-reared

Seasons:
October through March

Land: 500 private acres

Accommodations:
REMODELED FARMHOUSE
NUMBER OF ROOMS: 4
MAXIMUM NUMBER OF HUNTERS: 12

Meals: Can be catered by special arrangement; otherwise, eat in town.

Conference Groups: Yes

Guides: Trained dogs and guides

Dogs and Facilities:
Kennel for hunters' dogs, dog training

Shotgun Sports:
Informal Instruction

Other Services:
Birds cleaned and packed for travel

Other Activities:
Fishing

Rates:
Hunts priced per bird;
Accommodations: $25 / night;
Dog & guides from $50 / 1/2 day

Gratuity:
$10

Preferred Payment:
Cash or check

Getting There:
Fly to Greensboro and rent a car.

Contact:
C. J. Reynolds
Tobacco Stick Hunting
Preserve & Kennel
PO Box 310
Candor NC 27229
910/974-7100
Fax: 910/974-3866
EMAIL: tobaccostick@ac.net
WEB: www.tobaccostick.com

ECIL "C.J." REYNOLDS is a man who'll tell you the truth. And the truth he'll tell you is that there ain't no money in tobacco farming. That handwriting's been on the wall for a dozen years, long before the settlement of megaliability claims against tobacco companies. Do you believe C.J.? Why not. After all, he lives in Candor and he's a dog-breeding bird hunter.

Tobacco Stick is his family farm, so named for the stake on which green tobacco plants were skewered and hung to dry. The farm's 500 acres is now maintained as a regulated shooting preserve, where gunning for quail, chukar, pheasants and flighted mallards are offered from October through March. Fields of broomsedge and rowcrops are groomed for bird hunting. Bring your own dog or hunt over one of the classy English setters from C.J.'s kennel.

Blinds at a number of ponds that range in size from one acre to four hold pen-reared ducks. Ducks are gathered up at night. After you're securely set in your blind, the mallards are released and they head back to the pond from which they came. While this is not quite the same as hunting wild ducks—you know these babies are going to come—release duck shoots are marvelous for introducing children and spouses to the sport.

Often, gunners will combine a dawn-breaking duck shoot with a morning of upland bird hunting. Others arrive at midday, hunt birds in the afternoon, spend the night in the remodeled farmhouse with a catered southern-style dinner, shoot ducks before breakfast, and finish the day with another go for quail.

Tobacco Stick is located on the edge of the Uwharrie National Forest, about 45 miles south of Greensboro. Pinehurst is 20 miles east and Charlotte is less than two hours west.

[S O U T H]

Broxton Bridge Plantation

E h r h a r d t ,   S o u t h   C a r o l i n a

This lodge was saved from marauding Yanks by stalwart southern belles.

WITH GRANT besieging Richmond and Sherman having reached the Georgia coast, Yankee strategy turned Sherman north, heading for Columbia, South Carolina, and thence into North Carolina. Fighting a valiant delaying game, including a sharp fight in February 1865 at a bridge across the Big Salkehatchie River about 75 miles due south of the state capital, southern troops threw up a hasty fort and armed it with a dozen cannons. With a force of 6,000 troops, the Confederates held up the Union advance for four days.

You can walk the old fortifications and spend the night in an 1853 farmhouse that women and children stoutly defended from the advancing Yankees. The Old South lives here at Broxton, and among its fine traditions is hunting for bobwhite quail. Scores of fields on this 3,700-acre plantation are sown in milo, millet, corn, soybeans and lespedeza. You'll walk or ride and hunt with either Brittanies or pointers, as your preference dictates.

Along with field hunts for quail, Broxton offers flighted mallards shot from blinds over decoys. A skiff will carry you to your blind, and one is handicapped accessible. Groups of hunters can also enjoy tower shoots for pheasants. To play this game, use modified or full-choke tubes and number six shot. Most use 12-gauge guns, but those of unusual self-confidence can get away with a 20. Broxton is equally well know for its outstanding sporting clays courses—there are four on this plantation.

As you'd expect, accommodations here are southern elegant. With its highly polished random-width hardwood floors, the farmhouse bed-and-breakfast is furnished with antiques and reproductions. Beds are four-posters or brass, covered with handmade quilts. One of the five rooms includes a private bath, while the other four share two baths. Five additional rooms with private baths are found in outlying cabins. And on the menu, you'll discover country ham, fried chicken and corn pie.

VITAL STATISTICS:

GAME BIRDS:
DUCKS, PHEASANT, QUAIL
Source of Birds: Wild and pen-reared
Seasons:
October through February
Land: 3,700 private acres
Accommodations:
HISTORIC FARMHOUSE AND CABINS
NUMBER OF ROOMS: 10
MAXIMUM NUMBER OF HUNTERS: 19
Meals: Fine southern cuisine
Conference Groups: Yes
Guides: Trained dogs and guides
Dogs and Facilities:
Kennel for hunters' dogs
Shotgun Sports:
Driven birds, five-stand, shooting schools, sporting clays, tower or release shoots
Other Services:
Birds cleaned and packed for travel
Other Activities:
Big game, biking, bird-watching, boating, fishing, hiking, wildlife photography
Rates:
Hunts from $180 / gun; accommodations from $30 / person
Gratuity:
Hunter's discretion
Preferred Payment:
Cash, credit cards or check
Getting There:
Fly to Columbia, SC, or Augusta, GA, and rent a car.

Contact:
Jerry Varn
Broxton Bridge Plantation
PO Box 97, Hwy 601 S
Ehrhardt SC 29081
800/437-4868
EMAIL:
broxtonbridgeplantation@juno.com

Deerfield Plantation

St. George, South Carolina

Oh dear, guess you'll have to hunt quail now that your 10-pointer's cooling in the fridge.

VITAL STATISTICS:

GAME BIRDS:
QUAIL, TURKEY
Source of Birds: Wild and pen-reared
Seasons:
QUAIL: Late November through early-March
TURKEY: Mid-March through April
Land: 10,000 private acres
Accommodations:
RUSTIC PLANTATION HOUSE AND OUTLYING CABIN
NUMBER OF ROOMS: 7
MAXIMUM NUMBER OF HUNTERS: 20
Meals: Southern plantation-style
Conference Groups: Yes
Guides: Trained dogs and guides
Dogs and Facilities:
Kennel for hunters' dogs
Shotgun Sports:
Informal instruction
Other Services:
Birds cleaned and packed for travel
Other Activities:
Big game, bird-watching, fishing, wildlife photography
Rates:
From $295 / day inclusive
Gratuity:
10% - 15%
Preferred Payment:
Cash, MasterCard, Visa or check
Getting There:
Fly to Charleston and rent a car.

Contact:
Hugh Walters
Deerfield Plantation
709 Gum Branch Rd
St. George SC 29477
843/563-7927
WEB: www.huntersnet.com/deerfield

A BROAD FERTILE PLAIN rises gently from the swamps along the coast, and by the time you get inland 30 miles or so, the terrain supports vast farms of grain and some livestock. This is prime farmland. Fields support populations of bobwhite quail and deer. Wild turkey hang out in the woods.

Bucks of eight points or better are the main attraction at Deerfield. Yet small groups of hunters—generally no more than four, but sometimes as many as six at a time—can hunt quail on 1,500 acres that owner Hugh Walters manages expressly as a bird hunting preserve. Only one group of hunters is booked at a time. In a typical morning, they'll hunt 200 to 300 acres behind their own dogs, or setters or pointers from Deerfield's kennels. The terrain could be open pine woods or corn or sorghum. During the afternoon, the group will move to a different locale, perhaps concentrating on thick cover along field edges.

The turkey hunting here is grand. Hugh concentrates on long-beard toms—nine inches or better—and harvests a number of birds with 11-inch beards each year. Semi- and fully guided hunts are available. On the former, a guide will identify an area where birds have been roosting and feeding, and then take you into the field. The guide will explain the boundaries of your area, a river to the south, road on the east, and feed plots or fields to the north and west. Within those limits, you're free to move about on your own. On a fully guided hunt, you'll be accompanied by a guide who'll call or not, depending on your preference. During the afternoon, hunters will overlook feed plots where decoys have been set, although you may also hunt feed plots in the morning. It depends on where birds have roosted the night before.

When you see the old lodge at Deerfield, you'll know you're deep in the Old South. A deep front porch stretches along the front of this large 1900s vintage plantation house of unpainted clapboard. The plantation house contains five bedrooms, while a nearby guest cabin nestled in the trees offers two more. Meals are hearty, of course, and distinctly southern country cuisine.

[S O U T H]

Harris Springs

C r o s s   H i l l ,   S o u t h   C a r o l i n a

Therapeutic powers of gunning for quail are much in evidence at this fine old spa.

VITAL STATISTICS:

GAME BIRDS:
CHUKAR, PHEASANT, QUAIL, TURKEY

Source of Birds: Wild and pen-reared

Seasons:
UPLAND BIRDS: October through March

TURKEY: April

Land: 800 private acres

Accommodations:
STONE LODGE

NUMBER OF ROOMS: 8

MAXIMUM NUMBER OF HUNTERS: 8

Meals: Filet mignon, salmon, quail

Conference Groups: Yes

Guides: Trained dogs and guides

Dogs and Facilities:
Kennel for hunters' dogs, dog training

Shotgun Sports:
Five-stand, shooting schools, sporting clays

Other Services:
Birds cleaned and packed for travel, proshop

Other Activities:
Big game, golf

Rates:
From $375 / 1/2 day hunt for two

Gratuity:
10% - 15%

Preferred Payment:
Cash, MasterCard, Visa or check

Getting There:
Fly to Greenville/Spartanburg and rent a car or arrange for the lodge van for $60.

Contact:
Donny Roth
Harris Springs
PO Box 278
Cross Hill SC 29332
864/677-3448

I N THE GAY '90s, mineral springs were very popular vacation destinations. Waters of high sulphur content were thought to have healing properties (no doubt because, like most good medicines, they smell terrible). Families would take trains to the closest station and then pick up a horse-drawn stage from there. Wherever such springs welled up from the ground, you could expect to find a resort.

So it was with Harris Springs, a dozen or so miles northeast of Greenwood near the town of Waterloo. For the first quarter of the 1900s, with its fine hotel, dance hall and race track, this was a very popular resort. Fire ravaged the hotel in the midst of the Depression, and the resort withered and died.

Yet like Phoenix, a new resort—this one dedicated to shotgun sports—rose from materials salvaged from the dance hall and an adjacent bowling alley. At Harris Springs, you'll discover excellent preserve hunting for chukar, pheasants and quail. You and a friend—all parties contain no more than two hunters—will work native grasses beneath stands of pine, fields planted in feed, and over crops or thick edges where birds love to hide. Half- and full-day hunts are available. Come spring, it's time for turkey, hunted among hardwood ridges, creek bottoms, feed plots and abandoned farms.

Sporting clays is the center piece of Harris Springs. A 15-station course was designed by world-class shooter Dan Carlisle, who regularly gives clinics and offers personal instruction at the resort. Five-stand, a quail flush, a 40-foot tower and a pro shop complete the shotgunning facilities. Eight guest rooms are found in the fieldstone lodge. Meals are first class, with salmon, beef tenderloin and game fowl highlighting the menu.

Little River Plantation

Watch out! If you send your kids to camp here, they'll outshoot you come fall.

VITAL STATISTICS:

GAME BIRDS:
CHUKAR, DUCKS, PHEASANT, QUAIL, TURKEY
Source of Birds: Wild and pen-reared
Seasons:
PRESERVE: October through March
TURKEY: April
CAMPS: June, July and August
Land: 500 private acres
Accommodations:
REMODELED BARN AND MOBILE HOME
NUMBER OF ROOMS: 8
MAXIMUM NUMBER OF HUNTERS: 16
Meals: Country and hearty
Conference Groups: Yes
Guides: Trained dogs and guides
Dogs and Facilities:
Kennel for hunters' dogs, dog training
Shotgun Sports:
Five-stand, shooting schools, sporting clays, tower or release shoots
Other Services:
Birds cleaned and packed for travel, pro shop
Other Activities:
Big game, bird-watching, boating, canoeing, fishing, hiking, wildlife photography
Rates:
$60 / person / double occupancy; hunting priced per bird; camp: $975 / week
Gratuity:
Hunter's discretion
Preferred Payment:
Cash, credit card or check
Getting There:
Fly to Augusta and rent a car or Little River will provide transfer for $50 round trip.

Contact:
John Edens
Little River Plantation
PO Box 1129
Abbeville SC 29620
864/391-2300
Fax: 864/391-2304
EMAIL: lrplantation@wctel.net

AMONG THE CADRE of fine bird hunting lodges in South Carolina, Little River Plantation is somewhat unique. It's one of the few, and perhaps the only one, that offers a camp with an emphasis on shooting for youngsters age 12 through 15. Lasting a week, the camp features the Hunter Safety Course, instruction in shooting rifles, shotguns and bows, and lots of time on the sporting clays course. Campers will learn how to scout for turkey and deer. They'll practice turkey calling and study wildlife behavior and conservation. And there's the normal range of camp activities: fishing, canoeing and swimming. The camp is co-educational, with separate quarters for boys and girls. It's a great opportunity for kids (and for parents who want to introduce their offspring to the hunting and shooting sports in a safe and structured environment).

The danger of this is, of course, that with their sharp eyes and keen reflexes, kids schooled at Little River will outshoot their parents. So it's up to you guys to hone your skills as well. Little River's sporting clays course offers 50- or 100-round sessions, and there's also five-stand for quick tune-ups. On 500 acres of native grasses and sorghum, you can mix bags of quail, pheasant and chukar, or limit your hunt to any one of those species. Dogs and guides are optional. However, guests generally use a guide and a pointer, or a shorthair from the kennel if they do not bring their own. Shoots for flighted mallards are also available by special arrangements.

Sumter National Forest occupies a huge section of this area, and it's renowned for its abundance of long-beard Eastern turkey. Three- and six-day spring turkey packages that include lodging and meals as well as guide service are offered by Little River. One guide may serve two hunters, or each hunter may have an individual guide, depending on which package you select. Hunters on the three-day plan may harvest two turkeys, while those staying for six days get three. Little River offers accommodations in a remodeled barn and in a new, double-wide trailer. Meals are country and hearty.

[S O U T H]

Quail Valley Hunt Club

S h e l b y v i l l e ,   T e n n e s s e e

Stars from the Grand Ole Opry and Vols football rub shoulders at Quail Valley.

VITAL STATISTICS:

GAME BIRDS:
CHUKAR, PHEASANT, QUAIL
Source of Birds: Wild and pen-reared
Seasons:
September through April
Land: 400 private acres
Accommodations:
OLD FRAME FARMHOUSE
NUMBER OF ROOMS: 5
MAXIMUM NUMBER OF HUNTERS: 15
Meals: Home-cooked fried chicken and the like
Conference Groups: No
Guides: Trained dogs and guides
Dogs and Facilities:
Kennel for hunters' dogs, dog training
Shotgun Sports:
Sporting clays, tower or release shoots
Other Services:
Birds cleaned and packed for travel
Rates:
From $150 / gun;
room and board: $100/night
Gratuity:
$20 - $50
Preferred Payment:
Cash or check
Getting There:
Fly to Nashville and rent a car.

Contact:
Jim Walker
Quail Valley Hunt Club
506 Bryant Street
Shelbyville TN 37160
931/684-1772
Fax: 931/684-3819
EMAIL: walkerhull@cates.net

HARDWOOD RIDGES rise about 200 feet above gentle valleys in this, the south-central section of the Volunteer State. Limestone makes soils in the creek bottoms rich, and numerous springs issue forth. The most famous in this neck of the woods is the one at Lynchburg, where a certain potable beverage of high regard is distilled. You might sip a bit of it, cut with a dash of branch water, after chasing quail, chukar and pheasant on Jim Walker's preserve.

With 400 acres—much of it bottoms and most of it planted with lespedeza, sorghum and thigh-high cane—and a charming 1890s farmhouse like your great-great-granddaddy's, this hunt club draws big name clients from nearby Nashville (60 miles north) and its Grand Ole Opry. Porter Wagoner and Barbara Mandrell are regulars, as is former Tennessee Vols coach Johnny Majors. Once in a while, Senator Fred Thompson drops in for a visit.

After a brisk round of sporting clays on Jim's 13-station course—everybody's got to warm up before the hunt—you take to the 20 to 40 acres set aside for your hunt. Guides and dogs are optional, but most out-of-town guests don't pass up a chance to hunt over Quail Valley's fine Brittanies, German shorthairs or setters. Jim will send you out with the best dog he has that matches your shooting style.

And when you've walked the fields and bagged a few birds, you'll warm yourself before the fire in a log cabin that a woman in the hollow says is more than 200 years old. She should know, because her kin were born there. After taking the chill off, you'll head for the lodge, that old farmhouse beneath the trees. If it's warm enough, as it's apt to be in October or early November, you might pour yourself a little Mr. Jack, and go set on the porch swing and wonder what the rich folks are doin'.

74 Ranch Hunting Resort

Cambellton, Texas

A "must" on any tour of the great quail ranches of Texas.

VITAL STATISTICS:

GAME BIRDS:
DUCKS, QUAIL, DOVE
Source of Birds: Wild and pen-reared
Seasons:
DOVE: late September through early November
DUCKS: mid-September through late January
QUAIL: November through February
TURKEY: late March through April
Land: 27,000 private acres
Accommodations:
PRIVATE LODGE
NUMBER OF ROOMS: 15
MAXIMUM NUMBER OF HUNTERS: 28
Meals: Mexican, steaks, chicken, fish
Conference Groups: Yes
Guides: Trained dogs and guides
Shotgun Sports:
Five-stand, shooting schools, skeet, sporting clays
Other Services:
Birds cleaned and packed for travel
Other Activities:
Big game, bird-watching, fishing, hiking, wildlife photography
Rates:
Packages from $250 / day
Gratuity:
Hunter's discretion
Preferred Payment:
Cash, MasterCard, Visa or check
Getting There:
Fly to San Antonio and rent a car.

Contact:
Milo Abercrombie
74 Ranch Hunting Resort
PO Box 38
Cambellton TX 78008
830/579-7474
Fax: 830/579-4222
WEB: www.74ranch.com

FOR GENTLEMEN ENTREPRENEURS of the Lone Star state, quail hunting was as important to business as golf was to magnates unlucky enough to live where bobwhite didn't thrive. They'd travel around the state, frequently in their own aircraft, and hatch plans for new oil fields, real estate developments and the like. A regular stop on the circuit was the 27,000-acre 74 Ranch, owned by the Abercrombie oil family for more than three generations.

The 74 has an advantage over most of the other huge spreads. It is just 50 miles south of San Antonio, thus easily reachable by car. Long a cattle operation and privately managed for quail—a full-time biologist is on staff—this ranch was opened for commercial hunting about a decade ago. Its easy access and first-class accommodations made it a natural.

The hunting is outstanding. A week of teal shooting around stock tanks (man-made ponds to Yankees), kicks things off in mid-September. Then it's time for doves. Spend the morning shooting sporting clays, have lunch and a nap and head for the dove fields about 3 o'clock. Duck season comes in during the third week of October and runs for a month before taking a two-week hiatus in late November and early December before resuming and running through mid-January. October 31 marks the beginning of quail season. You'll gun for wild and pen-raised birds through the end of February. Typically, bird hunters ride in vehicles as dogs work through the grasses amongst stands of brush.

Rio turkey become legal during the end of March and closes on the first of May. Big game hunters will also find alligator and deer here, and are blown away when they encounter eland, zebra, giraffes and 15 other exotic game species (strictly for viewing, not hunting). Full- and half-day bird hunts are available as are three-day packages that include meals and accommodations in the fine lodge.

B-Bar-B Ranch

K i n g s v i l l e , T e x a s

Quality is the watchword at this quintessential south Texas quail resort.

VITAL STATISTICS:

GAME BIRDS:
QUAIL, TURKEY
Source of Birds: Wild
Seasons:
QUAIL: November through February
TURKEY: March and April
Land: 26,000 private acres
Accommodations:
LONG, LOW MODERN LODGE
NUMBER OF ROOMS: 16
MAXIMUM NUMBER OF HUNTERS: 16
Meals: Exquisite game fare
Conference Groups: Yes
Guides: Trained dogs and guides
Dogs and Facilities:
Kennel for hunters' dogs, dog training
Shotgun Sports:
Five-stand, shooting schools, sporting clays
Other Services:
Birds cleaned and packed for travel, proshop
Other Activities:
Big game, bird-watching, fishing, horseback riding, wildlife photography
Rates:
$850 / gun
Gratuity:
Hunter's discretion
Preferred Payment:
Cash, MasterCard, Visa or check
Getting There:
Fly to Corpus Christi and rent a car.

Contact:
Martin Miers
B-Bar-B Ranch
325 E County Road 2215
Kingsille TX 78363
361/296-3331
Fax: 361/296-3337
EMAIL: bbarb@rivnet.com
WEB: www.b-bar-b.com

MODERN YET RUSTIC, the B-Bar-B spreads long and low on manicured grounds beneath the trees just a few miles inland from the south Texas Gulf Coast. Operated as a bed-and-breakfast, the ranch's accommodations are elegant in comparison to most other bird hunting lodges. Rooms are spacious and decorated—but not over-done—in modern western motif. Each, as you'd expect, includes a private bath. Three-bedroom suites with Jacuzzi's are available. And there's a pool and hot tub.

Situated on an 80-acre remnant of the famed King Ranch, the B-Bar-B is an ideal jumping-off spot for hunting more than 26,000 acres of wild quail cover. No stocked birds here. Pointers range in front of the four-by-four pickup. You ride on a wide bench seat on top of the seven-kennel dog box. Scabbards for your shotgun are mounted on the side. When the dogs get birdy, your guide will stop the truck. You'll climb down from your vantage point, slip your gun from the scabbard and move in behind the dog. Bag limits are set by the state. So much scrub and grass is there that few plots are hunted more than twice or three times per season. Check out hunting for Rio Grande turkey while you're in this neck of the woods.

Lunch for quail hunters is special indeed. Out comes rice and beans, *carne quisada* and *pan de campo*, rustled up by a chuckwagon cook. Here, you're close enough to the border for everyone to take a siesta before returning to work. Back at the lodge, you'll expect and receive a gourmet dinner. Chose from quail with peach and jalepeno sauce, rabbit in white wine and ostrich steaks grilled with a secret marinade.

This is one of those lodges that a nonhunting spouse will enjoy. Tours of the King Ranch and museums highlighting the region's fascinating history are on the agenda. Shopping in Matamoras, Mexico, is but 90 minutes south. Baffin Bay and excellent fishing for redfish and speckled trout are also available.

Circle Rocking N Ranch

Texarkana, Texas

Business groups appreciate the excellent meeting facilities, as well as the hunting.

VITAL STATISTICS:

GAME BIRDS:
QUAIL
Source of Birds: Wild and pen-reared
Seasons:
All year
Land: 10,000 private acres
Accommodations:
MODERN, STONE LODGE
NUMBER OF ROOMS: 3
MAXIMUM NUMBER OF HUNTERS: 10
Meals: Family-style, country cooking
Conference Groups: Yes
Guides: Trained dogs and guides
Dogs and Facilities:
Kennel for hunters' dogs, dog training
Other Services:
Birds cleaned and packed for travel
Other Activities:
Big game, bird-watching, hiking, wildlife photography
Rates:
From $450 / day
Gratuity:
Hunter's discretion
Preferred Payment:
Cash, credit card or check
Getting There:
Fly to Texarkana and you'll be met by the ranch van.

Contact:
Fred R. Norton, Sr.
Circle Rocking N Ranch
PO Box 449
Texarkana TX 75504
903/793-4647
Fax: 903/793-4650

TEXARKANA—about 25 miles east of the ranch—is one of the most rapidly developing cities in this part of the country. Its favorable climate, good transportation and positive workers' ethic place it high on the list of potential business sites. And a number of companies that have located here over the past few years are finding the Circle Rocking N Ranch a dandy location for corporate meetings, with a little quail or deer hunting on the side.

West of New Boston, State Route 98 crosses Interstate 30, the main highway to Dallas, about 150 miles away. Four miles south on Rt. 98, on the left, is the yellow gate across the ranch's drive. Beyond the gate is 10,000 acres, or roughly fifteen square miles, of prime quail terrain that also harbors a fine deer herd. Much of the land is open, covered with grasses that are shaded here and there by occasional hardwoods. Tree-lined fencerows provide a good deal of cover. Creek banks, too, are heavy with brush. A large lake behind the lodge pulls in waterfowl, but they are not hunted commercially.

Hunters ride out to the fields in specially designed wagons and trucks. Parties of two hunters with a guide and a brace of pointers are the norm. Individuals and larger groups can also be accommodated. The Circle Rocking N specializes in custom hunts, tuned to meet the preferences and physical needs of its clients. The season here runs all year. If proper precautions for your dogs are taken—lots of breaks and lots of water—it's possible to hunt quail here in July! The best hunting, of course, is in November and December when grasses are dry and stubbly, leaves have fallen from the trees, and in the morning your breath leaves a trail in the air.

Parties of eight or more may book the lovely modern stone lodge, which includes guest rooms as well as meeting facilities for more than 100. Meals are provided with lodging and with some half-day and full-day hunt packages. Groups of fewer than eight hunters will find a range of motels and restaurants in New Boston.

Eagle Lake & Katy Prairie Outfitters

K a t y ,   T e x a s

VITAL STATISTICS:

GAME BIRDS:
DUCKS, GEESE, SANDHILL CRANES, PHEASANTS, CHUKAR

Source of Birds: Wild and pen-reared

Seasons:
DOVE and TEAL: September
CRANES: January through February
WATERFOWL: November through February
UPLAND GAME: November through April

Land: 52,000 private acres

Accommodations:
MOTELS IN NEARBY TOWN

Meals: Breakfast included

Corporate Groups: Yes

Guides: Included

Other Services:
Birds cleaned and packed for travel

Other Activities:
Bird-watching, fishing, wildlife photography

Rates:
From $125 / gun

Gratuity:
$50 - $100 day

Preferred Payment:
Cash or check

Getting There:
Fly to Houston and rent a car.

Contact:
James Prince
Eagle Lake & Katy Prairie Outfitters
PO Box 129
Katy TX 77492
281/391-6100
Fax: 281/391-6114

If goose hunting turns you on, you can't afford to miss hunting at Katy Prairie.

AT TIMES IT SEEMS that every goose in North America has found its way to the country around Katy, a town on Texas' coastal plain 30 miles west of Houston and Eagle Lake, another 30 miles to the southwest. Snows, blues, Ross', spec's, lesser Canadas—they're all here in such aggregated profusion that at times it's hard to carry on a conversation without shouting. Then, add the ducks: pintails, teal, mallard, wigeon, mottled ducks, tree ducks (when was the last time you bagged one of those?), gadwalls and shovelers. If that isn't enough, pick up teal early in the season and finish off with a sandhill crane in February. For a dessert, during mid-day, hunt the preserve for pheasants and chukar.

For more than 20 years, waterfowlers who are serious about their sport have been gunning with Eagle Lake and Katy Prairie Outfitters. Eagle Lake preserve is hard by a town of the same name near a river named Colorado that flows into the Gulf of Mexico. (That's right, this is another one.) Rice and other grains are big business in these flat, flat lands. And there's no better habitat for waterfowl hunters than a flooded rice field. Hunting is from blinds over decoys or pass-shooting where appropriate. A three-inch 12-gauge—choked modified and improved cylinder, if yours is a double gun—is the best medicine here. Pass-shooters may favor the 3 1/2-inch 12-bores or 10-gauges. In most applications, the 3-inch 12-gauge is enough. Smart alecks, or those who are damn good and patient shots, may sneak along a 3-inch 20—lots of fun on decoying ducks and, yes, geese. You'll hunt geese from fields strewn with 500 to 1000 decoys, and ducks in the rice fields.

Larry Gore, who started and owns this operation, will accommodate the needs of most shooters. Packages range from afternoon dove, waterfowl and upland bird hunts, but most clients opt for three- to five-day packages. He sees lots of corporate clients and offers a wide range of group memberships. But he's equally adept at meeting the needs of a solo hunter who has an extra day in his schedule and would like it spend it hunting birds. Accommodations are provided at motels in Katy, although a large, hot buffet breakfast is included. Another alternative is a quiet three-bedroom farmhouse—ideal for groups of six to eight—in Eagle Lake, where you'll do your own cooking or try the restaurants in town.

El Canelo Ranch

R a y m o n d v i l l e ,   T e x a s

The ranch in Texas where four-star lodging, dining and hunting all come together.

VITAL STATISTICS:

GAME BIRDS:
DOVE, DUCKS, QUAIL, TURKEY
Source of Birds: Wild and pen-reared
Seasons:
DOVE: mid-September through mid-November
DUCKS: late October through mid-January
QUAIL: late October through February
TURKEY: April
Land: 130,000 private acres
Accommodations:
ELEGANT SPANISH LODGE
NUMBER OF ROOMS: 5
MAXIMUM NUMBER OF HUNTERS: 13
Meals: Gourmet regional cuisine
Conference Groups: Yes
Guides: Trained dogs and guides
Dogs and Facilities:
Kennel for hunters' dogs
Shotgun Sports:
Sporting clays
Other Services:
Birds cleaned and packed for travel
Other Activities:
Big game, bird-watching, fishing, hiking, tennis, wildlife photography
Rates:
From $450 / day with meals and lodging / 3 day minimum
Gratuity:
Hunter's discretion
Preferred Payment:
Cash or check
Getting There:
Fly to Harlingen and you will be escorted to the lodge.

Contact:
R Ray Burdette
El Canelo Ranch
PO Box 487
Raymondville TX 78580
956/689-5042
Fax: 956/689-1089
EMAIL: elcanel@vista.com
WEB: furff.tamn.edu/~elcanelo

IN A FEW RARE INSTANCES, absolutely first-class accommodations mesh with equally fine bird hunting. The El Canelo Ranch is one of those. The ranch has been owned by Monica Burdett's family since shortly after Texas became a state. Her great-great-grandfather, a businessman, purchased the property to raise cattle. His father was an officer in the Mexican army, and his father before him served Spain in the early 1800s. History is deep here, but it does not hit you in the face. The inn on the ranch is far too genteel for that.

As you'd expect, the architecture of the inn echoes its Hispanic lineage. Yet, at the same time, it is modern. A massive mortared stone fireplace commands a cathedral-ceilinged living room that's paneled with taffy-colored planks. On either side of the fireplace are plush sofas that invite you to sit with a drink before dinner. The five guest rooms are equally charming, as is the sunny dining room with its French doors that open onto manicured grounds fringed with bougainvillea. For dinner, the chef offers dove in wine, filet of mignon with a sauce of green peppercorns, or beef or chicken fajitas grilled on mesquite.

Pointers or Brittany spaniels carry the workload when it comes to hunting quail. Under the guidance of Monica's husband, Ray, you'll be taken to the best of the 130,000 acres available for hunting. This terrain, about 20 miles inland from the Gulf Coast, rolls very little. Anacua, mesquite and clumps of cat's-claw offer protection for birds. Among the grass—coastal bluestem—are patches of cactus. Annual prescribed burns control and condition cover for bird hunting. Along with quail—definitely the main draw here—are dove (also superb) and ducks. At another ranch, Ray's guests hunt Rio Grande turkey. Big game hunters will find excellent whitetails as well as nilgai, a large (800-pound) slate blue antelope imported from India.

Commercial flights service Harlingen, 20 miles south of El Canelo. Brownsville and Matamoras, Mexico are 30 miles farther.

[**S O U T H**]

Greystone Castle Sporting Club

M i n g u s ,   T e x a s

File this hunt club under the heading of "you gotta see it to believe it!"

WHEN YOU'RE RACING WEST on Interstate 20, banging out of Fort Worth and makin' tracks for Abilene, cast your eyes south when you near Thurber, exit 367. There, if the light is right, the traffic not too heavy, and you believe your imagination, you'll see towers and battlements—more appropriate to England or Scotland—rising from the mesas. If you blink, you'll miss your glimpse of this builtmore folly, but unlike many such inanities, this one makes a sort of sense.

Texas is hot. Castles are built of stone. Thick stone walls stay cool. So what if it looks odd? The castle surrounds more than an acre, including 25 guest rooms with private baths, a huge meeting hall of 2,500 square feet, a lovely dining room and various lounges. Perched atop a mesa that rises some 200 feet above the surrounding sagey grasslands—and the ruins of Thurber, a ghost town — the views from the castle are stunning. What a place to watch the sunset after a day's hunting.

Greystone, endorsed by Orvis, hunts some 4,000 acres. From mid-October through March, you can hunt behind pointers for quail, pheasants and chukar. Four-by-fours will carry you to the field you and your guide have selected for the morning's hunt. If you hunt during the afternoon, it will be on different ground. Though there is some lift to it, most of the terrain is easily negotiated. You can hunt here too for wild ducks—mallards, wigeon, woodies, ringbills, scaup, pintails, gadwall and teal. Gunning is over decoys from blinds set up on the shores of small lakes and stock tanks in the area. Regulated mallard shoots are also offered. And you can take advantage of sporting clays, five-stand and skeet courses.

Also managed as a big game preserve, you can hunt axis deer, fallow and black buck, antelope, Sitka deer, oryx and sheep. Trophy whitetails are harvested here, as are wild turkey. The staff can offer bird and big game combination hunts. If you're so moved, there are bass and crappie in ponds and lakes. The only problem is figuring out how to get it all in during a three-day stay.

VITAL STATISTICS:

GAME BIRDS:
CHUKAR, DUCKS, PHEASANT, QUAIL
Source of Birds: Wild and pen-reared
Seasons:
UPLAND BIRDS: October through April
DUCKS: November through March
Land: 4,000 private acres
Accommodations:
STONE CASTLE
NUMBER OF ROOMS: 24
MAXIMUM NUMBER OF HUNTERS: 33
Meals: Fine dining
Conference Groups: Yes
Guides: Trained dogs and guides
Dogs and Facilities:
Kennel for hunters' dogs
Shotgun Sports:
Driven birds, five-stand, shooting schools, skeet, sporting clays, tower or release shoots
Other Services:
Birds cleaned and packed for travel, proshop
Other Activities:
Big game, biking, fishing, golf, hiking, wildlife photography
Rates:
From $600 / day
Gratuity:
Hunter's discretion
Preferred Payment:
Cash, credit cards or check
Getting There:
Fly to Dallas/Ft. Worth and rent a car.

Contact:
Porter Dunnaway
Greystone Castle Sporting Club
PO Box 158
Mingus TX 76463
800/399-3006
Fax: 254/672-5971
EMAIL: castle@our-town.com
WEB: www.greystonecastle.com

VITAL STATISTICS:

GAME BIRDS:
CHUKAR, PHEASANT, QUAIL

Source of Birds: Pen-reared

Seasons:
October through February

Land: 1,200 private acres

Accommodations:
IN NEARBY TOWN

Meals: Restaurants in town

Conference Groups: No

Guides: Trained dogs and guides

Dogs and Facilities:
Bring your own kennel

Rates:
From $100 / day

Gratuity:
Hunter's discretion

Preferred Payment:
Cash or check

Getting There:
Drive in from Amarillo or
Oklahoma City.

Contact:
Clydeene Harper
Harper's Hunting Preserve
Rt. 2, Box 484 WC
Booker TX 79005
806/435-3495
EMAIL: gamefarm@ren.net

Harper's Hunting Preserve

Booker, Texas

A basic preserve that's big on service and easy on the wallet.

IF YOUR TASTE RUNS TO no-frill pheasant preserves, and you find yourself in the vicinity of Amarillo or Oklahoma City, it might be worth a drive to Gilbert and Clydeene Harper's place outside of Booker. Booker is a tiny town two miles south of the Oklahoma border where Texas Routes 15 and 23 cross. This is big, softly rolling country, as arid as a starched khaki shirt. Sunny days outnumber those with cloud cover, but in the winter, the country gets down right cold. But, like the folks in Booker will tell you, it's dry cold.

Buffalo grass covers the landscape, broken by some grain crops and a pasture. Trees are at a premium. Sloughs hold moisture in their bottoms and thus provide the best cover. The drill here is as basic as it gets. The Harper's will set out your birds (not dizzied or rocked to sleep) before you're scheduled to arrive. They'll meet you at their farm where they raise game birds for other preserves. After swappin' howdy's and taking care of paperwork, you'll follow them in their pickup out to the stretch of countryside where they've planned your hunt.

The Harper's 1,200 acres offer as much variety as there is in this land, and weather conditions will determine where you hunt and how you hunt it. Assuming that winds are less than, say, 10 miles per hour (mere zephyrs in these parts), you may work a large field or a drainage down one side and then up the other. If it's blowing harder, and it usually does, you'll hunt into the wind down one side of the field, meet the Harper's pickup, and drive back to the end where you started. A short ride will return you to the downwind edge, and you'll hunt up the remaining half of the field.

There's no pro shop, no sporting clay games, no lodge, not even an office, unless you count the Harper's kitchen. Many of the folks who come in to work their dogs will spend a weekend, hunting the afternoon of the first day and the morning of the second. They'll overnight in motels in Booker or Perryton, 16 miles to the southwest, and eat in restaurants there.

Hawkeye Hunting Club

C e n t e r ,   T e x a s

A fine retreat for corporate meetings, and not bad for individuals either.

VITAL STATISTICS:

GAME BIRDS:
CHUKAR, PHEASANT, QUAIL
Source of Birds: Wild and pen-reared
Seasons:
October through April
Land: 160,000 private acres
Accommodations:
SIX MODERN LODGES
NUMBER OF ROOMS: 34
MAXIMUM NUMBER OF HUNTERS: 65
Meals: Diverse game menu
Conference Groups: Yes
Guides: Trained dogs and guides
Dogs and Facilities:
Bring your own kennel with your dog
Shotgun Sports:
Driven birds, five-stand, sporting clays, tower or release shoots
Other Services:
Birds cleaned and packed for travel
Other Activities:
Fishing, golf, hiking, horseback riding, tennis
Rates:
From $384 / 1/2-day hunt; accommodations and meals from $210 / night
Gratuity:
15%
Preferred Payment:
Cash, credit card or check
Getting There:
Fly to Shreveport, LA, and rent a car.

Contact:
Linda Masterson
Hawkeye Hunting Club
PO Box 2017
Center TX 75935
409/598-1003
Fax: 409/598-1005

JUST TO THE NORTHWEST of the upper reaches of Toledo Bend Reservoir, along the Louisiana border, is the small city of Center known for the manufacturing of plywood and other forest products. Eleven miles to the southeast is the nearest entrance to the Sabine National Forest, a 160,000-acre-plus tract once hotly contested by warring forces of Spain and the United States. Today, the forest is a haven for hunters and anglers.

Pines predominate in the forest and beyond its boundaries. Cotton and corn, historic crops, are still grown and much of the region is in pasture. About 60 miles from Shreveport, Louisiana, and Long View, Texas, and in the midst of the growing resort communities on Toledo Bend and Lake Sam Rayburn to the southeast, Center is becoming something of a sportsmen's headquarters. Quail and deer hunting are excellent in this region, as is turkey hunting and waterfowling.

For more than 45 years, Hawkeye Hunting Club has been serving individuals and corporations seeking quality gunning for pheasants, quail and chukar. The land here is best described as hilly, but it's not overly difficult. Much is covered with open pine woods shading sedge and grasses. Individual guides are assigned fields of 25 to 100 acres, and over the season, they know the land, and the behavior of the birds thereon extremely well. Pointers and German shorthairs are the norm here.

Hawkeye is designed especially for corporate guests. Six secluded lodges with five or six rooms each provide excellent opportunities for private meetings. Businesses may rent one or any number of the cabins, depending on the size of the group. The main lodge contains three mid-sized meeting rooms and one large room for plenary sessions. Meals are outstanding, featuring up to a dozen selections based on game and locally grown meat and fowl. Shotgun clays courses are available on site.

Herradura Ranch Inc

Cotulla, Texas

Wild quail thrive amid the scrub and creosote brush of arid south-central Texas.

VITAL STATISTICS:

GAME BIRDS:
CHUKAR, DOVE, PHEASANT, QUAIL, TURKEY

Source of Birds: Wild and pen-reared

Seasons:
QUAIL, PHEASANT, CHUKAR: October through March
DOVE: September
TURKEY: mid-April through mid-May

Land: Unlimited private acres

Accommodations:
PRIVATE RUSTIC LODGE
NUMBER OF ROOMS: 6 PLUS A BUNK HOUSE
MAXIMUM NUMBER OF HUNTERS: 26

Meals: Excellent, hearty fare

Conference Groups: Yes

Guides: Trained dogs and guides

Dogs and Facilities:
Bring your own kennel if you bring your dog

Shotgun Sports:
Sporting clays

Other Services:
Birds cleaned and packed for travel, proshop

Other Activities:
Big game, bird watching, boating, fishing, wildlife photography

Rates:
$1000 / day

Gratuity:
Hunter's discretion

Preferred Payment:
Cash or check

Getting There:
Fly to San Antonio and rent a car.

Contact:
David Schuster
Herradura Ranch Inc
PO Drawer 698
Cotulla TX 78014
830/373-4492
Fax: 830/373-4595
EMAIL: herradura@vista.com

JUST WHAT MARKS A QUAIL AS WILD? There are those who'll tell you that a quail ain't wild unless it came from a native hen's egg laid in a nest on the ground. Other's say that it's got to fly high and away from you or back over your head. Many folks spend a lot of time talking about flight-conditioned birds. Some gunners maintain that birds released a week or more before they're hunted either go wild or get eaten by hawks or foxes. And a few believe that a wild bird is any bobwhite that gets away from your shot.

Whatever suits your definition of wild, you'll find it in the wide-open spaces of the Herradura Ranch, located southeast of this little town half-way between San Antonio and Laredo. There's not a whole lot of relief to this land, but it's dotted with seven- to ten-acre ponds for watering grazing livestock. The Nueces River makes a big bend south of the ranch, and Piedra Creek flows just to the east. Quail buggies will carry you over the countryside while a brace of pointers races out front. Pheasants and chukar are available on request. Twenty-gauge guns with open chokes are favored. Snake chaps are provided for those who have a prudent streak.

On one-day hunts, most gunners arrive after lunch, hunt the afternoon, enjoy cocktails, hors d'ouevres and a fine dinner, before retiring to one of the six rooms or the bunkhouse. After breakfast, it's off to the quail fields again, then lunch and back to the airport. A more leisurely stay is, frankly, more fun. Along with quail, there are whitetails, wild boar, axis deer, red stags and black buck to be hunted. You'll also find turkey and dove in appropriate seasons. Stock tanks hold largemouth, and there's something to be said for just sitting in the gathering dusk on one of those golden days when the temperature's sliding slowly down through the 60s. A grass strip will handle many private aircraft, and Cotulla boasts an all-weather airport.

[S O U T H]

Joshua Creek Ranch

B o e r n e , T e x a s

Among all the great lodges of Texas, Joshua Creek glows with European polish.

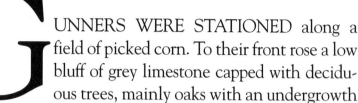

GUNNERS WERE STATIONED along a field of picked corn. To their front rose a low bluff of grey limestone capped with deciduous trees, mainly oaks with an undergrowth of thick grasses waving like burnished old brass in the low winter sun. Through the grass beneath the trees came the beaters, you could hear them, and ahead of the beaters flushed cock birds, their tails iridescent. The birds had the advantage, climbing for altitude and banking left and right in defiance of near-vertical shots. It was a driven bird shoot of near perfection, yet typical fare at Joshua Creek Ranch.

When Jim and Ann Kercheville bought the 1,000-acre ranch, which is 45 minutes north of San Antonio, they envisioned a gunning resort as fine as those they'd visited in Europe. But along with driven pheasants and flighted mallards, they offer hunting for bobwhite in open grasslands shaded by trees that look as if they've been transplanted from the African veldt. Cross Joshua Creek (more about that in a moment) and the cover takes on the look of the Dakota's plains and, it's here that you'll flush pheasants from beneath the noses of highly trained pointers. Even the bird dogs have a sense of where they are and they conduct themselves accordingly. A sporting clays course, strung through the heights and ravines of some 30 acres, offers tune-ups for those in need and serious competitions throughout the year. Deer and turkey are also available in season.

And then there's the lodge, a low-slung stone affair that sits atop a ledge of caprock overlooking the spring-fed Joshua Creek. You'll see rainbows rising in the impoundment below the lodge, and it is very difficult not to grab a fly rod and tell your hosts that you'll have dinner later. Meals are exquisite and accompanied by good vintages. Guest room options vary from bunks in the main lodge, to private rooms and suites in Long Haus, or a private home with three bedrooms and a kitchen.

VITAL STATISTICS:

GAME BIRDS:
CHUKAR, DUCKS, HUNGARIAN PARTRIDGE, PHEASANT, QUAIL

Source of Birds: Pen-reared

Seasons:
ALL: September through March

Land: 1,00 private acres

Accommodations:
PRIVATE STONE LODGE AND ANCILLARY HOUSES
NUMBER OF ROOMS: 12
MAXIMUM NUMBER OF HUNTERS: 40

Meals: Game, elegantly served

Conference Groups: Yes

Guides: Trained dogs and guides

Dogs and Facilities:
Kennel for hunters' dogs, dog training

Shotgun Sports:
Driven birds, sporting clays

Other Services:
Birds cleaned and packed for travel, proshop

Other Activities:
Canoeing, fishing

Rates:
From $900 / day, double occupancy

Gratuity:
Hunter's discretion

Preferred Payment:
Cash, MasterCard, Visa or check

Getting There:
Fly to San Antonio and rent a car.

Contact:
Ann Kercheville
Joshua Creek Ranch
PO Box 1946
Boerne TX 78006
830/537-5090
Fax: 830/537-4766
EMAIL: birdhunt@texas.net
WEB: www.joshuacreek.com

Krooked River Ranch Outfitters

H a s k e l l ,   T e x a s

A family-run operation where you'll find excellent wild quail, turkey, ducks and geese.

VITAL STATISTICS:

GAME BIRDS:
DOVE, DUCKS, GEESE,
QUAIL, TURKEY
Source of Birds: Wild
Seasons:
WATERFOWL: September through
mid-February
DOVE: September
QUAIL: early November through
mid-February
TURKEY: early April through mid-May
Land: 100,000 private acres
Accommodations:
PRIVATE AND COMFORTABLE LODGES
NUMBER OF ROOMS: 12 COMBINED
MAXIMUM NUMBER OF HUNTERS: 8 - 40
Meals: Family-style grilled chicken,
steaks, venison
Conference Groups: Yes
Guides: Trained dogs and guides
Dogs and Facilities:
Kennel for hunters' dogs
Shotgun Sports: Trap
Other Services:
Birds cleaned and packed for travel,
proshop
Other Activities:
Big game, biking, bird-watching,
fishing, hiking, skiing, wildlife
photography
Rates:
Multiple packages from $400 / day;
3 person minimum
Gratuity:
Hunter's discretion
Preferred Payment:
Cash, credit card or check
Getting There:
Fly to Dallas or Lubbock and rent a
car.

Contact:
Roy Wilson
Krooked River Ranch
Outfitters
PO Box 85
Haskell TX 79521
915/773-2457
Fax: 915/773-2541
EMAIL: krro@westex.net

WHEN YOU TOUCH DOWN in Lubbock, it's the flatness of the land that gets you. Were it not for huge, wheeled irrigators, the country outside the city would be one huge mirage, shimmering in the noonday heat. But as you head east, you drop off the caprock into the initial washes that coalesce to form tributaries to the Brazos. Beneath yellow cliffs, the land ebbs and flows and occasionally seems to plunge, only to rise steeply again across the way. Mesquite trees rise above the grassland and cacti. Mesquite look as if some demented hand planted them as groves, but they were not. The spacing between trees is more a measure of the need of each for a minimal amount of water to survive.

In spring, there is no place greener or more lovely on earth. Fall and winter draw the color from the land, leaving only yellows, grays and browns. All the better, because there's a chance—just a chance—that you'll see quail. From your perch atop the six-wheel John Deere ATV, you'll jounce along oil roads, watching a matched pair of pointers or setters flash back and forth among the mesquite, quartering and smelling for quail. You can see them from your perch, and when they get birdy, your guide will bring your conveyance to a standstill as you hustle off and move in toward the dogs. If it's been dry, bobwhite have a tendency to leak out from under a dog's point. Best not to waste time getting in position. One step, maybe three, and you've flushed the covey. Blurs of brown blast in many directions, one or two of which should give you at least a shot. Double guns are favored here for their speed as much as for their instant choice of choke. Twenties are plenty; 28-gauge are great fun. These birds are wild—owners Roy and Becky Wilson do no stocking at all—and they're fast, brother, fast.

Roy offers a pair of outstanding quail hunts. The first is at Caprock Lodge which offers two bedrooms with private baths, plus additional accommodations in the white ranch house. Here, you'll forget you're hunting in the twenty-first century. The second is farther southeast near Haskell, at Krooked River Ranch itself. Clear Fork of the Brazos has eaten away the plateau, leaving myriad microdrainages. Up on top, quail thrive in the groves of mesquite. Below is the lodge with its cottages for up to five hunters. Each cottage has a private bath. In both locations, meals are superb.

Los Cuernos Ranch

C o t u l l a ,   T e x a s

In this arid land, quail hunting is awesome, and accommodations are seldom finer.

VITAL STATISTICS:

GAME BIRDS:
CHUKAR, DOVE, PHEASANT, QUAIL, TURKEY
Source of Birds: Wild and pen-reared
Seasons:
DOVE: September
PRESERVE BIRDS: September through March
TURKEY: March and April
Land: 4,000 private acres
Accommodations:
PRIVATE LODGE
NUMBER OF ROOMS: 9
MAXIMUM NUMBER OF HUNTERS: 16
Meals: Regional cuisine
Conference Groups: Yes
Guides: Trained dogs and guides
Dogs and Facilities:
Kennel for hunters' dogs
Shotgun Sports:
Five-stand, skeet, sporting clays, tower or release shoots, trap
Other Services:
Birds cleaned and packed for travel, proshop
Other Activities:
Big game, bird-watching, fishing, horseback riding
Rates:
From $1500 each in groups of six or more
Gratuity:
Hunter's discretion
Preferred Payment:
Cash, Visa or check
Getting There:
Fly to San Antonio and rent a car.

Contact:
Greg Henicke
Los Cuernos Ranch
PO Box 697
Cotulla TX 78014
830/676-3317
Fax: 830/676-6496

THE HORNS OF A DILEMMA. Deer or quail? Here on the Nueces River, you can do both and more. The four-wheeler with the dog box and the seat above rocks over the faint trace through the brush and dry grasses. To your left is a run of cactus. Behind that rises a low curtain of mesquite. In the distance you see a buck—just a glint off its antlers but they must have been good-sized for you to see them at all—running through the trees. You're watching the buck and not thinking of the birds. Your guide jerks you back to the present with one word: "birds." Birds may be quail, pheasant or chukar, as is your choice. They're all waiting just for you on your section du jour. If you've come with a group and the competitive blood is flowing, book a tower shoot and let the high gun buy the drinks. He'll love it—there's an open bar. Talk about magnanimous. Play the same game with doves in September.

Meals are far better than most hunting lodge fare and built around wild game of the region. The 6,000-square-foot modern lodge displays Spanish antecedents. Guest rooms can be configured as singles, doubles or triples, with about half featuring private baths, while the others share. A large meeting room serves business clients, and an all-weather, lighted airstrip handles corporate jets as well as other private aircraft. Los Curenos specializes in corporate hunts, but you don't have to be doing business while you're hunting.

The Nueces River valley is sparsely populated and relatively little changed from the days when the first settlers moved into the region. It's not hard to imagine Mexicans riding north to the Alamo, or Indian towns along the life-giving river. Today, whitetails of Boone & Crockett stature haunt this area, as do black buck antelope, axis deer, feral hogs and turkey. Combination hunts can easily be arranged.

Mariposa Ranch-SK Corporation

Falfurrias, Texas

Some of the finest pointers in the world nail quail at Mariposa.

VITAL STATISTICS:

GAME BIRDS:
DOVE, QUAIL, TURKEY
Source of Birds: Wild
Seasons:
DOVE: mid-September through early November; late December through early January
QUAIL: November through February
TURKEY: mid-April through mid-May
Land: 45,000 private acres
Accommodations:
FOUR CHARMING HOUSES
NUMBER OF ROOMS: 30
MAXIMUM NUMBER OF HUNTERS: 30
Meals: Excellent regional cuisine
Conference Groups: Yes
Guides: Trained dogs and guides
Dogs and Facilities:
Kennel facilities can be arranged if need be
Shotgun Sports:
Five-stand
Other Services:
Birds cleaned and packed for travel
Other Activities:
Big game, fishing, golf, wildlife photography
Rates:
DOVE: from $750 / 2 days
QUAIL: from $3200 / 3 days
Gratuity:
Hunter's discretion
Preferred Payment:
Cash or check
Getting There:
Fly to Corpus Christi and rent a car.

Contact:
Danny Sullivan
Mariposa Ranch-SK Corporation
Rt. 1, Box 33
Falfurrias TX 78355
512/325-5752
Fx: 512/325-5827
Off season:
1000 N. Station
Port Aransas TX 78373
512/749-2926
Fax: 512/749-2927
EMAIL: whytmarlin@hotmail.com

WHEN YOU'RE TALKING ABOUT bird dogs, Rick Smith's name generally enters the conversation. His kennels in Pleasonton produce some of the finest pointers, setters and Brittanies in the world; his seminars help us anticipate what our dogs are about to do (and how to use that to our advantage during a hunt); and his bird hunting savvy has revolutionized the sport. He was among the first to design the welded aluminum dog boxes with benches that fit in the bed of a one-ton four-by-four pickup. That device allows hunters to ride atop the truck, savoring the desert panorama, while dogs hunt at a field trial pace. The action is fast, constant, and very, very productive.

Rick's the hunt master at Mariposa, and he runs about 85 digs on this 45,000-acre spread about 80 miles southwest of Corpus Christi. "Flat" describes this countryside of brush, buffalo grass, cactus and goatweed. Studded with occasional mesquite trees, the land is described by some as resembling the Serengeti. It is quail country. Danny Sullivan, whose family has owned the ranch for more than a century, manages the property for quail. Cattle keep cover grazed to manageable levels. Roads are grained to concentrate wild birds for relatively easy access. Generally, two hunters, but sometimes four, ride Mariposa quail rigs over the arid grassland; only two guns work each point. The hunting here is simply legendary.

While quail hunting dominates the ranch's schedule, dove hunting around water tanks can be very exciting. Shotgunners in the know try to schedule quail hunts in early November, when the doves are flying. Bobwhite in the morning, maybe a few more after lunch, then dove as the sun sets over a water hole. The ranch also offers deer, turkey and javelina.

Packages generally begin with an afternoon hunt on the day of your arrival, followed by a full day, and conclude with a hunt the morning of the day you depart. Guests stay in homes on the ranch with 12, 8, 6 or 4 bedrooms. You and your group will have a house all to yourselves. Parties will not be mixed without prior consent. And, as you'd expect with this operation, meals and service are absolutely first class. Most guests do not bring their own dogs to Mariposa; they'd rather see Rick practice what he preaches.

[S O U T H]

Possum Walk Shooting Preserve

H u n t s v i l l e ,   T e x a s

A fine Texas ranch where folks like you and me can afford to hunt.

VITAL STATISTICS:

GAME BIRDS:
CHUKAR, DOVE, PHEASANT, QUAIL
Source of Birds: Wild and pen-reared
Seasons:
DOVE: September through mid-October
PRESERVE BIRDS: mid-October through mid-March
Land: 1,350 private acres
Accommodations:
CAMP OR STAY IN NEARBY TOWN
Meals: Restaurants in town
Conference Groups: Yes
Guides: Trained dogs and guides
Dogs and Facilities:
Kennel for hunters' dogs, dog training
Shotgun Sports:
Five-stand, shooting schools, skeet, sporting clays, tower or release shoots, trap
Other Services:
Birds cleaned and packed for travel
Other Activities:
Big game, bird-watching, fishing, wildlife photography
Rates:
From $125 / gun
Gratuity:
Hunter's discretion
Preferred Payment:
Cash or check
Getting There:
It's about an hour drive north of Houston.

Contact:
Buddy Smith
Possum Walk Shooting Preserve
10 Bowden Rd
Huntsville TX 77340
409/291-1891

"**B**IRD HUNTIN'," Buddy Smith drawls, "was gettin' hard to come by for poor folks. 'Less you're a lawyer or an oil man, there weren't much place to shoot. So this is a preserve for bird hunters." That about sums up Possum Walk, 1,350 acres an hour or so north of Houston on the Dallas highway.

Buddy's a cattleman. And he'll be the first to tell you that raising beef and quail aren't supposed to go well together. But he figured out a way to restore wild native grasses by rotating his grazing more efficiently, and thus he created cover and feed for quail. You'll like it. The preserve is right on the line between Texas' piney woods and rolling plains. Oak trees and pine intermingle. In open fields, he's planted feed and cover strips. Along with bobwhite, you'll hunt pheasant and chukar. While east Texas isn't known for its dove hunting, the opening days of the season can be pretty good here.

Half of the hunt is working with a pointer or setter. Buddy makes no bones about it: dogs that only hunt preserve birds get lazy. So off and on during the season he takes his dogs south to hunt wild quail. And he encourages his guides to do likewise. While hunting on this preserve is all on foot, he likes his dogs to be of "Jeep huntin' quality." Many who hunt this preserve bring their own dogs.

Regulation skeet, trap and sporting clays are shot here as is a crazy game that Buddy calls five-stand dove tower. Hunters take stands under trees. Tower-mounted traps send birds past the branches just like flights of dove. No better way to practice for the season can be found.

Now, nobody is going to fly half way across the country to hunt at Possum Walk—though it's not a bad idea. More likely, hunters with business in Houston may drive up for an afternoon's shoot. Overnight accommodations are available through a nearby bed-and-breakfast. Campers will enjoy parking their rigs beneath the old pecan trees along the spring-fed creek that flows through the property. That gets my vote.

Texas Wings Sporting Charters

Austin, Texas

This mobile lodge finds birds, no matter where they've gone.

VITAL STATISTICS:

GAME BIRDS:
DOVE, QUAIL, TURKEY
Source of Birds: Wild
Seasons:
DOVE: September
QUAIL: November through February
TURKEY: April
Land: 60,000 private acres
Accommodations:
MOBILE LODGE
NUMBER OF ROOMS: 2
MAXIMUM NUMBER OF HUNTERS: 6
Meals: Tex/Mex, game
Conference Groups: No
Guides: Trained dogs and guides
Dogs and Facilities:
No facilities for hunter's dogs
Other Services:
Birds cleaned and packed for travel
Rates:
From $1,100 / gun / minimum 3 hunters
Gratuity:
5% to 10%
Preferred Payment:
Cash, MasterCard, Visa or check
Getting There:
Fly to Abilene/San Antonio and rent a car.

Contact:
Tosh Brown
Texas Wings Sporting Charters
PO Box 160818
Austin TX 78716
800/448-8994
Fax: 512/347-8339
EMAIL: Tosh@texwing.com
WEB: www.texwing.com

WHAT IT BOILS DOWN TO IS THIS: Sometimes the birds are where you ain't. You can't count on them being in the same place year after year, no matter how well you manage it. Some years will be better than others. The best bird hunting is often found in locales that haven't ever seen a habitable dwelling, let alone anything so posh as to be called a lodge. But leave it to Tosh Brown, colonel of Texas Wings, to come up with a better idea.

He simply moves his lodge to where the birds are best. We're not talking pup tents here, nor those heavy canvas jobs loved by the packhorse crowd. A pair of 33-foot office trailers configured into two bedrooms for a maximum of six hunters provides accommodations. A weatherport tent of the type favored by Alaskan bush operations serves as the kitchen, where a chef turns out near-gourmet dinners with a regional theme. All facilities are air conditioned, and you'll find cell phones and satellite television if you can't bear to be out of touch for a few days running.

Tosh spends most of his time prowling some 60,000 acres in northwest Texas, that lovely land of mesquite, cats-claw and thick tawny grasses where wild quail abound. Hills rise clear up the plain, then drop down again as incipient ravines give way to cracks in the rock which, with little prodding, seem to become canyons before you walk a dozen paces. It is a land of things that will stick you and sting you, but you don't care one iota. There are birds in these hills. Sometimes they're found in the cover beside seismic roads that have been "grained." But just as often, they're off in the brush or a field of sunflowers or wheat, and finding them is up to the dogs.

Of those, there are a plenty. More than two dozen pointers spend their days nose to the ground, nailing coveys left and right. A brace of Labs pull stand-by duty, handling retrieves and flushing birds when the need arises. Four-by-fours have been retrofitted as quail buggies. But with this outfitter, you'll spend a lot of time on foot, hunting behind the dogs, unless you feel compelled to ride the buggy. Normally, one party books this operation at a time; however, on those rare occasions when vacancies exist, Tosh will book singles and pairs. In either event, it's a good idea to get your name on the list early. Personal hunts of this quality are in high demand. Don't overlook doves in September and turkey in the delightful month of April.

[S O U T H]

Falkland Farms

S c o t t s b u r g ,   V i r g i n i a

One of the oldest shooting lodges in the South and a fine place for turkey, ducks and quail.

VITAL STATISTICS:

GAME BIRDS:
QUAIL, DUCKS, TURKEY
Source of Birds: Wild and pen-reared
Seasons:
QUAIL: September through April
DUCKS: November through January
TURKEY: mid-April through May
Land: 7,600 private acres
Accommodations:
CIRCA 1920S LODGE
NUMBER OF ROOMS: 7
MAXIMUM NUMBER OF HUNTERS: 14
Meals: Country and hearty
Conference Groups: Yes
Guides: Trained dogs and guides
Dogs and Facilities:
Kennel for hunters' dogs, dog training
Shotgun Sports:
Sporting clays
Other Services:
Birds cleaned and packed for travel
Other Activities:
Big game, fishing, horseback riding
Rates:
From $175 / gun / half-day; lodging and meals $80 / night for two
Gratuity:
Hunter's discretion
Preferred Payment:
Cash, MasterCard or check
Getting There:
Fly to Raleigh/Durham, NC, and rent a car.

Contact:
Thomas Rowland
Falkland Farms
1003 Falkland Landing
Scottsburg VA 24589
804/575-1400
Fax: 804/575-1400
EMAIL: falkland@halifax.com
WEB: www.shootingsports.com

PERHAPS THE LARGEST PRIVATE ESTATE in the East managed for bird and deer hunting is found in southern Virginia near the North Carolina border. With more than 7,600 acres, you never feel crowded here. The lodge, which was heavily remodeled in the 1920s (and recently updated), carries with it a vintage classic charm. Wide brick steps lead up to the long low porch that surrounds three sides of the lodge. A double-doored foyer takes you into a parlor where the Great Gatsby (had Fitzgerald made him a hunter) would have been quite at home. Mounts of Virginia whitetails taken on the farm grace the walls along with pictures of men in coats and ties, side-by-sides open over crooked arms, displaying turkey also from the plantation. Duck hunting was (and is) big here, too. And so, of course, are quail.

Scores of fields of Falkand Farms are managed for quail. You'll encounter coveys of native birds in food plots planted for deer and turkey. They thrive in fallow fields of broomsedge and along fencerows thick with honeysuckle and weed. You'll find them in the edges along streams and, once in a while, in woods that were recently clear-cut. How you hunt them is up to you. Bring your own pointer or setter if that's what turns you on. Or opt for one of Falkland's fine German shorthairs. In any event, you'll need a guide.

Seven miles of the Bannister and Dan rivers border the southern margins of the plantation. Between the junction of the two lies acres and acres of flooded timber. Wood duck hunting is outstanding early in the season, and then the parade of puddle ducks marches through as the season progresses. Swamps, small flowages and ponds on the farm itself provide additional opportunities. Often, guests will hunt ducks before breakfast and turn to quail afterwards. Deer hunting with shotguns and beagles in southside Virginia style is highly popular here. At times, it's possible to combine all three.

Come spring, the forests on Falkland resound with gobbling toms. Guides will position you so you'll have a clear shot and then will call in birds if you don't or can't do it yourself. Most gunners who book three-day hunts are successful.

FFF Kennels Hunting Preserve

Keysville, Virginia

Hunt quail and pheasant on lands hallowed by General Lee's great army.

VITAL STATISTICS:

GAME BIRDS:
CHUKAR, DUCKS, PHEASANT, QUAIL, TURKEY

Source of Birds: Wild and pen-reared

Seasons:
PRESERVE BIRDS: September through April
TURKEY: mid-April through mid-May

Land: 2,000 private acres

Accommodations:
REMODELED HOME
NUMBER OF ROOMS: 6
MAXIMUM NUMBER OF HUNTERS: 16

Meals: On special request

Conference Groups: Yes

Guides: Trained dogs and guides

Dogs and Facilities:
Kennel for hunters' dogs

Shotgun Sports:
Five-stand, tower or release shoots

Other Services:
Birds cleaned and packed for travel

Other Activities:
Big game, biking, bird-watching, boating, fishing, hiking, wildlife photography

Rates:
($25 / night

Gratuity:
Hunter's discretion

Preferred Payment:
Cash, MasterCard, Visa or check

Getting There:
Fly to Richmond and rent a car.

Contact:
Bill Hall
FFF Kennels Hunting Preserve
1975 Hwy 59
Keysville VA 23947
800/643-2606
Fax: 804/568-4017

DRIVING SOUTHWEST ON U.S. 360 toward Keysville from Richmond soon delivers you from the suburban sprawl. Strip malls and housing developments quickly give way to farms and pastures and second-growth woods. Your route crosses the axis of those last battles of the Civil War, when remnants of Lee's once great army made its desperate dash for the sanctuary beyond the Blue Ridge, only to be hounded to ground by Grant's well-supplied corps. Appomattox Courthouse is but 50 miles west of here. If you haven't yet, it's well worth a visit and a moment's contemplation on man's civility to man.

When you reach Keysville, you'll head south on State Route 59. The land here is rippled like a wind-blown sea. Fingers of little creeks probe the woods, which are harvested for pulp and chipboard. Small farms, once able to support families but not any longer, prevail. This is excellent habitat for quail, and a few native coveys are struggling to make a comeback. Wild bird hunting, however, is very limited.

That's why hunters make the trek to FFF Kennels and Hunting Preserve. Bill Hall, owner and breeder of setters, is a bird hunter. He needed a place to work his dogs. One thing, you know, kind of leads to another. Now he's managing 2,000 acres of mixed field and forest for bobwhite, pheasants and chukar. Meadows, overgrown with broomsedge and grains, are surrounded by stands of second growth. Winters are mild here and the cover holds up throughout the eight-month preserve season. Flighted mallards are released in the woods and sail toward a trio of ponds on the preserve. Bring and hunt your own dogs or use Bill's to retrieve your birds. Five-stand sporting clays is also shot here, and gobblers are hunted in spring.

A farmhouse on the preserve has been remodeled into a comfortable lodge. Six bedrooms with bunk beds provide overnight stays at a price that's hard to beat. Meals are not included, but if you want, they can be arranged.

Oak Ridge Estate

A r r i n g t o n ,   V i r g i n i a

An up and coming resort with a great staff in the wild lands south of Charlottesville.

VITAL STATISTICS:

GAME BIRDS:
DOVE, PHEASANT, QUAIL, TURKEY
Source of Birds: Wild and pen-reared
Seasons:
DOVE: September
UPLAND BIRDS: September through March
TURKEY: mid-April to mid-May
Land: 5,000 private acres
Accommodations:
SUBSTANTIAL BRICKHOUSE
NUMBER OF ROOMS: 5
MAXIMUM NUMBER OF HUNTERS: 10
Meals: Prepared by a skilled chef
Conference Groups: Yes
Guides: Trained dogs and guides
Dogs and Facilities:
Kennel for hunters' dogs
Shotgun Sports:
Driven birds
Other Services:
Birds cleaned and packed for travel
Other Activities:
Big game, biking, bird-watching, hiking, horseback riding, wildlife photography
Rates:
From $150 / gun for a full day; lodging and breakfast $50
Gratuity:
Hunter's discretion
Preferred Payment:
Cash or check
Getting There:
Fly to Charlottesville or Lynchburg and rent a car.

Contact:
Fred Clarkson
Oak Ridge Estate
2300 Oak Ridge Road
Arrington VA 22922
804/263-6695
Fax: 804/263-4168
EMAIL: oakrdg802@aol.com
WEB: www.sfi-sta.com/oakridge

WHAT DOES IT TAKE to make a great bird hunting lodge? Birds, certainly, and in this case quail and pheasant as well as doves and turkey; great guides and highly trained dogs; a place to stay and meals that reflect an ambience that matches the personality of the hunter; and finally, service—that all-too-seldom-found spirit of can-do accommodation. Oak Ridge gets high marks in all of these categories.

Let's start with the hunting, and that means with Fred Clarkson. He's a quiet, easy-going fellow who has spent 30 years hunting Nelson County. Some people take sheer delight in what they do, and Fred is one of those. You can tell it from the way his eyes twinkle when he talks about his program to raise pheasants and quail, and the feed plots he plants for deer, turkey, quail and doves. He loves to tell stories on himself, but you'll never hear him tell you a disparaging story about another client. Like the bobwhite he raises, Mr. Clarkson is a gentleman.

Oak Ridge covers some 5,000 acres in the foothill mountains between Charlottesville and Lynchburg. Of that, about 500 acres are set aside in eight fields planted with clover, switchgrass, lespedeza, sorghum and millet. Another pair of fields are rimmed with sunflowers and managed for dove. Dense stands of pine, open hardwood forests, and swamps along streams offer additional habitat favored by wild turkey. A new eight-point or better management policy is resulting in more bucks of bragging quality. Duck hunting is somewhat limited, but a hunt for resident geese (considered pests by local farmers) is under consideration.

Oak Ridge was carved out of wild western Virginia in the days immediately following the American Revolution. Bought around the turn of the last century by Thomas F. Ryan—a local boy who became one of the wealthiest men in America—the original estate was remodeled into an Italianate mansion, complete with its own railroad station, "crystal palace" greenhouse, vast stone dairy barns (where birds are now raised), and a number of other historic outbuildings. Guests reside in the former home of the farm manager. This house, more befitting the president of a local bank than a farmer, includes five bedrooms, four with private baths. A full commercial kitchen can prepare gourmet meals or simple and quick snacks for hunters on the go. So vast is the estate that you'll never see another hunter. When you and your group arrive, it's as if you own the place.

Primland Resort

Meadows of Dan, Virginia

You and your party reside in a house that overlooks thousands of foothills and scores of plots managed for pheasant and quail.

VITAL STATISTICS:

GAME BIRDS:
CHUKAR, DUCKS, PHEASANT, QUAIL
Source of Birds: Pen-reared
Seasons:
September through April
Land: 14,000 private acres
Accommodations:
PRIVATE VACATION HOMES
NUMBER OF ROOMS: VARIES FROM 2 UP
MAXIMUM NUMBER OF HUNTERS: 24
Meals: Fine restaurant fare or self-catered
Conference Groups: Yes
Guides: Trained dogs and guides
Dogs and Facilities:
Kennel for hunters' dogs
Shotgun Sports:
Driven birds, five-stand, sporting clays, tower or release shoots
Other Services:
Birds cleaned and packed for travel, proshop
Other Activities:
Big game, biking, bird-watching, fishing, hiking, horseback riding, tennis, wildlife photography
Rates:
From $300 / gun;
accommodations from $90 / night
Gratuity:
Hunter's discretion
Preferred Payment:
Cash, MasterCard, Visa or check
Getting There:
Fly to Greensboro, NC, and rent a car, or arrange for the lodge van to collect you for $50.

Contact:
Stephen G. Helms
Primland Resort
4621 Busted Rock Rd.
Meadows of Dan VA 24120
540/251-8012
Fax: 540/251-8244
EMAIL: primland@swva.net
WEB: www.primland.com

VIRGINIA'S SPINE KISSES 5,000 feet as it runs the length of the Blue Ridge from Front Royal to the North Carolina line. Off to the west is the Shenandoah Valley. To the east is a tortured land of low ridges and foothills that fade into the coastal plain. On both sides of the Blue Ridge, early settlers of Scotch-Irish extraction tried to wrest a living from hardscrabble farms nestled in tight valleys between steep slopes forested with oak, hickory, maple and sweet gum. Corn, hogs and cattle were the cash crops, and tobacco too. After a while, even subsistence was impossible, so thin was the soil. Eventually, timber companies bought up vast tracts, stripped the forest and moved on. Developers followed, but their success was limited. The hills east of the Blue Ridge are remote, yet not enough to draw the East Coast equivalent of Montana's California crowd.

All that bodes well for Primland, a 14,000-acre estate that's managed mainly for upland birds and deer. Feed plots of milo and sorghum are planted every spring for pheasants, chukar and quail. Like many of the better western preserves, birds are stocked throughout the season, not just before your hunt. As a result, these birds flush and fly as if they were born and raised here. European driven bird shoots are mounted in classic style at Primland. Gunners and loaders are stationed at points downhill from covers through which the beaters work. After each section is covered, gunners move on to new territory via horse-drawn wagon. A pair of ponds (stocked with bass) provide a venue for released mallard shooting. Gobbler hunting is available in the spring. The sporting clays course is always among the top courses in the country, and five-stand is also shot here. Primland maintains a kennel of 30 or more pointers, setters, shorthairs, Brittanies and Labs. Take your pick or bring your own.

Orvis endorsed, Primland is one of a network of international resorts; its sibling lodges include Luttrellstown Castle on the East Coast of Ireland and Domaine des Etangs near the Cognac region of France. As you'd expect, accommodations at Primland are first class. Guests reside in cottages, many of which were built as vacation homes. Meals are served in a restaurant or you may prepare your own.

Prospect Hall

K e a r n e y s v i l l e ,   W e s t   V i r g i n i a

Clays, birds and lodging, all less than two hours from Washington, D.C.

WHEN YOU THINK OF West Virginia, high and heavily forested mountains come to mind. Your vision fills with grouse and whitetails, and you're not wrong at all. But there's another West Virginia, a tail of land that swallows the point of land where the Shenandoah and Potomac rivers meet at Harper's Ferry.

This is rolling limestone countryside, open and cropped with fields of corn, wheat and beans. Here and there are isolated coveys of wild bobwhite, but, alas, quail are not prevalent enough for the prudent gunner to hunt. It is in this neck of the woods, on Opequon Creek, that Prospect Hall has established one of the finest preserves in the mid-Atlantic states.

Prospect Hall's 500 acres include varying terrain. Fields groomed for pheasant, chukar and Hungarian partridge flank the long gravel lane. Clumps of red cedar, patches of honeysuckle-entwined briars, and overgrown fencerows provide cover as do plots of milo, millet, corn and sorghum. Springers and English pointers do the work here; all you have to do is swing through the bird.

Tower shoots are immensely popular. Gunners line the base of a bluff that rises 100 feet above the floodplain. Atop the bluff rises a 50-foot tower. Pheasants are released from the tower and they sail down over the heads of the shooters, headed for the fields beyond. Shooting is fast and, well, frustrating. The club's 24-station sporting clays course rims the top of the bluff offering exceptionally challenging sport. Crazy quail, trap and skeet are also shot here.

Overnight guests are quartered in comfortable rooms in a white-columned mansion that dates from 1803. A nearby house contains fully modern conference facilities with full data connections for computers, a fax machine and copier. Lena's fried chicken and country fried steak are not to be missed. A membership club—initiation runs $2,500 and dues are $1,500 annually—Prospect Hall will host shooters who are potentially interested in membership at rates that are highly competitive.

VITAL STATISTICS:

GAME BIRDS:
CHUKAR, HUNGARIAN PARTRIDGE, PHEASANT
Source of Birds: Pen-reared
Seasons:
UPLAND BIRDS: September through April
Land: 500 private acres
Accommodations:
HISTORIC AND UPDATED FARMHOUSE
NUMBER OF ROOMS: 9
MAXIMUM NUMBER OF HUNTERS: 21
Meals: Fine southern cooking with a twist
Conference Groups: Yes
Guides: Trained dogs and guides
Dogs and Facilities:
Kennel for hunters' dogs
Shotgun Sports:
Skeet, sporting clays, tower or release shoots, trap
Other Services:
Birds cleaned and packed for travel, pro shop
Other Activities:
Big game, bird-watching, canoeing, fishing, golf, hiking
Rates:
Hunts from $100; lodging from $75 / night (advance reservation only)
Gratuity:
Hunter's discretion
Preferred Payment:
Cash, MasterCard, Visa or check
Getting There:
Fly to Dulles and rent a car.

Contact:
Matt Lohmann
Prospect Hall
Rt. 1, Box 370
Kearneysville WV 25430
304/728-8213
Fax: 304/725-3913
WEB: www.prospecthall.com

The Greenbrier Wingshooting Preserve

White Sulphur Springs, West Virginia

The great sporting traditions of the southern Appalachians and one of the finest resorts in North America merge here.

VITAL STATISTICS:

GAME BIRDS:
CHUKAR, GROUSE, PHEASANT, QUAIL, TURKEY

Source of Birds: Wild and pen-reared

Seasons:
CHUKAR, QUAIL, PHEASANT: September through March
RUFFED GROUSE: mid-October through February
TURKEY: late April through late May

Land: 3,000 private acres

Accommodations:
GRAND HISTORIC RESORT HOTEL
NUMBER OF ROOMS: 750
MAXIMUM NUMBER OF HUNTERS: 16

Meals: Elegant

Conference Groups: Yes

Guides: Trained dogs and guides

Dogs and Facilities:
Bring your own kennel

Shotgun Sports:
Five-stand, skeet, trap

Other Services:
Birds cleaned and packed for travel, pro shop

Other Activities:
Big game, biking, bird-watching, fishing, golf, hiking, horseback riding, tennis, wildlife photography

Rates:
Rooms from $558 / double occupancy; hunts from $225 / gun

Gratuity:
15%

Preferred Payment:
Cash, credit card or check

Getting There:
Fly to Greenbrier Valley/Lewisburg and rent a car.

Contact:
Neal Roth
The Greenbrier Wingshooting Preserve
300 West Main St
White Sulphur Springs WV 24986
304/536-1110
Fax: 304/536-7854
WEB: www.greenbrier.com

FOUNDED AS A SMALL COUNTRY INN before the close of the Revolutionary War and extensively expanded before the conflict that created the state of West Virginia, the Greenbrier has been a popular resort longer than the U.S. has been a country. Tourists first came to take the waters of the sulphur springs here, thought then to have special therapeutic powers. The Chesapeake & Ohio—now CSX—bought the hotel in 1910, back in the heyday of grand resorts that the railroads constructed to promote tourism (and passengers for their coaches).

Today, the Greenbrier tops everyone's list of fine resorts. It's earned Mobil Five-Star and AAA Five-Diamond rankings. Conde Nast readers rated the Greenbrier as the top resort destination in North America. As publicly adored as the resort is, the Greenbrier also has a secret side. At the height of the cold war, a massive underground bunker was added to house members of Congress in the event of a nuclear attack on Washington, D.C., three hours to the east and north.

When it comes to sports, most folks link the Greenbrier with golf, thanks to the Jack Nicklaus-designed course opened in 1979. But on 3,000 acres along Howard Creek is one of the finest upland game preserves in the nation. The preserve offers traditional hunts for pheasant, quail and chukar from September through April. Wild game includes ruffed grouse from mid-October to the end of February, and turkey from mid-April to late May. Deer, too, can be hunted by bow and muzzleloader. Staff at the Greenbrier will provide everything you need—you can even rent a pair of boots if you've managed to arrive without your own. Rates run about $225 for half-day upland bird hunts. The fee includes a guide and dog, but kennel facilities for visitor's dogs are not available. Bring your own.

At the Greenbrier's gun club, you'll have your pick of trap, skeet and five-stand courses. Informal instruction is available. Anglers will enjoy fly-fishing on the resort's private ponds and stream mileage.

MIDWEST

ARKANSAS, ILLINOIS, INDIANA, IOWA, KANSAS, MICHIGAN, MINNESOTA, MISSOURI, NEBRASKA, NORTH DAKOTA, OHIO, OKLAHOMA, SOUTH DAKOTA, WISCONSIN

THE PRAIRIE really begins in central Ohio and stretches west into Colorado. To the north in this region, glaciers depressed the land and left it damp on their retreat. This, of course, is pheasant country. You know the picture: endless fields of waving grasses cut by wet-weather sloughs grown thick with scrub brush. Along with pheasant, you'll find prairie chicken, sharptail grouse and Hungarian partridge. The farther south you head, the greater your chances of bumping into coveys of native quail.

Great rivers and their oxbows and cutoffs, as well as huge marshes and kettle ponds—another reminder of continental glaciers—are magnets for ducks migrating south on the Mississippi and Central flyways. Everybody waits for the first flocks of those big mallards from Canada, but makes do on woodies, teal, canvasbacks, wigeon, gadwall and you name it until they arrive. Goose

Arkansas
1 BAYOU METO LODGE
2 BLACK DOG HUNTING CLUB
3 QUAIL MOUNTAIN ENTERPRISES
4 TWIN RIVERS GUIDE SERVICE

Iowa
5 K-BAR-C HUNTING PRESERVE
6 OAKVIEW II HUNTING CLUB
7 TRIPLE H RANCH
8 WINTERSET HUNT CLUB AND LODGE

Kansas
9 BEAVER CREEK OUTFITTERS
10 FLINT OAK
11 JAYHAWK OUTFITTING
12 LaSADA HUNTING SERVICE
13 LIL' TOLEDO LODGE
14 RINGNECK RANCH INC
15 SHOW-ME BIRD HUNTING RESORT

Michigan
16 HUNTER'S RIDGE HUNT CLUB
17 WOODMOOR RESORT

Minnesota
18 CARIBOU GUN CLUB SHOOTING RESERVE
19 ELK LAKE HERITAGE PRESERVE
20 McCOLLUM'S HUNTING PRESERVE
21 MINNESOTA HORSE & HUNT CLUB
22 TRAXLER'S HUNTING PRESERVE

43 46 58 67

64 57

54 66

NORTH DAKOTA

31

32 33

MINNESOTA

23

20

19 24 25

WISCONSIN

17

MICHIGAN

47 62 68

SOUTH DAKOTA

60

53

21

71 69

18

22

51

70

48 61

44

59 56

55

65

63

16

52

IOWA

34 36

NEBRASKA

29

37

45 49 50

30 28

6

8

5

7

ILLINOIS INDIANA

OHIO

9

27

35

11 14 12

KANSAS

10

13

26

MISSOURI

15

42

40 39 38

3

OKLAHOMA

4

41

ARKANSAS

2 1

23 Voyageur Sportsman's Paradise
24 Wild Acres Hunting Club
25 Wings North

Missouri

26 Big River Hunting Club
& Kennels
27 Heartland Wildlife Ranches

Nebraska

28 Comstalk Hunting Club
29 K-D Hunting acres
30 Sandhills Adventures/Uncle
Buck's Lodge

North Dakota

31 Cannonball Company
32 Oak Lodge

33 Sheldon's Waterfowl &
Upland Bird Hunts

Ohio

34 Brier Oak Hunting Club
35 Hidden Haven Shooting
Preserve
36 Hill 'n Dale Club Inc
37 WR Hunt Club

Oklahoma

38 Bird-N-Buck Outfitters
39 Red Rock Ranch
40 Southern Ranch Hunting Club
41 Triple H Ranch &
Hunting Lodge
42 Western Cedar Co

South Dakota

43 Bass Pheasant Hunting
44 Big Bend Ranch
45 Biggins Hunting Service
46 Bob Priebe Pheasant Hunting
Country
47 Bush Ranch
48 Circle CE Ranch
49 Circle H Ranch
50 Cocks Unlimited
51 Dakota Dream Hutnts Inc
52 Dakota Hills Private Shooting
Preserve
53 Dakota Hunting Farm
54 Dakota Ridge
55 Don Reeves Pheasant Ranch
56 Forester Ranches
57 Great Plains Hunting
58 High Brass Inc
59 Medicine Creek Pheasant
Ranch Inc
60 Paul Nelson Farm
61 P&R Hunting Lodge
62 River View Lodge

hunting in the Missouri drainage and around Rochester, Minnesota, can be excellent.

So too is gunning for grouse and woodcock in the cutover forests of states whose northern lands border the Great Lakes. Perhaps the best ruffed grouse hunting in the U.S. is to be had in northern Michigan and Wisconsin, though Maine's woodland expanses—and the lack of hunting pressure there—would give it a run for its money.

Preserve hunts are a way of life in the Midwest, and you can find one within an hour's drive of most cities.

References:

WINGSHOOTER'S GUIDE TO IOWA
by *Larry Brown*

WINGSHOOTER'S GUIDE TO KANSAS
by *Web Parton*

WINGSHOOTER'S GUIDE TO
NORTH DAKOTA
by *Chuck Johnson*

WINGSHOOTER'S GUIDE TO
SOUTH DAKOTA
by *Ben O. Williams and Chuck Johnson*

WESTERN WINGS: HUNTING UPLAND
BIRDS ON THE NORTHERN PLAINS
by *Ben Williams and Russell Chatham*
(Illustrator)

ALL WILDERNESS ADVENTURE PRESS
800/925-3339

Resources:

ARKANSAS GAME AND FISH
COMMISSION
Information Section
2 Natural Resources Dr.
Little Rock, AR 72205
501/223-6300
800/364-4263 ext. 6351
web: www.agfc.state.ar.us

ILLINOIS DEPARTMENT OF
NATURAL RESOURCES
Lincoln Tower Plaza
524 S. Second St
Springfield, IL 62701-1787
217/785-0067
web: http://dnr.state.il.us

INDIANA DIVISION OF FISH
AND WILDLIFE
402 W. Washington St., Room W-273
Indianapolis, IN 46204
317/232-4080
web:
www.dnr.state.in.us/fishwild/index.html

IOWA DEPARTMENT OF
NATURAL RESOURCES
Wallace State Office Building
East Ninth and Grand Ave
Des Moines, IA 50319
515/281-5145
web: www.state.ia.us/wildlife

KANSAS DEPARTMENT OF
WILDLIFE AND PARKS
900 SW Jackson St., Suite 502
Topeka, KS 66612-1233
913/296-2281
web: www.kdwp.state.ks.us

MICHIGAN DEPARTMENT OF
NATURAL RESOURCES
Wildlife Division
Box 30444
Lansing, MI 48909
517/373-1263
web: www.dnr.state.mi.us

MINNESOTA DEPARTMENT OF
NATURAL RESOURCES
Division of Fish and Wildlife
500 Lafayette St
St. Paul, MN 55155-4001
612/297-1308
web: www.dnr.state.mn.us/

MISSOURI DEPARTMENT
OF CONSERVATION
2901 W. Truman Blvd., Box 180
Jefferson City, MO 65102-0180
573/751-4115
web: www.conservation.state.mo.us

NEBRASKA GAME AND
PARKS COMMISSION
2200 N. 33rd St., Box 30370
Lincoln, NE 68503
402/471-0641
web: www.npgc.state.ne.us

NORTH DAKOTA STATE GAME
AND FISH DEPARTMENT
100 North Bismarck Expy
Bismarck, ND 58501
701/328-6300
web: www.state.nd.us/gnf/

OHIO DIVISION OF WILDLIFE
1840 Belcher Dr
Columbus, OH 43224-1329
614/265-6300
web: www.dnr.state.oh.us/odnr/wildlife

OKLAHOMA DEPARTMENT OF
WILDLIFE CONSERVATION
1801 N. Lincoln
Box 53465
Oklahoma City, OK 73152
405/521-3851
web: www.state.ok.us/~odwc

SOUTH DAKOTA DEPARTMENT OF
GAME, FISH AND PARKS
523 E. Capitol
Pierre, SD 57501-3182
605/773-3387
web:
www.state.sd.us/state/gfp/index.html

WISCONSIN DEPARTMENT OF
NATURAL RESORUCES
PO Box 7921
Madison WI 53707
608/266-2121
web: www.dnr.state.wi.us

Bayou Meto Lodge

H u m p h r e y ,   A r k a n s a s

All you need to do is follow the guide's suggestions and shoot straight.

VITAL STATISTICS:

GAME BIRDS:
DUCKS, GEESE
Source of Birds: Wild
Seasons:
WATERFOWL: Mid-November through mid-January
Land: 1200 private acres
Accommodations:
MODERN, YET RUSTIC LODGE
NUMBER OF ROOMS: 11
MAXIMUM NUMBER OF HUNTERS: 10
Meals: Family. country cooking
Conference Groups: Yes
Guides: Guides and retrievers provided
Shotgun Sports:
Sporting clays
Other Services:
Birds cleaned and packed for travel
Rates:
$275 / day
Gratuity:
20%
Preferred Payment:
Cash or check
Getting There:
Fly to Little Rock and rent a car.

Contact:
Ronnie Hall
Bayou Meto Lodge
PO Box 98
Humphrey AR 72073
870/873-4815
Off Season:
14 Meadowview Circle
Cartersville GA 30121
770/386-0413
EMAIL: rhall5034@aol.com

I T WAS PITCH BLACK when you climbed into the johnboat at the landing and headed out into the marsh. Soon it gave way to timber. Overcast skies hid the stars and any moonlight, and the glow from nearby Humphrey simply wasn't enough to cut the dark. Yet your guide seemed to know where he was going. The boat glided through sloughs and around bends, and didn't hit anything in the process.

"We'll wait here," he said, shutting down the motor. And you sat in stillness so deep it lay on your face like a velvet mask. You did not know why the guide paused, other than that you must be somewhere near the hunting area. Then, as your pupils finished dilating fully, you could make out the shapes of the oaks standing in the water. "Why don't you lean against that tree," he suggested, pointing to a shape that looked like a water tower and seemed almost as tall. "Me and the dog'll set-up over there." Your offer to help with the decoys was politely turned down, and you understood: he had his own plan in mind and it was quicker and quieter if he put them out himself. It was only a dozen, and it wouldn't take long. Besides, you told yourself, "the less wading I do, the less apt I am to take a spill."

Effortlessly, the guide placed the blocks in a little opening. Then he, too, retreated to the shallows. You heard the whispered command to the Lab and the sound of water spilling from his coat as he climbed up onto a dry hummock in the swamp. Then came the silence, and 'fore long, the fast yet somehow heavy beat of wings. And a splash, then another and another. Four ducks were down in the decoys; you could see them moving. Too early, you knew when you peeked at your wristwatch, but it wouldn't be long.

At Bayou Meto, you'll shoot mallards, as well as gadwall, teal, pintails, wigeon and other ducks that happen to come your way. You'll hunt flooded green timber and rice fields from sunken blinds and stands among the trees. And when the ducking closes at noon, as it does in these parts, you'll stuff yourself with a hearty lunch and then battle the sleepy eyes for white-fronted, specs, snow and blue geese in fields during the afternoon. Country-style meals are served in the lodge, a large modern cypress-sided structure reminiscent of the regions century-old farmhouses. Located on the fringe of Bayou Meto, a 34,000-acre Wildlife Management Area, the lodge hunts some 1,200 private acres.

Black Dog Hunting Club

Stuttgart, Arkansas

One of the finest waterfowl clubs in the lower Midwest.

VITAL STATISTICS:

GAME BIRDS:
DUCKS and GEESE
Source of Birds: Wild
Seasons:
DUCKS: November through January
GEESE: November through March
Land: 50,000 private and public acres
Accommodations:
CABINS ADJACENT TO LODGE
NUMBER OF ROOMS: 4
MAXIMUM NUMBER OF HUNTERS: 16
Meals: Hardy meals with a regional flare
Conference Groups: Yes
Guides: Included
Dogs and Facilities:
Dog training
Other Services:
Birds cleaned and packed for travel
Other Activities:
Fishing
Rates:
$250 / day for morning hunt
Gratuity:
$25 / hunter
Preferred Payment:
Cash, MasterCard, Visa or check
Getting There:
Fly to Little Rock and rent a car.

Contact:
Todd & Gwen Brittain
Black Dog Hunting Club
PO Box 697
Stuttgart AR 72160
870/873-4673
EMAIL: blackdog@futura.net
WEB: huntarkansas.simplenet.com/blackdog

ROUGHLY 15 MILES SOUTHEAST of Little Rock, Stuttgart lies between the White and Arkansas rivers. The land is essentially flat, drained by sluggish streams that corkscrew on their way to one or the other rivers. Grain is grown here: soybeans where it's dry, and rice where it's not. Flooded timber—meaning stands of oak and cypress—abound. Further to the east are the broad bottoms of the meandering Mississippi River. If there were a better place to hunt waterfowl, nobody knows where it is. Millions of ducks and geese stream down the Mississippi flyway right into the barrels of Black Dog gunners.

You'll hunt mallards in green timber. The dog, at least, gets a stand on dry cypress. You stand in the water. Camo neoprene waders are the order of the day. In November and December, the best months for flooded timber hunting, the wind and water are cold. Dry land gunning for specs, blues and snows, as well as for mallards, pintails and teal will take you to bean fields. Type of blind is determined by which birds are working what areas. You may hunt from a pit, layouts or sleds. Set out the decoys or rely on pass-shooting, whatever your style. You'll have a look at enough bluebills to last a lifetime, as well as an infrequent can, redhead or goldeneye. And after duckin's done in January, you'll hunt extended seasons for snows.

Nobody goes home empty-handed, and the price is right reasonable. $325 per day buys morning and evening hunts along with lodging, meals, guides, dogs, and bird cleaning and packaging. The modern clubhouse spreads out below tall pines. Guest cabins for up to four hunters each are adjacent to the lodge. All baths are shared. Meals feature fine regional cuisine: catfish, duck gumbo, and barbecued steak and chicken. In business for more than a dozen years, Black Dog has made its mark by keeping parties small—seldom do more than five hunters share a blind. In the off season, owners Todd and Gwen Brittan train retrievers. They'll gladly take on your dog and occasionally have started and finished dogs for sale.

Quail Mountain Enterprises

V a n   B u r e n ,   A r k a n s a s

Quail huntin', lazy and laid back, the way it was meant to be.

VITAL STATISTICS:

GAME BIRDS:
CHUKAR, PHEASANT, QUAIL
Source of Birds: Pen-reared
Seasons:
October through March
Land: 500 private acres
Accommodations:
COUNTRY FARM HOUSE
NUMBER OF ROOMS: 2
MAXIMUM NUMBER OF HUNTERS: 6
Meals: Venison, quail, venison and chukar
Conference Groups: Yes
Guides: Trained dogs and guides
Shotgun Sports:
Informal clays
Other Activities:
Big game
Rates:
$250 / person
Gratuity:
Hunter's discretion
Preferred Payment:
Cash or check
Getting There:
Fly to Ft.Smith or Fayetteville and rent a car.

Contact:
Jerry or Gille Friddle
Quail Mountain Enterprises
811 Hynes
Van Buren AR 72956
501/474-9294
EMAIL: drathaarl@aol.com

DOWN HOME MIGHT BE the best way to describe this lodge in the Ozarks. It's the kind of place that time seems to have bypassed. Less than an hour from Fayetteville and Fort Smith, and within an easy haul of Branson, Missouri, Quail Mountains' 500 acres are well off the beaten path. Huge oaks shade the one-story white-sided farmhouse, which sits at the end of a dirt lane. Up the hill from the house is a roofed pavilion, a sort of screened house sans screen because the bugs aren't bad here, especially during bird season. Kennels for pointers and setters are nearby, tucked against the fringe of second-growth hardwoods. And the aroma from the open kitchen window is that of the preserve's trademark fried quail, venison chili or quail and dumplings.

Picture the Ozarks as a plate full of sugar cubes. The seams between the cubes have eroded into steep valleys, leaving the tops slightly rounded. Along the tops are fields of corn, milo and grasses planted to provide cover for birds. Birds here mean quail, chukar and pheasant bred and hatched in Quail Mountain's pens. For more than a decade, owners Jerry and Gille Friddle have been providing flight-conditioned game birds to dog trainers and hunting preserves in Arkansas and neighboring states.

You can hunt the Friddle's lands a couple of ways. About half of the hunters opt for a guide, dog and as many birds as their wallets will tolerate. But the other half typically bring their own dogs and take their choices of 25 quail, 12 chukar or eight pheasants for a fee of $130 for two gunners. These are half-day shoots. Full-day packages begin at $65 for guide and dog, with a per-bird fee for each quail released. A round of clays is included. Overnight packages feature a round on the clay pigeon range and your choice of quail, chukar, pheasants or a combo. Three meals and lodging run $250 per person or $900 for a group of four. In addition, Quail Mountain runs tower shoots throughout the season and will arrange them on other occasions by special request.

Twin Rivers Guide Service

Paragould, Arkansas

To be a successful duck hunter, you can't sit where the mallards ain't.

VITAL STATISTICS:

GAME BIRDS:
DUCKS
Source of Birds: Wild
Seasons:
WATERFOWL: mid-November through mid-January
Land: 3,000 private and public acres
Accommodations:
MODERN LODGE
NUMBER OF ROOMS: 4
MAXIMUM NUMBER OF HUNTERS: 16
Meals: Game, steak and fish
Conference Groups: Yes
Guides: Trained dogs and guides
Dogs and Facilities:
Kennel for hunters' dogs
Other Services:
Birds cleaned and packed for travel
Other Activities:
Big game, horseback riding
Rates:
$300 / day
Gratuity:
10%
Preferred Payment:
Cash, credit cards or check
Getting There:
Fly to Joneboro or Memphis and rent a car.

Contact:
Jerry Evans
Twin Rivers Guide Service
8143 Hwy. 34 West
Paragould AR 72450
870/586-0515
EMAIL: edwards@cswnet.com
WEB: www.arkansasduckhunt.com

IT'S HARD TO TELL which Jerry Edwards, the major domo of Twin Rivers, likes best—flying or duck hunting. During the season, he spends hour upon hour in the cockpit of a Cessna 172, looking at the patterns of migrating mallards. He believes, and rightly so, that all things being equal, where you find mallards in the evening is pretty close to where they'll be come shooting time next morning.

With 3,000 acres of flooded rice fields and green timber—all located near the David Donaldson Wildlife Management Area northwest of Paragould between the Black and Cache rivers—Jerry can assign hunters to productive areas with a minimum of guesswork. In the levees that separate his flooded rice fields, Jerry has sunk 24-foot-long steel tanks that serve as fine, dry blinds. These are plenty big enough to accommodate four hunters and a guide, the max allowed by state law.

As is the case elsewhere in Arkansas, mallards are the ducks of choice. The law allows four per day, but no more that two of them may be hens. If you shoot a pair of hens right off, you're through for the day. Nobody wants to risk going over limit. Best strategy is to hold off on mallards unless you can be 100 percent certain they're drakes, and spend your time on teal, pintails and woodies if you arrive early in the season.

While Jerry and his river-bottom farming partners have been hunting ducks in this area for years, they're fairly new to guiding, but they're headed in the right direction. They've built a new two-story lodge with a cathedral ceiling on the Black River. The lodge features four bedrooms, each with a private bath. Along with a game room for whiling away afternoons after the duck hunting's gone, there's a pleasant lounge where wild game dinners are also served.

K-Bar-C Hunting Preserve

D a v i s   C i t y ,   I o w a

*No hustle. No hype. Just good bird hunting
the way it's supposed to be.*

VITAL STATISTICS:

GAME BIRDS:
CHUKAR, PHEASANT
Source of Birds: Wild and pen-reared
Seasons:
PHEASANT, CHUKAR: September through March
TURKEY: April
Land: 960 private acres
Accommodations:
FARM-STYLE COTTAGES
NUMBER OF ROOMS: 5
MAXIMUM NUMBER OF HUNTERS: 12
Meals: Self-catered
Conference Groups: Yes
Guides: Trained dogs and guides
Shotgun Sports:
Shooting schools
Other Activities:
Big game, bird-watching, fishing, golf, hiking, tennis, skiing, wildlife photography
Rates:
From $100 / gun
Gratuity:
Hunter's discretion
Preferred Payment:
Cash or check
Getting There:
Fly to Kansas City or Des Moines, Iowa, and rent a car.

Contact:
Arnold Thompson
K-Bar-C Hunting Preserve
Box 168
Davis City IA 50065
515/442-2231
Fax: 515/442-2231
Off season:
EMAIL: kbarc@netins.net
WEB: www.huntingk-bar-c.com

WHEN PHEASANT HUNTERS close their eyes and dream of classic covers, they see miles and miles of thick prairie grasses broken by fields of corn stubble, overgrown fencerows, and occasional wet-weather stream channels filled with clumps of brush. It's country that calls to ringneck hunters with the same clarity of a cock's springtime holler. You owe it to yourself to hunt it at least once, and when you do, you'll come back time and time again.

The K-Bar-C Hunting Preserve is not one of those fancy, tricked-up places. That wouldn't be owner Arnold Thomspon's style. He's a guy who knows a thing or two about dogs and birds and loves to see them do their thing. With 960 acres just a click north of the Missouri border near the little hamlet of Linecity, Thompson runs hunts for wild cocks, preserve hunts for pheasants and chukar, and meets sanctioned by the National Bird Dog Challenge Association (NBDCA). In addition, there's hunting for turkey and deer, but only for archers.

Hunting here is pretty straight forward. Four pheasants and five chukars will be released before the beginning of each hunt. If you've opted to hunt with one of K-Bar-C's guides, you'll be taken to the fields and will go forth from there. If you're working your own dog, you'll be shown the area where you're supposed to hunt and be given general directions. Hunts are typically for three and a half hours and are scheduled for mornings and afternoons. Additional birds are available. The fee for this is a very reasonable $100. If you wish to stay overnight, Thompson has two housekeeping cabins that rent for a minimum of $100 per night ($25 each for four hunters).

Annually, K-Bar-C hosts NBDCA events where hunters pit the skills of their own dogs (and their own shooting prowess) against others of similar ilk. Categories have been established for pointing and flushing dogs, and for dogs and gunners with varying amounts of experience. Cash and merchandise are awarded to owners who accumulate the most points. Taking part in one of these events— entry fees are quite reasonable—is a great opportunity to see how you and your dog stack up. Spectators will enjoy seeing various dog breeds work game birds.

There's not much fancy about Iowa's Winterset Hunt Club,
unless you count the work by the German shorthairs, and that
over-your-shoulder, going-away double you nailed.

Flint Oak Farms offers first-class hunts for pheasants,
and some of the most challenging sporting clays courses in the
nation, a combination that's hard to beat.

[M I D W E S T]

Oakview II Hunting Club

Runnells, Iowa

More than a square mile of cover holds birds less than an hour from the center of the Midwest.

VITAL STATISTICS:

GAME BIRDS:
CHUKAR, PHEASANT, QUAIL
Source of Birds: Wild and pen-reared
Seasons:
September through March
Land: 700 private acres
Accommodations:
HOTELS IN DES MOINES
Corporate Groups: Yes
Guides: Trained dogs and guides
Dogs and Facilities:
Kennel for hunters' dogs, dog training
Shotgun Sports:
Driven birds
Other Services:
Birds cleaned and packed for travel
Other Activities:
Bird-watching, hiking, wildlife photography
Rates:
From $120 / gun
Gratuity:
Hunter's discretion
Preferred Payment:
Cash or check
Getting There:
Drive from Des Moines and get directions when you make reservations.

Contact:
Glen Neidleigh
Oakview II Hunting Club
12726 Hwy F 70W
Runnells IA 50237
515/966-2095
WEB: Best of Iowa.com/Oakview

WHAT'S IN A PRESERVE? When you sign up for a membership (even one-day hunts are often called memberships for liability insurance purposes), you're gaining access to private land where birds have been stocked. The preserve owner limits the number of hunters that gun over the preserve's fields and woods. Sure, preserves see heavy pressure, but they're also heavily stocked with game birds. The best preserves do their dead-level best to be sure that the birds they stock react in the same manner that wild birds do. How stocked birds are raised and conditioned, the style of holding pens (most preserves don't raise their own birds), and the manner in which they are released (are they dizzied by rocking or turned loose from a crate?), all determine how a bird performs when pointed or flushed.

Preserves are a godsend for hunters whose time is short. And those close to major cities see a lot of business entertaining. Less than 45 minutes from downtown Des Moines, Oakview II is an ideal location for a half-day business hunt. Owner Glenn Neideigh hunts 700 acres, a little more than a section, on rolling Iowa land east of the city. You'll find row crops left standing—milo, millet and grains of that ilk—overgrown fencerows and field edges, and occasional patches of brush. Dogs and guides are available. You won't find a pro shop and trap, skeet or sporting clays course. Gunning here is more like hunting your uncle's farm.

One-day "memberships" run in the neighborhood of $120 and for that, Neigdeigh will release five pheasants or a mixture of pheasants, chukar and quail. A dog and guide adds about $60 per day to the tab. "Business" memberships begin at $240. The more you pay, the more often you can hunt. For hunters whose work requires them to spend several weeks of fall or winter in Des Moines, the $475 plan—approximately 30 pheasants—will offer three or four good hunts for one or two guns. If you're in Des Moines, there are less pleasurable ways to spend a forced weekend or three. Advance reservations are important on this preserve, and meals can be arranged (also in advance) in the modern clubhouse. Lodging is available in town.

Triple H Ranch

Burlington, Iowa

OK. Burlington ain't in Illinois. It's in Iowa, with the birds.

VITAL STATISTICS:

GAME BIRDS:
CHUKAR, PHEASANT, QUAIL
Source of Birds: Pen-reared
Seasons:
September through March
Land: 1,000 private acres
Accommodations:
PRIVATE LODGE AND NEARBY MOTELS
NUMBER OF ROOMS: 7
MAXIMUM NUMBER OF HUNTERS:
7 OVERNIGHT
Meals: Family-style country cooking
Conference Groups: Yes
Guides: Trained dogs and guides
Dogs and Facilities:
Kennel for hunters' dogs, dog training
Shotgun Sports:
Driven birds, sporting clays
Other Services:
Birds cleaned and packed for travel
Other Activities:
Big game
Rates:
$220 / gun w/room and board
Gratuity:
Hunter's discretion
Preferred Payment:
Cash or check
Getting There:
Fly or drive to Burlington, Iowa, and rent a car.

Contact:
Keith A. Hoelzen
Triple H Ranch
16365 70th Ave South
Burlington IA 52601
319/985-2253

ONE LOUSY NIGHT I was flying back to New York via Chicago from Quincy, Illinois, and inclement weather grounded me in Burlington. Ever inquisitive, on the way from the airport to a hotel, I asked the cabby to tell me about Burlington, Illinois. (Hey, what did I know about the Midwest?) The driver turned, and in an accent redolent of Brooklyn, said "The first thing youse gotta know is it's in Iowa." He went on to mention the railroad and river and, god love us, pheasants.

Iowa is fine pheasant country, with a few quail thrown in on the south side. The border between Iowa and Minnesota marks the northern limit of bobwhite and the farther south you go, the more prevalent quail become. Once outside major cities, the land gets rural right quickly, and it doesn't take a whole lot of energy to imagine pheasants in every fencerow. Alas, fencerows are increasingly hard to find in Iowa. With the exception of CRP land and wildlife management areas, good pheasant fields are a vanishing species. That's what makes preserves like Triple H so popular.

Not much more than four hours out of Chicago via Interstates 88 and 74, and thence west on US Rt. 34 from Galesburg, Triple H is a destination for weekend shooters. At the end of the road you'll find 1,000 acres of excellent sedge, row-crops and thick field borders. No fancy bird buggies here; you'll ride a pickup with dogs in the back to your field for the afternoon. Then you'll follow the dogs. That may mean a bit of hustling to get up in position when one of the setters goes on point. Nothing wrong with that. Quail, pheasants, chukars or a combo are released in the numbers you specify. Triple H operates a fine sporting clays range where champion Jon Kruger occasionally gives clinics.

At the ranch, guests stay in a modern clubhouse with accommodations for seven shooters. If more than that have booked hunts, you may find your bed in a nearby Ramada, Best Western or Fairfield Inn little more than 15 minutes from the preserve. Pheasant dishes sometimes appear on Triple H's menu, but you'll also find steak and pork chops. After all, there's more to Iowa than game birds.

[M I D W E S T]

Winterset Hunt Club and Lodge

L o r i m o r ,   I o w a

Native prairie grasses plus sorghum equals birds in anyone's book.

VITAL STATISTICS:

GAME BIRDS:
CHUKAR, PHEASANT
Source of Birds: Wild and pen-reared
Seasons:
September through March
Land: 1,700 private acres
Accommodations:
1910 FARMHOUSE; MOTELS
NUMBER OF ROOMS: 3
MAXIMUM NUMBER OF HUNTERS: 12 IN THE LODGE
Meals: First-class dinners and breakfasts
Conference groups: Yes
Guides: Trained dogs and guides
Dogs and Facilities:
Kennel for hunters' dogs, dog training
Shotgun Sports:
Driven birds, trap
Other Services:
Birds cleaned and packed for travel
Other Activities:
Fishing
Rates:
$200 / day with lodging and meals
Gratuity:
Hunter's discretion
Preferred Payment:
Cash or check
Getting There:
Fly to Des Moines and rent a car.

Contact:
Curt Sandahl
Winterset Hunt Club and Lodge
3034 Heritage Ave
Lorimor IA 50149
515/462-2310

THERE WAS A TIME when Iowa was a prairie, that vast lush grassland underlain by rich black loam that stretched all the way from central Ohio to the Rocky Mountains. It took less than 100 years—closer to 50 actually—for the deep plows of the settlers to break the sod, turn the soil, and wear it out. Then came the years of depression and drought, and the heyday of fertilizer, clear-cropping and farming from fence line to fence line. Prairie grasses all but vanished.

Curt Sandahl bought the farm in 1972 and farms it today for corn and soybeans. But well aware of the resilience of tough prairie grasses, he began planting swaths of native cover along with sorghum and other food plot grains. The result is outstanding habitat and an increase in wild birds, and those that survive the season. Gunners have their choice of seven sections of the 1,700-acre lodge. Some are reasonably large, like the 350-acre parcel reserved for large groups. Some are small and thick. One section is open and rangy, ideal for a hunter who likes lots of walking with his gunning. And one is hilly enough to make you think you were hunting the grassy foothills of Montana.

Bring your own dog or use one from Curt's kennel. There, at any given time, you're likely to find labs, Brits, German shorthairs, and a handful of pointers and setters. A trap range is available should you want to hone your straightaways. And there's little doubt that you'll enjoy the farmhouse (circa 1910) with its three bedrooms and baths. Meals are almost as good as the hunting. The first night's dinner opens with hors d'oeuvres of oysters on the half shell, salmon, and cheese and crackers, then moves on to beef tenderloin, asparagus with lemon butter, and finishes with pie à la mode.

It's Curt's policy not to mix groups residing at the lodge, and on weekends he prefers parties of 10 or so. During the week, groups can be smaller. And if the lodge isn't available, a number of motels can be found within a twenty-minute's drive.

Beaver Creek Outfitters

A t w o o d ,   K a n s a s

Northwest Kansas isn't no-man's-land if a guy's toting a shotgun and looking for wild pheasants.

VITAL STATISTICS:

GAME BIRDS:
CHUKAR, PHEASANT, QUAIL
Source of Birds: Wild and pen-reared
Seasons:
CHUKAR, PHEASANT, QUAIL:
September through March
DOVE: September through October
TURKEY: April
Land: 2,000 private and public acres
Accommodations:
HISTORIC FRAME HOUSE
NUMBER OF ROOMS: 3
MAXIMUM NUMBER OF HUNTERS: 12
Meals: Hearty country with a flair
Conference Groups: Yes
Guides: Trained dogs and guides
Dogs and Facilities:
Kennel for hunters' dogs, dog training
Shotgun Sports:
Driven birds, sporting clays
Other Services:
Birds cleaned and packed for travel
Other Activities:
Fishing, golf, wildlife photography
Rates:
$300 / gun
Gratuity:
$10 - $50
Preferred Payment:
Cash, Discover, MasterCard or check
Getting There:
Fly to Denver and rent a car.

Contact:
Mark Leitner
Beaver Creek Outfitters
Rt. 1, Box 27
Atwood KS 67730
888-626-3948
Fax: 785/626-3795
EMAIL: phesnt@ruraltel.net

THE EXTREME NORTHWEST CORNER of Kansas, in the neighborhood of Atwood, is a vast tableland that tilts to the northeast toward Nebraska. High, limestone bluffs along the wide Beaver Creek (there are two) and its tributaries encompass wooded valleys providing game birds an extra degree of protection from harsh winter storms that sweep the region. Above the creeks, the land is sown in row crops and native grasses. Draws are tufted with clumps of plumb thicket and broadleafed shrubs. And owing to its relative isolation (Denver, the closest major city, is 200 miles west), bird hunting can be fabulous.

Beaver Creek hunts native pheasants and quail on 15,000 acres of leased land from mid-November through January. The terrain is not difficult; there's just a lot of it, and temperatures can be just this side of frigid. Truly wild birds are popular with Beaver Creek's clients, and the opportunity to hunt unspoiled area comes along rarely. State game limits apply. If, on the other hand, gunners prefer the certainty of filling a game bag, Beaver Creek operates a 2,000-acre preserve, where eight pheasants or chukar are released per day per hunter. This is a pick-up truck/shanks mare operation. You'll ride in the heated cab of a four-by-four to the fields for the day's hunt, and then walk from there. Owner Mark Leitner does his dead-level best to match terrain to the physical abilities and interests of guests. Here, new shooters (and those who haven't hunted in years) are very welcome. Dove are hunted here in September and October, and Turkey in the spring.

Hospitality is the name of the game, as far as Mark's wife, Monica, is concerned. She runs the kitchen, turning out pheasant in white wine with mushrooms and herbs from a recipe that was handed down from her grandmother. A few years ago, the couple remodeled one of the oldest frame houses in the county—dating from the 1890s—to include a new dining room and upstairs bedrooms for guests. There's not a room in the house that doesn't offer a view of the stunning countryside.

[M I D W E S T]

Flint Oak

F a l l   R i v e r ,   K a n s a s

Roll out of your Gulfstream, unlimber your shotguns, and run the sporting clays course before you set foot in the lodge.

VITAL STATISTICS:

GAME BIRDS:
CHUKAR, PHEASANT, QUAIL
Source of Birds: Wild and pen-reared
Seasons:
October through March
Land: 2,800 private acres
Accommodations:
A VARIETY TO MEET PERSONAL PREFERENCES AND BUDGETS
NUMBER OF ROOMS: 32
MAXIMUM NUMBER OF HUNTERS: 64
Meals: Superb traditional menu
Conference Groups: Yes
Guides: Trained dogs and guides
Dogs and Facilities:
Kennel for hunters' dogs, dog training
Shotgun Sports:
Driven birds, five-stand, shooting schools, skeet, sporting clays, tower or release shoots, trap
Other Services:
Birds cleaned and packed for travel
Other Activities:
Big game, bird-watching, fishing, hiking, wildlife photography
Rates:
Memberships from $2,750
Gratuity:
Hunter's discretion
Preferred Payment:
Cash, MasterCard, Visa or check
Getting There:
Fly to Wichita, KS, and rent a car.

Contact:
Jeff Oakes
Flint Oak
Rt 1, Box 262
Fall River KS 67047
316/658-4401
Fax: 316/658-4806

WRITING FOR THE *WICHITA EAGLE*, reporter Guy Boulton describes Flint Oak as the kind of hunting preserve that caters to folks who load up their corporate jets the way the rest of us load up our pickups. He's got a point. Since 1978, owner Ray Walton has invested some $10 million plus in developing, about 85 miles east of Wichita, what is one of the most sophisticated shotgunning resorts in the United States. Flint Oak is strictly a membership operation, and shooters must be guests of a member to hunt quail or run the championship clay courses.

Take the sporting clays course, for instance. A walkway of white gravel winds through swaths of manicured lawn to stations surrounding a lake. At each station a bronze sculpture of the bird imitated by the target reminds shooters what they're here for. Shooters wait their turn on raised decks, watching how the birds fly. But don't let its beauty beguile you; this course is totally electronically controlled, and the trapper who accompanies you can alter the speed and trajectory of any target. New shooters will find success here, and veterans of the tournament circuit will find it as tough as any in the country. Traditionalists will enjoy Flint Oak's trap and skeet ranges.

When you're shooting sporting clays here, it's hard for your eyes and mind not to wander into the sedgefields and brush beyond the pond. You know that it's fine cover for mixed bag hunts of chukar, pheasants and quail. Flint Oak maintains a kennel of championship-quality pointers and setters, along with guides known for their hunting savvy and their good manners. Field hunts are half-day affairs, which begin or end with lunch. European-style shoots are also available. Members with appropriate licenses can hunt deer, dove and turkey at no additional charge.

As you'd expect, lodging is exquisite, the peer of any of the best conference centers in the country. Meeting and break-out rooms are fully equipped with technology and facilities. Flint Oak has earned a platinum reputation from such companies as Bayer, Boyt, and Centurion Industries for its conference services. The ability to mix business with a wide range of outdoor sports makes Flint Oak an ideal location for building effective teams. Two pro shops offer everything from guns to incidentals, and the restaurant offers traditional cuisine—steaks, fish, fowl—served with style and grace.

Jayhawk Outfitting

Hill City, Kansas

Here's a place that would rather you did not come on opening day.

VITAL STATISTICS:

GAME BIRDS:
PHEASANT, QUAIL
Source of Birds: Wild and pen-reared
Seasons:
PHEASANTS and QUAIL: September through March
Land: 18,000 private acres
Accommodations:
MODERN LODGE
NUMBER OF ROOMS: 4
MAXIMUM NUMBER OF HUNTERS: 16
Meals: Family-style country cooking
Conference Groups: Yes
Guides: Trained dogs and guides
Dogs and Facilities:
Kennel for hunters' dogs
Shotgun Sports:
You may find a hand-trap somewhere
Other Services:
Birds cleaned and packed for travel, pro shop
Rates:
$495 / day
Gratuity:
Hunter's discretion
Preferred Payment:
Cash or check
Getting There:
Fly to Hays and rent a car.

Contact:
Gene Pimlott
Jayhawk Outfitting
PO Box 117
Hill City KS 67642
785/421-2284

WHAT YOU SEE when you race along Interstate 70 from Kansas City to Denver is mile after mile of grass. Prairie grass. Sometimes tilled and often grazed, the prairie is with you forever as you bucket along this thoroughfare. Some would be bored by the ride, but not you. You look at each thick patch of switchgrass or plumb brush and your mind whispers "pheasant" so loud that your companions can hear it over their argument about whether there's life for the Broncos after Elway.

Halfway between these two great football towns is a wide spot called WaKenney, and that's where you turn north towards Hill City and Jayhawk Outfitting. You'll like the lodge. Its big stone fireplace carries an ever inviting fire. Rooms offer various lodging configurations from single queen with private bath to a bunk room for eight. Any size group can be accommodated, and here, groups aren't mixed unless they want to be.

With more than 18,000 acres at his disposal, Gene Pimlott, the managing partner of this operation, can offer wingshooters land that's yet to be hunted. Quail and pheasant are released before the season opens, and you'll find some supplemental stocking when needed as the season progresses. Guides own and train their own dogs—mainly German shorthairs and Brittanies—and hunting parties never contain more than three hunters. "The terrain is pretty flat," says Gene. "We hunt a lot of wheat and milo stubble, and creek bottoms."

Best time to come is not on opening day. It's still pretty warm in Kansas then and hunting is harder on the dogs than it is on you. Wait until November and December when the mercury has found the freezing mark and your breath frosts in the early morning air. Then birds hold tighter, and each breath invigorates you and builds your appetite for more of Mary Lou's fine country cooking. This is purely a family operation, run by a group of nice folks who like having company that hunts.

LaSada Hunting Service

R u s s e l l , K a n s a s

Tight little covers provide lots of big birds on this land in the center of Kansas.

VITAL STATISTICS:

GAME BIRDS:
PHEASANT, QUAIL
Source of Birds: Wild and pen-reared
Seasons:
WILD: November through January
PRESERVE: February through March
Land: 5,000 private acres
Accommodations:
HOUSE IN TOWN
NUMBER OF ROOMS: 3
MAXIMUM NUMBER OF HUNTERS: 6 IN RENTAL HOUSE
Meals: Lunch during hunts, catered dinners available
Conference Groups: Yes
Guides: Trained dogs and guides
Dogs and Facilities:
Kennel for hunters' dogs
Shotgun Sports:
Five-stand, shooting schools, sporting clays, trap
Other Services:
Birds cleaned and packed for travel
Other Activities:
Bird-watching, fishing, wildlife photography
Rates:
From $150 / gun
Gratuity:
Hunter's discretion
Preferred Payment:
Cash or check
Getting There:
Fly to Hays, Kansas, and the lodge will collect you.

Contact:
Ron/Scott Young
LaSada Hunting Service
3720 183rd St
Russell KS 67665
785/483-3758
Fax: 785/483-6828
EMAIL: lasada@russellks.net
WEB: www.odsys.net/lasada

IF YOU POKE YOUR FINGER into the center of a map of Kansas, odds are you'll come pretty close to the town of Russell on Interstate 70. About four miles southwest of town is LaSada's headquarters. While this service offers preserve hunts for pheasant and quail, there's much that distinguishes it from most other bird hunting lodges and preserves.

LaSada emphasizes wild bird hunts on 5,000 acres during the Kansas season from November through January. You can harvest four roosters and eight quail per day. Unlike most guide operations, LaSada avoids those huge plots of CRP land. Sure they hold birds, but they're very difficult to hunt effectively. Instead, LaSada focuses on tight covers—a weedy fencerow that may run a mile or more; a draw choked with weeds and brush; thick growths on the edges of wet-weather streams or ponds. Gunners enjoy these hunts because it's easier to understand from whence a flush may come.

While you may encounter a pointer in LaSada's kennels, you won't see many. Rather, owners Ron and Scott Young prefer English springers. It may be a personal quirk on the Youngs' part, but once you hunt over these spaniels, you'll understand. First of all, they hunt close, and they're very thorough. Second, you can tell in a flash when the dogs are birdy, and since you've been able to keep up with them, you'll be there for the flush. Clients who insist on hunting over a pointing dog will enjoy LaSada's German wirehairs, another marvelous dog little seen in commercial hunting circles.

It's only after the regular bird season closes that LaSada switches operations to its 480-acre preserve. Half-day hunts for 10 quail or five pheasants are the norm. Corporate clients find these hunts very popular because they can mix them with morning or afternoon business meetings in LaSada's spacious clubhouse. Occasionally, they'll add a round of sporting clays, five-stand or trap.

Lunch is served on all of LaSada's hunts, but there are no accommodations at the preserve. However, the Young's own a house in Russell that rents for $60 dollars a night for up to six people. And, if that's taken—groups are not mixed—you'll find two or three motels in town.

Lil' Toledo Lodge

Chanute, Kansas

Waterfowling and pheasants couldn't be finer than what you'll find in this land of "ahhs."

VITAL STATISTICS:

GAME BIRDS:
DUCKS, GEESE, PHEASANT, QUAIL, TURKEY

Source of Birds: Wild and pen-reared

Seasons:
DUCKS: Late October through January
GEESE: Early November through early March
PHEASANT: September through March
QUAIL: Mid-November through January
TURKEY: Mid-October; late April through late May

Land: 2,500 private acres

Accommodations:
PRIVATE LOG LODGE AND CABINS
NUMBER OF ROOMS: 28
MAXIMUM NUMBER OF HUNTERS: 28

Meals: Hearty family-style

Conference Groups: Yes

Guides: Trained dogs and guides

Dogs and Facilities:
Kennel for hunters' dogs, dog training

Shotgun Sports:
Driven birds, five-stand, shooting schools, skeet, sporting clays, tower or release shoots, trap

Other Services:
Birds cleaned and packed for travel, proshop

Other Activities:
Big game, biking, bird-watching, boating, canoeing, fishing, golf, hiking, horseback riding, tennis, skiing, wildlife photography

Rates:
From $605 / day for two

Gratuity:
Hunter's discretion

Preferred Payment:
Cash, credit card or check

Getting There:
Fly to Tulsa or Wichita and rent a car.

RUNNING THROUGH southeastern Kansas, the Neosho River almost marks the western boundary of the Central Flyway. Flyways are, of course, imprecise thoroughfares, and borders are relative at best. Thousands of ducks and geese migrate through this neck of the woods, and the waters of the Neosho hold their share.

Yet to increase the odds a bit, Lil' Toledo has put in 391 acres of wetlands managed exclusively for ducks. In the center of it lies a 150-acre impoundment that, in summer, grows corn, millet, buckwheat, sorghum and alfalfa. Come fall, pumps are turned on and the area floods, providing waterfowl with the ultimate shallow-water smorgasbord. In each of the pond's two sections, islands have been built, and sunk in them are concrete blinds — heated, of course, in winter. This little bit of paradise is bounded on three sides by the Neosho. The set-up couldn't be finer.

Along with this man-made marsh is the river and a number of other ponds that offer gunning for ducks as well. Mallards, as always, are king. But early in the season, teal and wood ducks abound. There's a short duck season during the last week of October, but the real fun begins in the second week of November and continues through early January. Handicapped hunters are especially welcome at Lil' Toledo.

While waterfowling tops the agenda here, one wouldn't want to overlook pheasants and quail, the former being stocked and the latter mostly wild. And there's fall turkey in addition to spring gobblers. At Lil' Toledo, it's possible to take waterfowl, upland birds and turkey, all in one three-day outing. To do so, though, you'll have to really hustle. Add a couple of extra days and take a shot at a whitetail buck. And when the action's slow, there's always that pond with the lunker largemouth.

Accommodations are quite comfortable, but not the least bit pretentious. You'll stay either in the main lodge, cabins or in a bunk room, if that's your choice. Clay shooters will enjoy wobble trap, sporting clays, and skeet and trap ranges. And everyone likes the country cooking.

Contact:
Ron King
Lil' Toledo Lodge
10600 170th Rd
Chanute KS 66720
316/244-5668
Fax: 316/244-3639
EMAIL: liltoled@par1.net
WEB: www.liltoledo.com

Ringneck Ranch, Inc

T i p t o n ,   K a n s a s

You can park your plane and your bod in separate rooms at Keith's "Hanger."

VITAL STATISTICS:

GAME BIRDS:
CHUKAR, GEESE, PRAIRIE CHICKEN, PHEASANT, QUAIL

Source of Birds: Wild and pen-reared

Seasons:
PHEASANT and PRAIRIE CHICKEN: October through January
QUAIL: November through January
GEESE: Late November through late January

Land: 4,800 private acres

Accommodations:
PRIVATE LODGES
NUMBER OF ROOMS: 15
MAXIMUM NUMBER OF HUNTERS: 36

Meals: Home cooked meats and fowl

Conference Groups: Yes

Guides: Trained dogs and guides

Dogs and Facilities:
Kennel for hunters' dogs

Shotgun Sports:
Crazy quail

Other Services:
Birds cleaned and packed for travel, proshop

Other Activities:
Bird watching, boating, fishing, hiking, wildlife photography

Rates:
From $295 / gun

Gratuity:
Hunter's discretion

Preferred Payment:
Cash, credit cards or check

Getting There:
Fly to Salina or Wichita and rent a car.

Contact:
Keith Houghton
Ringneck Ranch Inc
HC61, Box 7
Tipton KS 67485
785/373-4835
Fx: 785/373-4059
EMAIL: ringneck@midusa.net
WEB: www.nckch.com/tic/ringneck.html

I N THE 1870S, when Keith Houghton's forebearers homesteaded this section of Kansas a few miles south of Tipton, they found prairie chickens, otherwise known as pinnated grouse. These near cousins of sharptails and sage grouse have all but disappeared with the demise of their namesake habitat. But in a few locations—northcentral Kansas being one—you can still hunt them, hidden in ambush as flocks of 50 birds or so wing from the grassland to dine in grain stubble fields.

As you know from the name, prairie chickens don't take center stage at Ringneck Ranch. It's cock birds that draw hunters from both coasts. In the main, you'll hunt for birds that were born in the wild, though owners Keith and Deb Houghton also do some supplemental stocking. A working ranch with hundreds of acres in grain crops, cover here varies from fencerows, to strips of milo and millet, to swaths of CRP land where the cover gets thicker and better every year. Along with pheasants, you'll hunt quail and, during the waterfowl season, geese. Guides are knowledgeable and professional and run some of the finest bird dogs— Brits, Vizslas, German shorthairs and German wirehairs, as well as Labs. This is a place that cares for its dogs as much as it cares for its guests. Crazy quail clays is available for gunners who need more practice.

Ringneck offers a number of packages for hunters. One focuses strictly on prairie chickens, and another offers both guided and unguided hunts for pheasants on other ranches. Quail can be added to pheasant hunts. And the grand casino is Ringneck's Wingshooter's Challenge, a two-day hunt for pheasant, quail, prairie chicken and geese with guide, dogs, accommodations and meals. The fee is $1,195 per person for a minimum of two hunters, and a third day can be added for another $200.

Guests stay on the ranch in one of three facilities: the ranch house, a private addition to the Houghton's home or the "Hanger," a multipurpose building containing four three-room suites with private baths and parking for pilot Keith's Cessna. No matter where they're quartered, guests gather for family-style meals built around Kansas beef, pheasants and delectable desserts. Ringneck also operates another ranch on the Republican River for hunters seeking a more secluded setting.

Show-Me Bird Hunting Resort

Baxter Springs, Kansas

"Where's the birds?" demanded Aunt Clara. If she'd been hunting here, she'd have had nothing to beef about.

VITAL STATISTICS:

GAME BIRDS:
CHUKAR, PHEASANT, QUAIL
Source of Birds: Pen-reared
Seasons:
September through March
Land: 800 private acres
Accommodations:
MOTEL IN NEARBY TOWN
Meals: Restaurant at motel
Conference Groups: Yes
Guides: Trained dogs and guides
Dogs and Facilities:
Kennel for hunters' dogs, dog training
Shotgun Sports:
Tower or release shoots
Other Services:
Birds cleaned and packed for travel
Rates:
From $115
Gratuity:
Hunter's discretion
Preferred Payment:
Cash, MasterCard, Visa or check
Getting There:
Fly to Joplin, MO, and rent a car.

Contact:
Kim Shira
Show-Me Bird Hunting Resort
2400 S.E. Quaker Rd
Baxter Springs KS 66713
316/674-8863

FROM THE NAME of this hunting service, you'd think it was in Missouri. It ain't, but lord it's so close. Baxter Springs is the last town in southeastern Kansas before you cross the line into Oklahoma to the south of the Show-Me state to the east. Did owner Kim Shira adopt Missouri's moniker for his own? Nope, it came from what he hears from hunters all the time: "Show me some birds!"

Well, birds you'll see in abundance, and if your swing is good, and your or the guide's dogs are working well, you'll fill your limit of chukar, pheasants or quail and possibly take additional birds as well. There's no limit at Show-Me. Any birds not harvested by previous hunters are yours, assuming that you hit 'em. Kim offers three basic packages: four pheasants or five chukar for $115 per gunner; six pheasants or seven chukar for $160 per hunter; or eight pheasants or nine chukar for $205 per hunter. All are half-day hunts and include an experienced guide and dog, bird cleaning and packaging. Your birds will be released on one of several farms in the area, and your party will have that farm to itself for the duration of the hunt.

While those are certainly reasonable hunts, perhaps the best deal is what Kim calls his "dog trainer's special." Instead of pheasants—which have a tendency to scoot out from under all but the staunchest point—a dozen bobwhite quail will be put out. You bring your own dog, and Kim provides a professional dog-trainer/guide. The dog trainer will teach you tactics to get the most out of your pointing or flushing dog. And you'll hunt a farm all to yourself. The fee for this is a mere $115 per person. Imagine a whole week of training sessions for you and your bird dog. At this rate, even writers could afford it!

Show-Me does not house guests on its property. Twenty-five minutes away in Joplin, Missouri, is a Ramada Inn that offers all the standard amenities.

[**M I D W E S T**]

Hunter's Ridge Hunt Club

O x f o r d ,   M i c h i g a n

Here on this horse-country farm are pheasant just the way you remember them.

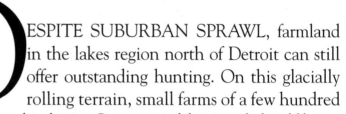

VITAL STATISTICS:

GAME BIRDS:
CHUKAR, HUNGARIAN PARTRIDGE, PHEASANT
Source of Birds: Pen-reared
Seasons:
August through April
Land: 600 private acres
Accommodations:
REMODELED FARMHOUSE
NUMBER OF ROOMS: 6
MAXIMUM NUMBER OF HUNTERS: 20
Meals: Restaurant with custom menu
Conference Groups: Yes
Guides: Trained dogs and guides
Dogs and Facilities:
Kennel for hunters' dogs, dog training
Shotgun Sports:
Shooting schools, skeet, sporting clays, tower or release shoots, trap
Other Services:
Birds cleaned and packed for travel, proshop
Other Activities:
Fishing, golf, hiking
Rates:
From $225 / 4 guns
Gratuity:
Hunter's discretion
Preferred Payment:
Cash, MasterCard, Visa or check
Getting There:
Drive from Detroit or Flint.

Contact:
Dave Fischer
Hunter's Ridge Hunt Club
3921 Barber
Oxford MI 48371
248/628-4868
Fax: 248/628-2770

DESPITE SUBURBAN SPRAWL, farmland in the lakes region north of Detroit can still offer outstanding hunting. On this glacially rolling terrain, small farms of a few hundred acres once engaged in dairying. Corn was raised for winter feed, and likewise, silage was chopped and stored. At one time, the native range of bobwhite quail extended through the region, as did the range of prairie chicken. Grouse and woodcock are reasonably plentiful here, drawn by coverts along creeks and in gnarly patches of second- or third-growth woods.

It is also pheasant country, though grounds where you can find and hunt them are increasingly sparse. That's where preserves like Hunter's Ridge come into play. Hunters think of this preserve as their own private farm. Small fields planted with corn, milo and sorghum, fencerows choked with weeds and vine, and plots of wood fringed with brambles at their margins all combine to present an ambience of the small farm of half a century ago. Along with ringnecks, chukar and bobwhite are released for each hunt in numbers determined by the package one purchases.

Hunter's Ridge is a membership club, but provisions can be made for guests. Trap, skeet, sporting clays, shooting schools, informal instruction—you'll find them all at Hunter's Ridge. In addition, there's a pro shop where firearms and accoutrements may be purchased on site. So too is lodging with six rooms upstairs (two with private baths) over the restaurant in the remodeled farmhouse.

Hunter's Ridge caters to corporate groups. A fully equipped conference room is available, as are requisite business equipment: fax, phone, data lines and copying. Often, morning meetings end with lunch, a round of sporting clays and then a quick hunt for ringnecks. On other occasions, businesspersons entertain clients on a leisurely hunt through the estate. Parents bring their youngsters to this preserve to introduce them to the shotgun sports, and many hunters kennel and train their dogs here.

Woodmoor Resort

Drummond Island, Michigan

Flights of woodcock filter into this little island off Michigan's U.P.

VITAL STATISTICS:

GAME BIRDS:
DUCKS, GEESE, GROUSE, WOODCOCK

Source of Birds: Wild and pen-reared

Seasons:
UPLAND: Mid-September through October
WATERFOWL: Early October through November

Land: 50,000 private and public acres

Accommodations:
NORTHWOODS LODGE AND COTTAGES
NUMBER OF ROOMS: 60
MAXIMUM NUMBER OF HUNTERS: 10

Meals: Game and seafood

Conference Groups: Yes

Guides: Trained dogs and guides

Dogs and Facilities:
Kennel for hunters' dogs

Shotgun Sports:
Shooting schools, sporting clays

Other Services:
Birds cleaned and packed for travel, proshop

Other Activities:
Bird-watching, boating, canoeing, fishing, golf, hiking, swimming, tennis, wildlife photography

Rates:
From $650 / day

Gratuity:
Hunter's discretion

Preferred Payment:
Cash, credit card or check

Getting There:
Fly to Chippewa County and rent a car.

Contact:
Reservations
Woodmoor Resort
33494 S. Maxton Rd.
Drummond Island MI 49726
906/493-1000
Fax: 906/493-5576
EMAIL: woodmoor@sault.com

COLUMBUS DAY is celebrated with delight here on Drummond Island. The joy has nothing to do with young Christopher, or the fact that on this date his stubby caravel finally made land. Often preceded by a frost or two, this long weekend marks the first flights of migrating woodcock, an event that gladdens the mien of any wingshooter whose tastes run to tight, boggy coverts and eager liver-and-white spaniels of pointing breed.

Drummond Island is an extension off the eastern tip of the Upper Peninsula. Around Drummond to the north flows the main channel. To the south and west is the outlet of Lake Michigan. Rising little more than 100 feet above the lake's surface, Drummond is forested with scrub—a reminder of its logging heritage—and pocked with shallow lakes and swamps, vestiges of kames and kettles of continental glacial origin. It is rich habitat for woodcock and ruffed grouse, and for ducks and geese as well.

In 1989, Woodmoor Lodge was constructed on the road that runs up the western, and more accessible, side of the island. Known for its golf and tennis, sailors tether their boats in the cove, and hikers wander the shoreline or follow nature trails through the woods. Canoeing and fishing are available as well.

Many wingshooters opt for the "Woodmoor Classic," three days of morning and afternoon hunts for ruffed grouse and woodcock. If one wants, shoots for released pheasant, chukar and Huns are also available as part of the "classic" package. You can save yourselves some dough by eschewing the pen-raised birds and taking your chances on wild fowl. Book the week after Columbus Day and you may also get in some gunning for ducks and geese. Fly-fishing for browns and salmon may also be substituted for a day of bird hunting.

Endorsed by Orvis, Woodmoor is known for outstanding rustic accommodations. Everywhere you look gives you the feel of being at a lodge in the northwoods as, indeed, you are. All guest rooms have private baths. Choose from a room in the massive wooden lodge, or from executive cottages with fireplaces that sleep from one person to five. You'll enjoy the chef's treatment of duck breast, and the scallop and shrimp linguine.

[M I D W E S T]

Caribou Gun Club Shooting Preserve

L e   S u e u r ,   M i n n e s o t a

Here's a preserve with a log lodge run by shooters who mind their peas and carrots.

VITAL STATISTICS:

GAME BIRDS:
CHUKAR, PHEASANT, QUAIL, TURKEY
Source of Birds: Pen-reared
Seasons:
UPLAND BIRDS: September through April
TURKEY: Mid-April through mid-May
Land: 700 private acres
Accommodations:
LOG LODGE
NUMBER OF ROOMS: 2
MAXIMUM NUMBER OF HUNTERS: 11
Meals: Self-catered
Conference Groups: Yes
Guides: Trained dogs and guides
Dogs and Facilities:
Kennel for hunters' dogs
Shotgun Sports:
Five-stand, skeet, sporting clays, tower or release shoots, trap
Other Services:
Birds cleaned and packed for travel, rifle and pistol range
Other Activities:
Big game, horseback riding
Rates:
$15 / bird; $12 / guide per hour
Gratuity:
Hunter's discretion
Preferred Payment:
Cash, Discover, MasterCard, Visa or check
Getting There:
Fly to Mankato and rent a car.

Contact:
Randy Voss
Caribou Gun Club Shooting Preserve
Rt 1, Box 26
Le Sueur MN 56058
800/672-3936

DEEP IN THE LAND of the Jolly Green Giant in Minnesota's blue earth country is a highly regarded shooting club and preserve that's served shotgunners for well over 40 years. You'll like the country. To the west, the Minnesota River flows through a valley about 200 feet below the prairie. Old glacial runoff channels add swales to the otherwise flat land. In some of these nascent valleys run wet-weather streams of ditches dug to facilitate the removal of standing water. Here and there, patches of hardwoods dot the landscape, but in the main, it's open country.

Randy and Earl Voss hunt about 700 acres where county Rt. 112 makes a right angle turn four miles south of Le Sueur. About 150 to 200 acres is in woods, some of it flat and the rest rolling gently. Annually, they groom 25 fields of corn, wheat stubble, alfalfa, grain sorghum and prairie grass. Each hunt has exclusive rights to one field, and the Voss' do their best to rotate fields to preserve cover.

Hunting here is not a high-priced affair. Dog and guide set you back $12 per hour or $50 for a half-day hunt. You buy the birds you hunt: Pheasants run roughly $14 each, and chukars are around $10 apiece. If you're a member, you can harvest scratch birds for $8 each. If not, you don't shoot more birds than you've paid for. Memberships begin at $100 for the first year, then drop to $50 per year. Members get a break on sporting clays, invitations to tower shoots, and opportunities to hunt wild spring gobblers. The club also maintains trap and skeet fields and a 325-yard rifle range. And twice a year, the club runs National Bird Dog Challenge Association sanctioned competitions.

Many preserves lack accommodations, but not Caribou. They've recently completed a cabin of white cedar log that sleeps 11 comfortably, and at rates that are very inexpensive. Many guests do their own cooking, barbecuing steaks or burgers on the gas grill on the huge front porch. Others ride into Le Sueur or Mankato for dinner. And if the log lodge is booked, both cities have an ample number of motels.

Elk Lake Heritage Preserve

Hoffman, Minnesota

Rolling prairie supports wonderful pheasant cover plus ponds where the ducks play.

VITAL STATISTICS:

GAME BIRDS:
CHUKAR, DUCKS, PHEASANT
Source of Birds: Wild and pen-reared
Seasons:
PRESERVE BIRDS: October through March
DUCKS: October through November
Land: 500 private acres
Accommodations:
TWO MODERN YET RUSTIC CABINS
NUMBER OF ROOMS: 4
MAXIMUM NUMBER OF HUNTERS: 11
Meals: Catered by special arrangement
Conference Groups: Yes
Guides: Trained dogs and guides
Dogs and Facilities:
Kennel for hunters' dogs, dog training
Shotgun Sports:
Driven birds, sporting clays
Other Services:
Birds cleaned and packed for travel
Other Activities:
Bird-watching, boating, fishing, golf, hiking, skiing, wildlife photography
Rates:
From $30 / night; pheasants from $12 each
Gratuity:
$25
Preferred Payment:
Cash or check
Getting There:
Fly to Alexandria and rent a car.

Contact:
Ed Loeffler
Elk Lake Heritage Preserve
PO Box 422
Hoffman MN 56339
320/986-2200

THE LAST GREAT GLACIAL SHEET to cover the Midwest smoothed the land yet left furrows for runoff along tongues of ice, benches and a zillion little lakes and ponds. Eventually, as the climate moderated, thick grasses grew, ribboned along watercourses with stands of cottonwood and willow. With the settling of the country, the few big trees were cut for lumber, and the sod was broken by ploughs. Row crops were planted on level lands, and the rest was put into pasture. Fences between fields grew up with weeds and wildflowers and provided marvelous habitat for native game birds: prairie chicken, ruffed grouse and gray partridge.

Hoffman is a small town about 15 miles south of Interstate 94 roughly two-thirds of the way from the Twin Cities of Minneapolis/St. Paul to Fargo. Interstate 94 is pretty much the northern boundary of naturally reproducing pheasants, although such lines are not hard and fast. Each year, the state stocks pheasants in selected areas. Some survive hunting, predators and climate.

The passion for bird hunting knows no geographic boundaries, and that's why Gary Peterson opened Elk Lake Hunting Preserve on Torstenson Lake a few miles north of Hoffman. On the preserve's 500 rolling acres, you can hunt pheasants and chukar from September through March. But manager Ed Loeffler will tell you that the hunting is best between September and December. Later, heavy snows blow across these northern prairies and pound field cover into a thickish mat. There is some shooting late in the season—March, that is—if the winter hasn't been too harsh. Along with preserve shooting, Elk Lake also rents duck blinds in October and November, and hunting for mallards, teal, canvasbacks, and pintails can be quite good. So, too, is the hunting for Canadas.

In a wooded area along the shore of Tortenson Lake, the preserve managers have created a good sporting clays range. And the lake itself is managed as a summer and winter fee fishery for walleye. Two cabins on the property provide accommodations. Meals can be catered or you can drive to nearby family restaurants.

McCollum's Hunting Preserve

B e j o u ,   M i n n e s o t a

Ya, so, did you ever hunt pheasants with a Doberman?

VITAL STATISTICS:

GAME BIRDS:
CHUKAR, PHEASANT
Source of Birds: Pen-reared
Seasons:
September through December
Land: 880 private and public acres
Accommodations:
PRIVATE LODGE
NUMBER OF ROOMS: 1
MAXIMUM NUMBER OF HUNTERS: 10
Meals: Dinners provided to lodge
guests
Conference Groups: Yes
Guides: Trained dogs and guides
Dogs and Facilities:
Kennel for hunters' dogs, dog training
Shotgun Sports:
Informal clays
Other Services:
Birds cleaned and packed for travel
Other Activities:
Bird-watching, hiking, cross-country
skiing
Rates:
Priced by the bird;
Guides and dogs $120 / full-day;
Lodging $15 / person
Gratuity:
10% - 15%
Preferred Payment:
Cash or check
Getting There:
Fly to Fargo, ND, and rent a car.

Contact:
Terry McCollum
McCollum's Hunting Preserve
Rt. 1, Box 9
Bejou MN 56516
218/935-2468

S O, WHERE DO YOU HUNT for pheasants when there's ten inches of snow on the ground and more on the way? Head for the northwest corner of the White Earth Indian Reservation about 50 miles northeast of Moorhead. The reservation covers about 1,000 square miles, and just to the east of it is Itasca State Park, the source of the Mississippi River.

Barren ground winters are rare up here. Snows can come as early as October. It all depends on the vagaries of the jet streams and those fronts that sweep across the Great Plains. During some weeks, the prairie rolls umber and tawny tan with dried sorghum, corn stubble and thick wild grasses. On others, only tips of the vegetation peeks above the snow. That's when hunting thick brush along watercourses can really pay off.

Even Terry and Theresa McCollum, who own and operate this family business, don't push the weather much. They close the hunting season at the end of December, before the weather really gets rough. But snow or not, from September on, Terry's out releasing birds on his 900 acres for gunners who want a quality shoot at a reasonable price.

Typical hunts will involve a mixture of hen and cock pheasants and chukar scattered in fields where the cover is best. Hunt with one of Terry's dogs or bring your own. Don't be surprised if you find yourself hunting over a canine odd-couple, like a Doberman and a Lab. Weird, you say? Well, Doberman's are known for their noses, and one like Terry's that's slow, sweet and gentle and whose fondness for people is not gastronomic, can be one hell of a flushing dog. The Lab comes along to bring back the birds you down. Guides are available too.

The McCollums provide lodging for up to 10 hunters in a cabin with complete kitchen facilities. Place an order for 45 birds, and you and your party can stay for free. Otherwise, guests are charged $15 dollars per night. If you feel lucky, after your hunt, head for the Shooting Star Casino 11 miles south at Mahnomen.

Minnesota Horse & Hunt Club

P r i o r   L a k e ,   M i n n e s o t a

Membership in this fine club won't entirely flatten your wallet.

VITAL STATISTICS:

GAME BIRDS:
CHUKAR, HUNGARIAN PARTRIDGE, PHEASANT, QUAIL
Source of Birds: Wild and pen-reared
Seasons:
UPLAND PRESERVE GAME: all year
WATERFOWL: October through November
Land: 700 private acres
Accommodations:
PRIVATE AND RUSTIC LODGES
NUMBER OF ROOMS: 9
MAXIMUM NUMBER OF HUNTERS: 36
Meals: Excellent regional cuisine
Conference Groups: Yes
Guides: Trained dogs and guides
Dogs and Facilities:
Kennel for hunters' dogs, dog training
Shotgun Sports:
Driven birds, five-stand, shooting schools, skeet, sporting clays, tower or release shoots, trap
Other Services:
Birds cleaned and packed for travel, proshop
Other Activities:
Biking, bird-watching, boating, fishing, golf, hiking, horseback riding, skiing, wildlife photography
Rates:
From $89 / night plus price per bird
Gratuity:
$20 - $100
Preferred Payment:
Cash credit card or check
Getting There:
Fly to Minneapolis/St. Paul and rent a car.

Contact:
Ken Larson
Minnesota Horse & Hunt Club
2920 220th St
Prior Lake MN 55372
612/447-2272
Fax: 612/447-2278
WEB: www.mnhorseandhunt.com

IF BUSINESS BRINGS YOU to the Twin Cities of Minneapolis/St. Paul more than once a year, then a membership in this fine club may be a worthwhile investment. As of this writing, for $400 per year, you have access to 700 acres of fields, forests and ponds; a first-class restaurant and charming guest accommodations (very competitively priced with the best in the Twin Cities); and a complete array of shotgun, rifle and pistol ranges.

First the hunting. Pheasants, chukar, Hungarian partridge, and bobwhite are released in nearly a dozen fields—all planted with cover crops such as sorghum, milo and millet—set aside for upland hunting. You'll work one field every half day, paying per bird for each released. Scratch hunts are also available. Use your dogs or the club's. The area south of the Twin Cities contains a number of small ponds and sloughs, reminders of the land's glacial sculpting. During waterfowl season, you'll find wood ducks and teal early and then mallards, bluebills, and an occasional canvasback. Blinds are maintained and guides with retrievers are available. Hunting licenses and waterfowl stamps are required.

For those times when birds aren't flying, the club offers an incredible range of shotgun clay games. Its sporting clays courses—five of them—are consistently ranked among the top handful in the nation. You'll also want to try out the club's trap and skeet fields. To alleviate crowding, there are two of each. Add a "crazy quail" course and a duck tower along with 50-yard pistol and 300-yard rifle ranges and you'll understand why the club is known as one of the most complete in the country.

Accommodations are strictly top flight. Choose from suites in the Hunter's lodge (excellent meeting facilities) or those in an atmosphere of an old country farmhouse. All contain kitchenette facilities. Most have private baths. And lest I forget, the restaurant is of a caliber equal to accommodations. Wild game, steaks and seafood grace the menu, and the restaurant boasts a cellar of vintage wines. Members receive a substantial discount on lodging.

[M I D W E S T]

Traxler's Hunting Preserve

L e   C e n t e r ,   M i n n e s o t a

A fine shooting ground where birds and hunters love the winter-hardy cover.

VITAL STATISTICS:

GAME BIRDS:
CHUKAR, DUCKS, PHEASANT
Source of Birds: Pen-reared
Seasons:
Mid-August through mid-April
Land: 800 private acres
Accommodations:
NEW AND RUSTIC LOG LODGE
NUMBER OF ROOMS: 6
MAXIMUM NUMBER OF HUNTERS: 12
Meals: Wild game and fish cuisine
Conference Groups: Yes
Guides: Trained dogs and guides
Dogs and Facilities:
Kennel for hunters' dogs, dog training
Shotgun Sports:
Driven birds, shooting schools, sporting clays, tower or release shoots, trap
Other Services:
Birds cleaned and packed for travel, pro shop
Other Activities:
Paintball in the off-season
Rates:
Priced per bird;
Accommodations $50 / night
Gratuity:
Hunter's discretion
Preferred Payment:
Cash, credit cards or check
Getting There:
Fly to Mankato and rent a car.

Contact:
Jeff Traxler
Traxler's Hunting Preserve
RR2, Box 223A
Le Center MN 56057
507/357-6940
Fax: 507/357-6940
EMAIL: thp@frontiernet.net

ITH MORE THAN 800 ACRES midway between the Twin Cities and Mankato, and only 75 miles from Rochester (location of Mayo Clinic), Traxler's Hunting Preserve is less than an hour and a half from most of the residents of Minnesota. In business for more than a dozen years, the preserve has earned a solid reputation for providing quality hunts at reasonable prices.

The land around Le Center is essentially prairie. An intermittent water course, artfully named "County Ditch No. 23," flows through the property. It drains into Le Sueur Creek west of the property and eventually into the Minnesota River. Birds — read that pheasants and chukar — are released into fields of 25 acres and up, depending on the number of hunters in a party. Over the years, Jeff Traxler has figured out the right mix of vegetation to provide cover for hunters and the birds throughout the season.

This, friends, is no mean feat. When the season opens in mid-August, the weather gods still have a handful of sultry 90° F days in store. You know how tough that kind of weather is on bird dogs (and hunters as well). Yet in the depths of winter, a sunny day still may nudge the thermometer up to 10°F, and that almost feels balmy. Thin cover — brougham along with strips of corn and sorghum — are planted for the early season. Dogs can work this without facing heat exhaustion, as long as hunters carry lots of water and observe the dog's behavior very carefully. But after the first snows, the game changes. Action switches to fields of sorghum and corn, thick cover that allows birds a maze of nooks and crannies where they can hole up. Paths mown through the strips make for easy walking for hunters. As the season wanes in late March and early April, action shifts back to short-grass fields, which have recovered a bit from the fall hunting. With four farms, there's always good land to hunt.

While upland birds are the main course here, Jeff also offers released mallard hunts. Gunners are positioned in the weedy brush around a pond and mallards are loosed from 150 yards away, deep in the woods. When the ducks break out of the trees, they're on the hunters who must be adept at pass-shooting to be successful. Populations of wild waterfowl are not sufficient enough in this area to permit hunting.

Voyageur Sportsman's Paradise

International Falls, Minnesota

Wild turkey as well as pheasants are found on this vest-pocket sized preserve.

VITAL STATISTICS:

GAME BIRDS:
CHUKAR, PHEASANT, QUAIL, TURKEY
Source of Birds: Pen-reared
Seasons:
All year
Land: 200 private acres
Accommodations:
IN NEARBY TOWN
Conference Groups: Yes
Guides: Trained dogs and guides
Dogs and Facilities:
Kennel for hunters' dogs, dog training
Shotgun Sports:
Sporting clays, tower or release shoots
Other Services:
Birds cleaned and packed for travel, proshop
Other Activities:
Big game, canoeing, fishing
Rates:
Priced by the bird
Gratuity:
Hunter's discretion
Preferred Payment:
Cash, MasterCard, Visa or check
Getting There:
Fly to International Falls and the lodge van will collect you.

Contact:
Ken & Sheila Bahr
Voyageur Sportsman's
Paradise
PO Box 1236
International Falls MN 55649
800/814-4868
Fax: 218/283-2473
EMAIL: paradise@northwinds.net
WEB: www.northwinds.net/Paradise

WHAT DO YOU DO WITH 200 ACRES of second-growth scrub, that hodgepodge of birch, poplar and firs of every description with a few tag alders thrown in just to keep your brush hogs busy? Create a bird hunting preserve? Not if you have good sense, you don't. But Ken and Sheila Bahr went blithely down the preserve course five years ago, and lo and behold, they're making a go of it, having fun, and introducing some birds to northern Minnesota that, if not totally exotic, are rare as proverbial hen's teeth.

Take wild turkey. How many preserves offer hunting for pen-raised toms? These aren't your lily-white butterball breeds, but genuine *Meleagris gallopavo*, the bird that Uncle Ben Franklin thought should become our national symbol. For the princely sum of about $80, Ken will order up a tom with your name on it and release it in the thick woods. Next morning, it's your job to go hunt it up. Naw, you don't get the services of a guide on this one. You must do your own calling. You don't, however, have to worry much about your Tom being distracted by hens other than the one you imitate with call and decoy. Why? Well, there just aren't many. Hunter success on this merry game runs about 50 percent. It isn't as easy as it sounds.

If talking turkey isn't your game, you can still hunt chukar, pheasant and bobwhite (pretty exotic this close to the Canadian border) with English setters in fields of buffalo grass or switchgrass. Hunts are priced per bird, and dog handlers can be included if you want. Some of Ken's clients forgo hunting with the setters in favor of taking Goldie, the Bahr's Lab. Goldie was raised with the setters and doesn't have the slightest idea that she's not one. She'll point, but it isn't the rock solid stand with right paw raised and feathers drifting in the wind. No, she does a jig like an Irishman who won the sweepstakes. That, plus the bird, is worth the price of admission. Should you be bored, go humble yourself with a round or two of sporting clays.

You'll find no lodging here. But nearby in International Falls is such a plethora of hotels, motels, and bed-and-breakfasts that every taste can be accommodated. Restaurants abound as well, and all are within a few minutes drive.

Wild Acres Hunting Club

P e q u o t   L a k e s ,   M i n n e s o t a

Walk the wild side or cross the fence into the game farm; either way you'll have fun.

VITAL STATISTICS:

GAME BIRDS:
CHUKAR, DUCKS, PHEASANT, QUAIL, TURKEY
Source of Birds: Pen-reared
Seasons:
September through December
Land: 500 private acres
Accommodations:
IN NEARBY TOWN
Meals: By special arrangement
Conference Groups: Yes
Guides: Trained dogs and guides
Dogs and Facilities:
Kennel for hunters' dogs
Other Services:
Birds cleaned and packed for travel
Rates:
Initial hunt $250 for party of four, plus birds
Gratuity:
Hunter's discretion
Preferred Payment:
Cash or check
Getting There:
Fly to Brainerd-Crowwing County and rent a car.

Contact:
Mary K. Ebnet
Wild Acres Hunting Club
HC 83, Box 108
Pequot Lakes MN 56472
218/568-5024
Fax: 218/568-4395
EMAIL: wildacres@uslink.com

YOU MIGHT SAY that Wild Acres, a 500-acre-plus preserve north of Brainerd in central Minnesota, suffers from a split personality. It's true. Over the last dozen years, Mary Ebnet, with a lot of help from her friends (and that includes customers), has created a preserve with two distinct faces. But this mom of ten (the youngest enters college as this book goes to press) would be the first to tell you that "suffers" is altogether the wrong word. Thrives is more like it.

On one side of the fence, there's a 350-acre natural hunting area. Open fields of prairie grasses, stripped with a mix of sorghum and millet, are interspersed among stands of oak, birch and pine. Fields are bordered by scrubby brush of thornapple, high bush cranberry and enough other native bushes to keep a plant taxonomist busy for a month. Here and there are ponds surrounded by stands of rushes and cattails. Into this natural conservatory, 150 or so pheasants, 50 to 60 chukar and the same number of quail are released before the season begins in September. As customers harvest birds, new ones are released. There's no dizzying these birds; they're wide awake and make for the thickest cover as soon as they're released. Along with upland birds, young wild turkey poults of eight to 10 weeks old are turned loose in early summer. They grow fat on a diet of acorns and insects during the summer and may be hunted during the fall. Mallards are also released for pass-shooting as they make their way toward the ponds.

Across the fence is the game farm, a more typical operation for the Midwest. Here a hunter makes a reservation, requests the number and kind of birds he or she wishes to hunt, and may even release them himself. There's no better way to tune up a hunting dog than by working it on birds of known location. This is a great place for training young shooters as well.

Hunting the natural area requires a $1,500 annual membership after the first hunt. With it comes guides, dogs and unlimited hunting (you still pay for your birds). When you think about the cost of a week of hunting bobwhite down south or pheasants in the Dakotas, the membership seems reasonable indeed. Accommodations are normally not available at the lodge—there are plenty of places to stay in nearby Brainerd. But you and your group may arrange for one of Mary's scrumptious dinners of pheasant with wild rice.

Wings North

Pine City, Minnesota

Why is a new preserve attracting rave reviews?
It's all in the family.

VITAL STATISTICS:

GAME BIRDS:
CHUKAR, PHEASANT, QUAIL
Source of Birds: Pen-reared
Seasons:
UPLAND BIRDS: mid-August through May
Land: 369 private acres
Accommodations:
IN NEARBY TOWN
Meals: By special arrangement
Conference Groups: Yes
Guides: Trained dogs and guides
Dogs and Facilities:
Dog training
Shotgun Sports:
Shooting schools, sporting clays, tower or release shoots
Other Services:
Birds cleaned and packed for travel, proshop
Other Activities:
Casino gambling
Rates:
By the bird; guides $50 / 1/2 day
Gratuity:
Hunter's discretion
Preferred Payment:
Cash, MasterCard, Visa or check
Getting There:
Drive from Minneapolis or Duluth.

Contact:
Thad Hughes
Wings North
Rt. 4, Box 274
Pine City MN 55063
320/629-5002
Fax: 320/629-4868

MAYBE THAD HUGHES didn't have a choice. He was raised in the bird hunting business; his dad owns Wild Wings of Oneka, a preserve about 15 miles northeast of Minneapolis. So when it came time to start a business, he took to the long grass like a ringneck pheasant and last year, opened Wings North about half-way between the Twin Cities and Duluth on Interstate 35. Since its opening in the fall of 1998, Wings North is attracting rave reviews on three counts: great birds and cover, good manners and common sense, and a real willingness to tailor hunts to the needs of its customers.

On 369 acres of reasonably level farm land, Thad has set up 11 hunting areas. Cover varies. Here you'll find fields of corn and sorghum, along with thickets of willow and cattails. There's heavy cover and medium cover and thin cover; you can pick what you like, depending on the season and your mood. No kennels are maintained at this preserve, but Thad's arranged with 30 to 35 guides to be available with their dogs—everything from pointers to a griffin—depending on what you want. Birds are released an hour or so before your hunt, but in such a way that they've wandered well away from the tracks of the ATV by the time you and your dog arrive. And come the depths of winter when snow depth is measured in feet, he'll use a snowmobile to groom a path that you can negotiate without snowshoes while your dog works the cover. Pricing is by the bird, with a five-bird minimum, and dogs and guides get $50 for a half-day hunt. The 10-station sporting clay's course offers NSCA registered shoots.

Is this a destination that you'd fly to? Of course not. But you might drive there and spend a couple days. It's a good operation run by a nice guy and his wife, who both have the right attitude. Doctor, lawyer, merchant, chief—everybody's treated with the same courtesy at Wings North. The clubhouse is new and comfortable; lunches are not generally provided but are available on advance notice. The town of Hinckley, 13 miles north, hosts a casino and a pair of large hotels. There you'll gamble with your money; at Wings North, you'll get your money's worth.

[M I D W E S T]

Big River Hunting Club & Kennels

F l e t c h e r ,   M i s s o u r i

Pheasants, ducks, geese—you'll find 'em all less than an hour from St. Louis.

VITAL STATISTICS:

GAME BIRDS:
CHUKAR, DUCKS, HUNGARIAN PARTRIDGE, PHEASANT, QUAIL, TURKEY

Source of Birds: Pen-reared, except for ducks and turkey

Seasons:
UPLAND BIRDS: September through March
DUCKS: November through February
TURKEY: Mid-April through early May

Land: 500 private acres

Accommodations:
WOOD-SIDED LODGE
NUMBER OF ROOMS: 3
MAXIMUM NUMBER OF HUNTERS: 12

Meals: Breakfast and lunch; dinners catered at guest's expense

Conference Groups: Yes

Guides: Trained dogs and guides

Dogs and Facilities:
Kennel for hunters' dogs, dog training

Shotgun Sports:
Driven birds, sporting clays, tower or release shoots

Other Services:
Birds cleaned and packed for travel

Other Activities:
Bird-watching, fishing, hiking, wildlife photography

Rates:
Priced per bird; lodging and breakfast $25 / night

Gratuity:
$25

Preferred Payment:
Cash or check

Getting There:
Fly to St. Louis and rent a car.

Contact:
Rich & Rose Baumgartner
Big River Hunting Club & Kennels
11444 Hwy WW
Flethcr MO 63030
314/452-3511
Off season:
610 Camborne
St. Louis MO 63125
314/892-7962

FORTY MILES SOUTHWEST of St. Louis, near the Washington County line, is the hamlet of Fletcher. Farming is big business here, but one of the more prosperous enterprises is Rich and Rose Baumbartner's Big River Hunting Club & Kennel. "This isn't the Cadillac of hunting clubs," laugh's Rich. "We're more like a Pontiac." Now he could have said "Chevy," but his friendliness, forthrightness, and the quality of his operation puts Big River a notch above run-of-the-mill preserves.

The 500 acres of his farm are planted in clover, lespedeza, switchgrass and fescue. Bands of milo 20 feet wide run down the middle of some of the fields. In others, they form horseshoes. He also plants corn and sunflowers for dove. Most gunners bring their own dogs, but Rich has a kennel of Brittanys and German shorthairs and a staff of guides for those who don't. Hunts are conducted in fields of 50 acres or so, ample space to chase a dozen and a half preserve birds. Most popular is the half-day shoot for three gunners. For $70 per gun or $210 total, Rich releases three pheasants, three chukars and a dozen quail. If the group wants a guide and dog, they must pony up another $40. Extra birds are available on request, and Rich can also set out flocks of Hungarian partridge. During the waterfowl season, you can hunt wild ducks and geese from the pair of three-man blinds on the perserve's pond, which is stocked with largemouth, smallmouth, crappie and catfish. Turkey are also hunted in the spring. A 10-station course sanctioned by the National Sporting Clay's Association is also found at this preserve.

Big River's lodge contains three rooms for sleeping. It functions like a bed-and-breakfast. For the princely sum of $25 per night, you have a clean, dry, warm and quiet (you don't snore, right?) bed as well as chow when you get up. Dinners can be catered in at your request. While open to the public, this is a membership lodge. And the way Rich puts it, walk-in shooters don't pay a premium or daily membership as they do at some lodges. Rather, members receive deep discounts.

Heartland Wildlife Ranches

Ethel, Missouri

This big game preserve offers some of the best birding and accommodations in the Midwest.

VITAL STATISTICS:

GAME BIRDS:
CHUKAR, HUNGARIAN PARTRIDGE, PHEASANT, QUAIL, TURKEY

Source of Birds: Wild and pen-reared

Seasons:
UPLAND BIRDS: October through March
TURKEY: Mid-April through early May

Land: 5,500 private acres

Accommodations:
PRIVATE TIMBER LODGE
NUMBER OF ROOMS: 8
MAXIMUM NUMBER OF HUNTERS: 16

Meals: Gourmet game

Conference Groups: Yes

Guides: Trained dogs and guides

Dogs and Facilities:
Kennel for hunters' dogs, dog training

Shotgun Sports:
Five-stand, sporting clays

Other Services:
Birds cleaned and packed for travel, pro shop

Other Activities:
Big game, bird-watching, fishing, hiking, wildlife photography

Rates:
From $1250 / gun

Gratuity:
Hunter's discretion

Preferred Payment:
Cash, credit cards or check

Getting There:
Fly to Kansas City and rent a car.

Contact:
Ty Brewer
Heartland Wildlife Ranches
10853 State Hwy VV
Ethel MO 63539-2303
660/486-3215
Fax: 660/486-3217
EMAIL: info@heartland-wildlife.com
WEB: www.heartland-wildlife.com

IN 1993, JAY AND KATHY BRASHER began to create their huge 5,500-acre wildlife ranch. Surrounded by high fence, it's stocked with whitetails, elk, red stag, American and Iranian sheep. If you're heart's set on a 400-Boone-and-Crockett-class bull, this is one place where the odds are fully in your favor, and it's only two hours from Kansas City. Sign up for an elk hunt in early October, then stay around for a couple of days for the finest preserve hunting you'll ever experience.

Endorsed by Orvis, Heartland offers gunners a mixed bag of wild and supplementally stocked quail, chukar, pheasant and Hungarian partridge. Hunts are generally scheduled for two or three days. On each, you'll be able to harvest 10 pheasants or a combination of seven pheasants and eight quail or chukar. In addition, you can bag three Huns. Cover is mixed between deep prairie grasses, standing row-crops and brushy open woods. Dogs and guides are provided, of course. You may hunt over your own dog.

On a typical hunt, you'll arrive at the three-story Rocky Mountain-style lodge about noon. After a brief orientation, it's off to the range for a round of sporting clays with informal instruction. Then, you get some exercise and shooting on your first afternoon hunt. Afterwards, while your birds are being cleaned and packaged, you relax with drinks before the fire, followed by a gourmet game dinner with desserts that are as deadly as they are delectable. Nobody needs sleeping pills here. Rooms (all with private baths) are furnished in period antiques. Two- and three-dimensional wildlife art abounds. You'll wake in the morning to steaming coffee, squeezed juice and a full country breakfast. The day's agenda contains morning and afternoon hunts, with lunch and a nap in between. Those who've booked two-day packages depart the following morning after breakfast. Those with the good sense to opt for three, head back to the fields. Turkey is hunted here in the spring.

A full-service pro shop offers items that will enhance your hunt. Lakes stocked with rapacious bass, and nature trails and indoor billiards offer diversions from the task at hand. Heartland caters to corporate groups and to families as well. The Amish country of northcentral Missouri offers some of the best, relatively undiscovered antiquing in the nation.

Comstock Hunting Club

B r o k e n   B o w ,   N e b r a s k a

Waterfowl and pheasants go hand in hand here in the vast open prairie.

VITAL STATISTICS:

GAME BIRDS:
DUCKS, GEESE, HUNGARIAN PARTRIDGE, PHEASANT, PRAIRIE CHICKEN, QUAIL, SHARPTAIL
Source of Birds: Wild and pen-reared
Seasons:
HUNS, PHEASANT, QUAIL:
September through March
PRAIRIE CHICKEN and SHARPTAIL:
September through December
WATERFOWL: October through mid-January
Land: 50,000 private acres
Accommodations:
NEW LODGE
NUMBER OF ROOMS: 8
MAXIMUM NUMBER OF HUNTERS: 16
Meals: Family-style
Conference Groups: Yes
Guides: Trained dogs and guides
Dogs and Facilities:
Kennel for hunters' dogs, dog training
Shotgun Sports:
Sporting clays
Other Services:
Birds cleaned and packed for travel, pro shop
Other Activities:
Big game, biking, bird-watching, boating, fishing, golf, hiking, horseback riding, wildlife photography
Rates:
$750 / day
Gratuity:
Hunter's discretion
Preferred Payment:
Cash, MasterCard or check
Getting There:
Fly to North Platte/Grand Island and rent a car.

Contact:
Cass McCaslin
Comstock Hunting Club
PO Box 58
Broken Bow NE 68822
308/872-2998
Fax: 308/872-6959

OLD JOKE: What's the favorite bumper sticker in these parts? Answer: "Kansas: Gateway to Nebraska." Nebraska offers some of the finest wildfowl hunting in the country. Its populations of wild pheasants and prairie chickens are thriving. Waterfowl abound in lands bordered by lakes and rivers, and in the pothole country as well. It's big country to be sure—big and open and reasonably easy to walk.

Comstock has established a good reputation for both its upland bird and waterfowl hunts. The former are conducted on 50,000 acres of mixed grain fields, CRP land, and plots planted with millet, milo, soybeans and corn. Cass McCaslin, the honcho of this operation, has organized plantings with the comforts of hunters in mind. The cover is stripped for easy access; only the dogs (English pointers, German shorthairs, and Labs) have to work hard. Full-day hunts are broken with lunch in the field or lodge, as seems to make the most sense.

While most hunters book into Comstock for upland birds, waterfowling on the nearby North Fork of the Loop and Clamus rivers is gaining in popularity. Woodies and teal open the season in October, and you'll also find some local mallards mixed in. As the season slips through November into December, local birds move out and larger, migrating mallards settle in. Blinds and decoys on the rivers and, sometimes, ponds are the normal *modus operandi*, but you may hunt in stubble fields as well.

Though plans are to double the size of the lodge from four bedrooms to eight in 2000, this is not one of those high volume operations. Corporations or groups of friends frequently book the entire place. Meals are built around family recipes, and nobody ever, ever goes away hungry.

K-D Hunting Acres

Tekamah, Nebraska

Fields nestle among ponds and creeks — and quail, pheasants, Huns and sharptail love it.

VITAL STATISTICS:

GAME BIRDS:
CHUKAR, PHEASANT, QUAIL
Source of Birds: Wild and pen-reared
Seasons:
October through March
Land: 1,200 private acres
Accommodations:
MOTELS IN TOWN
MAXIMUM NUMBER OF HUNTERS: 40
Meals: Pheasant dinners (lunch)
Conference Groups: Yes
Guides: Trained dogs and guides
Dogs and Facilities:
Kennel for hunters' dogs, dog training
Shotgun Sports:
Driven birds, sporting clays, tower or release shoots
Other Services:
Birds cleaned and packed for travel
Rates:
From $125 / gun
Gratuity:
Hunter's discretion
Preferred Payment:
Cash, MasterCard, Visa or check
Getting There:
Fly to Omaha and rent a car.

Contact:
Kim or Dee Snow
K-D Hunting Acres
2980 County Rd. 1
Tekamah NE 68061
402/374-1428

THIRTY-FIVE MILES NORTH OF OMAHA is one of the nation's top-flight and increasingly well-known hunting preserves. Like so many regulated shooting areas, this one started out as a fair-sized farm, but the uncertainties of the market for livestock sent Kim and Dee Snow into the shooting ground business. And they've prospered. Each year, more than 900 gunners from throughout the country come to K-D for pheasant, Hungarian partridge and quail.

While the Missouri River has worn a huge floodplain as it meanders between Iowa and Nebraska, the land above the river bottom rolls like a stormy sea. No 100-acre fields stretch 'til sunset; 300-acre pastures are virtually unheard of. Instead it's a patchwork of hilly, grassy plots of 10 to 20 acres, delineated by twisting creeks and little ponds. As the land nears water, its vegetation becomes thick with willows and brush. Otherwise, cover is native grass and clover. In this vicinity, wild birds are not wholly uncommon. The range of bobwhite extends a hundred miles or so north. Gray partridge are native, and you may find sharptail. Pheasants, of course, are king.

Gunners often bring their own dogs for half- or full-day hunts. If yours isn't travelling with you, then you have your choice of pointing German shorthairs or Labs. Both are splendid retrievers; it just depends on how you like to hunt.

With a number of motels four miles away in Tekama and a big city less than an hour away, K-D has not felt compelled to provide accommodations. Clean motel rooms in the neighborhood go for $25 to $30 per night. And so it is with meals. Fantastic baked pheasant dinners (read that lunches in urbanese) come with the hunts. Suppers and breakfast can be found easily at family restaurants in town.

Sandhills Adventures/Uncle Buck's Lodge

B r e w s t e r ,   N e b r a s k a

Bird hunters find prairie chickens as well as pheasants in the rounded hills on this ranch.

VITAL STATISTICS:

GAME BIRDS:
DUCKS, GEESE, GROUSE, PHEASANT
Source of Birds: Wild and pen-reared
Seasons:
SHARPTAIL, PRAIRIE CHICKENS: Mid-September through December
PHEASANT (WILD): November through January
PHEASANT, QUAIL (PRESERVE): September through March
GEESE: October through mid-January
DUCKS: October through January
Land: 12,000 private acres
Accommodations:
PRIVATE LODGE
NUMBER OF ROOMS: 10
MAXIMUM NUMBER OF HUNTERS: 20
Meals: Fine dinners of steak and shrimp
Conference Groups: Yes
Guides: Trained dogs and guides
Dogs and Facilities:
Kennel for hunters' dogs, dog training
Shotgun Sports:
Driven birds
Other Services:
Birds cleaned and packed for travel
Other Activities:
Big game, bird-watching, canoeing, hiking, horseback riding, wildlife photography
Rates:
From $950 / 3 days
Gratuity:
$100 / 3 day hunt
Preferred Payment:
Cash, MasterCard, Visa or check
Getting There:
Fly to Omaha and rent a car.

Contact:
Delten Rhoades
Sandhills Adventures/Uncle Buck's Lodge
Box 100
Brewster NE 68821
308/547-2210
Fax: 308/547-2255
EMAIL: unclebucks@neb-sandhills.net

THE COUNTY SEAT of Blaine County, Brewster sits virtually by itself in the middle of Nebraska. Twenty miles west is the Nebraska National Forest, and 30 miles-plus to the east is Calamus Reservoir State Recreation Area. Through the middle of this country flows the North Loup River, which Uncle Buck's Lodge borders. Hills are rounded and sweatered in switchgrass and bluestem. Level land along the rivers is sown in rye and corn. Canebreaks are common. There's some scrubby brush, but real woods are fairly rare.

While 2,500 acres of Sandhill's 12,000 acres are devoted to gunning for pen-raised quail and pheasant from October through March, it's the chance to bag a prairie chicken or two that draws most of the hunters. You'll walk and walk some more, prowling the hilly country if you want to get a shot. Where they were one day, they won't be the next. You may ambush them coming into a field, but don't bet your life savings. The lottery's a surer thing. Yet, if the morning is frosty, prairie chickens will covey up into flocks of 50 or more. Find a flock, swing through the bird, touch the trigger, and you're a winner! Off the preserve land, you can hunt for wild pheasant.

Duck hunting is high on the agenda here, too. You'll hunt mallards, redheads, pintail, canvasbacks, wigeon and teal from simple blinds on the edge of ponds. Geese come into stubble and corn fields. Both stand-up and layout blinds prove effective.

Four years ago, Sandhills completed a new three-story, cedar-sided western-style lodge. Upstairs are 10 guest rooms, eight with private baths. Below is the great room and the dining room where solid servings of steak and beef highlight dinner menus. Nearby cabins contain four more guest rooms.

Cannonball Company

Here the whole town's banded together to offer wingshooters great hunting.

VITAL STATISTICS:

GAME BIRDS:
HUNS, GROUSE, PHEASANT
Source of Birds: Wild
Seasons:
HUNS and SHARPTAILS: September through January
PHEASANTS: Early October through January
Land: 35,000 private acres
Accommodations:
MULTIPLE BED AND BREAKFASTS
NUMBER OF ROOMS: 40
MAXIMUM NUMBER OF HUNTERS: 40
Meals: Breakfast only
Conference Groups: Yes
Guides: Trained dogs and guides
Dogs and Facilities:
Kennel for hunters' dogs
Other Services:
Birds cleaned and packed for travel
Other Activities:
Big game, bird-watching, wildlife photography
Rates:
From $185 / gun / day
Gratuity:
Hunter's discretion
Preferred Payment:
Cash, MasterCard, Visa or check
Getting There:
Fly to Bismark or Dickinson and rent a car.

Contact:
Pat Candrian
Cannonball Company
PO Box 163
Regent ND 58650
800/920-4910
Fax: 701/563-4497
WEB: www.customdata.com/cannon ball

AMONG BIRD HUNTING operations, the Cannonball Company is quite unusual. It's a cooperative of farmers and townspeople who've banded together to offer the best they have to traveling bird hunters. And, what they offer is well worth thinking about.

Regent is a crossroads town about 40 miles southeast from Dickinson, a modest city some 60 miles from Montana on Interstate 94. Rising in White Lake National Wildlife Refuge, the Cannonball River winds first north, then southeast through the town of New England before reaching Regent. Low bluffs line the river, creating a valley where weeds thrive on the floodplain. Above the river, the prairie gently rolls. You know how it is: acres and acres of grass and grain, cut by sharp-shouldered stream courses too small and shallow to be called coulees. Cover in these is thicker. Prime hunting is found from early October into November. But late season hunts, when a crust of snow covers the ground and pheasants have become savvy to the ways of gunner and dog, can also be fun and productive. Because you have to work harder, rates are reduced. Limited deer hunting, packages expressly for Badlands sharptails, and prairie dog shoots are also available.

Cannonball hunts wild birds: pheasants, sharptails and Huns. Your guides are likely to be the owners of the cooperative: Jim Binstock, farmer; Pat Candrian, farmer, county commissioner and president of the North Dakota Association of Counties; Curt Honeyman, farmer and coach of the basketball team; and Monte Strand, farmer and member of the school board. All are licensed by the North Dakota Department of Game and Fish. Conversation on hunts ranges far afield from just that of birds and dogs.

At night you'll hole up in private homes that have been tastefully remodeled into bed-and-breakfasts. Some are located in town and others on farms on the prairie. If your group has special needs, other accommodations can be found. Dinners are found at restaurants in town.

❖ *A Willow Creek Guide* ❖

North America's GREATEST Bird Hunting Lodges & Preserves

[M I D W E S T]

Oak Lodge

M e n o k e n , N o r t h D a k o t a

Cocker spaniels are the busiest of bird dogs, and at Oak Ridge, you'll learn that they're among the best.

VITAL STATISTICS:

GAME BIRDS:
DUCKS, GEESE,
HUNGARIAN PARTRIDGE,
PHEASANT, SHARPTAIL
Source of Birds: Wild
Seasons:
HUNGARIAN PARTRIDGE and
SHARPTAIL: Mid-September through
December
PHEASANT: Mid-October through
December
WATERFOWL: October through
November
Land: 4,000 private and public acres
Accommodations:
REMODELED COUNTRY SCHOOL
NUMBER OF ROOMS: 4
MAXIMUM NUMBER OF HUNTERS: 8
Meals: Finest game cuisine
Conference Groups: Yes
Guides: Trained dogs and guides
Dogs and Facilities:
Kennel for hunters' dogs, dog training
Shotgun Sports:
Skeet and sporting clays close by
Other Services:
Birds cleaned and packed for travel
Rates:
$1,050 / 3 day / gun / minimum
party of four
Gratuity:
10% - 15%
Preferred Payment:
Cash or check
Getting There:
Fly to Bismark and you will be met.

Contact:
Tom Ness
Oak Lodge
6400 158th St.
Menoken ND 58558
701/673-3450

LORD LOVE AN ENGLISH COCKER. Never has there been a more meticulous breed. Leaving no blade unscented, cockers busily cast to and fro, working here, worrying there, poking about and always—well maybe not always, but usually—within easy gunning range. Of easy disposition, they'll sprawl in your lap if you let 'em. There's nothing they desire more out of life than to please.

If you hunt Oak Lodge's 4,000 acres, you'll hunt over cockers. Oh, you may find an English springer or two in lodge owner Tom Ness' kennel and perhaps one Lab for dirty work on ducks and geese. But in the main this is cocker country, and better bird hunting country than his area between the Missouri and the Dakota pothole country is very hard to find.

Getting underway in mid-September, the season opens with sharptails and Hungarian partridge. Best hunted soon after the season opens, stocks of sharpies and Huns have been on the decline. These birds native to the high prairie are unusually susceptible to bitter winters and cold, wet springs. A month later, pheasants come in, and during the first week or so of that season, combined hunts for all three upland birds are possible.

Pothole ducks—primarily pintails, gadwall, teal and mallards, but also canvasbacks and redheads—become legal game during the first of October. If mixing upland birds and waterfowl is your meat, link up with Tom in the third week of October. Later, in November, the potholes freeze over and waterfowling shifts to the Missouri. By then only the hardiest species remain. Geese too, hunted from layouts under magnum decoys, offer sport in November and December. Pheasants hold up pretty well through the end of the season in December, but the winds can be bitter cold. There is, however, no time that is more invigorating to hunt.

Four bedrooms with two baths in the basement of a charmingly remodeled schoolhouse accommodate hunters. You'll dine on exquisite game custom prepared by chef David Barberé, a Basque whose restaurant was a staple of the upscale crowd in nearby Bismark, the state capital.

Pheasants are the king bird in the grasses of the Midwest prairies. Native cocks are best hunted in late October and early November, but stocked birds can be shot from September to April.

Sheldon's Waterfowl & Upland Bird Hunts

S t r e e t e r ,   N o r t h   D a k o t a

With comfortable houses in town and combo hunts for birds and deer, this place is hard to beat.

VITAL STATISTICS:

GAME BIRDS:
DOVE, DUCKS, GEESE, HUNGARIAN PARTRIDGE, PHEASANT, SHARPTAIL, TUNDRA SWANS, SANDHILL CRANE, WILSON'S SNIPE
Source of Birds: Wild and pen-reared
Seasons:
DOVE, SHARPTAIL, HUNS: September through December
PHEASANT, DUCKS, GEESE, SWANS: October through November
Land: 41,000 private acres
Accommodations:
SMALL HOUSES IN TOWN
NUMBER OF ROOMS: 4 IN EACH HOUSE
MAXIMUM NUMBER OF HUNTERS: 30
Meals: Country meals with a German flare
Conference Groups: Yes
Guides: Trained dogs and guides
Dogs and Facilities:
Kennel for hunters' dogs
Shotgun Sports:
Informal instruction
Other Services:
Birds cleaned and packed for travel, proshop
Other Activities:
Big game, bird-watching, wildlife photography
Rates:
From $1,000 / 3 days / minimum party of 4
Gratuity:
$50 per person
Preferred Payment:
Cash or check
Getting There:
Fly to Bismark and the lodge van will pick you up.

Contact:
Sheldon Schlecht
Sheldon's Waterfowl &
Upland Bird Hunts
5034 48th R Ave.
Streeter ND 58483
701/424-3625
WEB: www.sportsmansweb.com/ sheldons

INTERSTATE 94 MARCHES ACROSS the southern third of North Dakota like a beeline. It may be the straightest stretch of highway in the country. About 120 miles west of the Minnesota border at exit 228, State Rt. 30 drops south for 15 miles or so to Streeter (pop. 160). Here you can hunt them all—dove, sharptails, Huns, pheasant, dark and light geese, ducks, sandhill cranes, tundra swans and Wilson's snipe—virtually every bird species legally taken in the state.

The owner of this wingshooter's emporium, Sheldon Schlecht, cut his teeth on waterfowling and now farms some 41,000 acres. This is grazing and row-crop country, and in between potholes that attract waterfowl come fall, he leaves plots of unharvested corn, sunflowers, millet, milo and oats. On some plots, pheasants are supplementally stocked, but in the main, you'll be hunting for wild birds.

No half-day in-and-out hunts these. Packages run from three to six days and typically include early morning, midday and afternoon hunts. You can mix and match. Hunt geese (north of Bismark an hour west on the Missouri River) at dawn, chase pheasants or sharptails after a late breakfast, come in for lunch, and finish up on ducks in the evening. Everything is provided, from airport pickup, guides, dogs, cleaning and packaging of game, meals and, of course, lodging. Your party of three or more will stay in its own house (not fancy, but private). Daily maid service is provided. Guides have dogs or you can bring your own. Sheldon recommends a 12-gauge, but the prudent hunter brings both a duck gun and a 20 for upland birds.

Farms around Streeter grow big deer. Week-long combo hunts for deer, waterfowl and upland birds may be the deal of the century. For $2400, you'll have a three-day deer hunt with a guaranteed shot at a legal buck (or you'll receive a $500 refund), and three days of duck, goose and upland game hunting.

Brier Oak Hunting Club

Bellevue, Ohio

Algonquins once mined flint where you'll be hunting upland birds among extensive native flora.

VITAL STATISTICS:

GAME BIRDS:
CHUKAR, PHEASANT, QUAIL
Source of Birds: Pen-reared
Seasons:
September through March
Land: 400 private acres
Accommodations:
IN NEARBY TOWN
Meals: Restaurants
Conference Groups: Yes
Guides: Trained dogs and guides
Dogs and Facilities:
Dog training
Shotgun Sports:
Five-stand, sporting clays
Other Services:
Birds cleaned and packed for travel
Rates:
From $82.50 / 4 birds
Gratuity:
$10 - $20 / gun
Preferred Payment:
Cash or check
Getting There:
Fly to Sandusky and rent a car.

Contact:
Kevin Schaeffer
Brier Oak Hunting Club
5316 Sandhill Rd
Bellevue OH 44811
419/483-4953
Fax: 419/483-7283
EMAIL: brieroak@belleviewo.com

WHAT SEPARATES ONE PRESERVE from another? Often it's just a little twist in perspective. Take Brier Oak, for instance. On the surface, there's little to differentiate this hunting ground just south of Sandusky from other conscientious and well-run operations that offer pheasants, chukar and quail.

But wait. When owner Kevin Schaeffer describes his planting program, two things immediately become crystal clear. This guy understands the land and he cares about its history. Get him to tell you about the flint quarries on the property, the pits where Algonquins mined that hard sedimentary silicate so prized for knives and points for arrows and spears. He'll bend your ear about the Indian raids on the property during the early 1800s, when Ohio territory was first enjoying statehood. He'll show you the old military road that follows the path the Indians cut through the highest and driest rise of his farm.

Kevin pores over soil maps and matches native grasses and other vegetation to the soil types where the plants were originally developed. This is part of the ancient bed of Lake Erie, and it's flat. Once swelled with glacial meltwater, after the lake drained, it left vast beaches. As soon as the climate permitted, prairie grasses colonized the area and tall pampas-like grasses—phragmites—took over where the land was moist.

If you hunt Brier Oak and are aware of its natural and social history, your visit will be much more interesting. With luck (more important, always, than skill), you'll knock down half a dozen or more pheasants. Hunt with your own dog, or one provided by a guide. If you want to hunt over a specific breed—a vizula or a German wirehair, for instance—all you have to do is ask, and Kevin will strive to provide.

This is a membership club, but nonmembers are perfectly welcome. Nonmembers pay a couple bucks more per bird. Accommodations and restaurants are easily available within a few miles.

Hidden Haven Shooting Preserve

S u g a r   G r o v e ,   O h i o

What's more difficult that a sporting clays double? Why a triple … and now you're really ready to hunt birds.

VITAL STATISTICS:

GAME BIRDS:
CHUKAR, PHEASANT, QUAIL
Source of Birds: Pen-reared
Seasons:
October through March
Land: 105 private acres
Accommodations:
IN NEARBY TOWN
Meals: Restaurants
Conference Groups: Yes
Guides: Trained dogs and guides
Dogs and Facilities:
Kennel for hunters' dogs, dog training
Shotgun Sports:
Driven birds, five-stand, shooting schools, skeet, sporting clays, tower or release shoots
Other Services:
Birds cleaned and packed for travel, pro shop
Rates:
From $360 / half day, for group up to 4 or so
Gratuity:
$50 - $75
Preferred Payment:
Cash or check
Getting There:
Fly to Columbus and rent a car.

Contact:
Ronald L. Blosser
Hidden Haven Shooting
Preserve
9192 Buckeye Road
Sugar Grove OH 43155-9632
740/746-8568
Fax: 740/746-8605

JUST WHEN YOU THOUGHT you had that sporting clays game figured out, there comes these guys, Richie Fritella and his son. Because shotgunners whose preference lies with pumps and autoloaders have been getting off easy, Messrs. Fritella devised a new demonic twist: three-shot sporting clays. Yep. Three targets. How about a springing teal, followed by a crossing pair on report? Or what about a smoking incomer, a bouncing bunny, and then a lazy crosser that dies the moment it comes into view.

You'd expect stuff like this to take root at Hidden Haven, an unpretentious-sounding shooting preserve about an hour south of Columbus on U.S. 33. At this writing, preserve owner Ron Blosser is president of the National Sporting Clays Association. At Hidden Valley, you'll find virtually every clay sport known to shotgun-kind.

But here in the sandstone country that eventually climbs into the foothills of the Appalachians, is a nifty run of fairly small fields given over to fine bird hunting. Hilltops are fairly flat, but not quite. And hill sides frequently steepen into cliffs that drop 70 feet or more to valley floors a quarter of a mile wide. Switchgrass predominates, but it's complemented by wild deer mix, canary grass and milo. Strips tend to withstand the winter.

Ron's kennel contains a number of Brittanies, a shorthair or two, and a Lab or two for cleaning up after the tower shoots. But in the main, gun dog duty is discharged by a handful of English setters, run by Randy Lawrence, a field editor for *Sporting Clays* magazine. Randy also trains dogs at Hidden Haven.

No accommodations are found on site here. Lancaster, a small city, is a handful of miles northwest toward Columbus. Most gunners are glad to get off the preserve to spend the night, lest that blasted three-shot sporting clays will trouble their dreams.

Tune up your shooting with a round of sporting clays before heading afield for birds. Many of the better wingshooting lodges and preserves offer clays games and shooting instruction.

Hill'n Dale Club Inc

M e d i n a ,   O h i o

For sporting clays and pheasants, businessmen are drawn to this preserve south of Cleveland.

VITAL STATISTICS:

GAME BIRDS:
CHUKAR, HUNGARIAN PARTRIDGE, PHEASANT, QUAIL
Source of Birds: Pen-reared
Seasons:
October through April
Land: 180 private acres
Accommodations:
OLD FARMHOUSE LODGE
NUMBER OF ROOMS: 3
MAXIMUM NUMBER OF HUNTERS: 10
Meals: Catering available with advance notice
Conference Groups: Yes
Guides: Trained dogs and guides
Dogs and Facilities:
Kennel for hunters' dogs
Shotgun Sports:
Driven birds, five-stand, skeet, sporting clays
Other Services:
Birds cleaned and packed for travel
Other Activities:
Fishing, hiking
Rates:
Nonresident memberships:
Approximately $850 / year;
hunts priced by the bird;
lodging $50 / night
Gratuity:
$30 - $40
Preferred Payment:
Cash or check
Getting There:
Fly to Cleveland and rent a car.

Contact:
Shawn Spindel
Hill 'n Dale Club Inc
3605 Poe Rd
Medina OH 44256
330/725-2097
Fax: 330/728-2129
WEB: www.hillndaleclub.com

OR MORE THAN 50 YEARS, this charming farm just west of a line drawn between Cleveland and Akron has provided hunting and clay shooting sport for members. Now under new management, Hill'n Dale has reduced rates for nonresidents of the northern Ohio area. This makes the preserve especially attractive to hunters with temporary assignments in the region or those whose business brings them in and out of the area on a regular basis.

At Hill'n Dale, you'll find bird hunting, fishing, sporting clays, and plenty of room to host corporate or conference events. Once a dairy farm, pastures are now sown in strips of mixed sorghum, milo and Sudan grass. Sudan grass provides hardy and tall cover that wears well in the winter. Other fields are planted with switchgrass, the old standby, one of the most durable prairie grasses. Hunting here is somewhat reminiscent of hunting on the plains. The terrain rolls a bit, but is easily negotiated. No steep coulees or canyons here. Hill'n Dale maintains three hunting zones of about 50 acres each.

Shotgunners will also enjoy the 25-station sporting clays course. Three stations feature overeater shots (always a treat), and a trap atop a 45-foot tower (even more of a treat) sails birds past gunners with frustrating regularity. Affiliated with numerous national organizations, the club hosts a number of registered tournaments during the year. Instruction and specialty shoots can also be arranged. More informal gunning is available at the hands of the wobble trap. Lakes are stocked with trout and bass . . . just in case your palate craves fish and fowl.

Recently remodeled, the farmhouse contains three bedrooms, which share a bath. Downstairs, the lodge offers a great room with a fireplace and a full commercial kitchen. While no meals are served, guests are welcome to cook for themselves or catering can be arranged with advance notice.

WR Hunt Club

Clyde, Ohio

You'll like this laid back preserve with bunks for hunters that want to spent the night.

VITAL STATISTICS:

GAME BIRDS:
CHUKAR, PHEASANT, QUAIL
Source of Birds: Pen-reared
Seasons:
UPLAND BIRDS: September through March
Land: 300 private acres
Accommodations:
RUSTIC LODGE
NUMBER OF ROOMS: 3
MAXIMUM NUMBER OF HUNTERS: 10
Meals: Homemade and very good
Conference Groups: Yes
Guides: Trained dogs and guides
Dogs and Facilities:
Kennel for hunters' dogs
Shotgun Sports:
Shooting schools, sporting clays
Other Services:
Birds cleaned and packed for travel, pro shop
Rates:
$25 / night by prior arrangement
Gratuity:
Hunter's discretion
Preferred Payment:
Cash or check
Getting There:
Fly to Toledo or Cleveland and rent a car.

Contact:
Robert or Betty Wright
WR Hunt Club
5690 CR237
Clyde OH 43410
419/547-8550

SOME PLACES FEEL LIKE HOME, and this preserve off the Ohio Turnpike about 20 miles southwest of Sandusky is one of those. Bob and Betty Wright own the preserve. What's special here is Betty's sense of humor: "Oh, we're a family operation, so I guess we can do what we want," she laughs. She's talking about the membership-only policy, in which the "only" doesn't apply. "Anyone can stay," she says. "We have some guys that drive up from Cincinnati [five hours south]. They have dinner, sleep over, eat full breakfasts [she chuckles as if she's sharing a secret] and then they hunt and go home. They live too far away to be members…wouldn't make sense. So we charge them the regular rate of $15 per night and add the daily membership fee…what is it, $10?…that's what they pay. Unless we're booked with members."

This is flat country, and everybody knows who's pounded their way over the interstate. Cornfields predominate. The preserve plants thick canary and Sudan grasses and also makes use of stubble fields from its farming operations. ("Bob's the farmer," Betty says. "I keep him in business with the preserve.") You'll find the normal bill of fare: pheasants, chukar and quail. Nonmembers pay by the bird. Pheasants run $17 each; chukar and quail are proportionately less. A gunning fee of $10 is also collected from nonmembers, and you'll pay $40 for a dog and guide for a typical half-day hunt. Sporting clays on the 20-station course are also available here.

The clubhouse is a two-story affair with a deck that overlooks the property. Lunch is the main meal and everybody fills up on pheasant soup (pheasant stewed in chicken broth with celery, onions, carrots and egg noodles) and a local version of a Philly Cheese steak: 1/3 lb. chopped beef patty, grilled onions and melted Swiss cheese on a grilled rye bun. There's pie ("If you ask nicely," you can hear Betty grin, "and we're in the mood"). "Pecan, peach, apple, coconut cream, elderberry… one guy wanted chocolate cream…I always thought that tasted kinda dumb…but he's a nice guy so we made it for him." This is a place to come back to.

[M I D W E S T]

VITAL STATISTICS:

GAME BIRDS:
PHEASANT, QUAIL, TURKEY
Source of Birds: Wild
Seasons:
UPLAND BIRDS: November through January
TURKEY: Mid-April through mid-May
Land: 150,000 private acres
Accommodations:
PRIVATE LOG LODGE
NUMBER OF ROOMS: 3
MAXIMUM NUMBER OF HUNTERS: 15
Meals: Solid country food of ample amount
Conference Groups: Yes
Guides: Trained dogs and guides
Dogs and Facilities:
Kennel for hunters' dogs
Other Services:
Birds cleaned and packed for travel
Other Activities:
Big game, fishing
Rates:
From $250 / day for 2 or more days
Gratuity:
Hunter's discretion
Preferred Payment:
Cash or check
Getting There:
Fly to Tulsa and the lodge van will meet you.

Contact:
Ron Thompson
Bird-N-Buck Outfitters
PO Box 442
Fairfax OK 74637
918/642-5509

Bird-N-Buck Outfitters

F a i r f a x ,   O k l a h o m a

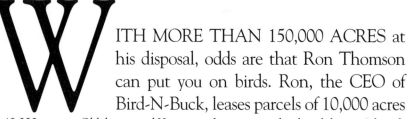

Tall grass prairies hold infinite numbers of wild birds, but finding them is up to you.

WITH MORE THAN 150,000 ACRES at his disposal, odds are that Ron Thomson can put you on birds. Ron, the CEO of Bird-N-Buck, leases parcels of 10,000 acres to 40,000 acres in Oklahoma and Kansas, and no matter what hand the year's breeding cycle has dealt, there's more than likely a place where populations are strong and hunters are scarce.

The mainstay of Bird-N-Buck Outfitters is 40,000 acres of tall grass prairie north of Fairfax along the Kansas Border, a couple of hours from both Oklahoma City and Tulsa. This is big country, and Ron runs pointers to cover it as best as he can. At times, clients hunt from horseback, watching the dogs cut back and forth. Hunters are supposed to rivet attention on the pointers, but eyes and minds wander, so vast is the horizon, so subtle the hues of sky, so mesmerizing the flow of clouds and grass from horizon to horizon. Here and there the prairie gives way to canyons, some defined by rocky bluffs, others headed up with thickets of plum. This is the best terrain for wild pheasants and quail, but not always.

At times, better hunting is found in agricultural regions in south-central Kansas, and Ron shifts his operations there. Wheat, milo and a little corn are the lead crops in this district. And at times, pheasant and quail hunting here can be extremely productive. Quail hunting on the semiarid ranchlands of western Kansas can also pay off. While Ron focuses most of his energy on wild birds, he also operates a 1,000-acre preserve where hunters—often corporate groups—chase pen-raised birds.

On the home spread, the main log lodge houses 14 hunters in a bunkroom and a pair of doubles with private baths. Everybody eats well. Dinners are legendary for thick slabs of steak and hand-sized pork chops. So large is dinner that most hunters forego a big breakfast in the morning, preferring to load up on grits, eggs, biscuits and gravy, and all those other health foods after the morning hunt. A 2,600-foot asphalt runway handles all but the largest private aircraft, and a hanger keeps planes out of the weather while their passengers hunt.

Red Rock Ranch

Marland, Oklahoma

On this ranch, the double gun rules the roost.

VITAL STATISTICS:

GAME BIRDS:
CHUKAR, PHEASANT, QUAIL
Source of Birds: Wild and pen-reared
Seasons:
November through mid-March
Land: 5,000 private acres
Accommodations:
LUXURY MOBILE HOMES
NUMBER OF ROOMS: 12
MAXIMUM NUMBER OF HUNTERS: 12
Meals: Hearty beef and fowl by professional chef
Conference Groups: Yes
Guides: Dogs and guides included
Dogs and Facilities:
Kennel for hunters' dogs
Shotgun Sports:
Wobble trap
Other Services:
Birds cleaned and packed for travel
Other Activities:
Big game, fishing
Rates:
$750 / gun
Gratuity:
Hunter's discretion
Preferred Payment:
Cash or check
Getting There:
Fly to Oklahoma City or Tulsa and rent a car.

Contact:
Bill Spires
Red Rock Ranch
30701 Badlands
Marland OK 74644
580/268-9663
Fax: 580/268-9107

THE ARKANSAS RIVER heads south from Nebraska into Oklahoma, and where it makes a huge bend to the east is the country occupied by Red Rock Ranch. Open land swells and ebbs like a Bach concerto. Hills are armored in tough prairie grasses: little and big bluestem, Indian and switchgrass. Hardwoods are like icing drizzled on a cake. Stands of black jack and post oak drip over some of the ridges and flow down into watercourses. Plum thickets are prevalent, as are feed plots of milo, wheat, clover and alfalfa.

Of Red Rock's 5,000 acres, about half are included in the preserve. The ranch has set aside 25 fields of roughly 100 acres each for release pheasant, quail and chukar hunts. Two gunners and a guide will have the field to themselves. You'll hunt one field in the morning and another in the afternoon and, should you overnight and plan to hunt after breakfast, you'll walk a field you haven't hunted before. No hunting the same field more than once here. Dogs there are aplenty: shorthairs, English setters, Brittanies, English pointers, and weimaraners. Typically, two gunners hunt with a single guide and dog, but other arrangements may be made on special request. Double guns are favored here over semiautos or pumps. You can sharpen your skills on the ranch's wobble trap game.

On the property, you'll find a pond stocked with trophy rainbows, which if you desire, can be cleaned and frozen for your trip home. You'll stay in mobile homes, especially configured so each bedroom has its own private bath. A trained chef provides hearty meals. The daily fee of $750 is inclusive, and an additional half-day hunt adds another half fee. While Tulsa and Oklahoma City are each about 90 miles from the ranch, the latter offers the better airport for traveling hunters. Transportation from the airport to the ranch and return can be arranged. Private aircraft fly into Ponca City, 11 miles north of the ranch.

[M I D W E S T]

Southern Ranch Hunting Club

C h a n d l e r ,   O k l a h o m a

Tower shoots, field hunts, and sporting clays keep gunners coming back to this elegant club.

VITAL STATISTICS:

GAME BIRDS:
PHEASANT, QUAIL
Source of Birds: Pen-reared
Seasons:
UPLAND BIRDS: October through March
Land: 832 private acres
Accommodations:
PRIVATE LODGE WITH TOUCHES OF ELEGANCE
NUMBER OF ROOMS: 6
MAXIMUM NUMBER OF HUNTERS: 28
Meals: Grilled steak, chicken, pork and barbecue
Conference Groups: Yes
Guides: Trained dogs and guides
Dogs and Facilities:
Kennel for hunters' dogs
Shotgun Sports:
Five-stand, shooting schools, sporting clays, tower or release shoots
Other Services:
Birds cleaned and packed for travel
Other Activities:
Bird-watching, boating, fishing, hiking, wildlife photography
Rates:
From $570 / 2 guns
Gratuity:
Hunter's discretion
Preferred Payment:
Cash, MasterCard, Visa or check
Getting There:
Fly to Oklahoma City and rent a car.

Contact:
Dean Caton
Southern Ranch Hunting Club
Rt. 2, Box 75
Chandler OK 74834
405/258-0000
Fax: 918/379-4226
EMAIL: southern@brightok.net
WEB: www.brightok.net/~southern

EEP FORK OF THE ARKANSAS RIVER rises a few miles west of this outstanding shotgunning resort, but as yet, the river has not had much time to cut a valley. The land here is about as flat as sheet cake, but it's pocked with numerous small ponds, and good-sized stands of hardwoods prevail. In between are verdant grasslands, prairies that become tawny as days shorten and temperatures fall.

Southern Ranch was one of the first to create a sporting clay's course, and its staff includes instructors certified by the United States Sporting Clays Association and the National Sporting Clays Association. Youth programs here have produced half a dozen national champions and one world champion. Along with clays, you can shoot a round or two of wobble trap.

While sporting clays provides year-round action, its birds—in particular a European-style pheasant shoot—that draws many hunters. From the top of a 50-foot tower back in the woods, pheasants are released one at a time. Birds streak for cover, over shooting butts and gunners, heading for thick brush beyond. Gunning is fast, there's no doubt about that, and shots are not always easy. A minimum tower shoot includes 120 birds for 10 hunters at a price of $175 per gun. And afterward you can do clean-up duty on birds that escaped the barrage.

Field hunts for pheasant and quail begin at $250 for a half day, and there's no limit to the number of birds you can harvest. Hunt over your own dog, or one of the ranch's pointers. The pheasants used by this ranch are brooded on the property, about 18,000 per year. They're kept in high mesh flight pens, and they're wild as March hare's when released. The season runs from October through March, but the gunning is generally best before December, when winter sets in.

Southern Ranch operates a top-flight lodge where accommodations range from a bunkhouse for eight to a palatial director's suite which must be seen to be believed. Dinners feature char-broiled steaks and smoked barbecue.

Triple H Ranch & Hunting Lodge

F r e d e r i c k ,   O k l a h o m a

On varied terrain, hunt dove, ducks, geese, quail and sandhill cranes.

VITAL STATISTICS:

GAME BIRDS:
DOVE, DUCKS, GEESE, QUAIL, SANDHILL CRANES
Source of Birds: Wild
Seasons:
DOVE: September through October
DUCK: Late October to early December, and mid-December through mid-January
GEESE: Late October to early December, and mid-December through early February
QUAIL: November through January
SANDHILL CRANES: Late October through late January
Land: 13,500 private acres
Accommodations:
PRIVATE LODGE AND BUNKHOUSE
NUMBER OF ROOMS: 8
MAXIMUM NUMBER OF HUNTERS: 32
Meals: Mexican, broiled steak, fish
Conference Groups: Yes
Guides: Trained dogs and guides
Dogs and Facilities:
Kennel for hunters' dogs
Shotgun Sports:
Sporting clays
Other Services:
Birds cleaned and packed for travel
Other Activities:
Big game, bird-watching, fishing, wildlife photography
Rates:
From $125 / gun
Gratuity:
$10 - $20
Preferred Payment:
Cash or check
Getting There:
Fly to Lawton (Ft. Sill) and rent a car.

Contact:
Joe E. Horton, M.D.
Triple H Ranch & Hunting Lodge
608 Cedar Lane
Frederick OK 73542
580/335-5385

PRESERVES HAVE A PLACE, to be sure. Hunters with limited time can be fairly well assured of finding upland quarry, be it pheasants, quail, Hungarian partridge or chukar. Preserves are dandy places to work birds, and they're ideal for introducing new hunters to the sport. Why? It's a controlled environment.

On the other hand, wild birds offer more of a challenge. Whether or not they flush better or faster or higher is a matter of endless debate. But everyone agrees that wild birds are generally harder to find. Even to come close, you need to know what they eat. You also need to know enough about their behavior so you can hazard an educated guess about where they'll be and what they'll be doing during any given day. And finally, there's that something special that comes with pitting your wits against the wiles of a native bird.

At Triple H, you won't find any pen-raised gamebirds. This is a hunting ranch, pure and simple. On about 13,000 acres—8,500 of Joe Horton's and another 5,000 or so he leases—you'll hunt dove, ducks, geese, quail and sandhill cranes. Terrain varies. In the main, it's not overly difficult. Hills are common, but they are neither steep nor long. Joe farms cotton, peanuts and wheat, but much of the land is in buffalo grass and sagebrush. Creeks are frequently rimmed with brush, salt cedar, oak and pecans. For quail, you'll walk and walk some more. But the other birds will keep you pretty much in one spot. Ducks and geese are hunted over decoys in either stand-up or layout rigs.

Triple H provides guides and dogs and recommends that you at least use their guides even if you bring your own dog. Probably a good idea: a local guide will be more likely to put you over game (and keep you out of trouble). And the price—$50 per full day—shouldn't be likely to break your bank. Nor is the cost of accommodations: if you opt for a room in the lodge with meals, guide and dog included, two nights will set you back $600. On the other hand, if you put up in the bunkhouse and do your own cooking, you can get away for as little as $125 per night. It's a do-it-yourselfer's dream. Both the lodge and the bunkhouse are remodeled residences.

[M I D W E S T]

Western Cedar Co.

Mooreland, Oklahoma

A square mile of bird hunter heaven with classic tower shoots to boot.

VITAL STATISTICS:

GAME BIRDS:
CHUKAR, DOVE, PHEASANT, QUAIL, TURKEY
Source of Birds: Wild and pen-reared
Seasons:
DOVE: September
PRESERVE BIRDS: October through March
TURKEY: April
Land: 640 private acres
Accommodations:
BUNKROOM AND BATH IN LOWER LEVEL OF TOM'S HOME
NUMBER OF ROOMS: 1
MAXIMUM NUMBER OF HUNTERS: 5
Meals: Country-fried steak and other goodies
Conference Groups: Yes
Guides: Trained dogs and guides
Dogs and Facilities:
Kennel for hunters' dogs, dog training
Shotgun Sports:
Tower or release shoots
Other Services:
Birds cleaned and packed for travel
Other Activities:
Big game, bird-watching, golf, wildlife photography
Rates:
Lodging and meals $45 / night
Gratuity:
Hunter's discretion
Preferred Payment:
Cash, MasterCard, Visa or check
Getting There:
Fly to Oklahoma City and rent a car.

Contact:
Tom Clark
Western Cedar Co
RR2, Box 120-A
Mooreland OK 73852
888/994-2500
Fax: 580/994-5495

HERE IN THE SANDHILL COUNTRY of western Oklahoma, the land swells and ebbs like a gentle sea. Native grasses cover the countryside, and they ripple with prevailing westerlies. Brush lines watercourses and sneaks into fields the moment a rancher's back is turned. Cedar is the farmer's nemesis. That's why Tom Clark's such a popular guy. He owns a machine that chops cedars to smithereens. Hence the name, "Western Cedar Co."

While he still hogs out these pesky conifers for grateful landowners, his real love is his section, an entire 640 acres—or one square mile—devoted to cover for birds, turkey and deer. About two-thirds of the section is devoted to plots of switchgrass, big bluestem and little bluestem. Tom's enrolled this acreage in the Conservation Reserve Program. The balance of the property is covered with heavy brush (yep, some of it cedars), providing deep habitat for deer, turkey and birds that have seen too much hunting pressure on neighboring ranches.

Tom's bird packages are based on a novel point system. A quail counts for one point; chukar, one-and-a-half points; and a pheasant, two. Rates are based on the number of points per gun: 10 points cost $160; 15 points, $210; 20 points, $260. The beauty of this system is that it allows hunters to shoot anything they flush, whether it be a pheasant, chukar or quail. Unlimited hunts—Tom calls them "Take no prisoner hunts"—begin at $300 for quail, climb to $400 for pheasant and chukar, and top out at $450 for as many birds as you can harvest in a day. Tower shoots are available for as few as five gunners.

In the field, you'll mainly hunt over pointers. They do flashy work in the field. But when it comes to tough retrieves, Tom brings forth his Chesapeake retriever Agnew (as in Spiro), who, like his namesake, seems to believe that a bird in mouth is better than two in the bush and is out for all he can get. Hunts generally include the noon meal, but full board and a bunk in the walk-out basement guestroom can be arranged.

Bass Pheasant Hunting

Kimball, South Dakota

Wild birds on the prairie, pen-reared birds on a full section — hunt both and then compare 'em.

VITAL STATISTICS:

GAME BIRDS:
PHEASANT
Source of Birds: Wild and pen-reared
Seasons:
September through March
Land: 3,000 private acres
Accommodations:
MOBILE HOMES
NUMBER OF ROOMS: 11
MAXIMUM NUMBER OF HUNTERS: 35
Meals: Homecooked
Conference Groups: Yes
Guides: Included
Dogs and Facilities:
Kennel for hunters' dogs
Shotgun Sports:
Driven birds
Other Services:
Birds cleaned and packed for travel
Rates:
$100 / day;
room and board, $50 additional
Gratuity:
Hunter's discretion
Preferred Payment:
Cash or check
Getting There:
Fly to Mitchell or Sioux Falls and rent a car.

Contact:
Patsy Bass
Bass Pheasant Hunting
R-2, Box 15
Kimball SD 57355
605/778-6842
EMAIL: pheasant@easnet.net

GOOD OL' I-90 HAMMERS out the westbound miles one after another across the flat prairie. It isn't flat. Not like you think. Slim rivers have shaved small valleys, and depressions hold small ponds, which in turn carry lots of ducks in the fall. Bird hunters will be impressed by the sheer extent of the grasslands. Unlike Minnesota, where fields are bounded by fences, the land along the interstate is increasingly open. Grasses go on forever, and your mind fills in the birds.

Jim and Patsy Bass run what might be called a pheasant ranch of about 3,000 acres. A 640-acre section, or one square mile, is devoted to preserve hunting. The rest is open land. In their farming operations, they use no herbicides or pesticides. The former eradicates weeds, which pheasants depend on for seed, and the latter removes insects, also important to pheasant diets. Though Jim and Patsy readily admit that they have no data to support their claim, the Bass' believe that the lack of herbicides and pesticides enhances the ability of pheasant to reproduce healthy clutches of young. About 100 acres of southward-facing slopes are set aside as a kind of nursery for hens.

Hunting here is a fairly straightforward affair. A converted school bus (the Ringneck Bus) ferries gunners out to the fields for the morning's mission. Use your own dog or one of the Bass', but in either event, you'll need a guide. Your limit, should you choose to fill it, is 15 birds per day. You'll either walk or hunt from an ATV. Should you and your party wish, driven bird shoots can be arranged. Guests stay in one of the trio of 70-foot-long mobile homes, or if they wish, head for the motels and restaurants of Chamberlain. Choose that alternative at your own risk. While there's nothing wrong with Chamberlain's accommodations, you'll be missing out on Patsy's fine home cooking. And that'd be too bad!

Big Bend Ranch

H a r r o l d ,   S o u t h   D a k o t a

The rule here is walk or get fat!

VITAL STATISTICS:

GAME BIRDS:
DUCKS, GEESE, HUNGARIAN PARTRIDGE, PHEASANT
Source of Birds: Wild and pen-reared
Seasons:
UPLAND BIRDS: September through March
DUCKS: October through January
GEESE: October through December
Land: 3,500 private acres
Accommodations:
MODERN LODGE AND CABIN
NUMBER OF ROOMS: 8
MAXIMUM NUMBER OF HUNTERS: 16
Meals: Elegant cuisine
Conference Groups: Yes
Guides: Trained dogs and guides
Dogs and Facilities:
Kennel for hunters' dogs, dog training
Shotgun Sports:
Five-stand, sporting clays
Other Services:
Birds cleaned and packed for travel, pro shop
Other Activities:
Bird-watching, fishing, wildlife photography
Rates:
From $1995 / 3 days
Gratuity:
Hunter's discretion
Preferred Payment:
Cash or check
Getting There:
Fly to Pierre and meet the lodge van.

Contact:
Alex or Annie Falk
Big Bend Ranch
21617 Joe Creek Rd
Harrold SD 57536
605/229-3035
Fax: 605/229-1888
Off season:
1301 N. 4th St
Aberdeen SD 57401
605/229-3035

BELOW OAHE DAM at Pierre, the Missouri strikes a southeast course for about 35 miles before it doubles back on itself, corrects course again, and continues another 20 miles or so to Chamberlain. The land here has its own stunning, timeless beauty. Gentle bluffs, some cut with cedar-filled coulees, rise from the river to khaki plains 400 feet above. On the north side of the river just west of the peninsula formed by the bend, is the locale hunted by this first-class operation.

Orvis endorsed, Big Bend provides all the amenities: hot tub for soaking muscles stretched in those long walks across the prairie; satellite television with football games from everywhere; eight rooms (four in cabins and four in the modern lodge), each with two beds and private baths; and an excellent kitchen. Just listen to the menu. For hors d'oeuvres, there's focaccia with marinara, chilled and peeled shrimp, and chicken quesadillas. Main courses feature the likes of prime rib complemented by strawberry spinach salad. For dessert, try the white chocolate raspberry cheese cake.

The rule here is walk or get fat, and walk you will. Pheasants and Hungarian partridge are released prior to and occasionally during the season on some 3,500 acres of high but not overly hilly prairie. Intermittent streams have carved channels in the topography and along some of the courses are little rock bluffs. These swales are thick with heavy grasses, though some of the flatter land may be in grain stubble when you hunt. Dogs of the day may be setters, shorthairs, pointers or labs. For those of a mind to, waterfowling can be added for an additional $100 per day. You'll hunt from blinds along the Missouri or over small lakes formed by dams on thin streams. The river is a major path for migrating fowl, and gunning can be heavy. Waterfowlers will start their days before sun-up, and will normally return in time for a hot lunch and an afternoon hunt for pheasants or Huns.

This is Crow Indian reservation country, and no visit is complete without a visit to tribal cultural heritage centers or attendance at Native American dance rituals. Both can be arranged by Alex or Annie Falk, owners and operators of Big Bend.

Biggins Hunting Service

Gregory, South Dakota

Time your hunt for the birds you want and then make a bee-line for Biggins.

VITAL STATISTICS:

GAME BIRDS:
CHUKAR, PHEASANT, QUAIL, TURKEY

Source of Birds: Wild and pen-reared

Seasons:
PHEASANT: September through March
TURKEY: early April through early May; October through late December

Land: 20,000 private and public acres

Accommodations:
MODERN LODGE AND FARM HOUSE
NUMBER OF ROOMS: 11
MAXIMUM NUMBER OF HUNTERS: 21

Meals: Hearty country-style

Conference Groups: Yes

Guides: Trained dogs and guides

Dogs and Facilities:
Kennel for hunters' dogs, dog training

Shotgun Sports:
Driven birds, five-stand, sporting clays, tower or release shoots

Other Services:
Birds cleaned and packed for travel

Other Activities:
Fishing, golf

Rates:
$430 / day

Gratuity:
Hunter's discretion

Preferred Payment:
Cash or check

Getting There:
Fly to Sioux Falls and rent a car.

Contact:
Gregg Biggins
Biggins Hunting Service
RR #3, Box 1
Gregory SD 57533
605/835-8518
Fax: 605/835-8257

IT'S THE AGE-OLD QUESTION every hunter asks: When's the best time to come? The old saw that any day hunting is better than the best day in the office notwithstanding, the answer really depends on what you want to do and how you like to do it. At places like Gregg Biggins', just a hoot and a holler north of the Nebraska state line, you have options galore.

September is the early season, when temperatures rest in the high 60s or low 70s most of the day. While warm, it's not too hot to work a dog for pheasants if you don't overdo it and carry plenty of water afield. Since South Dakota's pheasant season won't open until late October, you'll hunt birds released in cropland groomed as pheasant cover. While hunting these birds is fun, the real kick comes by combining pheasants and dove. Gun over millet or sunflowers in the afternoon, or ponds just as the sun slides under the horizon. Dove and pheasant combo hunts are best in the first three weeks of September. Any later and a hard freeze is apt to chase all the doves south.

South Dakota's pheasant season opens on the third Saturday in October. Hunts shift from preserve ground to the wide-open, rounded hills. You're hunting now for wild birds (or if they were stocked, it's been so long ago that they've forgotten all their bad habits). Opening day is the best of the best times. However, a week later, waterfowl season opens. Gregg pass-shoots geese, mainly Canadas, from pits. After a morning's gunning, you'll return to the lodge for an afternoon's hike behind a pointer, looking for cock birds. After a waterfowl/pheasant combo hunt, no one has any trouble sleeping. November's the best month for goose hunting, but it can hold up into December. Wild pheasants continue through the end of that month. The preserve season extends through March.

Licenses for spring turkey hunts are drawn in South Dakota, and it's best to apply by March of the year in which you want to hunt. Should your name not be drawn, hunting is available on the reservation of the Rosebud Sioux. Fall turkey hunting is an option in this state as well, but like spring hunting, you'll have to weather the draw. In any event, Gregg operates a nice lodge and has recently added a farmhouse for additional accommodations. Meals are traditional—steak and pheasant—and of ample proportions.

Bob Priebe Pheasant Hunting Country

C h a m b e r l a i n ,   S o u t h   D a k o t a

Hunt the prairie east of the river and stay the night right downtown.

VITAL STATISTICS:

GAME BIRDS:
PHEASANT
Source of Birds: Wild and pen-reared
Seasons:
October through December
Land: 1,000 private acres
Accommodations:
IN NEARBY TOWN
Meals: Restaurants of various types
Conference Groups: Yes
Guides: Trained dogs and guides
Dogs and Facilities:
Bring your own kennel if you bring a your dog
Other Services:
Birds cleaned and packed for travel
Other Activities:
Fishing
Rates:
$100 / day
Gratuity:
Hunter's discretion
Preferred Payment:
Cash or check
Getting There:
Fly to Sioux Falls and rent a car.

Contact:
Bob Priebe
Bob Priebe Pheasant Hunting Country
HC69, Box 36
Chamberlain SD 57325
605/734-6153
EMAIL: ipriebe@hotmail.com
WEB: www.chamberlainsd.org/priebe

THE VIEW FROM THE BLUFFS overlooking Chamberlain is stunning. Below is the Missouri, not so wide, but deep and blue-green in the morning sun. To the west, the prairie of olive and khaki struggles to rise from the valley of the river. But it's when you look to the north that you really see the contrast. East of the river, where Bob Priebe has been guiding pheasant hunters for more than a generation, the land is flat. Then it crumbles down a series of coulees into the river. Table above, river below. Pheasants are found on the tablelands.

All 1,000 acres of Bob's farm is managed for one thing: pheasants. He plants feed crops for the birds and mows paths through the fields to assure that you, at least, have easy walking. Guides work pointers or setters down the strips. Pheasants, not unused to this game, either flush or leak out the end of the field. Often they'll race to the end of the feed patch and then wait, apparently afraid to cross the openness to the next patch of cover. That's when you may get them, but only if you hurry. The country is big and open, and pheasants—even those reared in a flight pen—seem to know it. They'll flush and bank downwind and ride the current as if propelled with jets. If you want to nail these birds, you must pull ahead of them more than you'd think.

Bob offers no accommodations or meals on the farm. But not to worry. Chamberlain's long main street is lined with motels of varying price and attributes. Restaurants, too, vary in size and menu. Fast food fanatics will feel at home here, as will those who seek a well-built martini before or with dinner. Chamberlain's best full-service lodging is Cedar Shore's Resort, across the river in Oacoma. Licenses, shotgun shells and other hunting supplies are readily available in town.

Bush Ranch

P i e r r e ,　S o u t h　D a k o t a

Bring a 20 for ringnecks, a 12 for big Canadas and a cooler to carry home your plunder.

VITAL STATISTICS:

GAME BIRDS:
GEESE, PHEASANT
Source of Birds: Wild and pen-reared
Seasons:
GEESE and PHEASANT: October through December
Land: 20,000 private acres
Accommodations:
INDIVIDUAL CABINS
NUMBER OF ROOMS: 20
MAXIMUM NUMBER OF HUNTERS: 40
Meals: Walleye, beef, chicken
Conference Groups: Yes
Guides: Trained dogs and guides
Dogs and Facilities:
Dog training
Shotgun Sports:
Driven birds
Other Services:
Birds cleaned and packed for travel
Other Activities:
Big game, fishing
Rates:
Packages from $1490 / 3 days / minimum party of three
Gratuity:
Hunter's discretion
Preferred Payment:
Cash or check
Getting There:
Fly to Pierre and you'll be collected.

Contact:
Jeff Bush
Bush Ranch
18467 282 Ave
Pierre SD 57501
605/264-5496
Fax: 605/264-5435
EMAIL: jefbush@sullybuttes.net

LOCATED ON A PENINSULA surrounded by Lake Oahe, as the impounded Missouri River is called here, this ranch rides the catbird seat when it comes to hunting geese and pheasants. This run of the river coincides with the core of the Central Flyway. From across the midsection of Canada, geese funnel down the Missouri. Migrations begin in September, reach a peak in November, and taper off in December. If you want to add succulent goose breasts to that stock of wild game filets in your freezer, you'll have no better chance to do so than here, 30 miles north of the state capital in Pierre.

In stubble fields, ranch owner Jeff Bush uses an auger to punch 24-inch wide holes, four feet deep in the firm soil. This is your personal blind. Carry-lite, Big Foot and Outlaw decoys will be arrayed in such fashion as to provide a landing zone for geese and hide you at the same time. Drilled in a row, blinds are about three feet apart. It's the safest set-up Jeff knows.

You'll reach your blind in the pale dawn, get set, and (with luck) the geese will head out to feed soon thereafter. Jeff or another experienced guide will call the birds, and again, if dame fortune smiles, they'll come over, cup their wings, and settle into the spread. When you can see their eye's glint, they're close enough to take with a 20-gauge; however, for most of us, 12-bores deliver better medicine. The daily limit is two birds per gun. And if you've been triply blessed, a few fat northern mallards will pitch into your spread as well. That's a bonus. Sometimes it happens and sometimes it doesn't.

You'll need the 20 anyway. For pheasants, that is. Like many other bird hunting operations in this part of the country, Bush Ranch engages in supplemental stocking. Hundreds of birds, proportional to the anticipated harvest, are released before the preserve season gets underway in early September. They join native pheasants in crop, CRP and shelterbelts that Jeff's planted in cedar, green ash, plumb and chokecherry You'll also flush sharptails, Hungarian partridge, and prairie chickens, which may be taken in accordance with state seasons.

After a combo hunt for geese and upland birds, you'll return to a cabin with two beds and a bath. Cabins also boast kitchenettes, but everybody walks over to the ranch's steakhouse for dinner. On the menu, of course, is fresh walleye as well as various cuts of beef.

171

Circle CE Ranch

D i x o n ,   S o u t h   D a k o t a

Wild bird. Pen-raised bird. By the time the latter's run around the prairie for a month, you tell me the difference.

VITAL STATISTICS:

GAME BIRDS:
DOVE, PHEASANT

Source of Birds: Wild and pen-reared

Seasons:
DOVE: September through mid-October
PHEASANT: September through January

Land: 3,000 private acres

Accommodations:
MODERN LODGE
NUMBER OF ROOMS: 5
MAXIMUM NUMBER OF HUNTERS: 12

Meals: Pheasant and buffalo cooked family style

Conference Groups: Yes

Guides: Trained dogs and guides

Dogs and Facilities:
Kennel for hunters' dogs

Shotgun Sports:
Informal instruction

Other Services:
Birds cleaned and packed for travel

Other Activities:
Big game, bird-watching, boating, canoeing, fishing, hiking, wildlife photography

Rates:
From $250 / gun

Gratuity:
Hunter's discretion

Preferred payment:
Cash or check

Getting There:
Fly to Sioux Falls or Pierre and rent a car.

Contact:
Dick Shaffe
Circle CE Ranch
RR5, Box 98
Dixon SD 57533
605/835-8281

T HE WORLD CHANGES at the Missouri River. Cross at Chamberlain on Interstate 90 and you notice it immediately. If you're heading west on the interstate, you've been banging along on top of the prairie — fat, dumb and happy — and then bam! There's the river some 300 feet below you. The view is awesome. After shooting over the bridge into Oacoma, you're greeted with a modest sign: "The West starts here!"

Indeed it does. While elevations are similar, there's more relief to the land. Short cliffs define hillsides. Creeks snake irregular courses toward the river. Gone are the endless miles of row crops. Instead, range stretches to the horizon. Terrain stays the same after you turn south on State Route 47 and then west on Route 44, headed for Dixon.

This is the country of CE Ranch, tawny gold in autumn. Along with cattle, pastures contain buffalo. And plots have been planted in corn, milo, millet, and sunflowers. CRP land is heavy with wild grasses. Windbreaks and shelterbelts abound. It is country for pheasants. CE Ranch operates some 3,000 acres as a preserve. Ringnecks are released in August in preparation for the regulated shooting zone season, which begins September 1. The further into the season, the wilder the released birds become. By late September, it's hard to distinguish between native and pen-raised stock. But if you plan your hunt in September, you can get yourself into some fabulous dove hunting, along with pheasants.

A typical day at the ranch begins with a huge breakfast. You'll then hop into a small school bus for a ride to the area you'll hunt. Blockers are frequently posted at escape routes for ringnecks. Other hunters work their way down the fields. At noon, a ranch truck delivers a tailgate lunch. During the afternoon, you'll hunt back toward the ranch, arriving at sunset, and ready for drinks, dinner and a good night's sleep in the five-bedroom lodge that sleeps twelve. Indoor kennels are provided for your dogs and, should you have spare time on your hands (read that "limit out early"), you can fish the stocked pond for bass or bluegill, or take your car and go exploring.

Circle H Ranch

G r e g o r y , S o u t h D a k o t a

Call this the "Bronze Bird Triangle," because it's the center of bird hunting in South Dakota.

VITAL STATISTICS:

GAME BIRDS:
PHEASANT, GEESE and GROUSE
Source of Birds: Wild and pen-reared
Seasons:
Mid-September through mid-February
Land: 1,200 private acres
Accommodations:
LODGE AND BUNKHOUSE
NUMBER OF ROOMS: 11
MAXIMUM NUMBER OF HUNTERS: 26
Meals: Abundant family style
Conference Groups: Yes
Guides: Trained dogs and guides
Dogs and Facilities:
Kennel for hunters' dogs
Shotgun Sports:
Sporting clays
Other Services:
Birds cleaned and packed for travel
Other Activities:
Fishing, wildlife photography
Rates:
From $450 / gun
Gratuity:
5%
Preferred Payment:
Cash or check
Getting There:
Fly to Sioux Falls and rent a car.

Contact:
Pete Hegg
Circle H Ranch
1300 W 57th St
Sioux Falls SD 57108
605/336-2111
Fax: 605/338-1189

THIS LITTLE TOWN OF 1,200 down in the south-central part of the state is headquarters for a number of pheasant hunting operations. Few, however, offer traveling bird hunters a wider range of services than the Circle H. Not only is hunting for pheasants unparalleled, but you'll also find sharptails, geese, and great walleye fishing when seasons overlap.

First, the pheasants. Circle H includes more than 8,000 acres with swaths of brushy belts that provide cover when the weather sours, miles and miles of crop and native grassland, and sloughs which draw birds into dense vegetation. Terrain varies as well. Gentle hills give way to sharp-shouldered little draws. Cultivated fields seem endless. You may hunt your way up draws filled with chokecherry, with your bird dog or the guide's doing the hard work. Your job is to be ever vigilant. Who can predict the flush of a cock bird? And the chance of flushing a sharptail keeps you on your toes. Hen pheasant or grouse? You gotta decide before slapping the trigger. Custom hunts expressly for grouse and other hunts for Canada geese can be arranged by special request. To tune your gunning before the hunt, loosen up on the ranch's 13-station sporting clays range.

In 1993, Circle H completed a new timber lodge that sleeps 15 in five bedrooms and a loft. Another dozen gunners can be accommodated in a nearby bunkhouse. You'll enjoy winding down with a Finnish sauna after a full day tramping the fields, and that will put you in the mood for a cocktail from the open bar and a full-course family-style dinner. If you're a night owl, gambling at Indian casinos is readily available, or somebody can break out a deck of cards and run a game right here in the lodge.

Many corporate groups fly directly to the ranch's 2,100-foot grass strip. Others use the lighted runways at Gregory (3,800-feet) or Winner (4,500-feet with VOR approach). The ranch will provide transportation from these strips directly to the lodge. Sioux Falls, about three hours southeast, has the best commercial air service.

[M I D W E S T]

Cocks Unlimited

Gregory, South Dakota

At Bruce and Alice's you're treated like family (but don't have to help with the dishes).

VITAL STATISTICS:

GAME BIRDS:
PHEASANT
Source of Birds: Wild
Seasons:
Late October through mid-December
Land: 4,000 private acres
Accommodations:
MEDIUM-SIZED LODGE
NUMBER OF ROOMS: 8; 6 WITH PRIVATE BATH
MAXIMUM NUMBER OF HUNTERS: 18
Meals: Golden baked pheasant, prime rib, and homemade breads and pies
Conference Groups: Yes
Guides: Trained dogs and guides
Dogs and Facilities:
Kennels for hunter's dogs
Other Services:
Pro shop
Other Activities:
Fishing
Rates:
$335 / gun / day
Gratuity:
Hunter's discretion
Preferred Payment:
Cash, MasterCard, Visa or check
Getting There:
Fly to Sioux Falls and rent a car.

Contact:
Bruce Shaffer
Cocks Unlimited
RR2, Box 29
E. Hwy. 18
Gregory SD 57533
605/835-8479

SOMETIMES IT'S HARD to differentiate one lodge from another, especially when the territory that they cover is similar. All lodges are commercial operations, but some are more commercial than others. The finest of the commercial lodges function like well-run resorts. Everything happens just like clockwork. Hunters leave and return from the fields at precisely designated times. Meals are equally prompt. Staff is efficient and willing to do its best to meet any need you express. When you hunt at a lodge like this, you generally have nothing to worry about…but you seldom get a chance to know the folks who run it, or to make friendships that transcend time and distances.

On the other hand, there are places like Cocks Unlimited. Before dinner, you're liable to be standing in the kitchen with a libation in your hand, munching on a snack and talking with owners Bruce and Alice Shaffer like they were your second cousins. Dinner eventually gets served, and it's not late. It's just that the Shaffers have allowed a little extra time for visiting in the kitchen. The staff here cares about you. Often one member of a party, because of lack of experience or ability, will come in from the field skunked. Somehow Bruce or a guide will find an extra hour to take the hunter out to a bit of cover for a one-on-one hunt. Why not? Here, there's always time to go the extra mile.

Bruce hunts 4,000 acres of CRP land, corn and milo. Trees are few, so he's starting an aggressive planting program—mainly American plum, Russian olive, and skunk sumac. Walk and block hunting is standard bill of fare. And while Bruce has been favoring Labs over the 18 years he's been running the ranch, he's beginning to see the wisdom in hunting springer spaniels, especially early in the season. "Springers will outhunt a Lab anytime," he says with some sense of disbelief. And if their coats are clipped, they'll not gather the burrs that they'd normally carry by the end of the day. Sounds like a good idea, no?

Dakota Dream Hunts Inc

Arlington, South Dakota

Dinner is the meat-and-potatoes noon meal; afterwards you'll hunt over pointing Labs.

VITAL STATISTICS:

GAME BIRDS:
PHEASANT
Source of Birds: Wild and pen-reared
Seasons:
Mid-September through March
Land: 3,000 private acres
Accommodations:
IN ARLINGTON
Meals: "Dinner" at the lodge, supper and breakfast on your own
Conference Groups: Yes
Guides: Trained dogs and guides
Dogs and Facilities:
Kennel for hunters' dogs, dog training
Shotgun Sports:
Five-stand
Other Services:
Birds cleaned and packed for travel
Other Activities:
Bird-watching, fishing, hiking, wildlife photography
Rates:
From $285 / gun; lodging included
Gratuity:
Hunter's discretion
Preferred Payment:
Cash or check
Getting There:
Fly to Sioux Falls and rent a car.

Contact:
Doug Converse
Dakota Dream Hunts
20259 452nd Ave
Arlington SD 57212
605/983-5033
Fax: 605/983-4767
EMAIL: ddhunt@dtgnet.com
WEB: www.cruising-america.com/dakota

SNAKING DOWN FROM NORTH DAKOTA, the channel of the Missouri River pretty well defines the limits of the four vast continental glaciers known to have advanced across North America during the past million years. Ice sheets covered the land to the east of the river. Along the western margin of the ice sheet is a 70-mile wide band (about the same width as Florida's Everglades), that contains hundreds of ponds formed in depressions left by melting ice

Yet, South Dakota is semiarid. Rainfall is minimal. Thus many of the ponds in this belt only intermittently hold water. When they're driest, their rushes and cattails provide tremendous cover for wild pheasants. Ducks breed here too. Just above the northernmost limit of bobwhite quail, and a shade too far south and west for ruffed grouse, a few gray partridge are found here, as are sharp-tailed grouse, though it's on the eastern edge of their territory.

Dakota Dream Hunts operates a preserve of about 900 acres among more than 3,000 that's available for hunting during the regular season. Fields are planted in corn and other grains, and feed plots are sown with sorghum. Weeds and shelterbelts are nurtured to provide habitat that nurtures birds. Doug and Rich Converse, who own and operate the preserve, stock hens in the spring and cock birds in the fall. The result is a crop of pheasants that's virtually wild if not native. Most hunters go home with full limits. Hunting is on foot, often behind pointing Labs from the Convers' kennel, unless you care to bring your own. Full-day hunts are the rule.

This outfit does not offer accommodations at the ranch—they'll make reservations for you at reduced rates in any one of a number of motels near Arlington, about 10 minutes from the farm. What Dakota Dream does provide is dinner, and here that term means a farm-style noon meal of meat and potatoes with all the trimmings. Afterwards, it's tempting to find an overstuffed chair and snooze for a while, but you'll be better off if you shoot a round of clays from the humbling skat tower. Dakota Dream does not mix parties and caters to groups as well as individuals.

Dakota Hills Private Shooting Preserve

O r a l ,   S o u t h   D a k o t a

So what do you do when the temperature tops 50° in January? Hunt, man, hunt!

TWO DAYS BEFORE YOU ARRIVED, the temperature in this, the banana belt of South Dakota, took a nose dive. Chinook winds had bounced the February temperature up and down in the 40s and 50s, but a system swooped down out of the Canadian Rockies and the bottom fell out. Everything froze. You saw it on the news. You called Tom Laurig, who runs the preserve, and asked that ever-present question: What did the cold snap do to the hunting. Tom laughed and said, "Made it better. You'll see more birds in the next week than most guys see in a lifetime."

Braggadocio? Well, maybe. Tom's got a couple of marshy draws up his 1,200 acres. He calls them the Fossil Pit and Little Vietnam (about as much fun as wading through a rice paddy unless you know where to step). When they freeze, pheasants collect in the cattails. If you work the draws from the bottom up, it's possible to flush 500 pheasants in a day. Hunting them in the dead of winter, when there's just a skiffle (read that three or four inches) of snow on the ground is a treat. In September, Wilson's snipe hang out in these sloughs. They fly like woodcock, only they're a little smaller and their beaks are a bit longer. However, they're just as easy to miss.

Dakota Hills is in the extreme southwestern portion of the state on the Cheyenne River, about 60 miles south of Rapid City. Terrain rolls a good bit more than around Chamberlain. Crops are different too. You'll find more corn, along with milo, millet and Sudan grass. The ranch is irrigated, and brush lines ditches and open waterways. Planted fields are stripped for easy walking. Labs are the dog of choice here, and some of them point.

High on the bank of the Cheyenne, the lodge is of classic cathedral ceiling design. Floor-to-ceiling windows offer views of the Black Hills. Most rooms share baths, but two have private facilities. Meals are much better than average. A typical dinner might include smoked pheasant fettuccini with peapods, followed by key lime pie. Use the hot tub before dinner. If you do it afterwards, that's where your buddy will find you in the morning. The local airport handles corporate jets, and the lodge provides gratis transfers between the preserve and the commercial field at Rapid City.

VITAL STATISTICS:

GAME BIRDS:
CHUKAR, HUNGARIAN PARTRIDGE, PHEASANT, SHARPTAIL, SNIPE
Source of Birds: Wild and pen-reared
Seasons:
PRESERVE BIRDS: September through March
SHARPTAILS: September through December
Land: 1,200 private acres
Accommodations:
MODERN RIVER-FRONT LODGE
NUMBER OF ROOMS: 6
MAXIMUM NUMBER OF HUNTERS: 12
Meals: Outstanding regional cuisine
Conference Groups: Yes
Guides: Trained dogs and guides
Dogs and Facilities:
Kennel for hunters' dogs
Shotgun Sports:
Driven birds, sporting clays, trap
Other Services:
Birds cleaned and packed for travel, pro shop
Other Activities:
Bird-watching, fishing, wildlife photography
Rates:
From $2395 / 3 days
Gratuity:
10% - 15%
Preferred Payment:
Cash, credit card or check
Getting There:
Fly to Rapid City and you'll be collected.

Contact:
Tom Loving
Dakota Hills Private
Shooting Preserve
HC56 Box 90
Oral SD 57766
605/424-2500
Fax: 605/424-2399
EMAIL: dakhills@gwtc.net

Dakota Hunting Farm

Hecla, South Dakota

Bill turns wirehairs that nobody wanted into fantastic bird dogs. Hunt with him and you'll see!

VITAL STATISTICS:

GAME BIRDS:
CHUKAR, DUCKS, GEESE, PHEASANT
Source of Birds: Wild, pen-reared
Seasons:
DOVE: September
UPLAND BIRDS: September through March
WATERFOWL: October and November
Land: 20,000 private acres
Accommodations:
HUGE, WHITE 1900S FARMHOUSE
NUMBER OF ROOMS: 7 PLUS DORM
MAXIMUM NUMBER OF HUNTERS: 30
Meals: Country family-style
Conference Groups: Yes
Guides: Trained dogs and guides
Dogs and Facilities:
Kennel for hunters' dogs, dog training
Shotgun Sports:
Informal instruction
Other Services:
Birds cleaned and packed for travel
Other Activities:
Bird-watching, wildlife photography
Rates:
From $100 / day
Gratuity:
Hunter's discretion
Preferred Payment:
Cash or check
Getting There:
Fly to Aberdeen and the lodge will pick you up.

Contact:
Bill Mitchell
Dakota Hunting Farm
10095 Mitchell Rd
Hecla SD57446-6101
800/356-5281
Fax: 310/457-1169

NOW GERMAN WIRE-HAIRED pointers are not the most beautiful in dogdom. With their coarse and unruly white-tipped wirehairs and mottled coats of white and brown and black and grey, they look a bit like a dog designed by committee. But if you pay no attention to appearances, you'll find, as Bill Mitchell, owner of Dakota Hunting Farms has, that the German wirehair is one fine upland dog.

It takes heart and stamina to cover the big swaths of tough-grassed prairie, heavy plots of CRP ground, and dense stands of cattails and rushes along the edges of wet-weather water courses. Wirehairs are fast, efficient and friendly in the field. It's a joy to watch them slamming through brush. They seem to freeze on point before they come to a halt. And they're steady as Gibraltar. In sum, these dogs are a joy to hunt. And they'll make your experience at Dakota Farms special indeed.

"Oh yeah?" you yawn. Well there's more. Bill's wirehairs are orphans, dogs that nobody wanted. They're dogs once destined for the pound or to be put down. Numerous breed-specific rescue programs match such dogs—typically one- to four-year-old males with some training—with new owners who have the time, energy and financial resources to restore the dog to a productive life. (For more information on rescue programs, contact American Kennel Club headquarters in New York at 212/696-8245 or www.akc.org/rescue.htm)

You'll enjoy hunting over Bill's orphans as much as you'll like the no-nonsense way he runs hunts for dove, upland birds (chukar, Huns and pheasants), and waterfowl on some 20,000 acres along the border separating North and South Dakota. The only difference between hunting in one or the other is that North Dakota's seasons start and end a week or two earlier. Pheasants are the draw here, and over the last couple of years, Bill's hosted a few archers who hunt ringnecks with a long-bow and blunt-tipped arrows.

Guests stay in a huge old farmhouse from the early 1900s. You'll either sleep in one of seven bedrooms or the "dorm" on the top floor. Meals involve pheasant, beef, pork and lots of homegrown vegetables. Packages with lodging and with or without meals require a minimum 3-day stay. Fully guided, one-day hunts without lodging or meals are also available.

Dakota Ridge

A l t a m o n t ,   S o u t h   D a k o t a

Form a line and march across the prairie, jumping pheasants by the score—that's the way to do it.

VITAL STATISTICS:

GAME BIRDS:
GEESE, PHEASANT
Source of Birds: Wild and pen-reared
Seasons:
PHEASANT: September through March
GEESE: October through December
Land: 20,000 private acres
Accommodations:
MODERN LODGE WITH HANDICAPPED ACCESS
NUMBER OF ROOMS: 5
MAXIMUM NUMBER OF HUNTERS: 10
Meals: Pheasant, mashed potatoes and apple pie
Conference Groups: Yes
Guides: Trained dogs and guides
Dogs and Facilities:
Kennel for hunters' dogs, dog training
Shotgun Sports:
Informal instruction
Other Services:
Birds cleaned and packed for travel
Rates:
From $250 / gun
Gratuity:
Hunter's discretion
Preferred Payment:
Cash or check
Getting There:
Fly to Sioux Falls and rent a car.

Contact:
James Dailey
Dakota Ridge
RR2, Box 67
Altamont SD 57226
605/874-2823
EMAIL: dakridge@itctel.com
WEB: www.siteit.com/dakotaridge

A FEW YARDS FROM THE doorstep of the lodge, aptly named "Palace on the Prairie," your guide forms you into a skirmish line. (He won't yell, "Dress right, DRESS!" It ain't that close, but you get the idea.) Dogs, retrievers mainly, work close in front of you. Knee-high native grasses brush past your chaps, but the walking is easy. You hold your shotgun at port arms, trigger finger stretched to the front of the trigger guard or poised over the safety. You're ready, man, psyched on coffee and donuts, that sweet old caffeine rush boosting your adrenaline. You look down the line and you see a guy with a double, a side-by-side, broken over his shoulder. "How in hell," you wonder, "will he ever get on a bird."

To your left, you hear the raucous caw of a rising cock bird before that big old ringneck clears the weeds, two gunners down the line. Pop. A single shot. Guy with the double. Dead bird, and close too. Sounded like a 28. Naw, must be a 20. And so, of course, a bird flushes not ten feet in front of you. Your butt pad gets hung for a moment in your jacket. Seems like it's stuck for an hour. But somehow you manage to throw a shot after the bird. And down it comes. Feeling pretty pleased with yourself, aren't you? It goes on like that, a shot here, a double down the line…and everyone yelling "hen!" when a pheasant with no tail gets up. Soon, though, your group closes in on the lake. Birds that have been high stepping in front of the line begin to flush. It's like the first round of fireworks at the town picnic on the Fourth of July. Singles, a pair, more singles, then with the lakeshore less than 15 yards away, cocks flush like quail. Gunners empty their magazines. It's like the grand finale, only it isn't because you're only half-way into the morning hunt.

A mile and a half of frontage on Lake Alice is an ideal block for running down cock birds. And the lake itself, and a second ranch a ways to the west, provides better than average duck and goose hunting. Wheelchair-bound hunters can also get in on the action in a special cart that owner James Dailey uses. And the "Palace" is fully handicapped accessible. While some mom-and-pop operations rely on charm to overcome little glitches, this family-run pheasant farm is as professional as they come.

Don Reeves Pheasant Ranch

White Lake, South Dakota

Limits are guaranteed on this working farm.

VITAL STATISTICS:

GAME BIRDS:
PHEASANT
Source of Birds: Wild and pen-reared
Seasons:
September through March
Land: 900 private acres
Accommodations:
IN NEARBY TOWN
NUMBER OF ROOMS: 9
MAXIMUM NUMBER OF HUNTERS: 18
Meals: Family-style country cooking
Conference Groups: Yes
Guides: Trained dogs and guides
Dogs and Facilities:
Kennel for hunters' dogs
Other Services:
Birds cleaned and packed for travel
Rates:
$450 / 16 birds / 2 days / hunter; room & board, $40 / night / hunter
Gratuity:
Hunter's discretion
Preferred Payment:
Cash or check
Getting There:
Fly to Sioux Falls and rent a car.

Contact:
Dan Reeves
Don Reeves Pheasant Ranch
Rt. 2, Box 30
White Lake SD 57383
605/249-2693

SINCE 1984, DON REEVES has been running hunts from his 900-acre farm just off Interstate 90 midway between Mitchell and Chamberlain. This is old-fashioned, laid back, bring-your-most comfortable-boots kind of pheasant hunting. Let there be no mistake. This is a working farm, and much of the cover is corn, which stretches down long fields. Along with corn, you'll encounter occasional thick pockets of brush, shelterbelts and fence rows. Every year, gunners who hunt with Don harvest between 6,000 and 7,000 birds. This is one preserve that guarantees your limit.

Lots of walk-and-block hunting here, as both native and released birds sometimes get a little leggy. However, the flatness of the terrain—and it's generally level land, save those little swales that hold wet-weather streams or ponds—makes for easy, almost effortless walking. In fact, the terrain is so mild that it's readily negotiated by wheelchair-bound hunters. And Don, incidentally, holds an annual hunt for disable veterans.

Labs are the dog of choice with Don. He likes the steadiness of their retrieves and their thoroughness in covering a field. But he's not opposed to you using your own dogs. Actually, he welcomes it. It's always a joy to see another good dog at work (and, besides, it gives his Labs a day off). All breeds are welcome, and Don sets aside runs in his kennels for guests' dogs.

Guests stay in a pair of houses six miles away in Mitchell. The first has five bedrooms and two baths, and in the second a single bath serves four bedrooms. Owned and managed by Don's sister and one of her friends, you'll have the feeling of staying with family. Meals are ample as only country cooking can be. Only the most disciplined of hunters avoid foundering on stews and chilis served with home-baked bread at dinner (lunch, for you city guys). Supper is meat and potatoes followed by homemade fruit pies with ice cream. All of this is low-cal and designed to leave you lean and mean for the morning hunt. Right!

[M I D W E S T]

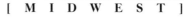

Forester Ranches

O a c o m a ,   S o u t h   D a k o t a

A generation of hunters has chased roosters with John Forester and most keep coming back.

VITAL STATISTICS:

GAME BIRDS:
DOVE, DUCKS, GEESE, HUNGARIAN PARTRIDGE, PHEASANT, PRAIRIE CHICKEN, QUAIL, SHARPTAIL, TURKEY
Source of Birds: Wild and pen-reared
Seasons:
DOVE: September
PRAIRIE CHICKENS & SHARPTAILS: September through December
HUNS and PHEASANT: September through January
DUCKS: October through December
GEESE: October through December (dark geese); March and April (light geese)
Land: 130,000 private acres
Accommodations:
INTIMATE MODERN LODGE
NUMBER OF ROOMS: 3
MAXIMUM NUMBER OF HUNTERS: 6
Meals: Steaks and chops
Conference Groups: Yes
Guides: Trained dogs and guides
Dogs and Facilities:
Bring your own kennel
Other Services:
Birds cleaned and packed for travel
Other Activities:
Big game, bird-watching, fishing, hiking, wildlife photography
Rates:
From $995
Gratuity:
10%
Preferred Payment:
Cash or check
Getting There:
Fly to Sioux Falls and rent a car.

Contact:
John Forester
Forester Ranches
PO Box 102
Oacoma SD 57365
605/734-5009
Fax: 605/734-5008

T O HEAR A SOUTH DAKOTAN TELL IT, the West begins at Oacoma, across the Interstate 90 bridge over the Missouri River from Chamberlain. To the east on the high bluffs, row crops predominate. But west of the river, rolling hills support pasture-land and vast tracts of native grasses. For more than 30 years, John Forester has been hosting wingshooters on his ranchlands here in south-central South Dakota and in north-central Nebraska. While hunting is essentially for wild birds, he does maintain a preserve where pheasants can be hunted from September through March.

Pheasants—wild ones, not preserve birds—are the main event here. But you'll also find Huns, sharptail and prairie chickens. Dove can be outstanding during the opening days of the season in September. October and November bring ducks and geese. Bobwhite are also available, as are turkey in the spring.

Combination hunts are very popular. Hunters choosing the top-of-the-line package can pursue dove, pheasant, prairie chicken, sharp-tailed grouse and Huns during a three-day hunt. It's possible to legally bag 26 birds per day, though few have ever pulled it off. This three day hunt sets you back $2,495. A saner approach targets dove in the morning and then a different upland species on each of three afternoons. Offered in September, this package runs about $1,595. Come October, waterfowl—ducks and geese—replace dove in the $1595 trip. Later in the year, attention hones in on trips for pheasant and partridge, or just pheasants if Huns aren't your thing.

John operates a small, three-bedroom lodge for up to six hunters. All bedrooms have private baths. Packages include all meals (steak, prime rib, chops, wild game), guides, dogs, shells, bird cleaning and field transportation.

Great Plains Hunting

Wessington, South Dakota

Only hunters seeking wild and native birds need apply.

VITAL STATISTICS:

GAME BIRDS:
GROUSE, PHEASANT
Source of Birds: Wild
Seasons:
PHEASANTS and HUNS: late October through late December
SHARPTAILS: September through late December
Land: 9,000 private acres
Accommodations:
PRIVATE HOME
NUMBER OF ROOMS: 6
MAXIMUM NUMBER OF HUNTERS: 12
Meals: Family-style
Conference Groups: Yes
Guides: Trained dogs and guides
Dogs and Facilities:
Kennel for hunters' dogs
Shotgun Sports:
Informal instruction
Other Services:
Birds cleaned and packed for travel
Rates:
$225 / day
Gratuity:
Hunter's discretion
Preferred Payment:
Cash or check
Getting There:
Fly to Sioux Falls and rent a car.

Contact:
Clyde Zepp
Great Plains Hunting
RR#2, Box 33
37984 211th St
Wessington SD 57381
605/883-4526

US ROUTE 281 cuts across Interstate 90 at the booming metropolis of Wessington and runs due north, meeting U.S. Route 14, 50 miles up the line. Wessington is a few miles west, a tiny town set on the prairie where Clyde and Dottie Zepp have been farming for a good bit of their lives. Owning some land and leasing other, this couple hosts hunters who are after only one thing: wild birds.

The argument over pen-raised versus wild-born birds will never be settled to anyone's satisfaction. By the time the season begins in late October, most hunters can't tell any difference between those cocks released in August and those who were born on the prairie a season or two earlier. Yet, there are more than a few hunters who say: "Look, I want to hunt native birds. It's my choice. And the fact that I'll flush fewer birds in a day, and maybe my game bag won't be as full, isn't important. I want to pit my skills and those of my dog against birds that have been dodging predators since the day they busted their shells. Just knowing that these birds were raised in the wild makes the hunt better for me."

If you hunt with the Zepp's, you'll hunt for wild birds. You'll be governed by the state's daily bag limits—three pheasants and sharptails, and five Hungarian partridge. The land you hunt will be private. How you hunt it depends on the weather, whether you're hunting over Clyde's dogs or yours, and your preferences and the length and strength of your legs. Terrain is marvelous: CRP ground, cornfields, strips of trees and brush, sloughs with cattails and rushes, and patches of nearly impenetrable weed.

As far as accommodations are concerned, you'll hang your hat in one of two houses separated by a pair of French doors. Bedrooms hold two hunters, and baths are shared. Dinners here revolve around hearty stews and steak. Guests are treated like family, not like business clients, and after a hunt you'll know you'll always have two good friends in the little town of Wessington.

High Brass, Inc.

C h a m b e r l a i n ,   S o u t h   D a k o t a

First-class hunts are found in the prairies near this town where you've got your own room and bath.

VITAL STATISTICS:

GAME BIRDS:
PHEASANT, PRAIRIE CHICKEN, SHARPTAIL
Source of Birds: Wild and pen raised
Seasons:
SHARPTAIL and PRAIRIE CHICKEN: September through December
PHEASANT: Late October through mid-December
Land: 50,000 private acres
Accommodations:
FIRST-CLASS MOTEL IN TOWN
Meals: Restaurant
Conference Groups: Yes
Guides: Trained dogs and guides
Dogs and Facilities:
Kennel for hunters' dogs
Shotgun Sports:
Shooting schools
Other Services:
Birds cleaned and packed for travel
Rates:
From $1,520 / 3 day / gun
Gratuity:
Hunter's discretion
Preferred Payment:
Cash or check
Getting There:
Fly to Sioux Falls and rent a car.

Contact:
Tom Koehn
High Brass Inc
RR1, Box 4X
Chamberlain SD 57325
605/734-6047
Fax: 605/734-5033
EMAIL: tkbrass@sd.cybernex.net
WEB: www.highbrass.com

TOM KOEHN AND HIS SON KELLY have it made. September finds them hunting ducks, geese and sandhill cranes in Saskatchewan. In January and February, they're chasing blue and bobwhite quail down in Mexico. But from October into December, they're concentrating on wild birds in South Dakota from their home base in Chamberlain.

Tom leases 50,000 acres, much of it CRP land in the area west of the Missouri. Hundreds of acres are planted in milo and sorghum. Native grasses and brush thicken in sloughs, creek beds and old dried-up, wet-weather lakes. Before entering a field, your party and guide will hatch a scheme. How can you best hunt this patch and contain the pheasants? These birds are not dumb. They know that it's better to leg it out rather than fly . . . if they can get away with it. It's your job, and the job of the dogs, not to let 'em pull it off. In the latter part of the season, you'll have a chance for prairie chicken and sharp-tailed grouse. With the amount of acreage that High Brass leases, odds are that the same plot won't be hunted any more often that two or three times a season, if that. The limit on pheasants during the season is three cocks. If you want a cooler full, arrange to hunt the High Brass preserve, where limits do not apply.

When the Koehns started this business a decade ago, Tom and Kelly debated whether they ought to operate a lodge. They decided against it for two reasons. First, they wanted to concentrate on the hunting and not running a resort. And second, they wanted each hunter to have a private room with its own bath. There's a wealth of merit in that decision. Hunters stay in a motel with indoor pool and hot tub. The restaurant offers excellent food—but it's not gourmet. And when you return from a hunt, hot snacks are available to accompany that first cold one of the day. Not bad. Chamberlain is a couple hours from Sioux Falls, but transportation from the airport is included in the package.

Medicine Creek Pheasant Ranch Inc

Vivian, South Dakota

The old barn on this historic farm has been remodeled just for you.

VITAL STATISTICS:

GAME BIRDS:
DUCKS, GEESE, PHEASANT, PRAIRIE CHICKEN, SHARPTAIL, TURKEY

Source of Birds: Wild and pen-reared

Seasons:
PHEASANT, SHARPTAIL, PRAIRIE CHICKEN, and TURKEY: September through December
DUCKS and GEESE: October through December

Land: 7,000 private acres

Accommodations:
FARMHOUSE AND REMODELED BARN
NUMBER OF ROOMS: 12
MAXIMUM NUMBER OF HUNTERS: 21

Meals: Hearty, regional fare

Conference Groups: Yes

Guides: Trained dogs and guides

Dogs and Facilities:
Kennel for hunters' dogs

Shotgun Sports:
Driven birds, trap

Other Services:
Birds cleaned and packed for travel

Other Activities:
Big game, fishing, golf, hiking

Rates:
From $800 / 2 days

Gratuity:
Hunter's discretion

Preferred Payment:
Cash or check

Getting There:
Fly to Pierre and you'll be shuttled to the lodge.

Contact:
Mike Authier
Medicine Creek Pheasant Ranch Inc
PO Box 63
1908 Medicine Creek Dr
Vivian SD 57576
605/683-6411
Fax: 603/683-4459
EMAIL: leroya114@aol.com

IN 1915, MIKE AUTHIER'S GRANDDAD built a barn on their ranch along Medicine Creek. It would store hay and protect cattle, milk cows, draft horses and other livestock from the bitter winds and snows of prairie winter. Tough native grasses thrived on the prairie, which hid astounding populations of sharptails and prairie chickens.

Today, this is pheasant country. And in September, hunters flood into the Dakotas to harvest cock birds. A few beat their way across Interstate 90 in sport utility vehicles or pickups with dog crates in the back. Others ride commercial airliners to Pierre, Sioux Falls and Rapid City. Some arrive via corporate aircraft, and others fly their own to private airports such as the landing strip at hamlets like Vivian, where I-90 and U.S. 83 cross.

Waiting for the migration of hunters are scores of outfitters, lodges and preserves. And among the best in this neck of the woods is this ranch along Medicine Creek. While the prairie has flattened a good bit west of the Missouri River, the land along the creek has more relief. You'll work 7,000 acres of pasture, ranch and cropland, two-thirds of it owned by the Authier family. Pointers and Labs help with the pheasants as well as with sharptail and prairie chicken. And the Labs are also essential on duck and goose hunts on the Missouri, about 30 miles to the north and east. Fall turkey hunting is also on the docket here.

At Medicine Creek, you only need to bring your gun, shells and gear. All else is provided. The barn has been remodeled into a comfortable lodge with five bedrooms (all with private baths), Jacuzzi, game room, and a bar that opens after the hunt. Seven additional rooms with shared bath are located in the main farmhouse. When the day's hunt is over, you may want to shoot a round of trap to figure out why in hell you keep missing those going-away shots. Meals sometimes feature buffalo and pheasant as well as traditional steaks and chicken. Rates include transportation from Pierre, about 30 miles north. Van service can be arranged from Rapid City and Sioux Falls, but flying to Pierre is a better option.

[M I D W E S T]

Paul Nelson Farm

Gettysburg, South Dakota

The sine qua non of pheasant lodges is found here on the tawny prairies.

VITAL STATISTICS:

GAME BIRDS:
HUNGARIAN PARTRIDGE, PHEASANT
Source of Birds: Wild and pen-reared
Seasons:
September through March
Land: 10,000 private acres
Accommodations:
EXCELLENT WINGSHOOTING RESORT
NUMBER OF ROOMS: 16
MAXIMUM NUMBER OF HUNTERS: 32
Meals: Elegant regional cuisine
Conference Groups: Yes
Guides: Trained dogs and guides
Dogs and Facilities:
Kennel for hunters' dogs, dog training
Shotgun Sports:
Shooting schools, sporting clays
Other Services:
Birds cleaned and packed for travel, pro shop
Other Activities:
Biking, bird-watching, fishing, wildlife photography
Rates:
From $2,895 / 3 days
Gratuity:
Hunter's discretion
Preferred Payment:
Cash, MasterCard, Visa or check
Getting There:
Fly to Pierre and you will be met.

Contact:
Paul Nelson
Paul Nelson Farm
119 Hilltop Dr
PO Box 183
Gettysburg SD 57442
605/765-2469
Fax: 605/765-9648
EMAIL: pdnelson@eaglepeak.com
WEB: www.paulnelsonfar.com

LIKE A SKIRMISH LINE, A BIT THIN, but in keeping with this town's namesake battlefield, eight hunters stretch across a field of thigh-high grass and grain. At the beginning, the walk is uneventful. But you can tell anticipation is intense; just look at white-knuckled fingers grasping forearms and pistol grips. Off to the right, one of the Labs is birdy—just watch its tail go. Then up flushes a bird. "Hen," somebody shouts. Two more steps and all hell lets loose. Ringnecks are flushing like fireballs from Roman candles. Shotguns pop. Birds fall. More cocks flush. It's crazy. You try to keep count of the birds you down — one, two, three — "hey, was that mine or yours?" you shout to the gunner on your right. Up jumps another, and you dump it with aplomb.

It's not always like this at Paul Nelson's, but most of the time it is. With 10,000 acres managed for game birds, by the time the first hunters arrive in September, this spread north of Pierre is chock-full of cocks. Your task is to pull five per day from the prairie grasses. Such a hard job. Maybe that's why you brought the 20-gauge gun.

When it comes to full-service, Paul Nelson and wife, Cheryl, invented the term. You're picked up at Pierre airport and enjoy their tender and professional mercies until you leave three days hence. Accommodations are equal to the best sporting lodges anywhere, and you'll have to travel a long way to beat truly gourmet presentations of pheasants and wild rice topped off by pecan pie. As a guest, you'll have unlimited use of the sporting clays range and open bar (in that order). Sanitary kennels and high-protein chow will be provided for your dog. Birds will be cleaned and packaged for your trip home.

Nelson's has an outstanding reputation among corporations as an excellent site for hosting clients or executive team building. Even so, individuals and small groups will find themselves right at home here. It's a place to which everyone wants to return.

P&R Hunting Lodge

D a l l a s ,   S o u t h   D a k o t a

Y'all could do worse that hunt the oldest little rooster ranch in Dallas.

VITAL STATISTICS:

GAME BIRDS:
GEESE, GROUSE, PHEASANT, TURKEY
Source of Birds: Wild
Seasons:
PHEASANT: October through late December
SHARPTAILS and GEESE: September through December
TURKEY: October through December
Land: 20,000 private acres
Accommodations:
FARMHOUSES AND MOBILE HOMES
NUMBER OF ROOMS: 14
MAXIMUM NUMBER OF HUNTERS: 20
Meals: Pheasant, pork, beef and turkey
Conference Groups: Yes
Guides: Trained dogs and guides
Dogs and Facilities:
Kennel for hunters' dogs
Other Services:
Birds cleaned and packed for travel
Other Activities:
Big game, fishing
Rates:
From $325 / day
Gratuity:
Hunter's discretion
Preferred Payment:
Cash, MasterCard, Visa or check
Getting There:
Fly to Sioux Falls and rent a car.

Contact:
Ruth Taggart
P&R Hunting Lodge
Rt. 5, Box 117
Dallas SD 57529
605/835-8050
Fax: 605/835-8036
EMAIL: prlodge@gwtc.net

YOU MIGHT CALL RUTH TAGGART the Queen Bee of the Golden Triangle. She's the "R" in P&R, and her husband, Paul, makes up the other half. Together they've been hosting pheasant hunters on their farm since 1964, the first commercial pheasant hunting in a triangle bounded by Gregory, Winner and Chamberlain up where Interstate 90 crosses the Missouri.

Dallas, South Dakota, is not a huge city. Population when pheasants are not in season runs something shy of 150. The town was named in 1907 by a pair of early settlers who evidently hankered for their hometown in Texas. It's not known whether the brothers were bird hunters, but the Taggarts came to it naturally.

It was a simple matter of economics. Anybody with insomnia has heard the ag report. Time was when that was about wind speed and drying conditions. But buried therein were reports from the Chicago futures market, an economic barometer far more volatile than the New York Stock Exchange. Wheat's up one day, down the next. Sow it in the spring; God only knows what a bushel will bring in the fall. Tossing the dice in a riverboat casino seems tamer by comparison.

The Taggarts thought so too. Back in 1964, a decade before wild pheasant hunting collapsed in the East, they saw a simple truth. Upland bird hunters would travel some distance and pay good money to hunt wild birds. You didn't need to run a preserve with the associated costs of buying and releasing a few thousand pheasants. If you protected the cover, and limited the number of hunters, you'd develop a new cash crop that only got better year after year. Hunt for geese, grouse and turkey as well, on more than 20,000 acres.

Ruth and Paul were right. They opened their homes to hunters and arranged for them to gun on their own farm and the farms of friends. Planting strips of corn, wheat and sunflowers for bird hunting generates more financial yield that the same grain brings per bushel. They put up additions to their homes, and added a couple of mobile homes as well. Everyone eats in the big quonset hut lodge. And indefatigable Ruth bustles about canning corn relish, baking bread and making sure that everything goes just the way it should. At this lodge you'll find everything the way it should be.

River View Lodge

P i e r r e ,   S o u t h   D a k o t a

What do you do after hunting ducks and pheasants? Laze before the fire and watch the river roll on.

VITAL STATISTICS:

GAME BIRDS:
DUCKS, GEESE, SHARPTAILS, PHEASANT
Source of Birds: Wild
Seasons:
SHARPTAILS: September through December
PHEASANTS: October through November
WATERFOWL: October through January
Land: 15,000 private acres
Accommodations:
WOOD LODGE AND CABIN
NUMBER OF ROOMS: 10
MAXIMUM NUMBER OF HUNTERS: 12
Meals: Country elegant
Conference Groups: Yes
Guides: Included
Dogs and Facilities:
Kennel for hunters' dogs
Shotgun Sports:
Sporting clays
Other Services:
Birds cleaned and packed for travel
Other Activities:
Fishing, wildlife photography
Rates:
$2,300 / 3 days / person
Gratuity:
Hunter's discretion
Preferred Payment:
Cash or check
Getting There:
Fly to Pierre and the lodge van will meet your flight.

Contact:
Jerome Jacobs
River View Lodge
109 River Place Dr
Pierre SD 57501
605/224-8589
Fax: 605/945-2216
EMAIL: upland@sd.cybernex.net
WEB: uplandriver.com

TO REACH RIVER VIEW LODGE, you won't have to plan on a half-day's rental car trek from a one-flight-per-day airport located in East Ox. Nope. River View is 20 minutes from downtown Pierre, the capital of South Dakota and about the same distance from the airport. Pierre, of course, is not a huge city, but you can buy a good cigar there, vintage wines, more than one brand of single-malt Scotch, and nontoxic shotshells for 20-gauge guns.

As the name suggests, the lodge overlooks the wide Missouri. On days when ducks are flying, the river carries the color of the leaden sky. On those bluebird days we all love to hunt, the river's as blue as it can be. You may be able to see the river and the dimpled dun green hills that rise beyond it from your room, one of ten at the lodge. Seven are found in the main building and four in nearby cabins. All rooms are private. This place caters to personal detail. A few weeks before you arrive, you'll receive a questionnaire asking your preferences for food, drink and reading material. (What, something more than the Cabela's catalog?) For corporate groups or others who must work, an alcove offers fax and copy machines, and the phone service is reliable enough for most modems. The menu varies depending on what you and your friends would like. Groups of up to 10 are the norm here, and only by special arrangement will the lodge host more than one group at a time.

Because hunting for wild pheasant in South Dakota begins no earlier than late morning, the daily regimen at River View is different. Hot coffee, juice and a snack greet you when you awaken; then it's off to pit blinds for geese. After they've come into your spread of decoys and you've bagged a pair, you'll return to the lodge for breakfast. Then comes pheasants on the grassy prairie, CRP land and fields of corn and milo. We're talking only wild birds here. After lunch, you may do more bird hunting, return to goose pits if you're shy a bird, or go jump ducks. Guides and dogs are provided, but you can bring your own pointer or setter if you wish. When you get back to the lodge, a drink and the sauna feels oh, so good. Typical hunts span three days and four nights and include cleaning and packaging of game as well as your transportation to and from the airport.

*Bill Mitchell has "rescued" dozen's of orphaned
German wirehairs and trained them to be fine pointers. Together they work
pheasants and waterfowl from Dakota Hunting Farms along
the border between North and South Dakota.*

*A mere 20 minutes from Pierre, South Dakota's capitol,
River View Lodge's duck and pheasant hunting is as excellent
as it is convenient for travelers.*

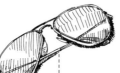

Rooster Roost Ranch

M i t c h e l l , S o u t h D a k o t a

Dean's Dream is a favorite with families and corporate groups.

VITAL STATISTICS:

GAME BIRDS:

PHEASANT

Source of Birds: Wild

Seasons:

Mid-October through mid-December

Land: 40, 000 private acres

Accommodations:

MODERN LODGE

NUMBER OF ROOMS: 4

MAXIMUM NUMBER OF HUNTERS: 10

Meals: Family-style country cooking

Conference Groups: Yes

Guides: Trained dogs and guides

Dogs and Facilities:

Kennels for hunters' use

Shotgun Sports:

Trap

Other Services:

Informal shooting instruction, birds cleaned and packed for travel

Other Activities:

Big game

Rates:

From $350 / day

Gratuity:

Hunter's discretion

Preferred Payment:

Cash or check

Getting There:

Fly to Sioux Falls and you'll be met.

Contact:

Dean V. Strand

Rooster Roost Ranch

25699 407th Ave

Mitchell SD 57301-5840

605/996-4676

DEAN STRAND HAD A DREAM. Fifteen years ago, he told his friends that he wanted to create a place where the hunting was just as good as it was when he was growing up. Now, folks around Mitchell are a pretty supportive lot. They said: "That's a nice idea, Dean. Go for it." But, not unlike Garrison Keillor's closet co-dependents of Lake Woebegone, they were probably thinking: "Ha, it'll never happen."

Well it did happen, and in spades. What was once a little 600-acre shooting area (little for this neck of the woods), now has 40,000 acres, managed and planted to propagate and nurture wild pheasants. Over the years, Dean's added tree lines to break up winds and provide cover, along with scores of food plots, ponds and brush to provide winter shelter. Since this is not a preserve, per se, hunters are limited to three birds, and the season runs from mid-October to mid-November, as set by South Dakota Game and Fish.

Over the years, "Dean's Dream," as it came to be called, prospered. In 1994, he and Sharon built a new lodge with four bedrooms, all with private baths. The following year they added heated kennels for clients' dogs. Guests who take commercial flights into Sioux Falls are met at the airport and driven to the lodge. Private aircraft can take advantage of Mitchell's all-weather field.

Unlike larger lodges, Rooster Ranch caters to families and small corporate groups. No more than 10 guests ever hunt out of the lodge. Dean likes to accompany each hunting party. That way he can find out exactly what each group needs and then do his best to fulfill it. Groups of six or more will have exclusive run of the lodge and Dean's leases. Those of fewer than six hunters will be matched to another small group.

Shallow Creek Pheasant Hunting

Wessington, South Dakota

With a pair of comfortable lodges, and birds in the bag, you'll know you've come to the right place.

VITAL STATISTICS:

GAME BIRDS:
HUNGARIAN PARTRIDGE,
PHEASANT, SHARPTAIL
Source of Birds: Wild and
pen-reared
Seasons:
September through March
Land: 2,500 private
Accommodations:
CEDAR LODGES
NUMBER OF ROOMS: 2
MAXIMUM NUMBER OF HUNTERS: 16
Meals: Family style
Conference Groups: Yes
Guides: Available on special request
Dogs and Facilities:
Kennel for hunters' dogs
Shotgun Sports:
Informal instruction
Other Services:
Birds cleaned and packed for travel
Other Activities:
Big game
Rates:
From $275 / gun
Gratuity:
Hunter's discretion
Preferred Payment:
Cash or check
Getting There:
Fly to Huron Regional and rent a car
or have Dan meet you.

Contact:
Dan Schilling
Shallow Creek Pheasant
Hunting
19941 373rd Ave
Wessington SD 57381
605/458-2462
Fax: 605/458-2204

WHAT'S IN AN ADDRESS? Take the location of Shallow Creek: 19941 373rd Ave. It's about halfway between 199th and 200th Street. Huh? Streets? Avenues? Visions of curbs and sidewalks, stoplights and parking meters? Hardly. Most of the rural roads that wear street numbers aren't even paved. Counties and states adopted the citified system using urban terms to make it easier for emergency services—fire, police and medical—to find precise locations in the endless prairie. All you have to remember is that streets run east and west while avenues go north and south. Just like Manhattan.

Here in Wessington, a small town in the center of the eastern half of South Dakota about 85 miles northwest of Mitchell, you couldn't be farther from the Big Apple. Grain elevators are the highest buildings you'll see, and the prairie—colored khaki in the fall—stretches to infinity, as does its sky. There is a very gentle roll to this land. In the last million years, it's been smoothed by glaciers. But by the time they reached this spot, they were running out of gas and lacked the energy to gouge the ground, leaving kettles for lakes or sinuous ridges called eskers. Row crops and pastures run to the horizon, interrupted by brushy swales and shallow stream courses, while acres and acres are left to grow wild in the Conservation Reserve Program. It is country for pheasants, sharptail grouse and Hungarian partridge.

To supplement wild stocks, Dan Schilling, who owns Shallow Creek Farm, releases about 600 pheasants a year on roughly 2,500 acres. As do most ranchers, Dan frees his birds in August, a few weeks before the season begins in September. By the time you arrive to hunt them—October and November are best—they'll have gone pretty well native. If you don't bring your own dog, you can hunt over one of his flushing Labs or German shorthairs. Hunt with or without a guide; it's up to you. Hunters who stay the night enjoy either of a pair of cedar-sided lodges, each consisting primarily of one large room with kitchen and bath facilities. And after hunting on those raw days of November, it'll feel good to warm your backside around the fat potbellied stove.

[M I D W E S T]

South Dakota Hunting Service

H e r r i c k ,   S o u t h   D a k o t a

If you can find a way, this is a place you'll come back to year after year.

VITAL STATISTICS:

GAME BIRDS:
DUCKS, GEESE, PHEASANT, SHARPTAIL

Source of Birds: Wild

Seasons:
PHEASANT, SHARPTAIL: September through mid-December
WATERFOWL: October through December

Land: 30,000 private and public acres

Accommodations:
PRIVATE LODGE IN NEARBY TOWN
NUMBER OF ROOMS: 8
MAXIMUM NUMBER OF HUNTERS: 20

Meals: Home cooking

Conference Groups: Yes

Guides: Trained dogs and guides

Dogs and Facilities:
Kennel for hunters' dogs

Other Services:
Birds cleaned and packed for travel

Other Activities:
Big game, fishing

Rates:
From $250 / day

Gratuity:
Hunter's discretion

Preferred Payment:
Cash or check

Getting There:
Fly to Pierre and rent a car.

Contact:
Mike Moody
South Dakota Hunting Service
PO Box 324
Herrick SD 57538
605/654-2465
WEB: www.onida.org/SDhunting service.htm

JUST ABOVE THE NEBRASKA BORDER is the little town of Herrick, where Mike Moody has been running a guiding service for the past decade or so. With 30,000 acres under ownership or lease, Mike puts hunters on wild game—birds, waterfowl, deer, and turkey. He's not the only outfitter in this region, heaven knows. But over the years he's built an enviable reputation. That's why those hunters who can, come back year after year.

Sloughs, treelines, CRP, rowcrop land, thickets—all hold pheasants. Working behind good dogs, yours or Mike's, you'll flush a number of birds. The daily limit is three cocks. If conditions are right, you may find yourself in gangs of sharptail as well. They erupt from cover like pheasants, but seem, somehow, faster. Maybe it's because they're somewhat smaller. Virtually everyone limits on pheasant, and those who make it a point to hunt early in October do well on sharpies as well.

Unlike many of the other outfits in the region, Mike has a thing about putting clients in waterfowl central. Long before dawn, he'll have you wading the marshes out to little hummocks where he's built dry-land blinds. As you slog in, you'll hear ducks flushing and gabbling into the night sky. Not to worry. They'll be back. You'll set a couple dozen decoys in the marsh. Then you'll sit back and wait. 'Fore long, the whistle of wings that ends in a splash tells you that the ducks are back. No doubt about it. In the gathering light, you see fat mallards bobbing before the blind. "Hyaa!" you shout, jumping to your feet. "Yaaaah!" And they flush, and a pair of the day's limit of six lies bobbing in the chop. The rest you shoot as they come in. After the prairie marshes freeze in November, action shifts to arms of Lake Francis Case, as the impounded Missouri is called in these parts.

Guests who don't drive in fly to Pierre, where they're met by Mike or one of his crew. Accommodations are found in a comfortable eight-bedroom lodge with shared baths.

South Dakota Pheasant Hunts

Nothing fancy about this preserve, just good shooting at a reasonable price.

VITAL STATISTICS:

GAME BIRDS:
PHEASANT
Source of Birds: Wild and pen-reared
Seasons:
September through March
Land: 900 private acres
Accommodations:
IN NEARBY TOWN
Meals: Local supper clubs and cafes
Conference Groups: Yes
Guides: Trained dogs and guides
Dogs and Facilities:
Kennel for hunters' dogs
Other Services:
Birds cleaned and packed for travel
Other Activities:
Biking, bird-watching, golf, hiking
Rates:
From $75 / day
Gratuity:
Hunter's discretion
Preferred Payment:
Cash or check
Getting There:
Fly to Watertown and you'll be driven to the preserve for a modest fee.

Contact:
Will Stone
South Dakota Pheasant Hunts
RR1, Box 260
Gary SD 57237
877/260-2686
WEB: www.itctel.com/~stohill

REMEMBER THAT OLD television show, *The Price is Right*? Well at this preserve right next to the Minnesota border 40 miles due west of Granite Falls, Minnesota, you won't have to spend a year's savings for a good pheasant hunt.

So what's a good hunt? Varies. For some guys, it's the chance to kill a lot of birds, more the better. For others, it's the opportunity to introduce a youngster or spouse to wingshooting, or to work a dog where pheasants are known to be. For some, it's like golf: a chance to cement business relationships or to improve teamwork among those who work together. For a few, it's nothing more than a walk in the tall grasses, shotgun at ready, mind halfway on the dog and halfway on the birds and, overall, kinda drifting with those cumulus clouds in the azure sky.

South Dakota Pheasant Hunts is not fancy or pretentious. There's no pro shop or sporting clays course or lodge touting a chef of dubious renown. Nope. Just 900 acres of sweet clover and prairie grasses—sloughs filled with thick cover so loved by pheasants—and corn and grain stubble. A single hunter is as welcome here as a half dozen. Groups of 10 or more will be divided for safety's sake. And groups will not be mixed; each will have exclusive use of a field for the day. Use your own dogs or Will Stone's, owner of the preserve. Some duck, goose and dove hunting can be arranged by special request.

Accommodations will be found in neighboring towns. Supper clubs and cafes provide varied menus. Northwest Airlines serves Watertown, South Dakota, about 50 miles to the west, and Will provides transportation to and from the airport for a reasonable charge.

Thunderstik Lodge

C h a m b e r l a i n ,   S o u t h   D a k o t a

Guess which former president was really bushed when he finished hunting here?

VITAL STATISTICS:

GAME BIRDS:
PHEASANT
Source of Birds: Wild and pen-reared
Seasons:
Late September through mid-December
Land: 6,000 private acres
Accommodations:
MODERN CEDAR LODGE
NUMBER OF ROOMS: 10
MAXIMUM NUMBER OF HUNTERS: 32
Meals: Regional cuisine that borders on elegant
Conference Groups: Yes
Guides: Trained dogs and guides
Dogs and Facilities:
Bring your own kennel if you bring your own dog
Shotgun Sports:
Sporting clays
Other Services:
Birds cleaned and packed for travel, pro shop
Other Activities:
Bird-watching, fishing, wildlife photography
Rates:
$2,495 / 3 days
Gratuity:
$100
Preferred Payment:
Cash, MasterCard, Visa or check
Getting There:
Fly to Sioux Falls and meet the bus.

Contact:
Nova Niewenhuis
Thunderstik Lodge
RR1, Box 10T
Chamberlain SD 57325
800/734-5168
Fax: 605/734-5994

O N A SUNNY DAY, and there are many in October here, grasslands surrounding Thunderstik glow like new gold. The river, a mile in front and below the red wood lodge is as blue and timeless as the sky. Across the river rise bluffs and coulees filled with cedar. Behind you stretches prairie without end. You know it holds pheasants, and you know that this lodge is the quintessential ringneck resort in the state.

For nearly a dozen years, Thunderstik's reputation has been growing. Among its clientele are former professional athletes, scores of CEOs, governors and a former President from Texas. They choose Thunderstik for three reasons: great cover that is superbly managed to nurture and protect wild and supplementally stocked pheasants; one of the best kennels of Labrador retrievers in North America; and outstanding care and feeding (equal emphasis on both) of guests.

A typical hunt at Thunderstik begins with waterfowling from blinds along backwaters that feed into Lake Francis Case, as the impounded Missouri is known here. After lunch, you'll work Labs in meticulously groomed fields of corn, prairie grasses and milo. Birds are plentiful, and the pair of Labs you hunt with know how to pin birds to keep them from leaking out the back door. You should have your limit of five birds well before the sun sets. There'll be time, then, to work in a round of sporting clays, or soak in the hot tub on the deck overlooking the river. If you prefer to hunt strictly for native birds—those that have not seen a pen— Thunderstik reserves several hundred acres just for you.

Meals are country elegant—lobster, buffalo, prime rib and pheasant. Reasonable vintages complement the entrée; desserts replace calories burned in the field. Ten rooms, eight in the main residential lodge and two in cabins nearby, are better than comfortable. Baths are shared. To ease access to Thunderstik, the lodge runs a charter bus from Sioux Falls airport. All you have to do is show up there, catch the bus, and your hunting vacation begins.

Tinker Kennels

Pierre, South Dakota

Pinnated grouse, sharptails, Huns, pheasants — Tinker's setters will find them all.

VITAL STATISTICS:

GAME BIRDS:
PRAIRIE CHICKENS, SHARPTAIL GROUSE, PHEASANT, HUNGARIAN PARTRIDGE
Source of Birds: Wild
Seasons:
GROUSE and PARTRIDGE: early September through late December
PHEASANT: Late October through late December
Land: 250,000 private and public acres
Accommodations:
MOTEL IN TOWN
Meals: Restaurants or grouse with Bob at home
Conference Groups: Yes
Guides: Trained dogs and guides
Dogs and Facilities:
Kennel for hunters' dogs, dog training
Shotgun Sports:
Informal instruction
Other Services:
Birds cleaned and packed for travel
Other Activities:
Bird-watching, horseback riding, wildlife photography
Rates:
$695 / day
Gratuity:
10%
Preferred Payment:
Cash, MasterCard, Visa or check
Getting There:
Fly to Pierre and you'll be met.

Contact:
Bob Tinker
Tinker Kennels
3031 Sussex Pl
Pierre SD 57501
605/224-5414
Fax: 605/224-2022
EMAIL: tinkerkennels@dakwest.com
WEB: dakotariveroutfitters

THEY CALLED THE PRAIRIE OF GRASS a sea and the wagons that rumbled across it schooners, and one of the men of the family walked a ways outboard of the lead wagons with a fowling piece crooked in his arm. He was on the lookout for two things: Sioux, which might or might not have been welcome—most probably the latter—and prairie chickens, which he probably had never heard called by their proper name: pinnated grouse.

Beneath you, saddle leather creaks. A trio of flashy English setters more at home in the quaily pine woods of Georgia romp through the grass, slashing right, cutting to the left, trailing whatever in hell it is that they smell and we can't. Following is a wooden wagon of the same vintage as the tumbled-down sodbuster's cabin (imagine raising six kids in that!) you see down in the flat along the Missouri below you. Bob, the Tinker of Tinker Kennels, rides point, shock collar control in his hand just in case the dogs need a jolt of remembering. This bit of technology, the flare of blaze orange against the grass, and your shotgun if you think about it, remind you that you're in the twenty-first century. Otherwise you'd be lost in the loveliest sort of way.

So what Bob does is hunt for the wild birds of the prairie on a quarter million acres. His quarry is sharptails, Huns, pheasants, and of course prairie chickens. You'll ride horses because the distances are as long as you can see and then some. And if you're not fixated on pheasant, as are so many gunners who trek to South Dakota, you'll hunt in the most glorious part of fall from early September into October. Should pheasant turn you on, hook up with Bob after the third week of October.

As this is being written, Bob's working on a lodge. However, he has an arrangement with a dog-friendly Best Western. Each hunter has a private room and private bath (two can share if they tolerate the other's snores). Meals either at Bob's ranch or restaurants in town are part of the package, as is transportation to and from the airport at Pierre.

P.S. Non-horseback hunts can be arranged if you wish.

Black Creek Ranch

D e e r b r o o k ,   W i s c o n s i n

Most folks come here for pheasants, but if they ask, Bill will let 'em in on the grouse.

VITAL STATISTICS:

GAME BIRDS:
PHEASANT and RUFFED GROUSE
Source of Birds: Wild and pen-reared
Seasons:
GROUSE: Mid-September through mid-February
PHEASANT: September through March
Land: 400 private acres
Accommodations:
ROOMS IN A PRIVATE HOME
NUMBER OF ROOMS: 3
MAXIMUM NUMBER OF HUNTERS: 8
Meals: Family-style (game only on request)
Conference Groups: Yes
Guides: Trained dogs and guides
Dogs and Facilities:
Kennel for hunters' dogs
Other Services:
Birds cleaned and packed for travel
Other Activities:
Big game
Rates:
Hunts: from $55;
Room: $55 / night / for two;
Meals: $25 / day
Gratuity:
Hunter's discretion
Preferred Payment:
Cash or check
Getting There:
Drive from Wausau or Green Bay.

Contact:
Bill Yunk
Black Creek Ranch
W13347 Hayes Rd
Deerbrook WI 54424
715/623-7290
Fax: 715/623-7290

UNNY HOW THINGS WORK OUT. For near-ly 40 years, Bill Yunk ran big game hunts out West. He'd organize hunts for elk, bear, deer, antelope, sheep—you name it. But about five years ago he decided to hang it up. He'd do a couple western hunts, for himself and maybe a friend, but that would be it. He spread his rug on 400 acres of north-central Wisconsin woodland, and thereupon entered the preserve business. "We thought it would be fun," you can hear the smile in his voice, "and, well, it is."

The country here was once farmed, but now it's mostly overgrown. Much of it has been logged (selectively) two or three times. Each year, new sections are cut and others reach different stages of maturity. That doesn't mean a whole lot to pheasant hunters. They're working plots of hardy native grasses ranging from 20 acres or so to more than 100, depending on the size of the group. No head-high corn here. "You hear a bird flush, you can't see it, don't know where it went, can't even see your dog. That's not fun," says Bill. Wild grasses grow about thigh high and they seem to weather harsh Wisconsin winters.

But the logged-over lands, especially those with three or four years of new growth after the harvest, offer splendid hunting for ruffed grouse. "We don't make a big thing of it," Bill maintains, "but I guess it's there if anybody wants it." Some hunters in the know make a grouse hunt an annual event. Woodcock don't seem to move through this area. "I saw two, no three last year," he says. Ducks are scarce as well. Both bear and deer are hunted here in the fall.

About 35 miles northeast of Wausau and 120 miles northwest of Green Bay on US 46, there's not much reason to be passing through Deerbrook unless you want to go hunting. But a number of business groups have found this preserve, its three-bedroom lodge, and its down-home meals nice and relaxing. Black Creek Ranch is utterly devoid of pretense. What you see is what you get, and what you get is pretty nice . . . and not overly hard on your wallet.

Burnett Game Farm & Hunt Club

B r o o k f i e l d ,   W i s c o n s i n

Waterfowling, to say nothing of pheasant hunting, is fabulous near this great marsh.

VITAL STATISTICS:

GAME BIRDS:
CHUKAR, DUCKS, GEESE, PHEASANT, QUAIL
Source of Birds: Wild and pen-reared
Seasons:
PRESERVE BIRDS: Mid-September through December
WATERFOWL: October through December
Land: 2,980 private acres
Accommodations:
PRIVATE RUSTIC LODGE
NUMBER OF ROOMS: 8
MAXIMUM NUMBER OF HUNTERS: 12
Meals: Breakfast only; others in restaurants
Conference Groups: Yes
Guides: Trained dogs and guides
Dogs and Facilities:
Kennel for hunters' dogs, dog training
Shotgun Sports:
Driven birds, shooting schools, trap
Other Services:
Birds cleaned and packed for travel, pro shop
Other Activities:
Big game, biking, bird-watching, boating, hiking, wildlife photography
Rates:
From $765 for annual membership; bed-and-breakfast $45 for two
Gratuity:
20%
Preferred Payment:
Cash, MasterCard, Visa or check
Getting There:
Drive from Milwaukee or fly a private plane to Juneau.

Contact:
Bob Voit
Burnett Fame Farm & Hunt Club
4430 Imperial Dr
Brookfield WI 53045
414/781-9156

WITH SOME 32,000 ACRES, the marsh near Horicon has been attracting bird hunters since the 1800s. During the most recent glacial advance, ice scooped out a depression that filled with water. But when the glaciers melted, the land rebounded and the one-time lake became shallower. Reeds and grasses, willow and alder thrive on the margins of these wetlands. During fall waterfowl migrations, the local population of 20,000 ducks swells to more than 100,000. Canada geese abound.

Burnett Game Farm, little more than an hour's drive northwest of Milwaukee, owns or leases a number of parcels adjacent to the marsh. On almost 3,000 acres, you'll hunt pheasant, chukar and quail. Terrain is mostly easy but not quite flat. Cover is normally lush, and at times it squishes underfoot. Pheasants love it. So do dogs—yours or theirs. Pointers, setters, and retrievers of virtually any description may be available for your use. Depends on which guides are on hand. When you call for reservations, you should make your wants known. Owner Bob Voit will do his best to oblige. Upland birds are stocked at regular intervals throughout the season. Thus they can acclimate to the cover before you arrive to hunt.

Mid- to late October may be the best time to hunt Burnett Farm. Hunker in a brushy fence row along a cornfield, not cut, but picked the old fashioned way. Set a few decoys in the field. With luck, ducks will trade off the marsh, looking for chow, and there you'll be. A 12-gauge welcoming committee. Later, after lunch, you'll kick up pheasants in cover that's hard to beat. And at the end of the day, you'll slide into your room with one of those dumb, happy grins that says, I'm ready for the sack. A rustic lodge on the preserve provides guest rooms (most with private baths). Breakfast comes with the room, but lunch and dinner are best found in one of the many cafes in the crossroads communities around the marsh.

If for no other reason than to visit Horicon Marsh National Wildlife Refuge and related state wildlife areas, Burnett Farm is one place you'll come back to time and time again. Established in the early 1940s as a breeding ground for redhead ducks, Horicon Marsh is a bird hunter's and bird watcher's paradise.

Timberdoodle Inn

P h i l l i p s ,   W i s c o n s i n

Hunt the rim of the world where grouse and woodcock are plentiful and people are not.

VITAL STATISTICS:

GAME BIRDS:
GROUSE, PHEASANT, WOODCOCK
Source of Birds: Wild and pen-reared
Seasons:
GROUSE: September through December
PHEASANT: September and October
WOODCOCK: September and October
Land: 505 private acres; 1.3 million public acres
Accommodations:
PRIVATE WOOD-AND-GLASS LODGE
NUMBER OF ROOMS: 4
MAXIMUM NUMBER OF HUNTERS: 8
Meals: Homestyle cooking
Conference Groups: Yes
Guides: Trained dogs and guides
Dogs and Facilities:
Kennel for hunters' dogs, dog training
Other Services:
Birds cleaned and packed for travel
Other Activities:
Big game, biking, bird-watching, boating, canoeing, fishing, hiking, skiing, wildlife photography
Rates:
$900 / 3 days
Gratuity:
Hunter's discretion
Preferred Payment:
Cash or check
Getting There:
Fly to Rhinelander and rent a car.

Contact:
Peter Jesunas
Timberdoodle Inn
N 11055 Brady Rd
Phillips WI 54555
715/339-2823
Fax: 715/339-2823

S O WHAT'S A TIMBERDOODLE? A big-eyed john, of course—that magic bird of damp alder coverts that marks the beginning of fall. You check birdy thickets each morning, looking for tell-tail streaks of white on still-green leaves of late summer's weed. In the soft earth, you scout for holes made by their probing beaks. Find chalking and evidence of feeding in the same spot, and the only soul you'll tell is your very best friend, the one who gave you the last Brittany pup from his bitch's litter.

We're talking woodcock here, birds of twittering helicopter flight that change direction just as you slap the trigger. We're also talking ruffed grouse, perhaps the quintessential upland bird. (Quail are birds of the lowlands, wouldn't you say, gentlemen?) We're talking heavy coverts of alder, aspen and balsam firs. You'll hunt from woodland roads on private and public lands in Price County, up in northern Wisconsin. Hunting for resident woodcock begins in September, but flight birds don't generally arrive until the middle of October. Grouse are on hand all of the time and are legal game from September through December. Peter Jesunas, who runs Timberdoodle Inn and Back Forty Guide Service, guns over drahthaar, a versatile pointing/flushing dog with tracking skills that are very valuable for finding crippled birds. On 500 acres, more or less, there's also hunting for pen-raised pheasants.

Typical hunts are day-long affairs beginning after a substantial breakfast and breaking for lunch in the field. At dusk, if you wish to hunt that long, you'll return to the modern wood-and-glass lodge, shower and sit down to dinner. Home cooking is the order of the evening here, and special diets are easily accommodated with advance notice. If beverages of fermented or distilled spirit suit your palate, bring them along.

ROCKY MOUNTAINS

COLORADO, IDAHO, MONTANA, UTAH, WYOMING

When six-by-six elk are whistling in the gray dawn and 20-inch rainbows are rising to that hatch matched by a #18 blue-winged olive, it's tough to concentrate on birds. Wingshooting in the rocky mountains may be the last great venue — open spaces, plenty of cover, and lots and lots of birds.

Pheasants, sharptails, chukar, Hungarian partridge, ruffed, blue and spruce grouse — you'll find them all. Vast ranches of native grasses rise between watersheds cut with draws filled with chokecherry, wild plumb and buffaloberry.

Surrounding these grazing lands are the mountains — high, cold and capped with snow. So stunning is the scenery that sometimes it's hard to concentrate on your pointer's trace.

Don't overlook ducks. Most of the major western rivers hold resident populations of mallards, wigeon and gadwall, along with teal. And when freeze-up comes in

Lodges:

Colorado

1 BUFFALO HORN RANCH
2 MT. BLANCA GAME BIRD & TROUT
3 SCENIC MESA RANCH
4 SPORTHAVEN LTD

Idaho

5 FLYING B RANCH
6 MALAD VALLEY UPLAND HUNTS
7 TETON VALLEY LODGE

Montana

8 BIG ISLAND SHOOTING PRESERVE
9 BIGHORN RIVER RESORT
10 EAGLE NEST LODGE
11 FETCH INN HUNTING PRESERVE
12 LAST STAND LODGE
13 ROCK CREEK OUTFITTERS

References:

WINGSHOOTER'S GUIDE TO IDAHO
*by Ken Retallic
and Rocky Barker
Wilderness Adventure Press*

WINGSHOOTER'S GUIDE
TO MONTANA
*by Ben O. Williams
and Chuck Johnson
Wilderness Adventure Press*

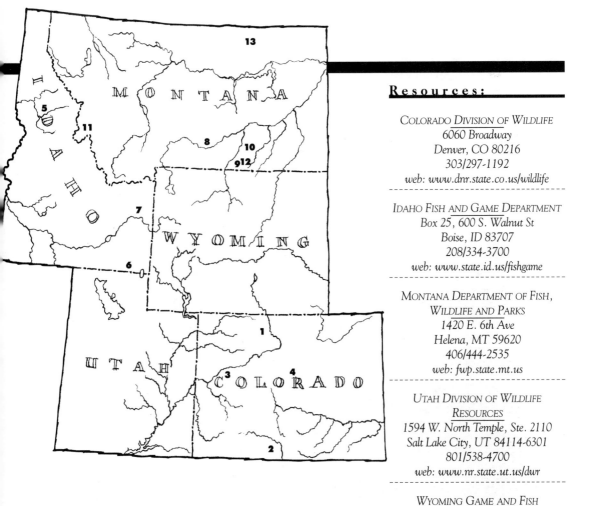

Resources:

COLORADO DIVISION OF WILDLIFE
6060 Broadway
Denver, CO 80216
303/297-1192
web: www.dnr.state.co.us/wildlife

- - - - - - - - - - - - - - - - - - -

IDAHO FISH AND GAME DEPARTMENT
Box 25, 600 S. Walnut St
Boise, ID 83707
208/334-3700
web: www.state.id.us/fishgame

- - - - - - - - - - - - - - - - - - -

MONTANA DEPARTMENT OF FISH,
WILDLIFE AND PARKS
1420 E. 6th Ave
Helena, MT 59620
406/444-2535
web: fwp.state.mt.us

- - - - - - - - - - - - - - - - - - -

UTAH DIVISION OF WILDLIFE
RESOURCES
1594 W. North Temple, Ste. 2110
Salt Lake City, UT 84114-6301
801/538-4700
web: www.nr.state.ut.us/dwr

- - - - - - - - - - - - - - - - - - -

WYOMING GAME AND FISH
DEPARTMENT
5400 Bishop Blvd
Cheyenne, WY 82006
307/777-4600
web: www.gf.state.wy.us

- - - - - - - - - - - - - - - - - - -

November, they move from pothole lakes and stock tanks to the sloughs and back channel bends of the rivers. Tailwaters like the Bighorn River hunt best.

Of all the places in North America, the Rockies offer the best opportunities for combining big game hunting and fishing with bird hunting, and many outfitters are delighted to offer cast-and-blast packages.

Give me a pair of Brittanies, a fine guide, a lively double, and a couple of cock birds like the ones you'll find at Nick Forrester's Bighorn River Resort in Ft. Smith, Montana, and I'll be happy for the rest of my life.

Buffalo Horn Ranch

M e e k e r ,   C o l o r a d o

Easy walking beneath the Flat Tops turns up pheasants and chukar aplenty.

VITAL STATISTICS:

GAME BIRDS:
CHUKAR, DUCKS, GEESE, GROUSE, HUNGARIAN PARTRIDGE, PHEASANT, QUAIL

Source of Birds: Wild and pen-reared

Seasons:
CHUKAR, HUNS, PHEASANT, QUAIL: September through October
BLUE GROUSE: September through early November
WATERFOWL: October into January

Land: 5,000 private and public acres

Accommodations:
PRIVATE LOG LODGE
NUMBER OF ROOMS: 24
MAXIMUM NUMBER OF HUNTERS: 24

Meals: Wild game cuisine

Conference Groups: Yes

Guides: Trained dogs and guides

Dogs and Facilities:
Kennel for hunters' dogs

Shotgun Sports:
Driven birds, five-stand, shooting schools, sporting clays, tower or release shoots

Other Services:
Birds cleaned and packed for travel

Other Activities:
Big game, bird-watching, canoeing, fishing, golf, hiking, horseback riding, skiing, wildlife photography

Rates:
From $495 / day

Gratuity:
Hunter's discretion

Preferred Payment:
Cash or check

Getting There:
Fly to Denver or Grand Junction and rent a car.

Contact:
Jim or Gail Walma
Buffalo Horn Ranch
13825 County Rd 7
Meeker CO 81641
970/878-5450
Fax: 970/878-4088
EMAIL: buffalohrn@aol.com
WEB: www.buffalohorn.com

MEEKER WAS ONE OF Teddy Roosevelt's hangouts, shared by cutthroats, bootleggers and other sundry outlaws. East of the town is the high Flat Top Wilderness with its deep pine forests and high alpine parks. Below this high plateau, the land becomes more arid, a tableau of rolling hills and sharp draws. Cover is mostly pinion pine, scrub oak, serviceberry and cedar. Grasses climb the flanks of the ridges before merging with stunted trees. It's good cover for chukars, pheasants and huns. And while there's a lot of it, it's fairly easy walking. You and your guide will ride a four-by-four out to the section you plan to hunt, and will lunch in the field unless you choose otherwise.

From the first of September through November, when snows put the finish on bird shooting, hunters work fields over pointers and setters for quail and pheasant. The edges of broad grassy pastures, particularly boundaries defined by intermittent creeks or brush-choked swales, are prime cover for Huns. You can bust a 12-bird covey once, twice, maybe three times before you have to hunt them as singles. And if you're willing to have a drink of water, pet the dog, tell lies about how come you missed that easy shot and otherwise sit tight for half an hour, the Huns will regroup. As you wait, you can hear the singles calling to each other. Chukars prefer high, dry rocky slopes. Buffalo ranch augments the wild birds on its 20,000 acres with pen-reared fowl. A nearby clays course allows gunners to hone shooting skills. Ducks and geese are also hunted here, as are blue grouse.

During bird season, elk and deer are also hunted on this ranch, but the only time wingshooters and big game hunters are likely to see each other is over dinner in the modern two-story, taffy-colored log lodge. Accommodations are easy on the bod. Most of the rooms have private baths and the others share. Rooms are made up daily, and meals—barbecue, steaks, chicken and wild game with all the fixin's—verge on fine dining.

And should you visit in September or October, by all means bring that five-weight. The ranch has a mile on the famed White River, and the Colorado and Yampa—to say nothing of the high lakes in the Flat Tops—are just a short drive away.

Mt. Blanca Game Bird & Trout Lodge

B l a n c a ,   C o l o r a d o

You'll need shotgun and fly rod when you visit the great white mountain.

VITAL STATISTICS:

GAME BIRDS:
CHUKAR, DOVE, DUCKS, GEESE, HUNGARIAN PARTRIDGE, PHEASANT, QUAIL
Source of Birds: Wild and pen-reared
Seasons:
DOVE: September
WATERFOWL: October through January
UPLAND BIRDS: September through April
Land: 6,000 private acres
Accommodations:
MODERN LODGE OF WOOD AND GLASS
NUMBER OF ROOMS: 8
MAXIMUM NUMBER OF HUNTERS: 16
Meals: Excellent regional and game cuisine
Conference Groups: Yes
Guides: Trained dogs and guides
Dogs and Facilities:
Kennel for hunters' dogs
Shotgun Sports:
Five-stand, shooting schools, skeet, sporting clays
Other Services:
Birds cleaned and packed for travel, proshop
Other Activities:
Big game, bird-watching, fishing, golf, hiking, horseback riding, skiing, wildlife photography
Rates:
From $900 / person / 4 days and 3 nights.
Gratuity:
Hunter's discretion
Preferred Payment:
Cash, MasterCard, Visa or check
Getting There:
Fly to Alamosa and rent a car.

Contact:
Mt. Blanca Game Bird & Trout Lodge
PO Box 236
Blanca CO 81123-0236
800/686-4024
Fax: 719/379-3843
EMAIL: mtblanca@fone.net
WEB: www.mtblanca.com

NEAR THE ARIZONA BORDER, an old volcanic mountain, its slopes pockmarked with cirques, rises a mile and a half above the surrounding arid plain. It is inescapable, this mountain, and it is apt to intrude on your thoughts as you swing on the bird flushing from beneath the pointer at your feet. You must not think of the mountain, or of the sparkling sky, or the ducks you will shoot this evening in the rushes by the lakes stocked with tippet-snapping trout. Your job is dropping the bird cleanly and quickly so as not to disappoint the dog who serves you so faithfully.

With 1,200 acres along Trinchera Creek, a few miles south of the Blanca airfield, this lodge is really one of those charming full-service outdoor resorts where you can play any number of shotgun or fly rod games. More than 6,000 acres is available for hunting. Dove and ducks are wild here. Quail, pheasant, chukar and Hungarian partridge are released before the season starts, and as need be on the section set aside as a preserve. Dogs range from Labs to pointers, and there are kennels if you want to bring your own. Rounds of sporting clays, five-stand and skeet may help your eye.

Though the elevation of the ranch's rolling terrain flirts with 8,000 feet, it's flat enough so that walking is reasonably easy. Anybody who plans to engage in strenuous activity at this elevation needs some conditioning. That may be the idea behind the trout ponds. Spend half a day handling rainbows in excess of three or four pounds and you'll be ready for a walk behind a dog in the stubble fields. Ducks are hunted from blinds with decoys.

Creature comforts at Mt. Blanca match the gunning. All rooms are tastefully decorated and include private baths. Meals verge on elegant; try Hunter's Choice, a 20-ounce ribeye stuffed with sautéed shallots, sweet peppers and mushrooms. After dinner, take a walk or sit and soak in the hot tub and sauna. Getting to sleep is never difficult at Mt. Blanca.

Scenic Mesa Ranch

Hotchkiss, Colorado

With the Gunnison at your back door, Scenic Mesa is the place to spend a week in October.

VITAL STATISTICS:

GAME BIRDS:
CHUKAR, DUCKS, GEESE, PHEASANT

Source of Birds: Wild and pen-reared

Seasons:
UPLAND BIRDS: September through February
WATERFOWL: December and January

Land: 9,000 private acres

Accommodations:
MODERN AMERICAN INDIAN-STYLE LODGE
NUMBER OF ROOMS: 3
MAXIMUM NUMBER OF HUNTERS: 6

Meals: Whatever you want (within reason)

Conference Groups: Yes

Guides: Trained dogs and guides

Dogs and Facilities:
Kennel for hunters' dogs, dog training

Shotgun Sports:
Sporting clays

Other Services:
Birds cleaned and packed for travel, proshop

Other Activities:
Big game, bird-watching, fishing, hiking, horseback riding, wildlife photography

Rates:
$650 / day

Gratuity:
$50 - $100

Preferred Payment:
Cash, Visa or check

Getting There:
Fly to Grand Junction and rent a car.

Contact:
Stan Stockton
Scenic Mesa Ranch
PO Box 251
Hotchkiss CO 81419
970/921-6200
Fax: 970/921-6343

THE NORTH FORK of the Gunnison flows down through a broad valley largely given to agriculture. It's cattle country with row crops planted in bottoms where there's moisture enough to bring in a harvest. The town of Hotchkiss has all the earmarks of an unpretentious farm community, especially when compared to others of similar size that have been all tricked up for the tourist trade. But five miles south of town is this Orvis-endorsed ranch, where you'll find outstanding wingshooting, as well as horseback riding, wilderness trips, historic tours and, yes, fly-fishing.

Scenic Mesa is a working ranch, raising bison for the market and for breeding. On its 9,000 acres, honcho Stan Stockton labors effectively to integrate good husbandry practices for his buffaloes and game birds. Grain plantings and water points are established to ensure a plentiful supply. Thick cover is maintained along wet-weather washes. Fence lines are allowed to become overgrown. Birds—pheasants and chukar—are released before the opening of the season in September, and by the time wingshooting reaches its stride in October, the birds are as wild as can be. Ducks and geese are hunted in the river bottoms and stubble fields in December and January.

The best time to hunt Scenic Mesa is in early to mid-October. Aspen are pure gold along the hillsides. Mornings are frosty yet warm to comfortable sweater weather by noon. A good walk behind a pointer usually brings a few birds to bag. Afternoons are best spent, though, across Green Mountain where the Gunnison cuts through Black Canyon. The Gunnison has earned a reputation as one of America's 100 best trout streams. The upper river near Almont is a fine freestone stream, and large browns play at the base of the 2,000-foot-deep canyon. Access to the canyon water is difficult but worth every minute of toil.

Hunters will find Scenic Mesa comfortable and intimate. The lodge has a strong southwestern flavor—lots of log and stucco with American Indian interior décor. With three rooms, each with private bath, you'll never feel crowded. Meals are family style and timed to hunting or fishing. There are no set menus, and special diets are easily accommodated. You'll work out the meal plan before you arrive. Be sure to ask about special recipes for bison.

Sporthaven Ltd.

B e n n e t t ,   C o l o r a d o

The greatest little bird house and clay range east of Denver.

VITAL STATISTICS:

GAME BIRDS:
CHUKAR, DOVE, HUNGARIAN PARTRIDGE, PHEASANT, QUAIL

Source of Birds: Wild and pen-reared

Seasons:
CHUKAR, HUNS, PHEASANT: October through April
QUAIL: All year

Land: 300 private acres

Accommodations:
IN NEARBY TOWN

Meals: Restaurants

Conference Groups: Yes

Guides: Trained dogs and guides

Dogs and Facilities:
Kennel for hunters' dogs, dog training

Shotgun Sports:
Five-stand, sporting clays

Other Services:
Birds cleaned and packed for travel

Other Activities:
Bird-watching, fishing, wildlife photography

Rates:
From $150 / gun

Gratuity:
$20

Preferred Payment:
Cash, MasterCard, Visa or check

Getting There:
Fly to Denver and rent a car.

Contact:
Dave Lincoln
Sporthaven Ltd
50500 E 72nd Ave
Bennett CO 80102
303/644-3030
WEB: www.sporthaven.com

GARY, A FRIEND OF MINE, commutes weekly from his home in northern Virginia to a job in Denver. At times, vagaries of airline schedules, weather or workload force him to spend weekends in the city. Thus marooned, Gary is separated from his sweet wife, has none of his usual hobbies to occupy mind and hand, and becomes a prime candidate for all sorts of trouble. He might have two pats of butter on his baked potato, an extra glass of wine with dinner, a rich chocolate dessert, or heaven forbid, go to a Denver Broncos game (unthinkable for a Redskins' fan). The vices of a big city like Denver prey heavily on middle-aged men from Millwood. But if Gary were a shooter, he'd be free of all temptation.

You see, less than 15 miles east of metropolitan Denver in the little town of Bennett is Sporthaven Limited, the ultimate sporting retreat. With only about 300 acres, you'd hardly think of Sporthaven as a destination for a bird hunting trip. However, if you're stuck in the city for one reason or another, Sporthaven is only 30 minutes down Interstate 70, and that makes it attractive indeed.

Quail are available all year round, and chukar, Huns and pheasants make their appearance from October through April. With a kennel of Brittanies and pointers, along with friendly guides, you can purchase a number of birds, have them released in one of several fields, and then go hunt them up. Is it like gunning for native wildfowl? Well, not quite. But it sure beats sitting in a motel room. While this is a membership club, one-day passes for $50 are available to non-members who wish to hunt. If you know you're going to be in Denver for a while, spring for the full $500 membership. That entitles you to bird hunts at reduced rates, and some fabulous dove hunting in early September. Guns — Weatherby and Winchester over/unders — can be rented. All you need to do is bring a pair of brush pants and old walking boots.

Members receive substantial discounts on rounds at the 30-station sporting clays course, can work out on the 3-D archery range, or fish ponds for bass in the three- to four-pound range. Accommodations are not found on site, but a range of motels and restaurants are nearby, and the preserve is within easy drive of the Denver airport.

Flying B Ranch

K a m i a h ,   I d a h o

*If Lewis and Clark came over the mountain
today, they'd stay at the Flying B.*

**VITAL
STATISTICS:**

GAME BIRDS:
CHUKAR, HUNGARIAN PARTRIDGE,
PHEASANT, QUAIL
Source of Birds: Wild and
pen-reared
Seasons:
UPLAND BIRDS: Mid-August through
mid-April
Land: 4,800 private acres
Accommodations:
LONG, LOW, LOG LODGE
NUMBER OF ROOMS: 14
MAXIMUM NUMBER OF HUNTERS: 19
Meals: Excellent regional cuisine
Conference Groups: Yes
Guides: Trained dogs and guides
Dogs and Facilities:
Kennel for hunters' dogs, dog training
Shotgun Sports:
Driven birds, shooting schools,
sporting clays
Other Services:
Birds cleaned and packed for travel,
proshop
Other Activities:
Big game, bird-watching, boating,
canoeing, fishing, golf, hiking,
horseback riding, wildlife photography
Rates:
From $2,750 / 3 days
Gratuity:
10%
Preferred Payment:
Cash, credit cards or check
Getting There:
Fly to Lewiston and you'll be
picked up.

Contact:
Bob Burlingame
Flying B Ranch
RR2, Box 120
Kamiah ID 83536
208/935-0755
Fax: 208/935-0705

FROM THE EAST, the road into Kamiah winds down the lovely and unspoiled Lochsa, which dumps into the Clearwater at Lowell. Down this watercourse came Lewis and Clark in 1805, moving peacefully through the lands of the Nez Percé. Native to this land, the Nez Percé had lived on agriculture and fish until the time of the expedition, when they adopted buffalo hunting in the style of the plains Indians. Gold claims in the 1860s pushed them from isolated valleys near Yellowstone, and a fearsome battle fought on Montana's Big Hole drove them into the Bitterroots and eventually back into the valley of the Clearwater, where they ranch today.

If you know this and more of the Nez Percé, you may think of it while walking the high and grassy hills humped up behind Flying B Ranch. You'll be intent, of course, on the doings of your pointer, waiting for her to lock onto a point, which means upland bird. But when you walk, you can't help but admire the grandeur of the peaks in the Clearwater National Forest to the east, and the waves of descending ridges to the west. Custom four-by-fours will carry you afield, and you may ride or walk from there as your senses dictate. Normally, a guide serves three hunters, and you'll gun over pointers and setters from among the Flying B's kennel of 50 bird dogs. Yes, you'll also find Labs and maybe a springer. Shooting schools are regularly held at the 11-station sporting clays course, and informal instruction is always available.

Along with bird hunting, the Flying B mounts expeditions for mule deer, elk, mountain lions and bear. There's fly-fishing for wild cutthroat in the Clearwater and Lochsa, and an icy pond on the ranch holds bruisers that will run you into backing. Steelhead and sturgeon also rate highly here.

The lodge is absolutely first class. Rooms are tastefully appointed with private baths and enough amenities to sooth even the most cynical vet of the travel wars. Meals feature regional cuisine prepared with gourmet flare. The Jacuzzi and sauna melt kinks from overstretched muscles, and the sigh of the night wind through the mountain grasses lulls you to sleep.

❖ *A Willow Creek Guide* ❖

North America's GREATEST Bird Hunting Lodges & Preserves

[R O C K Y   M O U N T A I N S]

Malad Valley Upland Hunts

M a l a d   C i t y ,   I d a h o

Park your RV, unlimber your shotgun, and chase a few pheasants in the lovely mountain-rimmed valley.

VITAL STATISTICS:

GAME BIRDS:
CHUKAR, HUNGARIAN PARTRIDGE, PHEASANT, QUAIL, SHARPTAIL
Source of Birds: Wild and pen-reared
Seasons:
PRESERVE BIRDS and HUNS: Mid-August through mid-December
SHARPTAIL: October
Land: 1,025 private acres
Accommodations:
IN NEARBY TOWN AND CAMPGROUNDS
Meals: Restaurants in town
Conference Groups: Yes
Guides: Trained dogs and guides
Dogs and Facilities:
Kennel for hunters' dogs, dog training
Rates:
$50 / membership
Gratuity:
Hunter's discretion
Preferred Payment:
Cash or check
Getting There:
On Interstate 15 just north of Utah line.

Contact:
Brett Rose
Malad Valley Upland Hunts
3400 W 2800 N
Malad City ID 83252
208/766-4208

I N A BASIN THAT'S ONLY 400 FEET SHY of being a mile high, Brett Rose runs a shooting preserve that's quite popular with hunters from Pocatello to the north and Salt Lake City to the south. This is a fairly straight-forward operation, and if you happen to be in the area after the preserve's mid-August opening, it's certainly worth a look.

Along the Malad River ("They call it a river, but you can jump across it in spots during a dry year," says Brett), he hunts about 400 acres of crested wheat grass, barley and wheat stubble. The balance of his 1,042 acres are higher up, mostly CRP land. There you'll work wheat and buffalograsses with sage, bitter- and buck- (also known as mountain mahogany) brush. Huns love the latter because of the shade it provides. And here, too, are sharptails. You and your party will have exclusive use of parcels ranging from 160 acres to 400 acres.

Prices for hunts are remarkably reasonable. Pay a $50 membership fee (good for the season) and a quartet of pheasants will set you back $60. Five chukar are similarly priced, as are six quail. If you happen on a Hungarian partridge or sharptail grouse, that's your good luck. There's no extra charge. Most hunters bring their own dogs and hunt without guides. But if you need a dog, one with a handler is available for $50 per half day. You'll hunt over one of Brett's English setters.

Malad is not a tourist Mecca, though no matter which way you look, you see tall mountains. Accommodations are available in two hotels: the Malad Hotel and the Village Inn. Many hunters park their motor homes on Bureau of Land Management or National Forest Service campsites.

Teton Valley Lodge

Driggs, Idaho

There's fine waterfowling at the back door to the Grand Tetons.

VITAL STATISTICS:

GAME BIRDS:
DUCKS, GEESE, GROUSE
Source of Birds: Wild
Seasons:
GROUSE: September through mid-October
WATERFOWL: October through January
Land: 600 private acres
Accommodations:
PRIVATE CABINS
NUMBER OF ROOMS: 22
MAXIMUM NUMBER OF HUNTERS: 30
Meals: Steaks, ribs, seafood
Conference Groups: Yes
Guides: Trained dogs and guides
Dogs and Facilities:
Kennel for hunters' dogs
Other Services:
Birds cleaned and packed for travel, pro shop
Other Activities:
Boating, fishing, hiking, horseback riding
Rates:
$850 / day for two
Gratuity:
10%
Preferred Payment:
Cash, credit card or check
Getting There:
Fly to Jackson, Wyoming, and rent a car, or use the lodge shuttle for $100 round trip.

Contact:
John Pehrson
Teton Valley Lodge
379 Adams Road
Driggs ID 83422
208/354-2386 or
208/354-8125
Fx: 208/354-2387
EMAIL: jpehrson@pd+.net
WEB: tetonvalleylodge.com

ONE OF THE OLDEST AND FINEST trout lodges offers great waterfowling, thanks to a bit of glacial geology and a burgeoning population of ducks and geese. First the landscape. The Grand Tetons, stunning with their soaring peaks, wow tourists who run the corridor from Jackson, Wyoming, to the southern entrance of Yellowstone. The eastern front of the Tetons is most often seen, and the back side in Idaho is not at all as spectacular. High plains climb toward the mountains, ascending into foothills that steepen into the mountains.

Ho hum? Well, hold on. Streams like Teton, Dick, and Warm creeks that drain the western slopes of the mountains level off quickly when they reach the plain. There they coalesce into the Teton River, a wide, shallow spring creek-like river that flows through a wetland before picking up speed and hustling out of the valley. Bordering the marshy ground are acres and acres of grassland and grain fields, the latter being the magnet for waterfowl. Given ample habitat and food, it's no wonder that gunning for mallards.

You'll hunt here the old-fashioned way, from wire-backed cattail blinds. Only two guns and the guide — and the obligatory Lab — hunt out of each blind. You'll move as the ducks do. There's goose hunting, too. They come into the field by the pond at 8:30 every morning with such punctuality that you can set your watch by 'em. Mallards are the staples of this operation, although you'll have a chance to shoot teal, pintails and bluebills as well.

After duck hunting's done in the morning, you've got a choice. Trade your 12-bore for a 20 and work the timber for ruffed grouse. You may find them a little easier than those of the Great Lakes woods or the ridges of West Virginia, but don't count on it. Or, if you're a mind to, the gray drake hatch on the Teton should be in full force, and you've just gotta unlimber your fly rod and give those 16- to 30-inch rainbows a go.

In business for more than 60 years, Teton Valley is one of the largest fishing lodges in the Rockies, but you wouldn't know it. Its frame cabins are clustered along the Teton like houses in a small village. Meals are not overly fancy, just good steaks, prime rib and seafood. The service, however, is outstanding; these folks know their business.

[R O C K Y   M O U N T A I N S]

Big Island Shooting Preserve

C o l u m b u s ,   M o n t a n a

Hunt pheasants and ducks on this huge island in the Yellowstone and overnight in your RV for free.

B RAWLING OUT OF THE MOST EXOTIC national park in the U.S., the Yellowstone River turns east at Livingston and scoots over gravel bars at the base of the Absaroka Mountains. During glacial times, the river's volume was much higher and the valley filled with cobble wrested from the mountains to the south and rounded by the tumbling currents. As flows diminished over the centuries, islands emerged. Annual runoff from snowpacks flooded them and deposited fine silt, enriching their soils. During summer, grasses thrive. Low spots are filled with heavy brush, and along the edges rise stands of cottonwoods.

John Sherwood and John Voorhis own one such island, a teardrop-shaped parcel of 123 acres between Columbus and Park City. Down the center runs a strip of hay fields allowed to grow wild. To the southwest lies a swamp. On the northeast side is a stunted forest of cottonwoods. As far as habitat for pheasant and chukar, this is hard country to beat. Not only do the owners stock it periodically during the season (as well as before your hunt), but wild birds pushed from fields along the river also often take refuge on the island. Gunning is normally good, and the river holds migratory waterfowl during the season. A dozen decoys set in the lee of a gravel bar will normally pull in birds. The best gunning comes in October and early November, coinciding with excellent hatches on the river. There's no better place than this for a combined upland game/trout trip.

And you can't beat the price of accommodations. Bring your camper or motor home and park it on the island for free when you book a hunt. You'll find many of the conveniences of a shooting resort: trap range, kennels for your dogs, and release shoots if gunning for high-flying birds turns you on. Guides and dogs are available if you so need. The towns along Interstate 90 offer a wide range of accommodations, often at reduced rates during the late fall.

VITAL STATISTICS:

GAME BIRDS:
CHUKAR, DUCKS, GEESE, PHEASANT
Source of Birds: Wild and pen-reared
Seasons:
UPLAND BIRDS: September through March
WATERFOWL: October through January
Land: 123 private acres
Accommodations:
CAMP ON THE ISLAND OR HOTELS IN TOWN
Conference Groups: Yes
Guides: Trained dogs and guides
Dogs and Facilities:
Kennel for hunters' dogs, dog training
Shotgun Sports:
Driven birds, shooting schools, tower or release shoots, trap
Other Services:
Birds cleaned and packed for travel
Other Activities:
Big game, bird-watching, boating, canoeing, fishing, hiking, wildlife photography
Rates:
From $125 / hunt
Gratuity:
Hunter's discretion
Preferred Payment:
Cash or check
Getting There:
Fly to Billings and rent a car.

Contact:
John Sherwood
Big Island Shooting Preserve
413 Shane Creek Rd
Columbus MT 59019
406/322-5339
Fax: 406/322-5562

Bighorn River Resort

Ft. Smith, Montana

Wonderful hunting for pheasants, Huns, sharptail and chukars in the land of the Crow.

VITAL STATISTICS:

GAME BIRDS:
CHUKAR, DUCKS, HUNGARIAN PARTRIDGE, PHEASANT, SAGE GROUSE, RUFFED GROUSE, SHARPTAIL

Source of Birds: Wild and pen-reared

Seasons:
UPLAND BIRDS sans PHEASANT: September through mid-December
PHEASANT: Mid-October through mid-December
WATERFOWL: November through mid-January

Land: 100,000 private acres

Accommodations:
PRIVATE LOG CABINS
NUMBER OF ROOMS: 7
MAXIMUM NUMBER OF HUNTERS: 14

Meals: Excellent cuisine with French overtones

Conference Groups: Yes

Guides: Trained dogs and guides

Dogs and Facilities:
Kennel for hunters' dogs, dog training

Shotgun Sports:
Five-stand, shooting schools, sporting clays

Other Services:
Birds cleaned and packed for travel, proshop

Other Activities:
Biking, bird-watching, boating, fishing, horseback riding, wildlife photography

Rates:
WATERFOWL from $1,800 / 4 days
UPLAND from $2,175 / 4 days

Gratuity:
10% - 15%

Preferred Payment:
Cash or check

Getting There:
Fly to Billings and rent a car.

Contact:
Nick Forrester
Bighorn River Resort
PO Box 7595
Ft. Smith MT 59035
406/666-9199
Fax: 406/666-9197
EMAIL: info@forresters-travel.com
WEB: www.forresters-travel.com

WERE IT NOT FOR YELLOWTAIL DAM, which impounds the Bighorn River, there probably wouldn't be as much of a town as there is now at Ft. Smith. And what there is isn't much, save a few fly shops, a grocery story and a couple motels that cater to anglers who can sleep almost anywhere. Below the town, a north road runs across the afterbay and climbs 1,500 feet or so up into the lands of the Crow Reservation. It winds along a tight canyon, the site of a buffalo jump from back in the days when there were buffalo. Indians herded the big bisons over a cliff here and easily harvested the meat, hides and horn from its base.

Today, this land of short grasses is grazed by cattle. Valleys, cut by streams that flow when it rains hard enough or when the snow melts, are often thick with plum, chokecherry and buffaloberry. Thick, gummy brown soil in these little valleys holds moisture, and grasses grow thick. It is the place where you'll find birds. Just what kind of birds you'll encounter, you won't know until they flush. But you can make a pretty good guess. The thicker the cover, the more likely you are to find sharptails. Huns seem to favor the edges and even open fields if the cover is more than eight inches deep. Chukars don't like creek bottoms at all, preferring instead rocky hillsides and low bluffs tufted with thin sage and brush. Pheasants know no reason or rhyme. They are where you find them.

Wild birds? What difference does it make? Like most lodge operators, Nick Forrester releases birds in advance of the season, and sometimes during it. But there's none of this dizzy-the-bird and stick it under a bush business so you and your bird dog can find it ten minutes later. Nick's guides are native Crow who grew up on the reservation. Some have attended college and now guide part time. You'll find them friendly and extremely knowledgeable about the land they're hunting. Dogs are springers, pointers or Labs, if you want them. At Nick's, you can also arrange to float the Bighorn for ducks, and throw nymphs or drys for big browns or 'bows.

Accommodations in honey-toned log cabins are first rate, and Francine, Nick's wife, is a trained French chef. Meals are delightful.

Eagle Nest Lodge

H a r d i n ,   M o n t a n a

Under new owners, Eagle Nest continues it tradition of excellent bird hunting under Montana's big sky.

VITAL STATISTICS:

GAME BIRDS:
DUCKS, GEESE, HUNGARIAN PARTRIDGE, PHEASANT, SAGE GROUSE, SHARPTAIL
Source of Birds: Wild and pen-reared
Seasons:
SAGE GROUSE, SHARPTAIL GROUSE and HUNGARIAN PARTRIDGE: September through mid-December
PHEASANT, WATERFOWL: mid-October through mid-December
Land: 42,000 private acres
Accommodations:
LOVELY LOG LODGE
NUMBER OF ROOMS: 7
MAXIMUM NUMBER OF HUNTERS: 14
Meals: Fine cuisine
Conference Groups: Yes
Guides: Trained dogs and guides
Dogs and Facilities:
Kennel for hunters' dogs, dog training
Shotgun Sports:
Shooting schools, sporting clays
Other Services:
Birds cleaned and packed for travel, proshop
Other Activities:
Fishing
Rates:
$1,000 / day or $3,400 / week
Gratuity:
$75 - $100 / day / guide
Preferred Payment:
Cash, MasterCard, Visa or check
Getting There:
Fly to Billings and rent a car or hire a shuttle at $160 round trip.

Contact:
Scott Moscato
Eagle Nest Lodge
PO Box 509
Hardin MT 59034
406/665-3711
Fax: 406/665-3712
EMAIL: s_moscato@progidy.net
WEB: www.eaglenestlodge

BIG NEWS HERE ON THE BANKS of the Bighorn, a stone's throw out of Hardin, is that Scott Moscato and John Tesenen have bought Eagle Nest from its founder, Alan Kelly. Al now manages the Orvis endorsed Wingshooting Lodges Program, one of which is, of course, Eagle Nest Lodge. You can expect the same, fine upland birds—pheasants, Huns, sage grouse, and sharptail grouse, as well as duck and goose hunting—that you knew under the previous owners.

Typical hunts begin right after breakfast. Guests, cup of hot coffee in hand, chat with guides about dogs, the weather and the acreage for the day's festivities. Pink noses of pointers and the darker snouts of shorthairs and Labs poke at the mesh in dog-box doors. Climbing into four-by-fours, parties disperse to ranches leased for bird hunting. Scott works with a handful of landowners whose lands total 42,000 acres. He rotates parties, so ranches are seldom hunted more often than once a week.

Terrain in these parts swells like an ocean troubled by a distant storm. Watercourses meander through flat bottoms of little more than a quarter-mile in width. Cattails and thick grass, interspersed with willow and occasional Russian olive, make these sloughs heavy walking. Yet it's cover loved by pheasants. Dogs will bust them out; you don't have to. Edges of stubble fields hold Hungarian partridge, and draws filled with plumb and chokecherry often hold families of sharptail. Pheasants and Huns are released during the season, but never just before your hunt the way some other lodges do. Sage grouse and sharptails are as wild as the wind.

Grain fields and ponds along the Bighorn attract more ducks and geese than you'd imagine. The wise gunner brings along a three-inch 12-gauge as well as a 20, though those who are good shots can do quite well, thank you, with the latter in three-inch chambering. Needless to say, it's foolish to come all the way to this glorious part of autumn's world without packing a five- or six-weight. There are few better venues than the Bighorn for a bit of fall fishing.

Accommodations in the toffee-hued log lodge are absolutely first class. Two guests share rooms decorated in western style with private baths. Meals are absolutely delightful—rack of lamb one night, swordfish the next. This is the kind of place that's not hard to get used to.

On the land of the Crow Reservation above the Little Bighorn, Dave Egdorf of Last Stand Lodge hunts sharptails that hide in brush choked ravines.

Fetch Inn Hunting Preserve

H a m i l t o n ,   M o n t a n a

The Bitterroot is a stunning land to hunt pheasants in the fall (and the fishin' ain't bad either!).

VITAL STATISTICS:

GAME BIRDS:
PHEASANT
Source of Birds: Wild and pen-reared
Seasons:
September through March
Land: 1,200 private acres
Accommodations:
PRIVATE LODGE
NUMBER OF ROOMS: 5
MAXIMUM NUMBER OF HUNTERS: 12
Meals: Self-catered
Conference Groups: No
Guides: Trained dogs and guides
Dogs and Facilities:
Kennel for hunters' dogs
Shotgun Sports:
Informal instruction
Other Services:
Birds cleaned and packed for travel
Other Activities:
Fishing
Rates:
Hunts from $180 / half-day; accommodations begin at $85
Gratuity:
Hunter's discretion
Preferred Payment:
Cash, MasterCard, Visa or check
Getting There:
Fly to Missoula and rent a car.

Contact:
Romey Harris
Fetch Inn Hunting Preserve
PO Drawer 1000
Hamilton MT 59840
406/363-5111
Fax: 406/363-6774
EMAIL: fox@montana.com
WEB: www.fetch-inn.com

UP WHERE the mountains begin to put the squeeze on the Bitterroot Valley is a first-class hunting preserve where ringnecks are king from September through March. Picture it: 1,200 acres of grassy river benches and stubble fields, tawny and golden in the waning sun of autumn. Stands of alder are yellowing, but the cottonwoods along the river are still green. They'll lose their leaves later. It's shirtsleeve weather in the fields, but winter's cold is climbing down from the 9,000-foot peaks of the Bitterroot Mountains to the west. Twice already this fall, Brandy Peak above the lodge to the west has worn a white beard. At night you can hear the wheezing whistles of bull elk. It won't be long until snow flies.

Working primarily with German shorthairs, parties hunt through the rich bottom cover. No high-seated Jeeps or mule-drawn wagons here. You walk behind the dogs, watching them consistently weave that figure-eight 10 to 15 yards ahead. When one bitch goes on point and the dog backs, you feel your shoulders tense, and you move your gun into the ready, port-arms carry. You are ready. Your guide tells you to ease up on the dog. You do, and the cock, iridescent and bronze, launches out of the grass with a cackle that'd wake the dead. No matter how often you hear it, you're still taken slightly by surprise. But you're not so startled that you can't drop him with the first barrel.

Up to nine hunters—three parties of three each—hunt the field managed by Fetch Inn. While you may bring and hunt your own dogs, you'll need a guide. Half-day and full-day hunts are available. If you come in September or October, by all means bring your fly rod. While the inn does not arrange fishing trips or provide gear to guests, you're more than welcome to fish the mileage of the river that borders the lodge's property.

Fetch Inn operates a modern yet rustic five-bedroom lodge. It's available on a first-come-first-served basis. The first party to book the lodge—be it only a single individual—has the sole use of it during her or his stay. Rates are reasonable: $85 for the first guest, and $50 for each additional member of the same party. The caveat: You'll sling your own hash unless you arrange to have dinner catered.

Last Stand Lodge

Hardin, Montana

Hunter, historian, naturalist, Dave Egdorf runs an excellent lodge for wild birds, trout and deer.

VITAL STATISTICS:

GAME BIRDS:
DUCKS, GEESE, HUNGARIAN PARTRIDGE, PHEASANT, SAGE HENS, SHARPTAIL, TURKEY
Source of Birds: Wild
Seasons:
DUCKS and GEESE: December through early January
TURKEY: mid-April to early May
UPLAND BIRDS: September through mid-December
Land: 500,000 private acres
Accommodations:
A-FRAME GUESTHOUSE AND MAIN LODGE
NUMBER OF ROOMS: 3
MAXIMUM NUMBER OF HUNTERS: 8
Meals: Very good and hearty fare with gourmet overtones
Conference Groups: Yes
Guides: Trained dogs and guides
Dogs and Facilities:
Kennel for hunters' dogs
Shotgun Sports:
Shooting schools, informal instruction
Other Services:
Birds cleaned and packed for travel
Other Activities:
Big game, bird-watching, fishing, hiking, wildlife photography
Rates:
$545 / day
Gratuity:
$25 - $50 / day
Preferred Payment:
Cash or check
Getting There:
Fly to Billings and rent a car.

Contact:
Dave Egdorf
Last Stand Lodge
PO Box 434
Hardin MT 59034
406/665-3489
Fax: 406/655-3492
EMAIL: egdorf@wtp.net
WEB: uswestdex.com/iyp.laststand

WHEN HE WAS A YOUNG BOY, Chief Plenty Coups of the Crow had a dream. He dreamed that all of the buffalo vanished into a hole in the ground, and out of the hole came different buffalo, ones with spots on their sides. Sitting under a tree by the hole was an old chief with gray braids. This was a strong dream, and he took it to the elders. "What does it mean?" he asked them. The wisest chief told him that it meant that all the buffalo would vanish, and in their place would come the white man's cattle. "Do you know who the old man is in your dream?" the chief asked Plenty Coups. "Yes," he replied, "It is I."

Plenty Coups believed the dream meant that the Crows should try to get along with the white man and join them in battle against the enemies of the Crow — the Sioux and Blackfoot. He believed that in so doing, the Crow would be able to retain rights to their native lands after the other tribes were defeated. Despite lost battles such as Custer's fight on the Little Bighorn, Plenty Coups' vision proved itself. The Crow Reservation covers nearly 2,000 square miles.

When you hunt with Dave Egdorf, you'll be hunting on private ranches within the reservation. Among them is a modest spread of 250,000 square miles that's as big as Montana's night sky. How do you hunt it? A little at a time. Birds — wild sharptail grouse and Hungarian partridge — seek cover in the thick brush that fills those wet-weather drainages that carve such tight, steep valleys on the rounded hills. The birds that flush — and there will be many — will sail over the brow of the nearest hill and settle out of sight. But you're a smart dude, and you've figured out that all you have to do is work the next draw. On a ranch of this size, it'll take a lifetime to work them all. Along with Huns and sharpies, you'll encounter pheasants and sage hens, all of them wild and none of them stocked. (Although he can arrange a stocked bird hunt.) Bird season begins to fade in November, but that's when waterfowling starts to reach its peak. Meriams turkey season opens in mid-April and runs through early May. And there's mule deer, antelope and elk in the fall.

If you come to Last Stand to hunt birds, don't forget a fly rod. It's the best time of the year for the browns and rainbows of the Bighorn.

Rock Creek Outfitters

H i n s d a l e ,   M o n t a n a

Help! Somebody's gotta thin out those pheasants and ducks up near the Canadian border.

VITAL STATISTICS:

GAME BIRDS:
DUCKS, GEESE, PHEASANT
Source of Birds: Wild
Seasons:
DUCKS and GEESE: October through January
PHEASANT: Mid-October through mid-December
Land: 3,000 private and public acres
Accommodations:
PRIVATE LODGE
NUMBER OF ROOMS: 3
MAXIMUM NUMBER OF HUNTERS: 6
Meals: Hearty beef and trimmings
Conference Groups: Yes
Guides: Trained dogs and guides
Dogs and Facilities:
Kennel for hunters' dogs
Shotgun Sports:
Informal instruction
Other Services:
Birds cleaned and packed for travel
Other Activities:
Big game, bird-watching, hiking, horseback riding, wildlife photography
Rates:
$1200 / week / gun
Gratuity:
$50 - $100
Preferred Payment:
Cash or check
Getting There:
Fly to Glasgow and you'll be picked up.

Contact:
Dean Armbrister
Rock Creek Outfitters
PO Box 152
Hinsdale MT 59241
406/648-5524
Fax: 406/648-5524
EMAIL: rock-creek-lodge1@juno.com
WEB: finditlocal.com/rock creek

IF YOU'RE LOOKING FOR A PLACE MORE than a little off the beaten path, you'll find it in Hinsdale. A small town on U.S. Rt. 2 less than 50 miles south of the Saskatchewan, Canada border, Hinsdale is located on the Milk River, which joins the Missouri below Fort Peck Dam. The country is wide open high prairie, broken by coulees that cut down from the plain to river bottoms below. Up here, the population is as sparse as the sky is big. That means, generally speaking, few bird hunters.

Bird season — pheasants, ducks and geese — runs from October into mid-December. At this time of year, most hunters, and guides for that matter, are hot in pursuit of whitetails and mule deer. Bird hunters are in reasonably short supply. The pheasants don't seem to mind. Working with pointers or retrievers, whichever you prefer, you'll work thick patches of grass and brush along the shores of Fort Peck Lake. Many hunters get their limits of three cock birds per day. At Rock Creek, you'll find excellent kennels for your dog.

Dean also hunts ducks and geese over decoys. You'll set up in stubble fields for geese, lying in a spread of decoys and watching the birds come closer and closer until the guide says "Now!" Ducks, hunted on sloughs that feed into Fort Peck or backwaters of the Milk, offer outstanding gunning in December and January. The season, however, opens on October 1, and it's quite possible to work in an early-season shoot.

Dean and Patti Armbrister are the owners of Rock Creek, and their lodge is only a couple of years old. Three bedrooms all have private baths and share a hot tub, which goes a long way to ease muscles stretched while chasing birds. Also soothing are sizeable meals of Montana beef, homemade breads and desserts that never met a calorie they didn't like. So how do you get to this bit of undiscovered bird hunting Mecca? Fly to Glasgow, Montana, and either Dean or Patti will pick you up at no extra charge.

WEST

ARIZONA, CALIFORNIA, NEVADA, NEW MEXICO, OREGON, WASHINGTON

FROM THE ARID reaches of New Mexico and Arizona up through California and the Pacific Northwest, the West, too, is a very diverse region. New Mexico and Arizona offer hunting for quail, but not many of the bobwhite variety. Here you'll encounter Mearn's, scaled, and Gambel's quail, birds that are somewhat fleet afoot and thus reluctant to hold still for a dog. Mourning dove and whitewings, too, provide fast gunning in the Southwest. Highlands and mountains offer a few blue grouse. Sharptails may also be found.

Dove are important in southern California, and the farther north you go, the more you get into lands of the valley quail. Among the best waterfowling in the West is to be had in the Sacramento Valley from the Capital north to Chico. Pintails (called "sprigs" here) are the big deal and they're hunted over flooded rice paddies known as "checks." In the northern grasslands of eastern Washington, you'll find good pheasant hunting as well as ruffed and sage grouse.

Lodges:

California

1 CAMANCHE HILLS HUNTING PRESERVE
2 GUNS & ROOSTERS HUNTING PRESERVE
3 HIGH DESERT HUNT CLUB
4 ROCK SPRINGS LODGE

Oregon

5 GREAT EXPECTATIONS HUNTING PRESERVE
6 TKO-THOMPSON KREIN OUTDOORS

Washington

7 PHEASANT VALLEY SHOOTING PRESERVE
8 R&M GAME BIRDS & SHOOTING CLAYS

References:

WINGSHOOTER'S GUIDE TO ARIZONA
by William "Web" Parton
Wilderness Adventure Press
800/925-3339

GAME BIRD HUNTING IN OREGON
Oregon Department of Fish and Wildlife
800/845-9448

Resources:

ARIZONA GAME AND FISH
DEPARTMENT
2221 W. Greenway Rd
Phoenix, AZ 85023
602/942-3000
web: www.gf.state.az.us

CALIFORNIA DEPARTMENT OF FISH &
GAME
Wildlife and Inland Fisheries Division
1416 9th St., Box 944209
Sacramento, CA 95814
916/324-7243
web: www.dfg.ca.gov/

NEVADA DIVISION OF WILDLIFE
Box 10678
Reno, NV 89520
702/688-1500
web: www.state.nv.us/cnr.nvwildlife

NEW MEXICO DEPARTMENT OF
GAME AND FISH
Box 25112
Santa Fe, NM 87504
505/827-7911
800/862-9310
web: www.gmfsh.state.nm.us

OREGON DEPARTMENT OF FISH
AND WILDLIFE
Box 59
Portland, OR 97207
503/872-5268
web: www.dfw.state.or.us/

WASHINGTON DEPARTMENT OF
FISH AND WILDLIFE
600 Capitol Way North
Olympia, WA 98501-1091
360/902-2515
web: www.wa.gov/wdfw/

[W E S T]

Camanche Hills Hunting Preserve

I o n e ,   C a l i f o r n i a

Mild of climate, rich in cover, scenic as a postcard . . . and birds too!

VITAL STATISTICS:

GAME BIRDS:
CHUKAR, DUCKS, PHEASANT
Source of Birds: Pen-reared
Seasons:
September through March
Land: 1,485 private acres
Accommodations:
IN NEARBY TOWN
Meals: Breakfast and lunch served
Conference Groups: Yes
Guides: Trained dogs and guides
Dogs and Facilities:
Kennel for hunters' dogs, dog training
Shotgun Sports:
Driven birds, five-stand, shooting schools, skeet, sporting clays, trap
Other Services:
Birds cleaned and packed for travel, proshop
Other Activities:
Bird-watching, wildlife photography
Rates:
Nonmember shoots from $150
Gratuity:
15%
Preferred Payment:
Cash, MasterCard, Visa or check
Getting There:
Fly to Sacramento and rent a car.

Contact:
Larry Skinner
Camanche Hills Hunting Preserve
2951 Curran Rd
Ione CA 95640
209/763-5270
Fax: 207/763-5803

TO THE EAST of the Sacramento Valley the land begins to climb into the foothills of the Sierra Nevada. It is lovely country, not so arid as further south. Hills are studded with black and valley oak, almost as if they'd been planted as groves. But they weren't. They just look that way. Beneath the trees roll endless grassy hills. In the low spots on the valley floors wave acre upon acre of harding, canary reed, and perla—perennial grasses favored by upland fowl. Hillsides or those that have been manicured (for that's what they seem) are lush with a carpet of habitat rye. There is no brush, or very little of it, in sight.

In winter, the climate here is delightful. Farther up the valley from Colusa to Chico, where pintails fly, winters can become terrible. But here the land is just southward enough so it's seldom too cold to really hunt. Sill, the best times are October and March.

Camanche Hills is a membership club. For $2995, you can become a lifetime member. Once in, dues are but $200 a year. For that price, you get a heck of a break on the price of birds and on rates for sporting clays and release duck shoots. Even if you're not a member, you can try out the preserve hunting for $25 per pheasant and $15 per chukar. If you want to pass-shoot ducks—released over a dry lake bed because California Game and Fish feels that to do so over water would attract wild birds—you're welcome to sign up for $150. Ten ducks are released per gun. How many you take, well, that's up to you. Pointers of various ilk are employed on upland hunts, and it's up to Labs and Chessies to bring in mallards that meet with lethal doses of steel shot.

The club includes no accommodations, but why should it? Less than a quarter of a mile away, on the shores of Lake Camanche, are a number of hotels, motels and bed-and-breakfasts. Restaurants are abundant. And, by the way, fishing in the reservoir for trout, bass and crappie is much better than good.

Guns & Roosters Hunting Preserve

V i s a l i a , C a l i f o r n i a

OK, *who wants to hunt birds with* black powder? *It's a real blast.*

VITAL STATISTICS:

GAME BIRDS:
CHUKAR, PHEASANT
Source of Birds: Wild and pen-reared
Seasons:
November through March
Land: 2,100 private acres
Accommodations:
IN NEARBY TOWN
Meals: Restaurants
Guides: Trained dogs and guides
Other Services:
Birds cleaned and packed for travel
Rates:
$60 / 3 pheasants or 5 chukar
Gratuity:
$10 / gun
Preferred Payment:
Cash or check
Getting There:
Drive in from Fresno or Bakersfield.

Contact:
Dave Hamilton
Guns & Roosters Hunting Preserve
31661 Rd 160
Visalia CA 93292
559/798-1966
Fax: 559/798-1062
EMAIL: birddog@lightspeed.net

IN CALIFORNIA, full-service hunting lodges specializing in birds are few and far between. And there aren't as many preserves as you might think. Many hunters get by with hunting on public land, but like most overpressured acreage close to population centers, getting by is just about all you can say for it.

Here and there, though, are good quality preserves, and Guns & Roosters fits into that category. With more than 2,000 acres of wheat and alfalfa managed for pheasants and chukar, Guns & Roosters offers fee hunting from November through March. Bring your own dog or use one of owner Dave Hamilton's German shorthairs.

Dave has been in this business for nearly a decade, and he's learned a couple of things. One: The less contact pen-raised birds have with humans, the more likely they'll fly as if they were wild. Dave trained a couple of neighbors to raise birds just the way he wants, and the result is a bird that will flush or run to escape. Hunting here is a matter of keeping up with a well-trained dog. If you're not on the bird soon after the shorthair goes on point, you'll have to work the bird again.

A second revelation concerns drainage checks, those shallow canals that carry life-giving irrigation water to grain and forage fields. For years, the ditches and berms were sprayed with herbicides to retard weed growth. Such, though, is no longer the practice. The checks grow up with natural vegetation, pruned here and there as logic dictates. Not only does the luxuriant brush provide a place for released birds to hide, but Dave's noticing an increased number of wild birds on his spread.

At Guns & Roosters, you won't find fancy clay games or driven shoots of European style. What you have here is a basic preserve with good birds and quality cover. Juniors, women, black-powder gunners (a real kick in more ways than one) and archers are welcome here. Morning or afternoon hunts can be arranged, often on short notice during the week. Visalia is a small city more or less halfway between Fresno and Bakersfield. Should you wish to stay the night, you'll find a number of motels and a few bed-and-breakfasts in town. Restaurants, of course, are abundant.

High Desert Hunt Club

G o r m a n ,   C a l i f o r n i a

West of Tejon Pass is a little road that leads to the greatest bird hunting close to L.A.

VITAL STATISTICS:

GAME BIRDS:
CHUKAR, PHEASANT, QUAIL
Source of Birds: Wild and pen-reared
Seasons:
October through March
Land: 8,100 private acres
Accommodations:
NEARBY BED-AND-BREAKFASTS OR MOTELS
Meals: Lunches of fresh salads, homebaked breads and desserts
Conference Groups: Yes
Guides: Trained dogs and guides
Dogs and Facilities:
Kennel for hunters' dogs, dog training
Shotgun Sports:
Driven birds
Other Services:
Birds cleaned and packed for travel, pro shop
Other Activities:
Fishing, hiking, wildlife photography
Rates:
From $150 / gun
Gratuity:
$20
Preferred Payment:
Cash, MasterCard, Visa or check
Getting There:
Fly to Los Angeles and rent a car.

Contact:
Lisa McNamee
High Desert Hunt Club
PO Box 89
Gorman CA 93243
888/425-4868
Fax: 949/863-0633
WEB: www.highdeserthunt.com

LEAVING LOS ANGELES, Interstate 5 climbs out of the congested valley into a welter of arid ridges and high rolling mountains. Just before you crest Tejon Pass and start down into California's Great Valley, State Rt. 138 breaks off to the east. It's the trail into a bit of the Golden State that time has, thankfully, overlooked. The club hunts 8,000 acres. Lush meadows crossed here and there by bright cold-water creeks grow green even in the driest seasons. From these gentle glens rise canyons with their scree and truncated ledges. In between are swaths of brown grasses and rabbit brush.

Two species of quail thrive in the dry grasses. You may take only ten valley quail per day; the bag on bobwhite is unlimited. Outcrops and talus are favored by chukar, a bird that is native to southern sections of central California. Meadows, brushy fencerows and weedy watercourses provide cover for pheasants.

This is an utterly first-class preserve offering a variety of hunts. Popular programs include a day-long for quail, chukar and pheasant. Nineteen birds are released per hunter, but there's no limit on the number harvested (with the exception of valley quail). Lunch, dogs and a guide are included as is cleaning and packaging of birds at the end of the hunt. A less expensive version limits gunning to ten valley quail and five chukar. Bring your own dog or hire a guide and dog for an additional fee. Lunches can also be ordered if you wish. Special hunts for individual species can also be arranged.

High Desert is known in the L.A. area for its fine continental shoots for driven pheasants. Beginning with a continental breakfast, gunners then move to the butts for a morning's gunning. Professional dog handlers run retrievers to pick-up downed birds. After lunch in the hacienda, hunters may work up pheasants that escaped unscathed from the morning's shooting.

While overnight accommodations can be arranged at Willowbrook (a charming bed-and-breakfast of the Victorian era), or at motels on the Interstate, elegant lunches are served in the Adobe Hacienda, the oldest building in Antelope Valley. Corporate groups are quite at home here as are guys who just want to work their dogs on a few good birds.

Rock Springs Ranch

P a i c i n e s ,   C a l i f o r n i a

Just a quick ride from the bay area puts you in the lap of luxurious bird hunting.

VITAL STATISTICS:

GAME BIRDS:
CHUKAR, HUNGARIAN PARTRIDGE, PHEASANT, QUAIL (BOBWHITE and VALLEY)

Source of Birds: Wild and pen-reared

Seasons:
VALLEY QUAIL: Late October through January
BOBWHITE and CHUKAR: September through May
HUNGARIAN PARTRIDGE: October through February
PHEASANT: October through March

Land: 19,000 private acres

Accommodations:
PRIVATE LODGE OF WOOD AND GLASS
NUMBER OF ROOMS: 6
MAXIMUM NUMBER OF HUNTERS: 12

Meals: Gourmet regional cuisine

Conference Groups: Yes

Guides: Trained dogs and guides

Dogs and Facilities:
Kennel for hunters' dogs

Shotgun Sports:
Five-stand, wobble trap

Other Services:
Birds cleaned and packed for travel, pro shop

Other Activities:
Big game, bird-watching, hiking, wildlife photography

Rates:
$800 / gun / day

Gratuity:
Hunter's discretion

Preferred Payment:
Cash, MasterCard, Visa or check

Getting There:
Fly to San Jose and rent a car, or the lodge will provide at $250 roundtrip.

Contact:
Nola or Ken Range
Rock Springs Lodge
11000 Old Hernandez Road
Paicines CA 95043
800-209-5175 or
408-385-5242
Fax: 831/385-5270
EMAIL: covey@sirius.com
WEB: www.rockspringsranch.com

WITH HALF A DOZEN YEARS under its belt, Rock Springs Ranch—in the mountains 75 miles southwest of San Jose—is earning an enviable reputation as one of the best wingshooting lodges in the United States. Nola and Ken Range, managers of operations since it opened in 1994, are unstinting in their commitment to quality. This is one of very few California ranches open to the public for bird and big game hunting. Quail, especially valley quail, is the name of the game here, but you'll also hunt pheasant, chukar and Hungarian partridge.

Native to the xerophytic brushlands of southern California and Nevada, valley quail wear waistcoats of ruddy pearl beneath their slate gray jackets. They have a reputation for running ahead of even the best pointers, according to Ben Williams, who knows such things. But he'll tell you not to believe a word of it. In the waning days of the season, as food and water become more scarce, valley quail tend to gather in flocks that are difficult to approach. But once you bust them up, you can work singles and doubles to your pointer's content.

Valley quail are the only wild game birds (unless you count turkeys and mallards) that are hunted on Rock Springs' 19,000 acres. But the low and rounded hills in the rain shadow of the Coast Range and the fields in the intervening valleys—farmed to promote wildfowl—offer bird hunting as challenging as you want to make it. Equally fun are released bird shoots. A high hill serves as the tower, and gunners are stationed in butts around its perimeter. First come pheasants, flyer after flyer after flyer, and you shoot until you're barrel's too hot to hold. Pigeons, too, are released from the hilltop, and the gunning begins anew. Afterward you'll sit in the shade of weathered oaks and lunch on the likes of grilled steak, chicken, guacamole and desserts whose very description will loosen your belt at least one notch.

And that's only the midday meal. An afternoon hunt works up a second appetite for dinner of rack of lamb accompanied by excellent vintages from the cellar and finished with port and cigars. As you'd suspect, the lodge's six guest rooms, all with private baths, are exquisitely furnished.

Great Expectations Hunting Preserve

K i m b e r l y ,   O r e g o n

Only one party at a time hunts this Shangri-La of rolling fields deep in the mountains.

VITAL STATISTICS:

GAME BIRDS:
CHUKAR, PHEASANT, QUAIL
Source of Birds: Wild and pen-reared
Seasons:
September through March
Land: 550 private acres
Accommodations:
PRIVATE TIMBER LODGE
NUMBER OF ROOMS: 4
MAXIMUM NUMBER OF HUNTERS: 8
Meals: Chef prepares or you do
Conference Groups: Yes
Guides: Trained dogs and guides
Dogs and Facilities:
Kennel for hunters' dogs, dog training
Shotgun Sports:
Sporting clays, tower or release shoots
Other Services:
Birds cleaned and packed for travel
Other Activities:
Big game, bird-watching, fishing, wildlife photography
Rates:
From $150 / up to 4 guests; birds and guides additional
Gratuity:
Hunter's discretion
Preferred Payment:
Cash or check
Getting There:
Fly to Redmond and rent a car.

Contact:
Jerry Russell
Great Expectations Hunting Preserve
HC82, Box 234
Star Rt. 2
Kimberly OR 97848
541/934-2117

SELDOM does land fire the imagination like the terrain of central Oregon in the vicinity of the Umatilla National Forest. High grassy meadows, glowing golden in the waning day's sun, fall off into valleys plush with forest along the river only to rise again in the distance and climb ridges that steepen with altitude, finally becoming barren mountains, perhaps brushed with snow when you arrive.

So much of the sporting West has gone tourist-commercial, but not Great Expectations. Halfway between Kimberly and Monument, this lodge is on the way to nowhere else. If it's tranquility you're seeking, it's here in ample supply. And the lodge, a modern ranch, is only booked by one party at a time. If you happen to be a gourmet cook, bring your own herbs and vintage wines, and let your tastes run rampant in the fully-equipped kitchen. But if, on the other hand, you prefer that another perform the culinary art (hey, let's get real here, wash the dishes?), you can arrange to have a chef prepare dinner for two or more.

Great Expectations hunts more than 550 acres of thick grass and grain fields. Cover is mixed here; about one third of the preserve is planted in crops specifically chosen to nurture upland species. Otherwise, the birds — pheasants, chukar, bobwhite and valley quail — have to fend for themselves. They don't have much to worry about. Grass fields range up hillsides. You'll find a few stubble fields. Along creek beds, brush becomes denser. Hunting without a dog is not recommended. Guides and pointers, setters or flushing retrievers are available. A championship-caliber sporting clays course, designed by Dan Carlisle, is available for your use.

The thing to do here is to gather a group of four—two couples where spouses hunt are ideal—and book the lodge for a weekend. Plan to arrive on a Friday afternoon. Loosen up with a round of sporting clays, then hunt the fields for the rest of the afternoon. Cook dinner yourselves, but bring the chef in for breakfast and lunch the next day. Hunt the morning, fish for trout in the afternoon or go looking for sabertooth tigers in the John Day Fossil Beds National Monument to the east. After a lazy dinner, hit the sack early, grab coffee and a quick bite for breakfast and wrap it up with a morning hunt. A great weekend, no?

TKO-Thompson Krein Outdoors

Heppner, Oregon

Three lodges, three different ranches — Guess you'll have to spend an extra week.

VITAL STATISTICS:

GAME BIRDS:
CHUKAR, PHEASANT
Source of Birds: Wild and pen-reared
Seasons:
September through March
Land: 70,000 private acres
Accommodations:
THREE LODGES
NUMBER OF ROOMS: VARIES WITH LODGE
MAXIMUM NUMBER OF HUNTERS: VARIES
WITH LODGE, BUT NO MORE THAN 13
Meals: From full-service to self-catered
Conference Groups: Yes
Guides: Trained dogs and guides
Dogs and Facilities:
Kennel for hunters' dogs
Shotgun Sports:
Driven birds, sporting clays, tower or release shoots
Other Services:
Birds cleaned and packed for travel
Other Activities:
Big game, bird-watching, wildlife photography
Rates:
From $395 / day
Gratuity:
Hunter's discretion
Preferred Payment:
Cash, MasterCard, Visa or check
Getting There:
Fly to Pendleton or Portland and rent a car.

Contact:
Bob Krein
TKO-Thompson Krein Outdoors
58588 Balmy Fork Rd
Heppner OR 97836
541/676-5005
Fax: 541/676-8995
EMAIL: bobkrien@ptinet.com
WEB: www.ruggsranch.com

ORTHEASTERN OREGON is an arid land, ideal for growing grass and little else. Here, north of the Umatilla National Forest, trees are at a premium. A little brush breaks up valleys along creeks. In the main, though, it's just miles and miles of benchland . . . and pheasant land. In this Mecca for bird shooters, Thompson Krein Outdoors (TKO) runs preserve-style hunts on 70,000 acres, provides lodging on three ranches, and offers gunners a fine sporting clays course in the rimrock canyonland along Rhea Creek south of Ruggs.

Each of the ranches covers slightly different ground. Ruggs Ranch is the signature lodge. Sitting atop a bench, the vista from the dining room stretches across miles and miles of open range. Sleeping 13 in comfort, the ranch includes five bedrooms, each with a private bath. Two stone fireplaces warm backsides chilled by the winds of early winter. Meals are excellent. The lodge has kennel facilities for guests' dogs, and the terrain around the lodge is generally easy walking (there's just a lot of it).

In Balm Fork Lodge, just across the broad ridge coming down from mile-high Coalmine Hill, you'll see leaded glass windows and old pine floors that date this white frame house back to the late 1800s. When it comes to meals, you can either do your own cooking, take potluck with the restaurants in Heppner, or arrange for meals at extra cost. You'll be glad to know that Balm Fork features a heated kennel for your dogs. Guests pick from seven bedrooms and share a hot tub.

North of Heppner is the smallest of the trio: Willow Creek Ranch. Here the foothills of Ruggs and Balm Fork have smoothed out a bit, but you're still deep in grasslands. With four bedrooms, a living room with a wood stove, and a fully equipped kitchen, this is a do-it-yourself hostelry. Bring your own food and beverages or rely on diners in Lexington or Heppner, each about four miles away.

[**W E S T**]

Pheasant Valley Shooting Preserve

L a C r o s s e ,   W a s h i n g t o n

America has a second great prairie—the Palouse—and it hunts as well as the other one.

VITAL STATISTICS:

GAME BIRDS:
CHUKAR, DUCKS, GEESE, PHEASANT

Source of Birds: Wild and pen-reared

Seasons:
PRESERVE BIRDS: September through April
WATERFOWL: October through December

Land: 4,000 private acres

Accommodations:
PRIVATE HOME
NUMBER OF ROOMS: 3
MAXIMUM NUMBER OF HUNTERS: 6

Meals: In nearby restaurants

Conference Groups: Yes

Guides: Trained dogs and guides

Dogs and Facilities:
Kennel for hunters' dogs

Shotgun Sports:
Sporting clays

Other Services:
Birds cleaned and packed for travel

Other Activities:
Big game, bird-watching, hiking, wildlife photography

Rates:
Hunts from $250;
accommodations $100 / houseful

Gratuity:
Hunter's discretion

Preferred Payment:
Cash, MasterCard, Visa or check

Getting There:
Fly to Spokane and rent a car.

Contact:
Jerry Townsend
Pheasant Valley Shooting Preserve
PO Box 201
LaCrosse WA 99143
509/549-3912
EMAIL: jtownsen@televar.com

ROUGHLY SPEAKING, the region south and west of Spokane is a high prairie of rich, thick grasses, extensive grain farms and very few trees. It's known as the Palouse, so named for a Native American peoples whose ancestral home was here and whose descendants live in the area around LaCrosse, about 60 miles south of Spokane.

This prairie is not of the gently rolling kind. Low cliffs of basalt define box canyons. The land heaves like a sea troubled by an on-shore storm. It's a welter of pockets, swales and little draws, and that's what makes hunting here so fantastic. Pheasants and chukar, even those that have been released recently, will take advantage of the terrain. Hunt the bottoms along the Palouse River or the hills above it. Waterfowling can be excellent, and it adds only $100 to the price of a pheasant hunt.

Pheasant Valley's sporting clays course also draws raves. Preserve owner Jerry Townsend has taken a canyon and hidden his traps therein. With 40 positions and unlimited variation, you never get the same birds twice. They sail low and fast along the top of the cliff, zing through the grass like a Hun that's chased by a dozen 7 1/2s from a 20-gauge. High incoming shots fade just when you've got a line on them. Birds seem to spring up from nowhere. No dodging trees here as in most eastern courses. It's all open, so the only excuses are yours. One hundred targets constitutes the course here; plan to wear your bird hunting boots and long pants.

Overnight accommodations for up to six are provided in a fully furnished house. Meals will be taken at area restaurants. Campgrounds are available for RV owners.

R&M Game Birds & Shooting Clays

L y l e ,   W a s h i n g t o n

The drive up the scenic valley along the Columbia is almost as much fun as the hunt at R&M.

VITAL STATISTICS:

GAME BIRDS:
CHUKAR, PHEASANT, QUAIL
Source of Birds: Wild and pen-reared
Seasons:
All year
Land: 1,100 private and public acres
Accommodations:
IN NEARBY TOWN
Meals: Restaurants
Conference Groups: Yes
Guides: Trained dogs and guides
Dogs and Facilities:
Kennel for hunters' dogs, dog training
Shotgun Sports:
Five-stand, shooting schools, sporting clays
Other Services:
Birds cleaned and packed for travel, proshop
Other Activities:
Big game, biking, bird-watching, boating, canoeing, fishing, golf, hiking, horseback riding, skiing, wildlife photography
Rates:
Based on number of birds released
Gratuity:
Hunter's discretion
Preferred Payment:
Cash, MasterCard, Visa or check
Getting There:
Drive from Portland.

Contact:
Rodger Ford
R&M Game Birds &
Shooting Clays
495 Fisher Hill Rd Hill
Lyle WA 98635
509/365-3245
Fax: 509/365-4868
EMAIL: rm@gorge.net
WEB: www.americaoutdoors.com/r&m

RIVING FROM THE WEST, you'll leave Portland heading up the south bank of the Columbia on Interstate 84. Once you pass Troutdale, it won't be long until you enter the Mt. Hood National Forest; its 11,000-foot namesake volcano has been on your right, guiding you since you left the city. At Hood River, you'll leave the Interstate, cross the river to White Salmon and follow State Rt. 14 for another dozen miles to Lyle, where the wild and scenic Klickitat River flows into the Columbia from the north.

This river valley is nothing short of absolutely stunning. Valley walls rise 1,000 feet from the broad alluvial floor. Taking Fisher Hill Road, you'll wind up from the valley, breaking onto a broad plateau of mixed forest. A few miles farther and you come to R & M preserve. Up on the plateau, the terrain rolls oh-so-gently. Fields of bulbgrass, alfalfa and native ground covers make walking relatively easy. So captivating is the view of Mt. Hood to the south, that it's almost impossible to keep your mind focused on the birds in the bush. You must, of course. R&M raises pheasants and chukar for its own preserve as well as for others.

On the property is an outstanding sporting clays course, the first to be sanctioned by National Sporting Clays Association back in 1989. Guests who return year after year are delighted to find that the course continues to evolve. It may not be the same as when you shot it last. Regional tournaments are held regularly, yet novice shooters can be successful on this course as well. Shooting schools and clinics are scheduled throughout the year.

Open all year—the weather is benign enough for all but hunts in July and August—R&M offers a nice diversion for shotgun sportsmen traveling in RVs. Campgrounds abound, as do motels and restaurants for those not driving their accommodations.

ALASKA

NOBODY THINKS OF Alaska as a place to hunt birds. You go there for rainbows with weights that nudge double digits, for salmon the size of small toddlers, for brown bear and moose and caribou, but not for upland birds or waterfowl. Well, maybe it's time to think again.

Cold winds out of the Arctic get ducks moving early. They stream down from the Bering Sea, crossing Bristol Bay, the peninsula, and the islands of the panhandle. They filter into Kodiak and Afognak islands with each cold front. You wake up in the morning and they're there: mallards, gadwalls, wigeon, green-winged teal, shovelers, redheads and canvasbacks. While dabbling ducks have beat it out of Alaska by mid-October, sea ducks hang around much of the winter. Hunt for oldsquaws, harlequins and scoters in the chill, wet winds of November and December. Geese, too, frequent Alaska's south coast. Major species include brant, Canadas

Lodges:

1 ALL ALASKA OUTDOORS INC

2 CHRIS GOLL'S RAINBOW RIVER LODGE

3 CRYSTAL CREEK LODGE

References:

ALASKA FISHING AND HUNTING GUIDE
Christopher M. Batin
Alaska Angler Publications
P.O. Box 83550
Fairbanks, Alaska 99708-3550
(907) 455-8000

Resources:

ALASKA DEPARTMENT OF FISH AND GAME
Box 25526
Juneau, Alaska 99802
(907) 465-4100
web: *www.fishgame.state.ak.us*

ALASKA

and white-fronted geese.

As for upland birds, you won't find many wild pheasants. But grouse — blue, ruffed, sharp-tailed and spruce — can be plentiful in the interior of the state. Ruffs have been introduced in Sustina and Kenai areas. Ptarmigan needed no introduction. You'll encounter rock, whitetail and willow, and they can be quite sporting, especially if you hunt them with a vibrant pointer whose footfalls, like a fox, make them nervous as can be.

Wile it's difficult to imagine planning a trip to Alaska just to hunt birds, there are those who might. They'd be well advised to tote a three-inch 20-gauge, and a few boxes of 7 1/2s and three-inch steel fours or twos for waterfowl. And they ought to haul along a six-weight as well. Never know when you'll need to fight off one of those rainbows.

[A L A S K A]

All Alaska Outdoors, Inc.

S o l d o t n a ,   A l a s k a

Ducks and grouse and ptarmigan (three species), all for the serious collector.

VITAL STATISTICS:

GAME BIRDS:
DUCKS, GROUSE, PTARMIGAN
Source of Birds: Wild
Seasons:
GROUSE and PTARMIGAN:
mid-August through March
DUCKS: September through
mid-December
Land: Unlimited public acreage
Accommodations:
LOVELY RUSTIC YET MODERN LODGE
NUMBER OF ROOMS: 8
MAXIMUM NUMBER OF HUNTERS: 20
Meals: Regional game and seafood
Conference Groups: Yes
Guides: Trained dogs and guides
Dogs and Facilities:
Kennel for hunters' dogs
Shotgun Sports: Sporting clays
Other Services:
Birds cleaned and packed for travel
Other Activities:
Big game, bird-watching, boating,
canoeing, fishing, hiking, horseback
riding, skiing, wildlife photography
Rates:
Packages from $1,450 / person /
7 nights
Gratuity:
Hunter's discretion
Preferred Payment:
Cash or check
Getting There:
Fly to Anchorage and rent a car.

Contact:
Bob Ledda
All Alaska Outdoors, Inc.
PO Box 208
Soldotna AK 99669
907-262-4868
Fx: 907/262-1349
EMAIL: allakout@alaska.net
WEB: www.allakaska.com

NOBODY COMES TO ALASKA just to hunt birds. But if your travel plans fall after the first week in August, you might just want to pack a scattergun too. The season opens with ptarmigan and spruce grouse, and moves on to ducks three weeks later. Ducks close in mid-December, but if you're hardy enough, you can shoot grouse and ptarmigan to your heart's content all the way through the end of March. If you plan to do that, bring your snow shoes.

Spruce grouse and ptarmigan are birds that upland gunners love to hate. "No sport," they chorus. "They're dumb, just sit there and look at you," say others. "About as much fun as hunting pigeons around a bird feeder." Sure, these natives to the Kenai Peninsula lack the type "A" behavior so typical of the ruffed grouse of eastern forests or native-bred bobwhite quail. Their flush is nowhere near as explosive as a sharptail or wild Hungarian partridge. There's even a four-mile hike on All Alaska's roster where you'll normally jump 400 birds on a given day. Still, they can be challenging to hunt. So focused on one group are you as you approach, that you completely miss seeing another bunch that flushes from the low brush by your left knee. Some hunters try to collect all three species: white-tailed (so named for that feature), rock (found in dryer land and lacking the reddish color of the willow), and willow (more russet than brown and preferring thickets of alder and willow, hence the name). If you hunt upland game, you'll probably do so over a highly skilled Drahthaar (German wirehair pointer).

Ducks are also plentiful. Mallards, teal, gadwall, pintail and wigeon are found in Redoubt Bay, a short flight from the lodge. Later, as the season moves into mid-October, hunting for sea ducks picks up. Typical bags are mixed with goldeneyes, harlequins, oldsquaws, scoters and eiders. Labs do the retrieving work. Decoys and pass-shooting are used, depending on the birds and weather conditions.

Bird hunting peaks with runs of fall steelhead, rainbows and grayling. Some silver salmon remain in the river systems at that time. Most visitors combine fishing and gunning for upland birds. Accommodations, as you'd expect, are excellent. Located on a lake in Soldotna, the three-story lodge is the ideal jumping-off point for explorations of the Kenai Peninsula.

Chris Goll's Rainbow River Lodge

Iliamna, Alaska

Did those fool hens fool you again? Well, spruce up your shooting!

VITAL STATISTICS:

GAME BIRDS:
DUCKS, GROUSE, PTARMIGAN
Source of Birds: Wild
Seasons:
UPLAND: Mid-August through November
WATERFOWL: September through November
Land: 900 square miles
Accommodations:
MODERN GLASS-FRONTED LODGE
NUMBER OF ROOMS: 6
MAXIMUM NUMBER OF HUNTERS: 12
Meals: Excellent cuisine based on choice meats and regional seafood
Conference Groups: Yes
Guides: Trained dogs and guides
Shotgun Sports: Trap
Other Services: Birds cleaned and packed for travel, pro shop
Other Activities:
Big game, bird-watching, canoeing, fishing, hiking, wildlife photography
Rates:
$500 / day; $3,500 / week
Gratuity:
Hunter's discretion
Preferred Payment:
Cash, MasterCard, Visa or check
Getting There:
Fly to Iliamna and meet the air taxi.

Contact:
Chris Goll
Chris Goll's Rainbow River Lodge
PO Box 330
Iliamna AK 99606
907/571-1210
Off Season:
PO Box 1070
Silver City NM 88062
505/388-2259
Fax: 505/388-2261

YOU MIGHT THINK THAT THIS RIVER is so named because it's a pot of gold, and in a way you'd be right. Hoglike rainbows up to 23 pounds wallow in this river at the tail of the salmon spawn. Feeding on flesh and eggs, these 'bows aren't overly choosy. Bend some orange-colored yarn on a hook and cast upstream and across the current. Throw a mend in your line, and then maybe another for good measure. Odds favor a massive strike. If not persnickety, these fish are pugnacious. You'll catch half a dozen in the morning and more in the afternoon. That is, unless you take a break for a little bird hunting.

Washed by flood and formed by glaciers, rivers in the Iliamna area are mainly bordered by bars of sand and gravel. Stands of willow thrive along the rivers and behind rise loden forests of spruce and fir. Perfect habitat for spruce grouse. *Dendrapagus canadensis* is not highly rated as upland game birds go. They're called "fool hens," but that sobriquet is apt to fool hunters as well.

Some will sit like brown bumps on a log as you approach. Others flush wildly, artfully dodging through the forest and vanishing behind their namesake conifer just as you pull the trigger. "Fooled you, ha!" they seem to chortle. Ruffed grouse, if found far enough from hunting pressure, occasionally behave the same way. Ptarmigan, too, inhabit this region, though they're found in more open tundralike terrain. It, too, has a dubious reputation among eastern gunners of grouse and wild quail. But swinging on a flushing bird, and letting it get out a bit before shooting, is always a challenge.

Along with grouse and ptarmigan, ducks (particularly mallards, pintails, gadwall and teal), are common on the sloughs and ponds of the region. A handful of decoys set in the early morning will provide more action that you can imagine. Ducks are seldom decoy-shy, and limits are very generous. The only question is how many ducks can you shoot before you have to go fishing. Tough life.

Guests stay in rustic cabins complete with private baths, and dine on exquisite fare, after drinks and hors d'oeuvres before the fire. Accommodations are limited to no more than 12 per week at Rainbow River Lodge. Since bird hunting peaks with the height of rainbow run, booking a year in advance is imperative.

[A L A S K A]

Crystal Creek Lodge

D o l l i n g h a m ,   A l a s k a

The waterfowlers' ultimate cast and blast.

VITAL STATISTICS:

GAME BIRDS:
DUCKS, GEESE, PTARMIGAN
Source of Birds: Wild
Seasons:
PTARMIGAN: Mid-August through mid-April
DUCKS and GEESE: September through October
Land: 10 million acres
Accommodations:
PRIVATE LOG LODGE ON LAKE
NUMBER OF ROOMS: 14 w/PRIVATE BATHS
MAXIMUM NUMBER OF HUNTERS: 20
Meals: Elegant Alaskan cuisine
Conference Groups: Yes
Guides: Trained dogs and guides provided
Other Services:
Birds cleaned and packed for travel
Other Activities:
Fishing
Rates:
$5,500 / week / person
Gratuity: 10% - 15%
Preferred Payment:
Cash or check
Getting There:
Fly to Dillingham and the lodge van will meet you.

Contact:
Dan Michels
Crystal Creek Lodge
Box 92170
Anchorage AK 99509
800/525-3153
Fax: 907/245-1946
EMAIL: crystalc@alaska.net
WEB: www.crystalcreeklodge.com

AT THIS FIRST-CLASS establishment (Orvis' lodge of the year in 1997), wise anglers pack along a 12-bore or maybe a 20 when they sign up for a week of fall fishing. Tucked on a little springlike creek that feeds into Nunavaugaluk Lake 25 miles north and west of Dillingham, ducks are flying at the same time silver salmon and rainbows reach their peak runs of the season. Habitat fishing is nothing short of awesome. Scores of potholes left by glacial ice dot the lowlands southwest of the lake. The first cold fronts of Autumn, bred in the Arctic, push flights of mallards, gadwalls, wigeon, greenwing teal, shovelers, redheads and canvasbacks to the south. Many of these birds have never heard a shotgun, and they decoy readily.

That's just how Dan Michels, owner of Crystal Creek, likes to see it. Hunters, two to a blind with guide and retriever, wait in the early morning gloaming as the ducks begin to fly. You can hear them tuning up in the distance, that raucous cacophony that fires expectations. If early morning isn't your bag, sleep in or go fishing. Ducks fly all day here in the early season, and they'll be willing when you're ready. You'll also find good gunning for lesser Canadas, blues, specks and brant. Limits are generous: 10 ducks per day and nearly as many geese (subject to annual change). And, if a spot of upland shooting tickles your fancy, ptarmigan are generally abundant and close by.

Some of the ponds that Dan hunts are close to saltwater, thus the environment may be harsh on that lovely over-under. Bring a pump for ducks and geese, and a double for ptarmigan. Steel shot is required for waterfowl. Dan can supply camo if you don't want to pack yours.

September is a magic time in Alaska. Most tourist/anglers have beaten it back to the lower 48. It's possible to fish some of the most popular rivers without seeing another fisherman. Silver salmon are at their peak and rainbows are going strong. And Arctic char aren't half bad. This is probably the best of Alaska's months. (Why am I telling you this?)

The low, modern wooden lodge fits comfortably among a few spruce on a little bay of the lake. A fire on the stone hearth invites you to sink into a plush leather couch and relax. Guest rooms are comfortable motel-style with private baths, and the lodge boasts a whirlpool as well. Meals here are as good as the waterfowling and fishing.

CANADA WEST

ALBERTA, BRITISH COLUMBIA, NORTHWEST TERRITORIES, SASKATCHEWAN, YUKON TERRITORY

WHILE YOU'LL FIND some spruce and blue grouse, along with a smattering of ptarmigan and ducks in British Columbia, it's not until you're east of the soaring peaks of the Canadian Rockies that wingshooting in western Canada really gets interesting. The vast plains of Alberta and Saskatchewan nurture some ducks, but the main affair is migrations from the vast tundra of the Northwest Territories, where duck hunting begins early in September. Here are greater and lesser scaup, bluebills, bufflehead, scoters, ringnecks, mallards, goldeneye, wigeon, pintail and teal. Add white-fronted and snow geese.

Sharp-tailed grouse and gray partridge are also native to these provinces. Ruffed grouse, also native, are widely scattered. Upland hunts are offered as adjuncts to duck hunts, which are often available to hunters who book for deer, or to anglers seeking late season pike and lake trout.

Lodges:

Alberta
1 BITTERN LAKE LODGE
2 WESTERN GUIDING SERVICE

Northwest Territories
3 TROUT ROCK LODGE (ENODAH WILDERNESS TRAVEL)

Saskatchewan
4 HIGH BRASS - SASKATCHEWAN
5 MAKWA RIVER OUTFITTERS
6 MONTGOMERY OUTFITTING SERVICE

Resources:

DEPARTMENT OF ENVIRONMENTAL PROTECTION
Petroleum Plaza, South Tower
9945 108 St., 9th Floor
Edmonton, Alberta
T5K 2G8, Canada
780/944-0313
web: www.gov.ab.ca/env/

SASKATCHEWAN ENVIRONMENT AND
RESOURCE MANAGEMENT
524-3211 Albert St.
Regina, Saskatchewan
S4S 5W6, Canada
306/787-2931
web: www.gov.sk.ca/govt/environ/

TOURISM SASKATCHEWAN
500-1900 Albert St.
Regina SK
S4P 4L9 Canada
web: www.sasktourism.com

TRAVEL ALBERTA
300-10155 102nd. St.
Edmonton AB
T5J 4G8 Canada
800/661-8888; web: explorealberta.com

MINISTRY OF ENVIRONMENT
WILDLIFE BRANCH
PO Box 9374
Station Provincial Gov't
Victoria, British Columbia
V8W 9M4, Canada
250/387-9731
www.env.gov.bc.ca

TOURISM BRITISH COLUMBIA
865 W. Hornby St.
Vancouver BC
V6Z 2G3 Canada
604/660-2861
800/663-6000
web: www.travel.bc.ca

DEPARTMENT OF RESOURCES
WILDLIFE AND ECONOMIC
DEVELOPMENT
GOVERNMENT OF THE
NORTHWEST TERRITORIES
Box 2668
Yellowknife, Northwest Territories
X1A 3P9, Canada
867/873-7184
web: www.rwed.gov.nt.ca

NWT ARCTIC TOURISM
PO Box 610
Yellowknife NT
X1A 2N5 Canada
800/661-0788
web: www.nwttravel.nt.ca

DEPARTMENT OF
RENEWABLE RESOURCES
Fish & Wildlife Branch
Box 2703
Whitehorse, Yukon Territory
Y1A 2C6, Canada
867/667-5715
web: www.gov.yk.ca/

TOURISM YUKON
Box 2703
Whitehorse, Yukon Territory
Y1A 2C6, Canada
867/667-5340
web: www.touryukon.com

NUNAVUT TOURISM
P. O. Box 1450
Iqaluit, NT
X0A 0H0, Canada
800/491-7910
web: www.nunatour.nt.ca

Bittern Lake Lodge

E d m o n t o n ,   A l b e r t a

Hunt greenheads from North America's largest flocks of mallards.

VITAL STATISTICS:

GAME BIRDS:
DUCKS, GEESE, HUNGARIAN PARTRIDGE, SHARPTAIL
Source of Birds: Wild
Seasons:
WATERFOWL: Sept. through October
HUNGARIAN PARTRIDGE: Mid-Sept. through October
SHARPTAIL GROUSE: October
Land: 1,000 sq. miles, private
Accommodations:
MODERN WOOD LODGE AND RUSTIC FARMHOUSE
NUMBER OF ROOMS: 8
MAXIMUM NUMBER OF HUNTERS: 16
Meals: Steaks and prime rib
Conference Groups: Yes
Guides: Trained dogs and guides
Dogs and Facilities:
Kennel for hunters' dogs, dog training
Shotgun Sports: Sporting clays
Other Services:
Birds cleaned and packed for travel
Other Activities:
Bird-watching, fishing
Rates:
$425 / day
Gratuity:
Hunter's discretion
Preferred Payment:
Cash or check
Getting There:
Fly to Edmonton and Kevin will meet you.

Contact:
Kevin Rolfe
Bittern Lake Lodge
9243 62nd St
Edmonton AB
T6B 1N9 Canada
780/448-0381
Fax: 780/448-1724
EMAIL: outdooredge@westworld.ca

TO THE EAST AND SOUTH of Edmonton, the land begins to resemble Swiss cheese, so dotted with potholes it becomes. Grain fields— wheat, barley and peas—surround these little glacial kettles, and the food provides a high-protein diet for ducks. The formula is a no-brainer. That's why this area has the highest concentration of breeding mallards in North America. And along with an abundance of greenheads, there are enough gadwall, pintails, wigeon, canvasbacks, redheads, scaup and, of course, blue-winged teal to keep you busy.

How many ducks will you see? Lodge owner Kevin Rolfe, whose been guiding for more than two decades, claims that it's not uncommon to watch 2,000 mallards settle into Bittern Lake's shallows in less than an hour. You won't hunt the lake though; all ducking is done from dry-land blinds on grain fields or jump-shooting over the little ponds. Limits are generous — eight mallards per day — and as many Canada geese as well. Ducks and geese work the same fields, but at different times of the day. Most gunners — four to a blind but only two shoot at the same time — hunt Canadas in the morning and ducks as the sun sets over the prairie. Then it's back to the comfortable California-style lodge that overlooks the lake for libations and dinner. If there's spare time, grab a fly rod and go play with the Jurassic rainbows in the trout pond.

What you won't find many of in this patch of prairie are upland birds. For Hungarian partridge and sharptail grouse, the venue switches to the dry lands north of Medicine Hat, about 350 miles southeast of Bittern Lake. "A totally different ecosystem with some speargrass and a little bit of pear cactus," says Rolfe. Gone are the labs of the waterfowl lodge. Here a brace of springers and Brittanys rule the kennels. Upland birds aren't as concentrated as the ducks. Before hunters arrive, guides run farm roads, scouting and spotting. When you arrive, they're ready to put you on birds. Accommodations are found in a fine old farmstead that's been remodeled to sleep eight hunters. Here, one guide serves two hunters.

Bittern Lake is one of those well known places where the reputation is justly deserved. You can read about it in *Shooting Times* and a host of other magazines. Most who book into this operation spend three days waterfowling and two on upland birds.

Western Guiding Service

E m p r e s s ,   A l b e r t a

Exotic to many, sandhill cranes are fine fare for gun and table.

VITAL STATISTICS:

GAME BIRDS:
DUCKS, GEESE, HUNGARIAN PARTRIDGE, SANDHILL CRANES, SHARPTAIL

Source of Birds: Wild and pen-reared

Seasons:
CRANES and GEESE: September through October
HUNGARIAN PARTRIDGE: September through November
DUCKS: September through December
SHARPTAIL GROUSE: October

Land: 50 sq. miles, private

Accommodations:
RUSTIC LODGE
NUMBER OF ROOMS: 9
MAXIMUM NUMBER OF HUNTERS: 9

Meals: Family-style

Conference Groups: Yes

Guides: Trained dogs and guides

Dogs and Facilities:
Kennel for hunters' dogs

Other Services:
Birds cleaned and packed for travel

Other Activities:
Big game, bird-watching, wildlife photography

Rates:
$1,200 / 3 days

Gratuity:
10%

Preferred Payment:
Cash or check

Getting There:
Fly to Medicine Hat, Calgary, or Saskatoon and rent a car, or the lodge will collect you for $150 round trip.

Contact:
Dave Molloy
Western Guiding Service
Box 191
Empress AB
T0S 1E0 Canada
403/565-3755
Fax: 403/565-3755

WITH WINGS SPANNING more than six feet, a red-capped head, and a rattling call which sounds most like a much amplified cat with laryngitis (you can hear it for more than a mile), the sandhill crane is not what you'd call usual upland game. But game it is, and an important species to boot here in the grain fields along the Saskatchewan border. Sandhills breed in the northern Canadian tundra, but also in Rocky Mountain and northern Great Lakes states in the U.S. Best hunting is found in Canada, over decoys. Sandhills are wary, spooky almost. Good camouflage is important. Limits are generous — five per day as of this writing — and the breasts, pounded, marinated and then cooked rare on the grill, are delicious.

Dave Molloy, owner of Western Guiding Service, has made something of a specialty out of hunting sandhills, but that's not all that's on the agenda here. Geese are high on the list — Canadas, white-fronted, Ross', Richardson's — as are ducks, primarily but not exclusively mallards. Geese are hunted over stuffers, in the main, but silhouettes are also used for white-fronted geese.

A typical day begins sometime before 4 a.m., when you're rousted out of the sack, fed a couple of cups of coffee, some juice and muffin, and stowed in the pick-up for a short trek to the field of the morning. There, ensconced in a blind, you'll wait for geese, cranes or ducks that occasionally land amongst the dekes. Gunning is normally fast. You can take up to eight Canadas, five sandhills, and ten snows per day. By 10:30 you're sitting down to breakfast at the lodge. Then, if your constitution permits, you'll walk off those eggs and flapjacks chasing sharptails and Huns over Labs or your own pointers, along brushy sloughs through the grain fields. Dusk may find you back in a blind. Or, should you have reached the limit on geese (yours or the province's), you may jump ducks over potholes.

At Dave's comfortable lodge, you won't fine many late-night poker games. After beef and potato dinners, most hunters stumble wearily into bed, oblivious to the calls of cranes migrating overhead.

[C A N A D A - W E S T]

Trout Rock Lodge (Enodah Wilderness Travel)

Y e l l o w k n i f e ,   N o r t h w e s t   T e r r i t o r i e s

There's great duck hunting just a short hop from Yellowknife, with grouse to boot.

VITAL STATISTICS:

GAME BIRDS:
DUCKS, GEESE, GROUSE
Source of Birds: Wild
Seasons:
ALL: September to mid-October
Land: Unlimited private and public acres
Accommodations:
PRIVATE LODGE AND FRAME CABINS
NUMBER OF ROOMS: 3 CABINS
MAXIMUM NUMBER OF HUNTERS: 12
Meals: Game cuisine
Conference Groups: Yes
Guides: Trained dogs and guides
Dogs and Facilities:
Kennel for hunters' dogs
Shotgun Sports: Trap
Other Services:
Birds cleaned and packed for travel
Other Activities:
Big game, bird-watching, boating, canoeing, fishing, golf, wildlife photography
Rates:
$1,125 / 3 days
Gratuity:
Hunter's discretion
Preferred Payment:
Cash, American Express or check
Getting There:
Fly to Yellowknife and catch the air taxi.

Contact:
Ragnar Wesstrom
Trout Rock Lodge (Enodah Wilderness Travel)
Box 2382
Yellowknife NWT
X1A 2P8 Canada
867/873-4334
Fax: 867/873-3825
EMAIL: ducks@enodah.com
WEB: www.enodah.com

WHEN CONTINENTAL GLACIERS scraped across the Northwest Territories they leveled and smoothed the land, leaving depressions that filled with groundwater and a good bit of terrain that can't decide whether it's wet or dry. All that adds up to some of the best landscape in the world for waterfowl, and Ragnar Wesstrom plunked his lodge right smack in the middle of it.

Trout Rock Lodge is a collection of timber cabins and wall tents firmly perched on a granite outcrop on the north edge of Great Slave Lake. Don't worry, the outcrop is about a mile and a half square and it's of substantial enough elevation so you won't get your feet wet no matter how hard the wind blows. Around the island are vast shallow channels that grade into marsh as they near the shore. The whole area is a staging ground for waterfowl before their southern migration. You'll find them all here: greater and lesser scaup, bluebills, bufflehead, scoters, ringnecks, mallards, goldeneye, wigeon, pintail and teal. Add Canada geese and you've got enough to keep you more than busy for the typical three-day stay. Many guests do their best to collect one drake from each species—quite a challenge, you'll agree. Decoys and blinds are employed here as are guides who use Labs and Chesapeakes to retrieve your birds.

Islands in the lake hold significant populations of grouse—spruce, sharptail and ruffed, according to Ragnar. Walk woods roads without a dog and you'll do just fine. Gunning is best in mid-September, and if you like hurling big spoons, you may connect with a trophy pike.

Despite its location high in Canada's wilderness, regular air connections to Yellowknife allow most American's to reach the lodge in one day's travel. Once there, you'll enjoy fine northern hospitality and some of the finest game cooking—when was the last time you put a fork to musk ox?—anywhere. More timid palates will find beef, chicken and fish to their liking.

High Brass - Saskatchewan

Quill Lakes, Saskatchewan

So much to hunt, so little time. Gotta decide: ducks, geese, cranes, grouse? Your choice.

VITAL STATISTICS:

GAME BIRDS:
CRANES, DUCKS, GEESE, GROUSE, HUNGARIAN PARTRIDGE
Source of Birds: Wild
Seasons: September
Land: Unlimited private and public acres
Accommodations:
PRIVATE NATURE LODGE
NUMBER OF ROOMS: 12
MAXIMUM NUMBER OF HUNTERS: 12
Meals: Game-based country cooking
Conference Groups: Yes
Guides: Trained dogs and guides
Dogs and Facilities:
Kennel for hunters' dogs
Other Services:
Birds cleaned and packed for travel
Rates:
From $1,520 / 3 days
Gratuity:
Hunter's discretion
Preferred Payment:
Cash or check
Getting There:
Fly to Regina and rent a car.

Contact:
Tom Koehn
High Brass - Saskatchewan
RR1, Box 4X
Chamberlain SD 57325
605/734-6047
Fax: 605/734-5033
EMAIL: tkbrass@sd.cybernex.net
WEB: www.highbrass.com

PRIORITIES. Remember your priorities. That's the name of the game when you're hunting waterfowl with Tom Koehn's operation 120 miles north of Regina in the Quill Lakes area. When you arrive in September, ducks, geese and sandhill cranes will be staging for their winter migration south. Ruffed and sharptail grouse will also be active, as will Hungarian partridge. In short, you'll have reached this little outpost on the edge of the prairie at the time when everything is almost perfect.

So, what to do? Canada game laws help. Geese can't be hunted after high noon in Saskatchewan. If you want to shoot Canadas, snows, whitefront or Arctic species, you'd best hie yourself out to the stubble fields before daylight. That means lunch and a choice between puddle ducks (mallards, gadwalls, wigeon, pintail) or divers (canvasbacks, redheads, buffleheads and bluebills). Bluewing and greenwing teal are everywhere. So too are shovelers. Pick your poison (with an eye to the weather). Jump-hunt sloughs and ponds? Decoys in marshes or the lake? Pass-shoot the edges? Up to you.

Then there are sandhill cranes. Many gunners demur at shooting these magnificent birds, which are nearly four-feet in length and their wings stretch six feet or more. On the East Coast, cranes are exotic, meaning they are rarely seen. Their winter range includes Mexico and southern Louisiana. Occasionally, they are encountered in the Everglades. But here in central Saskatchewan, populations are huge, and they are considered a highly desirable game bird. Shoot one, serve it over wild rice, and you will have finally encountered a wildfowl that tastes as good as wild turkey. Grouse and Huns will be hunted if opportunity permits.

You'll find accommodations here to be very clean and comfortable, if a bit spartan. Most rooms contain two to four beds and share baths. Rather than eating in cafes, a full-time cook prepares simple and satisfying game dinners—crane or ducks if you'd like. This is a great outing to fill the freezer with waterfowl in their prime. Bring a big cooler. Pack your clothes in it on the way up, and fill it with ducks for the trip back.

[C A N A D A - W E S T]

Makwa River Outfitters

M a k w a ,   S a s k a t c h e w a n

Deer hunters at Ken's place demanded to hunt ducks too. What's an outfitter to do?

VITAL STATISTICS:

GAME BIRDS:
DUCKS, GEESE
Source of Birds: Wild
Seasons:
September through mid-December
Land: 200,000 private and public acres
Accommodations:
PRIVATE LODGE
NUMBER OF ROOMS: 3
MAXIMUM NUMBER OF HUNTERS: 8
Meals: Home-style and hearty
Conference Groups: Yes
Guides: Included
Dogs and Facilities:
Kennel for hunters' dogs
Other Services:
Birds cleaned and packed for travel
Other Activities:
Big game, golf
Rates:
$300 / gun
Gratuity:
$20 day
Preferred Payment:
Cash, MasterCard, Visa or check
Getting There:
Fly to Saskatoon and rent a car.

Contact:
Ken Dopko
Makwa River Outfitters
Box 89, Makwa SK
S0M 1N0 Canada
306/236-4649
Fax: 306/236-4716
EMAIL: k.dopkp@sk.sympatico.net
WEB: www3.sk.sympatico.ca/sons

WHEN THE LAST of the continental glaciers left Saskatchewan about 12,000 years ago, it left a vast tableland that slopes to the east. The northernmost portion of Saskatchewan is tundra, which, southward, grades into boreal forest. Pines and spruce blanket most of the land, broken by clearcuts. Thin rivers drain hundreds of lakes and ponds lying in areas left by melting ice; it's the first way station on the southern flights of waterfowl that migrate in the fall.

Ken Dopko and his wife, Kathy, have been guiding and hosting whitetail hunters since the early 1990s. But when waterfowl season opened in September, they'd sneak away for a little duck and goose hunting on their own. Occasionally, they'd take along deer hunters who'd bagged their bucks (140 B&C is typical). The hunting was very good, and everyone who went suggested that Ken offer waterfowling as an option separate from big game. This year he took them up on the idea.

Within five miles are a number of big, shallow lakes. Reeds and rushes along shore provide excellent cover for blinds. An airboat carries hunters to remote sections where the birds have been working. In addition, fields of field pea, oat, barley, and wheat stubble draw waterfowl. Both pit and layout blinds are available. You'll hunt in the midst of a spread of decoys primarily for geese: greater and lesser Canadas, specks, and snows. Kennels are available for hunters' dogs. As yet, Ken does not provide retrievers, but that's on his agenda. While the season opens in September and continues through mid-December, hunting is best in the first month and a half.

At some lodges, you load up at what seems like midnight and drive for an hour or so before reaching the land for the day's hunt. Not so here. You'll roll out of bed in the comfortable log cabin, eat a breakfast that's as substantial as you want, and pile into the four-by-fours for the drive of no more than 15 minutes to the bog or field du jour. As you surmise, Makwa River is a small and very personal operation. Two or three hunters share rooms and a common bath in the lodge that's adjacent to the main house. Dinners are family affairs skillfully prepared by Kathy. But when it comes to breakfast, you're the cook. You'll find everything in the fridge, just where Kathy said it would be.

Montgomery Outfitting Service

Morse, Saskatchewan

Ah, the open prairies and their exuberant sharptails and Huns, to say nothing of pothole ducks.

VITAL STATISTICS:

GAME BIRDS:
DUCKS, GEESE, HUNS, SHARPTAILS

Source of Birds: Wild

Seasons:
UPLAND BIRDS: September through October
WATERFOWL: September through November

Land: 300,000 private acres

Accommodations:
ELEGANT COUNTRY INN
NUMBER OF ROOMS: 13
MAXIMUM NUMBER OF HUNTERS: 26

Meals: Fine dining with game entrees

Conference Groups: Yes

Guides: Trained dogs and guides

Dogs and Facilities:
Kennel for hunters' dogs

Other Services:
Birds cleaned and packed for travel, informal shooting instruction

Other Activities:
Big game, golf

Rates:
From $1,250 / 3 days

Gratuity:
$100

Preferred Payment:
Cash or check

Getting There:
Fly to Regina and rent a car.

Contact:
Doug Montgomery
Montgomery Outfitting Service
Box 92
Morse SK
S0H 3C0 Canada
306/629-3752
Fax: 306/629-3752

THERE IS NO PRAIRIE like the Saskatchewan prairie. From horizon to horizon, it rolls on endlessly, its mantle of grass and grains—more of a mane, really—undulates with the incessant winds. To walk the prairie is to feel a tranquility, like sailing on a calm sea. No noise intrudes. The mind is free. Brisk air purges the soul. At the end of the day, you feel like you've walked through another time, another era, and you are refreshed.

That you carried a shotgun was almost, but not quite, incidental. And the Lab worked close enough so you were not pushed to be where you needed to be to get off a good clean shot. That was good. When you hit that covey of Hungarian partridge the first time, and 20 birds erupted from the stubble, you thought you were in heaven. Huns are everything you ever dreamed for quail, and more. They're bigger, about as fast, and after you bump the covey two or three times, will separate as singles. Then it's time to stop. Sit and stroke the Lab's floppy ears and listen to the singles calling and homing in on each other.

Sharptails, too, are found here. They erupt from brushy wet-weather watercourses. First comes one, then maybe a pair, then a single and a trio and another pair. You never know when the flush of sharptails has ended until it does. By then your gun's long been empty, and if you're fortunate, the Lab will be trotting back to the guide with your first bird.

Morse is a click west of Ducks Unlimited's 15,000-acre Thunder Creek project, an effort to restore critical breeding and nesting grounds for resident and migratory waterfowl and related species. Fifty miles of intermittent creek channel meanders through the prairie here, and the project is restoring spring flows to provide staging areas for migrant waterfowl and molting areas for resident birds. This means fine gunning for mallards and Canada geese hunted over water and grain.

Doug Montgomery's inn draws high praise from former guests. The nine rooms in the lodge itself and the four in the nearby cabin all have private baths. Meals are scrumptious and often feature game. They are served on china and accompanied by reasonable vintages.

CANADA EAST

MANITOBA, NEW BRUNSWICK, NEWFOUNDLAND/LABRADOR NOVA SCOTIA, ONTARIO, PRINCE EDWARD ISLAND, QUEBEC

F ROM THE PRAIRIES of south-ern Manitoba, with its fabulous marshes that nurture most of the ducks that migrate down the Central and Mississippi flyways, to the Maritime Provinces, where grouse and wood-cock are unparalleled, Canada's eastern provinces provide some of the best bird hunt-ing in the world.

Hunker down in a blind in the rushes fringing the shallows at the end of virtually every lake in Manitoba and the ducks will come. Most fishing camp operators also guide duck hunts. Limits are generous. Geese and duck hunting can be very good along the St. Lawrence Seaway in Quebec, and on Prince Edward Island.

In the Maritimes, grouse and woodcock are the primary quarry, hunt-ed over pointers, setters or spaniels. Hunting for these species often coincides with the last week or so of the season for Atlantic salmon — life can be tough. Bring a 20-gauge as well as an eight-weight. You'll need both to hunt ptarmigan in Quebec's Ungava region, and to chase pheasants and trout in the streams of Nova Scotia.

Lodges:

Manitoba
1 CHESLEY'S RESORT
2 CROOKED CREEK LODGE
3 STANLEY'S GOOSE CAMP
4 WEBBER'S DYMOND LAKE LODGE

New Brunswick
5 MIRAMICHI INN
6 SHEPODY PHEASANT PRESERVE
7 THE OLD RIVER LODGE

Newfoundland/Labrador
8 GREY RIVER LODGE
9 TUCKAMORE LODGE & OUTFITTERS

Nova Scotia
10 LANDSDOWNE LODGE

Ontario
11 CALL OF THE NORTH

Prince Edward Island
12 WILD GOOSE LODGE

Quebec
13 DIANA LAKE LODGE/HIGH ARCTIC ADVENTURES

Resources:

DEPARTMENT OF NATURAL RESOURCES
*Box 22, 200 Saulteaux Crescent
Winnipeg, Manitoba
R3J 3W3, Canada
204/945-6784 or
800/214-6497*

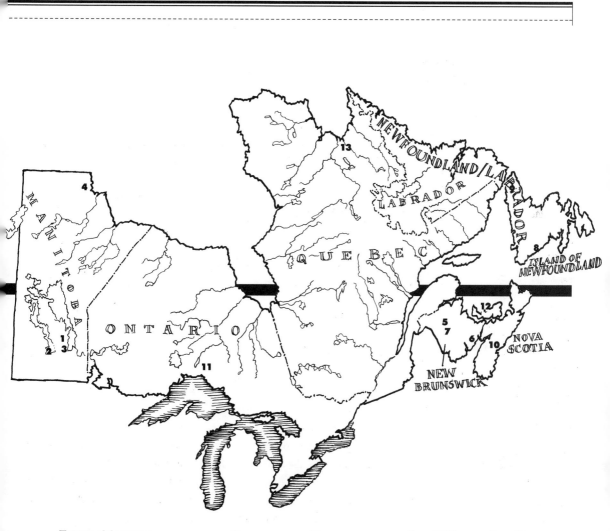

TOURISM MANITOBA
21 Forks Market Road
Winnipeg MB
R3C 4T7 Canada
204/945-3777
800/665-0040
web: www.gov.mb.ca/natres

DEPARTMENT OF NATURAL
RESOURCES & ENERGY
Fish & Wildlife
Box 6000
Fredericton, New Brunswick
E3B 5HI, Canada
506/453-2440
web: www.gov.nb.ca

INLAND FISH AND WILDLIFE DIVISION
Building 810 - Pleasantville
PO Box 8700
St. John's, Newfoundland
A1B 4J6 Canada
Ph: 709/729-2815

DEPARTMENT OF TOURISM,
CULTURE AND RECREATION
PO Box 8700
St. John's. Newfoundland
A1B 4J6 Canada
709/729-6857
www.gov.nf.ca

DEPARTMENT OF NATURAL RESOURCES
Box 698
Halifax, Nova Scotia
B3J 2T9, Canada
902/424-5935

MINISTRY OF NATURAL RESOURCES
Information Center
900 Bay St.
Toronto, Ontario
M7A 2C1, Canada
416/314-2000
800-667-1940
web: www.mnr.gov.on.ca

FISH & WILDLIFE DIV., DEPT. OF
TECHNOLOGY AND ENVIRONMENT
Box 2000
Charlottetown, PE
C1A 7N8 Canada
902/368-4683
web: www.gov.pe.ca

MINISTERE DE L'ENVIRONMENT
Dept. of Recreation, Fish and Game
Box 88, 675 Boule. Rene-Levesque Est.
Quebec, QC
G1R 4Y1 Canada
800/561-1616
web: www.mef.gouv.qc.ca

TOURISME QUEBEC
1010 Sainte-Catherine Ouest
Room 400
Montreal, QC
H3B 1G2 Canada
800/363-7777
web: www.tourisme.gouv.qc.ca

Chesley's Report

P e t e r s f i e l d ,   M a n i t o b a

Good duck and goose hunting near Manitoba's famed marshes needn't cost an arm and a leg.

VITAL STATISTICS:

GAME BIRDS:
WATERFOWL
Source of Birds: Wild
Seasons:
WATERFOWL: September through November
Land: Unlimited acres
Accommodations:
COTTAGES AND MOTEL ROOMS
NUMBER OF ROOMS: 8
MAXIMUM NUMBER OF HUNTERS: 30
Meals: Home cooked steak, veal, roasts
Conference Groups: Yes
Guides: Trained dogs and guides
Dogs and Facilities:
If you bring your dog, bring a kennel
Other Services:
Pro shop
Other Activities:
Bird-watching, boating, fishing, golf, horseback riding, swimming
Rates:
From $750 / 3 days
Gratuity:
Hunter's discretion
Preferred Payment:
Cash, MasterCard, Visa or check
Getting There:
Fly to Winnipeg and rent a car or arrange for the lodge van at $40.

CONTACT:
Kimberly Isfjord
Chesley's Report
Box 220
Petersfield MB
R0C 2L0 Canada
204/738-2250
Fax: 204/738-4486
EMAIL: chesley@sympatico.mb.com
WEB: www.chesleys.com

UNDER THE TREES by the spring-fed waters of Netley Creek sprawls an RV Park with lodge, motel rooms and cabins. The creek opens into a marsh by the same name, one of hundreds of wetlands left by the drainage of Lake Agassiz. You won't find Lake Agassiz on many maps, but at the time of the retreat of the latest stage of continental glaciation—about 10,000 years ago—Lake Agassiz inundated huge sections of Saskatchewan, Manitoba, Ontario and a bit of North Dakota and Minnesota. Larger than the Great Lakes combined, even at their glacial meltwater highs, the bed of Lake Agassiz is now pocked with a thousand little ponds, and some huge lakes as well, including Lakes Winnipegosis, Manitoba and Winnipeg.

The Netley Marsh is hard by the west end of Lake Winnipeg. It's a breeding ground for ducks and geese, and pulls in its share of migrating waterfowl as well. Each morning, well before the sun tinges the sky, you'll meet your guide. Depending on where you'll hunt—and the area offers virtually unlimited opportunities—you'll either head off in a boat from the dock, or pull the boat off toward some lake that only the guide knows the name of. Guides work overtime finding where birds are flying. They'll do their best to snug the boat into a copse of thick reeds with just enough open water to hold a few decoys and the ducks they'll pull in. Geese are gunned from pit blinds in cut-over barley field stubble.

Accommodations vary. Cottages with two bedrooms sleep up to six and boast kitchen facilities. Motel rooms can sleep four (if you're willing to share double beds) and include kitchenettes as well. Complete hookups are provided for RVs. You can either sling your own hash or walk over to the lodge for meals, as most hunters do. Who wants to cook if you don't have to?

Snows fly over Webber's Dymond Lake Lodge near Churchill,
Manitoba, on the western shore of Hudson Bay.

On a bench overlooking the Little Southwest Miramichi, in
New Brunswick, sits the Miramichi Inn, known for
combining woodcock, grouse and Atlantic salmon.

Crooked Creek Lodge

S t .   A m b r o i s e ,   M a n i t o b a

Here's a lodge where waterfowlers really feel at home.

VITAL STATISTICS:

GAME BIRDS:
DUCKS, GEESE, SHARPTAIL & RUFFED GROUSE
Source of Birds: Wild
Seasons:
GROUSE: Mid-September through November
WATERFOWL: September through November
Land: Unlimited public and private acres
Accommodations:
MODERN WOOD-AND-GLASS LODGE
NUMBER OF ROOMS: 6
MAXIMUM NUMBER OF HUNTERS: 12
Meals: Cooked as only Theresa can
Conference Groups: Yes
Guides: Included
Dogs and Facilities:
Bring your own kennel
Other Services:
Birds cleaned and packed for travel
Other Activities:
Big game, fishing
Rates:
$250 / day
Gratuity:
Hunter's discretion
Preferred Payment:
Cash or check
Getting There:
Fly to Winnipeg and rent a car.

Contact:
Aime Lavellee
Crooked Creek Lodge
Box 23
St. Ambroise, MB
R0H 1G0 Canada
800/292-3973

FIVE YEARS AGO TWO BROTHERS, AIME and John Lavellee, decided to open a hunting lodge on the fringe of the great Delta Marsh, south of Lake Manitoba. They came to this decision naturally. Since 1900, their forebears guided waterfowlers. They learned from their father and uncles and cousins. The Lavellees are well known in these parts.

Gunners have a choice of hunting ducks in the marshes that surround the lodge, or driving for an hour or so east to private acreage that the brothers lease in the vicinity of Oak Hammock Marsh, the great waterfowl propagation project run by Canadian Ducks Unlimited, the Province of Manitoba and the government of Canada. If you hunt geese, you'll head out early — about 4:30 a.m. — to be hidden in makeshift blinds by sun up. In front of you will be a spread of magnum decoys. Most get their limits by noon.

Duck hunters rise at the same time, but have a more leisurely time of breakfast. Still, before dawn, you and your guide will be loading decoys in the pram and shoving off into channels that lead to little ponds in the marsh. You'll set 15 to 20 decoys, seldom more, snug yourself deeply in the rushes nearby, and wait for the ducks to come. That they will—mallards, pintails, canvasbacks, and redheads. Most of the other duck species found in North America make an appearance in the Delta Marsh at one time or another. Normally, you'll reach your limit well before noon. After that (and a full lunch), you have a choice: hunt upland sharptail or ruffed grouse, or deer should it be the season.

Crooked Creek Lodge is a comfortable place, a cut above others in this neck of the woods. Built in the mid-1990s of wood and glass, the lodge boasts a greatroom with mounts of impressive whitetails (all local) and waterfowl. Six bedrooms each sleep two, and all share a pair of baths. Meals here are substantial, and often feature hearty soups and duck roasted in a secret way known only to Aime's aunt, Theresa, the cook. Guests clamor for seconds and thirds and forget to leave room for her pies.

Stanley's Goose Camp

Balmoral, Manitoba

Hunt the Oak Hammock Marsh area, where tens of thousands of ducks and geese stage for winter migrations.

VITAL STATISTICS:

GAME BIRDS:
DUCKS, GEESE
Source of Birds: Wild
Seasons:
September through November
Land: 2,000 private and public acres
Accommodations:
MODERN LODGE
NUMBER OF ROOMS: 4
MAXIMUM NUMBER OF HUNTERS: 8
Meals: Family-style beef and fowl
Conference Groups: Yes
Guides: Trained dogs and guides
Dogs and Facilities:
Kennel for hunters' dogs
Other Services:
Birds cleaned and packed for travel
Other Activities:
Big game, bird-watching, wildlife photography
Rates:
$1,100 / 3 days
Gratuity:
Hunter's discretion
Preferred Payment:
Cash or check
Getting There:
Fly to Winnipeg and rent a car.

Contact:
Daryl Stanley
Stanley's Goose Camp
Box 164
Balmoral MB
R0C 0H0 Canada
204/467-8216
EMAIL: dfstanl@ibm.net

A TORRENT OF DUCKS AND GEESE from vast northern Canada pours south in early autumn like water shooting out of the just opened penstocks of a dam. And not unlike the flow of a tailwater, the birds surge along for a while, only to eddy up in huge wetlands along their paths to wintering grounds near the Gulf coast. Just 20 miles north of Winnipeg is the massive Oak Hammock Marsh, a 9,000-acre remnant of 118,000 acres that once comprised St. Andrews Bog.

In the late 1890s, farmers began to drain the bog. By 1960, only 625 acres remained. Gone, too, were most of the waterfowl. But then began a series of discussions between Ducks Unlimited Canada and the governments of Manitoba and Canada, which resulted in a partnership to restore portions of the bog. Miles and miles of dykes were built to contain water. Nesting islands were constructed and predators were controlled. Under management by Ducks Unlimited Canada and provincial wildlife resource agencies, the waterfowl population has flourished — and residents of Winnipeg have a marvelous wildlife education, research and interpretation center right on their doorstep.

No visit to the region is complete without a tour of Oak Hammock, and hunters at Stanley's Goose Camp, a small intimate lodge that hunts 2,000 acres near the marsh, often make it a point to stop in. A long time operator in the region, Daryl Stanley makes it a point to provide personal service. The lodge hosts no more than eight hunters at a time, and they're housed two to a room in modern quarters. Meals feature hearty fare: steaks, roast beef, filet mignon. Weather determines your hunt, but mainly you'll gun for geese early, and fill in with ducks later in the day. Most shooting is over decoys from blinds, though there is some pass-shooting as well. The season runs from September through November, with the best hunting from mid-September through the end of October.

[C A N A D A E A S T]

Webber's Dymond Lake Lodge

C h u r c h i l l , M a n i t o b a

Get the first crack at migrating Canadas and other geese, high near the shore of Hudson Bay.

VITAL STATISTICS:

GAME BIRDS:
DUCKS, GEESE
Source of Birds: Wild
Seasons:
GEESE: Early through late May
DUCKS and GEESE: Early through late September
Land: 40 square miles, public
Accommodations:
MODERN CABINS
NUMBER OF ROOMS: 7
MAXIMUM NUMBER OF HUNTERS: 16
Meals: Excellent game cuisine
Conference Groups: Yes
Guides: Trained dogs and guides
Other Services:
Birds cleaned and packed for travel
Other Activities:
Big game, bird-watching, boating, canoeing, fishing, hiking, snowmobiling, wildlife photography
Rates:
From $1,600 / 3 days
Gratuity:
Hunter's discretion
Preferred Payment:
Cash, Visa or check
Getting There:
Fly to Churchill and catch the shuttle flight.

Contact:
Mike Reimer
Webber's Dymond Lake Lodge
Box 304
Churchill MB
R0B 0E0 Canada
888/932-2377
Fax: 204/675-2386
EMAIL: webbers@capcom.net
WEB: www.webberslodges.com

IT DOESN'T LOOK LIKE MUCH, this cobbled together blind of willow, driftwood and saltgrass. But there's not much else here near the tidal flats of Hudson Bay. The countryside seems to stretch clear to the far horizon. To the north and west are hundreds of square miles of tundra, with marshes and kettle ponds too numerous to count, let alone name. But each one breeds its levy of ducks and geese, and with the shortening of daylight and the first rumples in the jet stream, waterfowl begin to stir. Like the vast air armadas of World War II's D-Day, wave after wave of waterfowl head south. Their first stop is often a little patch of water called Dymond Lake, 15 miles west of Churchill on Hudson Bay.

You know the ducks: greenwinged teal, shovelers, pintails, scaup, blacks and mallards. And there are geese too, squadrons of them: giant and lesser Canadas, snows and blues, Ross' and even a few brant. With nearly 40 square miles at his disposal, owner Doug Webber has ample room to hunt. Yet he finds that, in the main, most of the shooting is within a half mile of the log lodge. Geese are normally the first order of business here, and most gunning is over decoys. Daily bag limits are so generous that there's no way you can tote home all the geese you harvest. "We give them to an elder at the local church," Doug explains. "Many elderly families live in town, and they have no one to hunt for them. They need the meat." Limits on ducks are also ample. You'll pass-shoot them from atop eskers, or jump them from pothole ponds.

Modern cabins heated with wood or propane stoves and lit with electricity — some with private baths — accommodate hunters. Two rooms are handicapped accessible. Nearby is the main lodge where dinners are served. The marinated goose breast, stuffed with sliced japalenos and cooked on the grill, is heavenly enough without a dessert of Bavarian apple tort.

Miramichi Inn

Red Bank, New Brunswick

Coverts come alive with grouse and woodcock, and André's Irish setters find them with aplomb.

VITAL STATISTICS:

GAME BIRDS:
CHUKAR, DUCKS, GEESE, GROUSE, QUAIL
Source of Birds: Wild and pen-reared
Seasons:
WOODCOCK: Mid-September through mid-November
DUCKS & GROUSE: October through December
GEESE: early October through December
CHUKAR & QUAIL: May through November
Land: Unlimited public and 100 private acres
Accommodations:
PRIVATE LODGE
NUMBER OF ROOMS: 9
MAXIMUM NUMBER OF HUNTERS: 12
Meals: Scrumptious regional fare
Conference groups: Yes
Guides:
Trained dogs and guides
Dogs and Facilities:
Kennel for hunters' dogs, dog training
Shotgun Sports:
Five-stand, shooting schools, sporting clays, tower or release shoots
Other Services:
Birds cleaned and packed for travel
Other Activities:
Big game, fishing
Rates: $370 / day
Gratuity: Hunter's discretion
Preferred Payment:
Cash, MasterCard, Visa or check
Getting There:
Fly to Miramichi and rent a car.

Contact:
André Godin
Miramichi Inn
1100 Halcomb Road
PO Box 331
Red Bank NB
E9E 2P3 Canada
506/836-7452
Fax: 506/836-7805

HOW DO YOU TRAIN an Irish setter to be a bird dog? Just ask André Godin, impresario of the Miramichi Inn. "I read him *Grouse Feathers*, eh. Spiller, he knew the birds, that man. These dogs are smart, so maybe they learn," André grins. "Now what can it hurt?" Believe him or not. But André's Irish know how to hunt. They're not flashy, hard-chargin' dogs. Leave that to the field-trial boys. Determination, steadiness and reliability are what André looks for in dogs, and if they don't measure up, off to pure petdom they go.

André's lodge sits among birch and firs on a bank high over the little Southwest Miramichi. In mid-October, the best of angling and upland bird hunting coincide for a few glorious days. Atlantic salmon are making their final runs of the season. If there's a bit of rain, those holding in the long finger of the bay at Chatham will make their run upstream. And, should there be dirty weather to the north, flights of woodcock will have come in during the night to join native birds lurking in the poplar scrub along the river. In ones and twos, they'll sift down through maples, birches and beech. On the ground, they'll scurry past grouse fat on berries. These are the birds that await André's guests.

Come during the week of the fifteenth. In the days before salmon season closes, throw General Practitioners across the expresso-colored waters. Cast, retrieve, take a step or two, and cast again. The very rhythm dispels any hint of boredom, and when a salmon slashes your fly, you'll know without being told why this is the sport of kings. After a few days, bird season comes in. Fish in the morning after salmon have rested the night. And after a lunch of cream of fiddlehead soup, take that sweet little 20 of yours and march behind one of André's setters. They prance through the wood like diminutive red ponies, noses held high. You'll want to laugh, so improbable is the sight. But whoa, the nose is down, right foot up, tail stiff with a weird crook to the left. Now all you have to do is figure out which route through the impenetrable cover favored by this grouse or woodcock. Bon chance!

And when you're done for the day, there's a hot shower in your room, fresh and dry clothes, a drink before the fire, and regional cuisine that verges on exquisite. Sporting clays and hunts for released quail and chukar help tune shooters before the hunt.

[C A N A D A   E A S T]

Shepody Pheasant Preserve

A l b e r t   C o u n t y ,   N e w   B r u n s w i c k

What Pebble Beach is to golf, Shepody is to upland birds.

VITAL STATISTICS:

GAME BIRDS:
DUCKS, GEESE, GROUSE, PHEASANT, WOODCOCK

Source of Birds:
Wild and pen-reared

Seasons:
PHEASANT: September through December
WATERFOWL: October through November
GROUSE: October through mid-November
WOODCOCK: Mid-September through mid-November

Land: 400 private and unlimited public acres

Accommodations:
PRIVATE LODGE
NUMBER OF ROOMS: 4
MAXIMUM NUMBER OF HUNTERS: 10

Meals: Family-style farm cooking

Conference groups: Yes

Guides: Trained dogs and guides

Dogs and Facilities:
Kennel for hunters' dogs, dog training

Shotgun Sports:
Five-stand, sporting clays, tower or release shoots

Other Services:
Birds cleaned and packed for travel

Other Activities:
Biking, bird-watching, boating, hiking, horseback riding

Rates:
From $200 / day / double occupancy

Gratuity:
Hunter's discretion

Preferred Payment:
Cash, Visa or check

Getting There:
Fly to Moncton and rent a car.

Contact:
Lynn and Claude Dixon
Shepody Pheasant Preserve
R R #2
Albert County NB
E0A 1A0 Canada
506/882-2667
Fax: 506/882-2625
EMAIL: gamebird@nbnet.nb.ca
WEB: www.shepodypreserve.com

THE TERRAIN HERE IS CANDY for the eye. To the east, below the cliffs, the Bay of Fundy floods with 30-foot tides—among the highest in the world—twice a day. Shepody Mountain rises behind the preserve. Between the bluffs and the mountains is the rolling farm of 400 acres that Claude and Lynn Dixon have crafted into a magnificent hunting preserve.

The Dixon's have divided their farm into five zones. Some are steep and verge on being wooded with lots of heavy undergrowth. Others undulate gently — land that's suitable for meadow or row crops, though it's expressly managed for hunting. Areas of marsh and a duck pond provide opportunities for waterfowlers. Additionally, hundreds of acres of public ground and private lands to which Claude has access offer gunning for ruffed grouse and woodcock. English pointers, Brittanies, springers and Labs constitute the canine corps, all managed by guides who know the land and the birds as well as their dogs. Many clients drive up from the states of New England, bringing young dogs that need a week in the field before the hunting season begins in earnest at home. Clay games—sporting, five-stand and trap—are on the docket for those whose reflexes need sharpening.

The lodge is a small, intimate affair with four bedrooms that serve a maximum of ten hunters. Six or eight is a more normal number, and it seems that hunters of similar yet eclectic interests tend to show up. Conversations over pheasant potpie and vegetables grown on the farm and canned for winter, range widely.

Tourist sites and locales of significant natural heritage are located nearby. Most who come to Shepody manage a visit to Fundy National Park, down the highway to the south. Others are content to spend their time at the preserve, walking out to the cliffs, should their visit be appropriately timed, to watch the full harvest moon draw the tide up the bay.

A great Irish setter beats it across a beaver pond, telling
the hunters they'd better hurry up if they want to find this
New Brunswick grouse or woodcock.

The Old River Lodge

B l i s s f i e l d ,   N e w   B r u n s w i c k

Think all the north woods are alike? Trust your guide. He knows better.

VITAL STATISTICS:

GAME BIRDS:
GROUSE and WOODCOCK
Source of Birds: Wild
Seasons:
WOODCOCK: mid-September through mid-November
GROUSE: October through November
Land: Unlimited private and public
Accommodations:
PRIVATE LODGE
NUMBER OF ROOMS: 10
MAXIMUM NUMBER OF HUNTERS: 9
Meals: Fine regional cuisine
Conference Groups: Yes
Guides: Trained dogs and guides
Dogs and Facilities:
Kennel for hunters' dogs
Other Services:
Birds cleaned and packed for travel
Other Activities:
Bird-watching, canoeing, fishing, golf, hiking, wildlife photography
Rates:
$400 / gun / day
Gratuity:
$10 - $ 30 / day
Preferred Payment:
Cash or check
Getting there:
Fly to Frederickton, NB, and rent a car.

Contact:
Alex Mills
The Old River Lodge
42 Greene Road
Blissfield NB
E9C 1L4 Canada
506/365-7568
FAX: 506/365-7134
EMAIL: raamlaw@nb.sympatico.ca

ALONG THE RIVER, maples and birch flash fiery against somber spruce and pines. Overhead, mares' tails dance across a sky so blue it makes your heart weep with joy. Your Brittany quivers with energy just barely contained. And you, dubbed "old stoneface" by your wife because of your spontaneity in expressing your emotions, are grinning like the kid who found the pony tethered to the fencepost on Christmas. Your guide's eyes twinkle; he's seen days like this before, but every time they happen, they're good.

In the old van, you've jounced down some sandy logging road that has no name and never will. Along the way, you've seen grouse. You didn't want to stop. It just made you more anxious to get to the covert. All these woods look alike. Why there, not here? you ask, and are rewarded with, "It's better where we go." Trust him? Why not? What do you know? So eventually he wheels the van down into a ditch and up into a trace that leads to a clearing where logs were piled a decade ago.

The land is fringed with second-growth poplar, ferns as high as your thigh, thickets of brush and berry, and clumps of pine and spruce not more than 30 feet high. This cover is perfect for you and your Brit. You know it inside. And that makes you happy. You know that in the fringe of this cutover land there will be grouse and woodcock. You see no fresh tire tracks, no litter of cans or a tell-tail empty hull. Though on public land, this covert has not been hunted yet this season. You're getting it fresh. And that, man, has turned you on. Your guide sees you and knows too. And later, when the day is done and you've counted 20 jumps—four of which brought grouse to bag and a couple of woodcock to boot—you can't help but grin. It's just a bird, and a little orange and white dog, and a patch of woods, and a cheerful guide. How could they strike you so dumb with joy? They just do.

On a hillside overlooking the Southwest Miramichi rises The Old River Lodge. Around the lodge are cabins of timber. Prime rib, lamb, and roast turkey are typical entrées, often preceded with the lodge's signature seafood chowder. Rooms in the lodge share baths, but those in the cabins are private.

Grey River Lodge

Shoal Harbour, Newfoundland

What's a red grouse by any other name? Read on to find out.

VITAL STATISTICS:

GAME BIRDS:
PTARMIGAN
Source of Birds: Wild
Seasons:
Mid-September through November
Land: Unlimited public acres
Accommodations:
WOOD FRAME LODGE
NUMBER OF ROOMS: 2
MAXIMUM NUMBER OF HUNTERS: 4
Meals: Hearty Canadian fare
Conference Groups: No
Guides: Trained dogs and guides
Dogs and Facilities:
If you bring a dog, bring a portable kennel
Other Services:
Birds cleaned and packed for travel
Other Activities:
Big game, boating, fishing, hiking, wildlife photography
Rates:
From $1,400 / week
Gratuity:
$100
Preferred Payment:
Cash or check
Getting There:
Fly to Deer Lake and catch the helicopter shuttle, included.

Contact:
Tony Tuck
Rocky Ridge Lodge
PO Box 62
Shoal Harbour NF
A0C 2L0 Canada
709/466-2440
Fax: 709/466-2536
EMAIL: greyltd@terra.nlnet.nf.ca

WILLOW PTARMIGAN are not highly regarded among neophyte bird hunters—especially those who have never shot them. "You can walk right up on them," uplanders say. "No self-respecting grouse will let you do that." "Dumb birds," retorts another wingshooter for whom the wild bobwhite is without peer. Yet the willow ptarmigan is found in northern latitudes circling the globe. And in areas like the UK, where human population is high (and bird populations correspondingly low), these birds are held in much greater esteem. Gunning season in the British Isles opens on the Glorious Twelfth of August, and the most coveted quarry is the famous red grouse. What's a red grouse? Nothing but a willow ptarmigan that's yet to change colors.

When the season opens in Newfoundland in the middle of September, ptarmigan have yet to change color. Their reddish brown hews blend with foliage of blueberry and marshberry. They may let you get close, but it takes a sharp eye to see them. A social bird, as fall fades toward winter, ptarmigan begin to gather in increasingly large groups. As their flocks get larger they become more skittish, and thus more challenging to hunt. Cold weather brings on the final color shift — to pure white. Ever try to shoot a white bird against a snowy mountain or a grey white sky? Fun, huh?

Tom Tuck runs ptarmigan hunts on the tundra near his two-bedroom lodge on the Grey River in south-central Newfoundland. Some anglers know the Grey for its good runs of Atlantic salmon, while hunters may know the area for caribou and moose. And a growing number of bird hunters know it from their days hiking over the low brush of muted oranges, greens and browns behind setters.

Tuck runs Gordons, Irish and English, aristocratic dogs to be sure. They range widely over the tundra, and it's your job to maintain contact with the dog. You'll lose sight of him for sure, but if you keep heading in the direction where you last saw him, you'll eventually find him, often as not holding a point. Forget electronic beeping collars. They'd work, but the technology intrudes on your solitude. Just be certain that your rubber boots fit well, and that you're in shape for a good hike. When you return to the lodge, you'll find a substantial meal of chicken, fish or steak well underway, but not before you've soothed your aching bones and exalted soul with a dram of the distilled spirit.

251

Northern Newfoundland, around Grey River Lodge near
Shoal Harbour, holds fine populations of ptarmigan.

Tuckamore Lodge & Outfitters

Main Brook, Newfoundland

For ducks and ptarmigan, fine hospitality and great food, sportsmen flock to the tip of this island.

VITAL STATISTICS:

GAME BIRDS:
DUCKS, PTARMIGAN
Source of Birds: Wild
Seasons:
Mid-September through
early December
Land: Unlimited public acres
Accommodations:
SWISS-STYLE LODGES
NUMBER OF ROOMS: 9
MAXIMUM NUMBER OF HUNTERS: 18
Meals: Eclectic regional cuisine
Conference Groups: Yes
Guides: Trained dogs and guides
Other Services:
Birds cleaned and packed for travel
Other Activities:
Big game, bird-watching, canoeing,
fishing, hiking, skiing, wildlife
photography
Rates:
From $1,000 / person / double
occupancy
Gratuity:
Hunter's discretion
Preferred Payment:
Cash or check
Getting There:
Fly to St. Anthony and you'll be met.

Contact:
Barb Gegne
Tuckamore Lodge &
Outfitters
PO Box 100
Main Brook NFLD
A0K 3N0 Canada
888-865-6361 or
709-865-6361
Fax: 709/865-2112

TUCKAMORE IS NOT YOUR USUAL hunting lodge. It's more of a wilderness retreat that also offers bird hunting—ptarmigan, spruce grouse, sea ducks—as well as bear, caribou and moose. In the summer, guests fish for Atlantic salmon and brook trout. They watch whales and puffins. And they stay in either of Barb Genge's delightful Scandinavian-style inns. Guest rooms have private baths. There's a sauna to soothe aches, and menus feature the likes of crab au gratin appetizer, grilled T-bones or spare ribs, and strawberries with ice cream for dessert.

All you need to bring is your toothbrush, shotguns and shells, and distilled spirits of your choice. Despite what critics say, ptarmigan hunting is worthwhile indeed. Early in the season, they're as brown as speckled hens and not easy at all to see against the heather-colored tundra. Barb and her guides hunt two areas. The first and perhaps best is the White Hills above Locks Cove. It's the same ground where caribou roam, and you may see them in the distance. You'll also encounter spruce grouse in these parts. Delectable as table fare, spruce grouse are not shy of humans. They'll present opportunities for you, but only where poplar and brush are thick along streams and ponds.

The other bird hunting ground lies 14 miles offshore in the Grey Islands. This is really special and worth the trip. Shorebirds and waterfowl are migrating; you'll see species that summer in the Arctic not so far to the north. The islands are low, rocky and covered with tundra. The broad Atlantic forms the backdrop. You'll see hundreds of birds, but a couple of boxes of shells ought to bring you your limit. Sea ducks are also hunted in this corner of Newfoundland.

Don't expect flashy setters or spaniels here, or staunch Labs, either. You're more likely to be accompanied afield by a beagle or two. Odd, you say? Well, this is practical Newfoundland, and the old saw: "Make do, do without; use it up, wear it out" has more than a bit of credence here. Beagles have good noses, will help find downed ptarmigan, and will run you a varying hare if you want.

Landsdowne Lodge

Upper   Stewiacke,   Nova   Scotia

Would you believe great ringneck hunting in Canada's Maritimes?

VITAL STATISTICS:

GAME BIRDS:
DUCKS, GEESE, GROUSE, PHEASANT, SNIPE
Source of Birds: Wild
Seasons:
UPLAND GAME (except pheasant) and WATERFOWL: October through December
PHEASANT: October through November
Land: Unlimited private and public acres
Accommodations:
TWO PRIVATE LODGES
NUMBER OF ROOMS: 5
MAXIMUM NUMBER OF HUNTERS: 10
Meals: Regional cuisine
Conference Groups: Yes
Guides: Trained dogs and guides
Dogs and Facilities:
Dog training
Other Services:
Birds cleaned and packed for travel, pro shop
Other Activities:
Big game, canoeing, fishing, golf, hiking
Rates:
From $363 / day
Gratuity:
Hunter's discretion
Preferred Payment:
Cash, Visa or check
Getting There:
Fly to Halifax and rent a car.

Contact:
Brent Ferris
Landsdowne Lodge
RR 2
Upper Stewiacke NS
B0N 2P0 Canada
902/671-2749
Fax: 902/671-2021
WEB: www.outdoors.com/lands downelodge

I N THE EARLY 1950s, the province of Nova Scotia stopped stocking pheasants. No sense in it, game managers reasoned. They'd either make do on their own, or they wouldn't. But on this little chunk of Canada that would be an island were it not for the isthmus at the New Brunswick border, pheasants thrived. Rumor has it that here you'll find the biggest population of ringnecks east of the Mississippi River.

A couple of factors give life to the notion. First, southern Nova Scotia is bounded on three sides by oceans or bay. Temperatures are moderated by ocean currents; what would be snow in Maine and New Brunswick falls as rain on Nova Scotia. Second, the boom in big farming that killed wild pheasant hunting in Pennsylvania and the southern tier of New York never made it to the Maritimes. Farms are small here, mostly dairy with some row crops grown for local feed. Fencerows abound. In short, there's cover for pheasants like the U.S. mid-Atlantic states haven't seen in decades. It's not unusual to flush 20 birds in a day, and with that number, how hard can it be to get a couple of cocks?

Along with pheasants there are grouse and woodcock hunted along forest roads, abandoned farms and the overgrown orchards that once made New Hampshire and Vermont so famous. You'll also flush an occasional Wilson's snipe. Add a measure of ducks — woodies early in the season, then mallards, gadwalls and pintails — along with goose hunting from pit blinds in grain fields, and you've got yourself quite a hunt. Should you time your trip for mid-October, there's a better than good chance of tagging an Atlantic salmon or two in the Stewiacke, which flows past the lodge. Imagine: grouse, pheasant, woodcock, snipe and salmon all in one trip!

Accommodations are much better than average. Guests stay in large cabins constructed of cedar and knotty pine. Meals run the gamut from seafood to roast beef. And though there's room for more, no more than half a dozen hunters are in residence at any given time.

You'll ride a DeHavilland Beaver to reach Diana Lake Lodge,
west of Kuujjuac in Quebec's Ungava region. Out the back door, you'll
kick up coveys of ptarmigan as if they were quail.

You'd never believe that Landsdowne Lodge, hidden in
the woods near Upper Stewiacke, Nova Scotia, offers the hottest
wild pheasant hunting in the East.

[C A N A D A   E A S T]

Call of the North

G e r a l d t o n ,   O n t a r i o

Now which of these grouse fooled you:
ruffed, spruce, or sharptail?

VITAL STATISTICS:

GAME BIRDS:
GROUSE
Source of Birds: Wild
Seasons:
Mid-September through
mid- December
Land: Unlimited public acres
Accommodations:
PRIVATE CABINS
NUMBER OF ROOMS: 23
MAXIMUM NUMBER OF HUNTERS: 50
Meals: Self-catered
Conference Groups: No
Guides: Optional at $150 / day
Dogs and Facilities:
Bring your own kennel
Other Services:
Birds cleaned and packed for travel
Other Activities:
Big game, biking, bird-watching,
boating, canoeing, fishing, golf,
hiking, wildlife photography
Rates:
From $395 / 5 days / person,
double occupancy
Gratuity:
Hunter's discretion
Preferred Payment:
Cash or check
Getting There:
Drive to Geraldton or fly to Thunder
Bay and rent a car.

Contact:
Joe & Paula Bosanac
Call of the North
Box 607 Hwy 11
Geraldton ON
POT 1M0 Canada
800/801-4080
Fax: 807/854-0824
EMAIL: bosanac@cancom.net

L IKE A BIG ARC FROM NORTH BAY, Canada's Rt. 11 climbs up the border between Ontario and Quebec, passing through Cochrane, Kapusksing, and Hearst until you eventually come to Geraldton, and then to Thunder Bay. North of the highway is wilderness. Dirt roads, some growing up with grasses, cut back and forth, winding deeper into the woods. Logging operations have left the forest in a transition. In places you'll see the evidence of last season's cuts. In others, the woods are in stages of succession, and that means virtually endless habitat for ruffed, sharptailed and spruce grouse.

The difference among the species isn't academic. Ruffed grouse, the most prevalent grouse of the family *phasianidae*, which also includes ptarmigan, chukar, prairie chickens, pheasants and quail, is the mainstay of these northern woods. Smaller, and known variously as the "fool hen" or Franklin's grouse, spruce grouse are disparaged for their unwillingness to fly (except at the last minute, of course; then they dart behind the maple flaming golden in the October morn). Spruce grouse are only slightly smaller than their cousins. Sharpies, on the other hand, seem to be the most communal of the three. Where you find one, there's generally more. And when you bump into a covey, unlike quail, they seldom flush all at once. After the first three take off, the others wait until they're sure that hunters have unloaded their guns. Then it's their turn to flush.

Do you need a dog to hunt grouse in this cutover country? In a word, yes. While it's possible to walk up your limit — especially early in the season — finding downed or disabled birds is very difficult without a dog. And later on, after the birds may have seen a shotgunner and become a bit skittish, a good pointer, setter or spaniel will help you find birds. However, none of these birds holds with the same patience as a woodcock, so either your legs have to be long enough to keep up with the dog, or the dog must work close to you. Which do you prefer?

Joe Bosanac, your host here, is himself a grouse hunter. In his camp he provides housekeeping cabins. Guests bring their own food, bedding, and electric appliances (like an electric coffee maker or toaster oven). It's a 250- to 300-mile trek to the lodge from major U.S. border crossings, but driving is probably best, especially if you're traveling with a dog, portable kennel, food and bedding.

Wild Goose Lodge

Some of the best of North America's waterfowling is found on PEI.

VITAL STATISTICS:

GAME BIRDS:
DUCKS, GEESE
Source of Birds: Wild
Seasons:
WATERFOWL: Early October through early December
Land: 1,000 private and public acres
Accommodations:
PRIVATE TWO-STORY LODGE
NUMBER OF ROOMS: 6
MAXIMUM NUMBER OF HUNTERS: 20
Meals: Family-style regional cuisine
Conference Groups: Yes
Guides: Trained dogs and guides
Shotgun Sports:
Five-stand, skeet, trap
Other Services:
Birds cleaned and packed for travel
Other Activities:
Golf
Rates:
$800 (Canadian) / 3 days
Gratuity:
Hunter's discretion
Preferred Payment:
Cash, credit cards or check
Getting There:
Fly to Charlottetown or drive from Boston.

Contact:
Jim Duggan
Wild Goose Lodge
RR 2
Kensington PEI
COB 1M0 Canada
902/886-2177
Fax: 902/886-8367
EMAIL: wildgeese@pei.sympatico.ca
WEB: www.wildgooselodge.com

AS THE FALL GETS DEEPER, the emerald fields of this charming island province turn tawny, basing golden as the first light off the Atlantic sweeps inland under low-hanging clouds. Freshwater wetlands ripple with wild rice harvested by beaters with sticks in their canoes. Ducks, of course, feed on the rice, but Canada geese — the main event at this lodge — ride the morning sun into barley and potato fields.

For more than half a century, gunners from North America and Europe have come to PEI to hunt geese, but this lodge is one of the very few that cater expressly to hunters. Owner Jim Duggan leases more than a dozen fields, all within a half-hour's drive from the lodge. Hunting is from blinds over decoys. Labs are on hand to do the retrieving work. Limits are generous—five per day with ten in possession. Goose hunting comes first here, always. But when the birds are in the bag, you'll have a chance to head out to Malpeque Bay for pass-shooting at teal, mallards, blacks, and hybrids of the latter two.

Located in Kensington, where the island is narrowest, Wild Goose Lodge offers two accommodation plans. The deluxe program provides three days of breakfasts and dinners, guides and accommodations for $800 per gunner. Those who like to sling their own hash can save a few bucks. Made of cedar, the lodge contains six self-contained units, each with kitchenette, private bath, and room for up to four to six hunters.

If you go to PEI, plan to spend a day or two exploring. The ends of the island are rugged and remote. You'll find historic fishing villages, wooden lighthouses and streams that carry some salmon in summer. The central core of the island is a tourist Mecca come summer. At Cavendish is the house of *Ann of Green Gables* fame. Throughout the island, you'll find charming churches built with buttresses designed for stone but articulated in white frame. Seafood is abundant, as is wild rice, a few pounds of which ought to find its way home with you and your geese.

[C A N A D A   E A S T]

Diana Lake Lodge

K u u j j u a q ,   Q u e b e c

Up near Ungava Bay, this fine lodge is known for superior fishing and excellent ptarmigan gunning.

VITAL STATISTICS:

GAME BIRDS:
PTARMIGAN
Source of Birds: Wild
Seasons:
Late August to late September
Land: Unlimited public acres
Accommodations:
PRIVATE LODGE
NUMBER OF ROOMS: 4
MAXIMUM NUMBER OF HUNTERS: 10
Meals: Game prepared by an excellent French chef
Conference Groups: Yes
Guides: Trained dogs and guides
Dogs and Facilities:
Kennel for hunters' dogs
Other Services:
Birds cleaned and packed for travel
Other Activities:
Big game, bird-watching, boating, canoeing, fishing, hiking, skiing, wildlife photography
Rates:
From $3,495 U.S. / week
Gratuity:
$100 - $200
Preferred Payment:
Cash, MasterCard, Visa or check
Getting There:
Fly to Montreal and catch the plane to Kuujjuaq.

Contact:
Joe Stefanski
Diana Lake Lodge/High Arctic Adventures
PO Box 1053
Kuujjuaq, QC
J0M 1C0 Canada
800/662-6404
Fax: 603/532-6404
Off Season:
33 Gibbs Rd
Jaffrey NH 03452
WEB: higharcticadv.com

IN SOME REMOTE CORNERS OF THE WORLD exist overlapping seasons that allow sportsmen and women to do it all: trophy big game hunting, reel-screaming fishing, and upland bird hunting. Such locales are few and far between, and often only one of the sports is really good and the others end up being so-so.

That's not the case at Diana Lake Lodge, 25 miles northwest of the outpost community of Kuujjuaq, not far from the southern tip of Ungava Bay. Well known for its caribou, the region boasts outstanding angling for Arctic char, lake trout and brook trout with fly or spinning tackle. What most folks don't think about is bird hunting. Maybe they're too busy with caribou or fish, but willow ptarmigan are fun and not so easy as they look.

The season is long, stretching from late August through April, but the best hunting is found in the first month. That's when the tundra delivers its full bounty of crowberries, blueberries, lowbush cranberries, willow buds just set for the next season, and seeds of every description. Ptarmigan feed with abandon, preferring warm, sunny slopes, as if to soak up as much heat as possible before the coming brutal winter.

At this time of the year, dogs are not really needed to hunt these birds, but they help. A good pointer will find the first single, and you can bet that in the immediate vicinity is a covey of a dozen others. Ptarmigan don't seem to group as tightly as quail in a covey, though. So when you flush the bird that the dog pointed, the others—hidden in the low ground cover within a 15- to 20-yard area — may erupt as well. That, friends, makes for some interesting gunning. Does a dog help? Well, yeah. And Joe Stefanski, a principal in the operation of Diana Lake, keeps his Brittany around for just that purpose. You can bring yours as well. Air freight is much more reasonable than you'd believe. Do you really need a dog? Well, not really.

Diana Lake Lodge is comfortable with hot showers and flush toilets. The lodge boasts something you don't find in most suburban ranches, and that's a French chef. Price for a week inclusive is $3,495 U.S. If you want a caribou, add another $500 and the pick of the bulls is yours.

MEXICO

YOU KNOW THE OLD SAYING, "Practice, practice, practice . . ." Well, Mexico is just the place to get in all the practice you need. You, your guide and bird boy will get to the fields before 9 a.m. and, from then until noon, you'll shoot at dove after dove after dove. Some you'll hit and many you'll miss, but you'll be presented with the same shots over and over until you get it right.

In Mexico, gunning for waterfowl is as good, if not better than it is in Arkansas or Manitoba. Many outfitters offer combination trips for dove and ducks, and those on the eastern side of the country also provide hunts for bobwhite and blue or scaled quail.

Most hunters stay in established tourist resorts and soak up the total experience — adobe quarters with tile roof, authentic Mexican cuisine, bottled water and libations. Transporting a firearm into Mexico can be a problem, and it can be expensive. Best bet: Ask your outfitter if he has one you may use.

Wide open and arid, Mexico is known for its whitewing and mourning dove hunts, as well as for its waterfowling.

L o d g e s :
1 ALCAMPO HUNTING ADVENTURES
2 HIGH BRASS - MEXICO
3 LAS PALOMAS DE LOMA COLORADA
4 PANCHO VILLA/INTERNATIONAL ADVENTURE
5 THE AVILES BROTHERS

Alcampo Hunting Adventures

Hermosillo, Mexico

So, before you shoot so much that your barrels melt, maybe you can figure out why you miss those crossing shots.

VITAL STATISTICS:

GAME BIRDS:
DOVE
Source of Birds: Wild
Seasons:
November through March
Land: 200,000 private acres
Accommodations:
PRIVATE LODGE
NUMBER OF ROOMS: 6
MAXIMUM NUMBER OF HUNTERS: 18
Meals: Mexican cuisine
Conference Groups: Yes
Guides: Bird boys provided
at your expense
Other Services:
Birds cleaned and packed for travel
Other Activities:
Big game
Rates:
$1,495 / gun / 3 days
Gratuity:
$120 guide; $48 birdboy
Preferred Payment:
Cash or check
Getting There:
Fly to Hermosillo and Alcampo staff
will meet you.

Contact:
Javier Artee
Alcampo Hunting Adventures
Blvd. Hidalgo #39-Bis
Hermosillo Sonora
83260 Mexico
52-62-125510
Fax: 52-62-174119
Off Season:
PO Box 6909
Nogales AZ 85628
52-62-125510
EMAIL: hunting@alcampo.com.mx
WEB: www.alcampo.com.mx

THE RIO SONORA drains the famous green belt of Mexico, land of some of the finest whitewing and mourning dove shooting in all of Mexico. With more than 200,000 acres under lease, there's little doubt that you'll find enough gunning to keep your barrels hotter than they've ever been in the good old U.S. of A. Alcampo's program is headquartered in Hermosillo and Kino Bay, at the mouth of the river.

The typical drill is to head out to shooting fields early. You'll leave the lodge at six in the morning and drive an hour or so to the field of the day. Once there, you and your bird boy will agree on a location. Shells, refreshments and midday meals are all provided. Your job is to figure out why you're missing the simple shots while nailing those difficult doubles. After lunch, and a siesta if you're like me and must, there's more gunning. Afterwards, the cold beer tastes so good and you'll unwind on the drive back to the lodge. Guests who stay at Bahia Kino typically have three full days of shooting; those who use Hermosillo as their headquarters generally spend two and a half days in the field.

If you're traveling to Mexico, you'll want to have Alcampo handle permits for your shotgun, unless you choose to use one of theirs (not a bad idea). You're allowed to bring two shotguns and 100 rounds of ammo per gun into the country, but permits may be expensive. Discuss, too, the cost of bird boys and shells. If you want to bring home your doves, pack some of your gear in a cooler and include a duffel. Then you can fill the cooler with doves and the duffel with your gear. And don't forget a good pair of boots, lightweight khaki or camo clothing, and a down or fleece vest. A Gore-Tex rain jacket or similar shell can be a real advantage too.

Whether you opt to hunt out of Hermosillo or Bahia Kino, accommodations will be modern, with all conveniences. Hunters usually share rooms. And this is the place to fill up on excellent fajitas, seafood and wonderful homemade flan. If you're a fan of fancy booze like LaFroig, then bring it along. Otherwise, you can make do nicely with local potions.

[**M E X I C O**]

High Brass - Mexico

P i e d r a s   N e g r a s ,   M e x i c o

A U.S. host and Mexican guides partner for the quail hunt of a lifetime.

VITAL STATISTICS:

GAME BIRDS:
QUAIL
Source of Birds: Wild
Seasons:
January and February
Land: 100,000 private acres
Accommodations:
MODERN MOTEL
NUMBER OF ROOMS: 10
MAXIMUM NUMBER OF HUNTERS: 10
Meals: Restaurants
Conference Groups: Yes
Guides: Trained dogs and guides
Dogs and Facilities:
Kennel for hunters' dogs
Other Services:
Birds cleaned and packed for travel
Rates:
From $1,520 / 3 days
Gratuity:
Hunter's discretion
Preferred Payment:
Cash, MasterCard, Visa or check
Getting There:
Fly to San Antonio and rent a car for the trip to Eagle Pass.

Contact:
Tom Koehn
High Brass - Mexico
RR1, Box 4X
Chamberlain SD 57325
605/734-6047
Fax: 605/734-5033
EMAIL: tkbrass@sd.cybernex.net
WEB: www.highbrass.com

GUYS and gals who journey to Mexico to hunt bobwhite and blue quail often think they've died and gone to heaven. When was the last time you jumped 30 to 40 coveys a day of 12 to 15 birds per covey? Maybe on a preserve, but not in the wild. That's, however, just what you can expect from the High Brass hunt on the plains south of Piedras Negras, right across the river from Eagle Pass, Texas.

For the past several years, Tom Koehn has been hunting this area. He's leased 100,000 acres, most of it reasonably level grass, brush, mesquite, and yes, cactus and cat's-claw. His system is straight forward. In the weeks before the hunting begins, Tom's crew grains the roads on the ranches he plans to hunt. That draws birds from miles around. On the morning of the hunt, he arrives with a short caravan of vehicles. Dogs and gunners are loaded on Jeeps and off they go down the roads, pointers sweeping to either side. Dogs get birdy. Hunters dismount. Guide tells hunters to work in on the dogs. Birds flush all over the place. Wow! Crazy shooting! Then, back in the Jeep 'til the next point. Terrain is generally pretty easy walking. Good boots and brush pants are a must. At noon, the action stops. Out comes the grill and a moment later quail or chicken is sizzling over mesquite. Cold beverages are welcome. Though it's January, it's dry.

Later that night, you'll shower in your room at a new motel that offers a wing for the exclusive use of Tom and his hunters. Dinners will be held either in the motel restaurant or at places in town. Tom works with an outfitter who handles border crossings and gun permits, which cost $200 for two guns. If you'd rather leave your guns at home, you can rent 20-gauge Beretta 390s during your hunt for $75. Ammo needs to be ordered in advance, a detail Tom will handle through his local outfitter. Because of the logistics involved, it's best to book early in the year.

Hunting in Mexico need not be overly burdensome if it's arranged through a bona fide outfitter whose references you've checked thoroughly. Otherwise, let the gunner beware.

Las Palomas de Loma Colorada

San Fernando, Mexico

Fall opens with doves then moves on to ducks and quail, and never will your gun barrel grow cold.

VITAL STATISTICS:

GAME BIRDS:
DUCKS, GEESE, QUAIL, DOVE
Source of Birds: Wild
Seasons:
DUCK, QUAIL, GOOSE: November through February
MOURNING DOVE: August through December
WHITE WING DOVE: August through October
Land: 500,000 private acres
Accommodations:
HISPANIC STYLE PRIVATE LODGE
NUMBER OF ROOMS: 13
MAXIMUM NUMBER OF HUNTERS: 30
Meals: Fine regional cuisine
Conference groups: Yes
Guides: Trained dogs and guides
Dogs and Facilities:
Kennel for hunters' dogs
Shotgun Sports:
Five-stand, sporting clays
Other Services:
Birds cleaned and packed for travel
Other Activities:
Swimming
Rates:
From $1,295 / 3 days
Gratuity:
$75 / day
Preferred Payment:
Cash, MasterCard, Visa or check
Getting There:
Fly to McAllen Texas and the lodge van will take you the rest of the way.

Contact:
Drew Butterwick
Outdoor Adventures
Worldwide
PO Box 202
Linn TX 78563
800/375-4868
Fax: 956/380-3723
EMAIL: info@oaww.com
WEB: www.oaww.com

TROUBLE WITH DOVE HUNTING in most parts of the U.S. is too few birds to learn anything. You get them in ones, twos and threes. In a good day, you'll swing on maybe 25 birds, but often only half that number. As they dart and swoop, you vary your lead. You try to swing through them. You shoot ahead and you shoot behind. There's always plenty of time to contemplate your misses, but seldom enough birds to let you keep experimenting until you get it right.

That's one of the reasons gunners flock to Las Palomas de Loma Colorada, that great shooting resort 85 miles south of the border town of McAllen, Texas. Over sorghum fields that stretch to the foothills of the mountains, you'll see literally tens of thousands of whitewing dove. During the August through October season, shooting can be so frantic that wise clients bring two guns in case one fails. Guests are accompanied by bird boys who make sure that your pockets are filled with shells and your cooler is chock-full of iced soft drinks.

As October fades, action shifts to quail and waterfowl. Quail are utterly wild here, and acreages are vast. Hunters ride bumper or over-dog box seats mounted on four-by-fours. Each truck carries eight pointers, and two are generally worked at one time. Driving the truck, the guide watches the dogs and is in constant radio contact with others from the lodge. If your field is slow, you'll move quickly to one that isn't. On a typical day, you'll flush upwards of 20 coveys. Waterfowling for puddle ducks and geese is equally fantastic. Hunt ducks early and quail the rest of the day.

If there ever were a shooting lodge that pampers you, Los Palomas is it. Known for its gracious service and excellent cuisine, the lodge is more aptly described as an ultimate resort for shotgunners. Sporting clays with a registered National Sporting Clays Association instructor is always available. Swim up to the bar in the heated pool and refresh your libation. Drift to sleep in the hammock on your patio. The price for all of this is surprisingly reasonable; less, in fact, than some lodges of lesser caliber in the United States. One caveat: Make your plans early. Permits to bring a shotgun into Mexico take time and are not inexpensive.

[M E X I C O]

Pancho Villa Hunting Club

M e r i d a ,   M e x i c o

Quail, ducks, off-shore fishing and the mysterious Mayan ruins—what a vacation!

VITAL STATISTICS:

GAME BIRDS:
DUCKS, QUAIL
Source of Birds: Wild and pen-reared
Seasons:
January through March
Land: 500,000 public acres
Accommodations:
MODERN RESORT
NUMBER OF ROOMS: 60
MAXIMUM NUMBER OF HUNTERS: 40
Meals: American plan
Conference Groups: Yes
Guides: Trained dogs and guides
Other Services:
Birds cleaned and packed for travel
Other Activities:
Fishing, golf
Rates:
From $1,450 / double occupancy
Gratuity:
Hunter's discretion
Preferred Payment:
Cash, MasterCard, Visa or check
Getting There:
Fly to Merida and take a taxi to the hotel.

Contact:
Charles Stevens
Pancho Villa/International
Adventure
20 Worthington Access Dr
308 Mikel
Maryland Hts. MO 63043
314/434-0506

WITH CONVENIENT FLIGHTs across the Gulf of Mexico from Houston, Miami and New Orleans, the Yucatan Peninsula offers shotgunners an opportunity for world-class duck and quail hunting in an international resort setting. A low, flat limestone peninsula, Yucatan was the seat of the great Mayan civilization and now thrives as a tourist destination. The climate in the north, around Merida, capital of the state, is hot and dry. Extensive wetlands rim the coast.

For more than 25 years, Pancho Villa has been offering waterfowling in a vast 180-square-mile marsh. Species include bluebills, gadwall, pintail, scaup, teal and wigeon. You'll hunt from blinds over decoys with native guides. Limits are extremely generous, generally at least twice that of the United States. Quail fit in this picture too. Flushes of 12 to 15 coveys of 20 birds or so each are not uncommon in the sisal fields near the marsh. Experienced guides work trained pointers. While the land is flat, hunting in sisal is much more difficult than the broom sedge and buffalograsses in the U.S. Brush pants and eight-inch boots add significantly to your comfort.

International Adventure, U.S. agent for Pancho Villa, handles all of the details. Charles Stevens, manager, will arrange permits for your shotguns. Shells are available through the club. Typical packages include three morning duck or quail hunts, transportation to and from hunting areas, guide service and dogs, double occupancy in the Hacienda Inn Hotel, and all meals.

The half-day hunting schedule frees your afternoons for trips to the ruins of the ancient city of Uxmal. Flourishing between 600 and 900 AD, Uxmal exhibits classic Mayan architecture. Especially interesting are stone friezes, the Governor's Palace, and the Pyramid of the Magician. The Gulf provides fishing. There's also tennis, golf and shopping, while a hundred-mile trip in a rental car will deliver you to Cancun.

The Aviles Brothers

M a z a t l a n ,   M e x i c o

This town across the bay from Cabo San Lucas is headquarters for hunting and fishing.

VITAL STATISTICS:

GAME BIRDS:
DUCKS
Source of Birds: Wild
Seasons:
November through March
Land: Unlimited private and public acres
Accommodations:
PRIVATE LODGES OR HOTELS IN TOWN
NUMBER OF ROOMS: 10 IN LODGE
MAXIMUM NUMBER OF HUNTERS: 20
Meals: Seafood and game
Conference Groups: No
Guides: Yes
Other Services:
Birds cleaned and packed for travel
Other Activities:
Bird watching, fishing, golf
Rates:
From $1,529 / person, double occupancy / 5 days/4 nights
Gratuity:
10% - 15%
Preferred Payment:
Cash or check
Getting There:
Fly to Mazatlan and be met.

Contact:
Roberto Aviles
The Aviles Brothers
PO Box 221
5 De Mayo
Mazatlan Sinaloa
82000 Mexico
52-69-81-6060
Fax: 52-69-14-6598

IN LATE FALL, waterfowl from the Pacific, Central and Mississippi flyways converge at Mazatlán, Mexico's principal port city on the Pacific. Across from the tip of Baja California, the city lies below the Tropic of Cancer. A large lake, Laguna Caimanero, lies south of the city, into which flows the Rio Presidio. Along lakes and ponds of fresh and brackish water, you'll hunt over decoys from blinds, boats, and airboats where the water is really shallow. Waders are generally not required (though a prudent hunter might slip a pair of ultralight breathables into his duffel).

The season opens in November with hunting for teal (blue, green, and cinnamon), pintails, and tree ducks. As the season progresses, teal become less numerous and wigeon, bluebills and shovellers begin to dominate. Bag limits are very generous—20 per day—with the exception of pintails, where you're limited to five. Duck hunts are often combined with gunning for mourning and whitewing doves. Bring your own shotgun or rent one from the "Brothers." And fresh or saltwater fishing can also be arranged. English-speaking guides will be available for your party.

The Aviles Brothers have been guiding hunters and anglers for more than a generation, but they do not own a resort or lodge. Rather- they put you up in those run by friends in the vicinity of Esquinapa down Federal Route 15 from Mazatlán. Guests may stay in a hotel in Esquinapa, a typical small Mexican town with market and chapel, or the beachfront Los Angeles Ranch out of town. Though Mazatlán, with a population of 200,000 or so, is a lovely old city that overlooks Olas Altas Bay, it lacks much of the tourist hype of Cabo San Lucas across the Gulf of California. Still, this is a tourist area that caters specifically to hunters and anglers. And its location on the northern fringe of the tropics ensures that it never really gets cold. Temperatures range from the high 60s to the low 90s, even during the coolest months of winter.

*Tom Huggler, wingshooting author, considers ptarmigan
a vastly underrated game bird. It is, after all, the same
as the red grouse of Scotland.*

State and Province Index

GAME INDEX